Beyond Expectations

Tale of a civil servant in and out of office

ಐಂಡ

R. D. Pradhan

Beyond Expectations

First Edition - February 2016

© Author

ISBN - 978-93-83572-81-6

All rights reserved. No part of this book will be reproduced, used or stored in any form without the prior permission of the Publisher.

The views expressed in this book are those of the author and do not necessarily represent the views of Vishwakarma Publications.

Published by:
Vishwakarma Publications
283, Budhwar Peth, Near City Post,
Pune- 411 002.
Phone No: (020) 20261157 / 24448989
Email: info@vpindia.co.in
Website: www.vpindia.co.in

Cover Design
Abhishek Darekar - Vishwakarma Publications

Typeset and Layout
Chaitali Nachnekar - Vishwakarma Publications

Printed at
Repro India Limited, Mumbai

Dedication

I would like to dedicate 'Beyond Expectations'

To

Lopa,

Who Shared Every Moment of My Life,

My Ambitions and My Achievements,

From IAS Probationer's Life

To, Raj Bhavan.

Preface

This is an autobiography of a former civil servant. Why should one impose this on readers?

I believe I have much to share with others. This is the life story of a public servant who served India between 1952-86. In a way, my life and the era in which I spent my professional life is almost extinct. India has transformed from a poor and hungry nation into a potential economic giant.

Circumstances had forced me into a career that was not my first choice. Was it my luck or an example of a famous quote: 'We are all creatures of circumstance'! At every critical stage of my life, destiny would lead me into the unknown and the unexpected areas that would open new vistas.

In a way, I became a witness to the transformation of a slave India into a Republic. I was born in 1928 into an average middle class family in Kokan on the western coast and brought up in Mumbai. It was my good fortune that my father was posted in Delhi/Simla between 1935-41. I got exposed to north India and learnt Urdu and Hindustani. Pre-partition Delhi was predominantly inhabited by families that lived there during the Mughal rule. They were known as Hindustanis. Along with Bengalis who came there with the shifting of British India's capital from Calcutta to Delhi in 1911, they were the social milieu of Delhi. Thus in my formative years I was brought up in a cosmopolitan and secular capital.

During 1942, I was in Poona, where Mahatma Gandhi was under arrest in the Aga Khan Palace. My grandmother was a Congress worker who had courted jail in 1931. With her I was at the Congress House on 9th August to demonstrate on arrest of our leaders. One boy standing by my side was killed by a bullet. His statue stands in the square of village named Wakad on old Pune-Mumbai Road. I often wonder that but for him I may have become the first martyr of 1942 Quit India movement. Dead and of no consequence to India. I believe that today most freedom fighters have that thought in their mind.

Later, at the Fergusson College established by Bal Gangadhar Tilak, I got lessons in political science. Thus born and brought up in a politically vibrant atmosphere, I was a young man enthused with idealism of Nehru and his vision of India when India became independent on 15th August 1947.

I joined the IAS in April 1952, the year in which India's first General elections were held. The first session of the House of People was convened in January 1953. There was shortage of ushers. We probationers were drafted to undertake that task and we witnessed the historic opening of the First session by the President of the Republic of India, when Dr. Rajendra Prasad addressed a joint session of both the Houses of the Parliament. For us it was exciting to meet and escort the great leaders of our Freedom movement, including Pandit Nehru, Abul Kalam Azad, S. K. Kriplani and several others. Thus I became a witness to the birth of India's finest democratic institutions.

I had a somewhat unorthodox career neither connected to my educational background nor to family. Generally plum postings were for sons and son-in-laws of the ICS. It was understood that if there was a plum job with any kind of extra perks going, only those with family connection with those in power would be considered. Believe it or not, I turned down several such jobs. Yet my destiny would land me in those postings. Not only in India but abroad as well.

During thirty four years in the IAS, I would serve in districts of then "the Bombay state" which formarly used to be in the princely states that are now in Gujarat and in western Maharashtra as well. I would meet the former rulers of these states, still living in opulence with their privileges and handsome purses. At a young age, I would serve a great Maratha leader Yashwantrao Chavan in Bombay and Delhi and get to know several freedom fighters. I would work in the Government of India in the Defence and the Commerce ministries. For over a decade, I would serve India abroad at Geneva in the diplomatic capacity as well as a UN civil servant at the highest bureaucratic level, and visit over fifty countries all around the globe. I gave up that lucrative career to return to serve my country but again my fate-line catapulted me back to the United Nations to occupy a high level political post. That was at the direction of Mrs. Indira Gandhi the Prime Minister of India. It was again my fate that at her instance I was recalled to be the chief secretary of Maharashtra. That led me to the post of the Union Home secretary in Delhi to work with the young Prime minister Rajiv Gandhi. I became an instrument to work on the Punjab Accord to lead towards curbing the secessionist movement and four years later restoring peace in that frontier state. I also negotiated and signed on behalf of the Central government accords with AASU in Assam and with the Mizo National Front in case of Mizoram. Both led restoration of democratic regime and brought peace and tranquility to the northeast after decades of insurgency. It was Rajiv Gandhi who gave me free hand to deal with these matters. Though much older to him I found myself in tune with his vision of a resurgent and modern India. In return I got respect and friendship that I described in my book 'Working with Rajiv Gandhi'.

My more memorable second life started after my retirement from the IAS on June 30, 1986. I was awarded Padma Bhushan for an exceptional 'Public Service' and I became a governor at the age of 58. Thereafter I became an MLC in Maharashtra.

In the course of my life, I had several opportunities to meet Pandit Nehru. I met the great Govind Ballabh Pant, the redoubtable freedom fighter and the Home minister of India. I also had the opportunity to meet Lal Bahadur Shastri who succeeded Pandit Nehru. I met Mrs. Indira Gandhi when she was the president of the Congress 1958 and during her prime ministership between 1982-84 on several occasions, as the chief secretary of Maharashtra.

My second life started after my retirement from the IAS on June 30, 1986. I became a governor at the age of 58. Thereafter I became an MLC in Maharashtra. I would work with both Rajiv Gandhi and Narsimha Rao, when they were in and out of office. In the last phase of my active public life, I worked as a close aide of Mrs. Sonia Gandhi.

1952 was the fourth batch of direct recruitment to the IAS. We considered ourselves as elitists and worthy successor service to the ICS that was created by the British to administer a continent. For us, thirty seven of 1952 batch it was a matter of great pride that we were at the Metcalf House, named after a great British administrator. We had fiercely competed against each other to get selected. On completion of our probation, we were to compete with ourselves. Many would fall by the way side in first fifteen years.

Pandit Nehru was opposed to the continuance of any all India service. Writing about the future of the ICS he wrote in his autobiography, "But of one thing I am sure that no new order can be built up in India so long as the spirit of the ICS pervades our administration and our public services". It was Sardar Vallabhbhai Patel, the redoubtable Home Minister of India who advocated creation of a new 'All India administrative service' to maintain the highest possible standards of efficiency.

Money was not an incentive. I joined at a salary of Rs350 per month. In my last post I got Rs3500 per month. But what I got in return, was the respect and a sense of satisfaction of working in the service the nation. When we met Nehru in 1953, he said, "I am the first servant of the people of India and all of you are public sevants". That's what motivated us.

I was fortunate that my first posting as an Assistant collector was under V. Shankar, ICS. He had worked with Sardar Patel as his private secretary. From him I learnt how Sardar Patel insisted on formation of a non-political, permanent civil service with dedication to a high degree of integrity, impartiality and objectivity that would serve loyally the government of the day.

Looking back, what I got out of my life is unbelievable. It has taken several twists and turns. I got fame, friendship and admiration of many. I have shared slices of that life in five books so far. My first one on 'Working with Rajiv Gandhi'; Second 'The Debacle to Revival – Y. B. Chavan as the Defence Minister 1962-65'; Third 'The Inside Story of 1965 War' and the last 'The Dragon's Shadow over Arunachal'. I also wrote an anecdotal book titled 'Never A Dull Moment'. I have enjoyed sharing all that with my readers. Now past eighties I believe, I must present the story of my life as a whole before it is late.

I trust that my autobiography may serve to throw light on some persons and events of India's contemporary history including Mrs. Sonia Gandhi, who has emerged as the most enigmatic political figure of this millennium. That is what has motivated me to write: BEYOND EXPECTATIONS.

Foreword

When a comprehensive post-independence administrative history of India is written, the pride of place is likely to be given to the administrative cadres that have manned the civil services of India. The doyen of these numerous All India and Central Services has been the Indian Administrative Services (IAS) the successor to the famed Indian Civil Service (ICS) that the British had established in their governance of India.

The IAS, of which Mr. R. D. Pradhan was a member of the 1952 batch, was formed initially as the All India Administrative Service, in 1946, when the Indian independence negotiations were in full swing, and then renamed the IAS in 1947. The first recruitment to the IAS took place from amongst the cadres of armed forces officers that were soon to be demobilized after the Second World War. The first recruitment by examination to the IAS, on the patterns of the recruitment to the ICS, took place in 1948. In the first five years of such recruitment, for the 1948 to 1952 intakes, the numbers selected were just over 30 per annum. Keep in mind that the recruitment to the ICS, from the time it had been set up in the mid-1850s to the time the last formal examinations were conducted in London and India in 1939, had been over 50 men per

- Sumit Muzumdar, Professor of Technology Strategy, University of Texas at Dallas, USA, is author of several articles on Indian Civil Servants and is currently engaged in writing History of the Indian Civil Service.

year. Thus, even compared to ICS officers of the past, the 1948, 1949, 1950, 1951 and 1952 batches of IAS officers, obtained via the so-called regular recruitment (RR) route, were a rather exclusive lot.

When a comprehensive history of the Indian members of the ICS, which is yet to be written, is penned, I believe that among these men, the stalwarts who built India would be the officers who were development-oriented, and the stalwarts who ruled India would be the officers that were politically oriented. These builders and rulers would make up the top ten percent who would have had a hand in the transformation of the nation. The development administrators might rightly be called 'The Men Who Built India,' and the political administrators would be called 'The Men Who Ruled India.' Of course, the latter classification or title is hardly original, as it was used by the late Mr. Philip Mason, himself an ICS officer, as the title of his 1950s history of the ICS.

Going by my experience as a son of the system, and here I have to declare my interest as my late father Anil K. Majumdar was a member of the Bombay cadre 1949 batch of the IAS. Based on observations, it is my belief that many of the early IAS officers who went to become political administrators could also be classified as the men who ruled India. In my view, R. D. Pradhan, as a political administrator is justified as being called one of such men who ruled India. He has written a detailed autobiography, of a part of his life and career which gives a considerable amount of insight into how a man, and for that matter after 1947 a woman too, might become a political administrator, and have a hand, in whatever manner, in the creation or reformation or transformation of a nation.

A little of further background is useful. The British, as a colonial power, governed India with the use of ICS officers. But, the British had also to deal with the Princely States that made up over forty percent of the land mass of India. Thus, the Indian administration had to be in political relationship with the States and their respective Princes, and for this purpose, the British had established an unofficial Indian Political Service, consisting of ICS officers and Army officers seconded to the Foreign and Political Department, which operated directly under the Viceroy. These Politicals, as they were called, were unique, and many of their practices had a distinct impact on how the post-independence IAS officers who became politically-oriented learned their trade. The few Indian members of the Foreign and Political Department went on to occupy important positions in international diplomacy as India's political plenipotentiaries in various countries.

Only seven Indian ICS officers, the late Messrs. C. S. Venkatachar ICS (1921), who had a major role as Secretary in the Ministry of States in the 1950s; K. P. S. Menon ICS (1921); Muizuddin Ahmed ICS (1933); A. N. Jha ICS (1935); Hareshwar Dayal ICS (1936); S. Sen ICS (1938) and V. M. M. Nair of the 1942 ICS batch, were Politicals. Mr. Pradhan has been one of the few from the first five batches to have achieved membership of the great and good club, after a career that has included being the Chief Secretary of Maharashtra state, the Union Home Secretary and finally the first Governor of Arunachal Pradesh. All of these are top jobs. Along the way, he has been a diplomat on behalf of India, at the General Agreement of Trade and Tariffs (GATT), as it was then, and the United Nations Conference on Trade and Development (UNCTAD), as well as a staff member of the United Nations. He has also held the temporary Governorship of Bihar. These distinctions entitle him to the top ten percent categorization. Therefore, it is important to glean from his autobiography what might make for such categorization and what one could make of it.

When a person joins the IAS, there is no rule or logic stating that a person be classified as politically or development oriented. It all depends on the luck of the draw, on one's initial cadre placement, on one's initial place of posting, on one's initial Collector(s) who have trained them in the districts, and on one's aptitudes that only surface after a few years in the field.

Three useful ideas in assessing the contents of this volume further are imprinting, transference and founding conditions. Mr. Pradhan was allotted to the Bombay cadre of the IAS. As had been the norm, when a Marathi speaking officer was allotted to the ICS or IAS cadre of the Bombay province or state, till 1960 she or he would be assigned to the Gujarat part of the state for training to meet their language requirements, and he commenced his service careers in the districts of what is now Gujarat. In true tradition, Mr. Pradhan also commenced service in Gujarat, and perhaps it is his subsequent posting in the Banaskantha district that led to his becoming a political administrator.

Mr. Pradhan's sojourn at Mount Abu, then a part of the Banaskantha district, was under the redoubtable

Collectorship of Mr. V. Shankar, an ICS officer of the 1932 batch of the Bombay cadre, who had achieved notice as being one of Sardar Patel's right hand men. Mr. Shankar had been the Private Secretary to the Deputy Prime Minister and Home Minister, as Sardar Patel was, and then was Joint Secretary in the Ministry of States helping Sardar Patel and later his successor as Minister in the integration of the Indian Princely States into the Indian Union. He was Mr. Pradhan's boss and his mentor, and that is important.

Mr. V. Shankar imparted lessons in style and courage, but of more significance was the advice to consider the personal angle since behind every file was a human or a family concern. This is an important piece of advice for a budding political officer as politics is the art of the possible, and engendering all possibilities involves an understanding of human psychologies. Seeing another person's point of view is vital. In the final analysis, it is the political psychology associated with all human interactions that matters in generating outcomes. It is invaluable to have been taught these lessons early in one's career.

Mr. Pradhan's early experiences in wearing several hats, all at once, in the small hill station that is Mount Abu, as the Assistant Collector, Sub-Divisional Magistrate, Forest Officer, President of the Municipality and the Superintendent of the Hill Station, would have been of consequence in learning to be adept in multi-tasking, negotiating and compromising with himself in his various Mount Abu avatars and getting to know the views of the various officials embodied in his own persona.

After Banaskantha, Kolhapur is where the seeds of Mr. Pradhan's career success were truly laid. Kolhapur was the epicenter of the Samyukta Maharashtra Movement (SMM) as well as the hometown of that Great Maratha Shivaji. By his own admission, Mr. Pradhan would shed his 'Poona personality'. I am not sure what that is. But, let us assume that Poona being a quiet, academic and intellectual sort of place, a Poona Personalitywala would be a reticent, introspective, non-dashing, studious, sober and almost invisible character. Mr. Pradhan's sojourn as the Kolhapur Collector would make him a good communicator, driven by a spirit of enterprise, dash, grit and energy. I would add that such a sojourn might also provide a budding Collector turned political administrator the wherewithal to project one's personality, hold one's nerve and remain outwardly calm and serene, even though one was quaking inside.

Mr. Pradhan's subsequent experiences have included being Private Secretary to the Defense Minister, Mr. Y. B. Chavan, where one of his tasks was making a précis for political consumption of the famous Henderson-Brooks report on the infamous 1962 NEFA debacle that the Indian Army had suffered, being Home Secretary in the Government of Maharashtra, and being the Union Home Secretary. The last post enabled Mr. Pradhan to negotiate three historically important agreements that have had substantial consequences for keeping intact the political fabric of the Indian nation. These have been the Punjab Accord, with Harcharan Singh Longowal, bringing to an end the civil strife in the Punjab, the Assam Accord bringing to an end the student strife in Assam and the Mizoram Accord, bringing to an end the separatist strife in Mizoram. For that, he was awarded Padma Bhushan – a rare recognition of his services to the nation.

In sum, the present volume is an interesting recollection of half a century of experiences of one of India's foremost political administrators, a person who has been a fitting successor to the Politicals of old, and its contents shed intimate light on many key political events of our time.

Sumit K. Majumdar
Professor of Technology Strategy
University of Texas at Dallas
Richardson, TX, USA

Prologue

Like many others, I joined the IAS, in April 1952 most unexpectedly. Was it destined ?

One Saturday in the month of October 1951, I had gone to visit my friend and classmate since school days. I enjoyed visiting Vitthal Mavinkurve in the Saraswat colony in Poona because his mother was very kind to me. After we had the usual tea and repast, Vitthal suggested walking over to PTI office, a few minutes of walking distance. Results of the Competitive examination were expected to be announced that afternoon. On entering the PTI office we were excited to find that names of the successful candidates had already started ticking on the tele-printer tapes. Both of us were intently watching each name and praying to our Gods. Soon names of the thirty candidates had come out. We were getting increasingly anxious because it was known that only about thirty-five or so candidates would be taken that year. Suddenly, my prayers seemed to have been answered. The tele-printer started knocking off : RAMCHANDRA DATTATRAYA PRADHAN.

Both of us anxiously waited for Vitthal's name. That did not appear. He was disappointed but decided to celebrate my selection. When we went back to his home, there was considerable excitement on my success. He and his mother must have been dejected on Vitthal's failure, but they did not allow that to affect their joy at my success. For me, it was a touching moment and a very much mixed pleasure. In his mother's face, I saw the joy of my late mother. I have not forgotten their joy at my selection.

Why was I selected? I, who did not want to join government service but instead aspire to follow footsteps of some eminent educationists in Poona and go to Oxford/Cambridge for higher studies. Was it a destiny that was to take me to high positions, national and international recognition and nearness to high and mighty of India? Now over eighty decades old I often wonder, why good fortune followed in whatever I attempted and did – in a vocation that was not my first choice.

Was my late mother guiding my destiny? Her death in February 1951 had in fact led me to appear for the IAS. Perhaps my securing a place in IAS, was the fulfillment of a dream - not mine, but my mother's. On the day I graduated with a high First Class, she told everyone that 'My Ram is going to be ICS and become Governor one day.' She did not know then, that the ICS had ceased to exist and I did not know that the IAS had replaced it. However, her one desire had come true. Thirty-six years later her second desire would also come true, when I would become the Governor of the Arunachal Pradesh. Between those two events, I would enjoy years of fulfillment and a career in which I did not spend a dull moment.

I had been brought up in Poona (now Pune) of the 40's. It was inhabited by parochial-minded and self-opinionated middle class, who claimed to be superior to others and there were evidences of that all around. The old city, around Shaniwar-wada housed families, who had for generations been known for their erudition and scholarship. New parts of the city such as the Shivajinagar was a home to retired government officials, professionals and intellectuals working as professors and lecturers in colleges or doing research in numerous institutions. Their way of living and thinking were in tune with their attitude towards life. Money could not earn respect and, in fact, too much money invited contempt. Frugal living, dedication to work and sacrifice for higher purpose in life, were taken for granted.

This was well illustrated by the example of the founders of the Deccan Education Society including Bal Gangadhar Tilak, Mahadev Govind Ranade, Vishnushastri Chiplunkar, who promoted the New English School and Fergusson College in 1880's. They took a vow to serve the Society for life on a monthly salary of less than rupees sixty. Later two of the Principals of the Fergusson College, Sir Raghunathrao Paranjpye and G. S. Mahajani, both Wranglers from Cambridge, worked for the Society and the College on monthly salary of less than rupees one hundred fifty.

In 1940s' Poona was a medium size town with a population of just over one and half lakh.(1,50,000) New residential areas of Shivajinagar were developing fast with small bungalows. All students moved around on their bicycles and played on the sports grounds of the two Gymkhanas or whiling away evenings at two Irani restaurants named 'Lucky' and the 'Good Luck'. Drinking cups of tea, then priced one anna (6 paisa now) we discussed endlessly our future that was intimately connected with India's, as the 1942 freedom movement was on and we exchanged notes on daily happenings and news paper reports of Hitler's armies attacking Leningrad. The two restaurants were thus the hub of heated discussions and clearing houses of gossip that we thought was great information.

In our college, inspired by Bal Gangadhar Tilak, such was the ethos, that brighter students never thought of joining government service. They looked forward to professions such as engineers, doctors or lawyers or joining their traditional family vocations in trade and commerce. Only mediocre ones looked for clerical jobs in government offices. Not many aspired for higher level appointments. Service with foreign government was looked down and generally shunned during last few years of the British Raj because of politically surcharged atmosphere prevailing in Poona.

Even after attaining independence, surprisingly in a city where so many Indian Civil Service (ICS) officers had settled down to enjoy their post-retirement life, no one talked or briefed students about the Indian Administrative Service (IAS) formed by Sardar Patel as successor to the Indian Civil Service (ICS), to serve independent India.

I was a product of that atmosphere. It was therefore logical that after getting a first class in the B.A. examination with mathematics, I thought of joining the new Post-Graduate Department of Statistics of the University of Bombay. Statistics was considered a new field, with immense potentialities for carrying out research work; also offering employment in big multi-national companies, as well as in the banking and insurance sectors. During the first year of the post-graduate course my tutors were very happy that I had shown aptitude for research and already attempted some original work in the field of Operational Research.

At the start of second year, I learnt that my mother who suffered severe stomach pains, had cancer. She was operated in the Tata Memorial Hospital in Bombay by an eminent surgeon, who assured that she should be able to survive for at least four-five years. However, within three months, the pains recurred and the doctors advised that there was nothing that they could do except to put her under sedatives. It was middle of the academic year. One night I decided to quit the hostel to attend to her. My father had retired six months earlier and was trying to settle down in Poona. I thought that I could be of some use to both of them. On the advice of some friends of the father, we took her to Pen, a place about sixty kilometers from Bombay for treatment. We were told that a Vaidya, a practitioner of Ayurvedic medicine could cure cancer. Call it a miracle, she really started recovering and within two weeks the pain subsided and the growth disappeared. We invited the eminent doctor from Bombay who had attended her. He was greatly puzzled to find that the carcinogenic growth was indeed shrinking in size. To our misfortune, one morning we learnt that the Vaidya had died in sleep. No one knew, what medicine he was administering. According to his family, the medicine formulated with some rare herbs and roots had been passed on to him by his mother with a strict injunction that the knowledge should not be passed to anyone. Within ten days of the Vaidya's death my mother died.

I had lost the better part of the second term and there was no question of my appearing for the M.A. examination to be held in the month of April. Instead of sitting at home, on the urging of some friends I joined the Gokhale Institute of Politics and Economics to work on the National Sample Survey (NSS). The work was related to field of statistics and the job would also earn me handsome monthly salary of Rs250 per month. One day, some one casually mentioned that V. S. Bhir had appeared for some competitive examination and had been selected to join the Defence Accounts Service in a senior position. Bhir was a brilliant student and we had occupied adjoining rooms at the Fergusson college hostel for four years. I knew something about the Defence Accounts Department because my father, who had joined that Department as a clerk had taken over thirty-five years to become the Deputy Accountant General. Bhir would start his career at that level. I decided to try my luck at the competitive examination. I immediately secured a form from Union Public Service Commission (UPSC) and managed to file it at the Commission's office in New Delhi almost on the last date.

I found to my horror that, for the examination to be held that year in September 1951, UPSC had prescribed two additional higher papers for the Indian Administrative Service (IAS) and the Indian Foreign Service (IFS). The standard of those papers would be comparable to that of post-graduate level. With examination hardly four months away, I felt it safer to rely on the good old history and selected the European history and World history in addition to the mathematics/statistics and usual compulsory papers.

As the examination was in September, I had hardly four months to prepare for the competitive examination. I decided to join the Department of Statistics next term, in case I did not qualify. Some good friends did not fail to advise me that I was making a mistake. I could do brilliant work in the academic field and I should continue with my post-graduate studies in statistics. Some of them bluntly told me that with my poor 'Poona personality', I could never expect to qualify at the viva-voce. They continued to give me their unsolicited advice even after I had received a call for the interview on the basis of the marks in the written examination. That was great for my morale!

Between the written examinations and call for interview there was a period of four months. One day I learnt that Sir Raghunathrao Paranjpye, and some retired ICS officers had decided to offer one hour of their time each week to 'train' candidates for appearing at the viva voce examination. For that they held 'Tea Meetings' at the Law College each Thursday. Apart from the manners and mannerism to face the interview panel, they tried to instill certain degree of confidence in candidates to communicate in English. At the beginning there were about fifteen other candidates. After the written examinations, we were reduced to four or five. It was exhilarating to sit at the table with eminent persons who had achieved so much in their lives. There was Sir Raghunathrao Paranjpye, who after retiring from the Fergusson College, had gone as India's High Commissioner to Australia. S. B. Dhavale, an ICS, had retired as a Judge of the Patna High Court; Prof. Patwardhan from the Indian Education Service and a couple of other retired ICS officers. Most of the candidates, who had initially started attending these meetings had dropped out, because they found it futile to spend time with these 'old fogies' who had their own ideas about the All India Services examination and how the viva-voce ought to be conducted. However, I decided to stick around, because of the unique opportunity to meet and get to know such distinguished personalities.

My interview in Delhi was fixed for 3 January, 1952. In those days candidates dreaded appearing before the Chairman of the UPSC, R. N. Banerjee, ICS (Retd.), who had been the first Union Home Secretary after the independence. He had a formidable reputation for tearing to pieces candidates appearing before him by shouting and browbeating them. That afternoon there were five candidates waiting as sacrificial lambs. First two candidates came out crest-fallen within less than ten minutes. On entering the room I got a taste of the Chairman's well-known bullying. As he was sitting with his back to a window and I faced the light filtering through the window, I could not see his face. I only heard a booming voice shouting at me across the room asking me to take my seat at the opposite end of the large size oval table. Banerjee was glowering at me from the other end and was trying to cow me down with his glare. He was flanked by eight other members, four on either side. In Poona, I had been repeatedly warned that if I did not know the correct answer, it would be best to reply that 'I do not know'. Accordingly I replied to the first four-five questions from the Chairman. With a great show of indignation he shouted, 'Then tell us what do you know'.

As I could not reply to that question with my stock answer 'I do not know', I stared back at him for a moment.

Apparently, he decided to relent and pass me on to other members. I recollect that Dr. H. N. Kunjru, M. P. and Hareshwar Dayal, ICS, who was then Joint Secretary in the Ministry of External Affairs, were very kind to me and tried to find out what I knew. Very soon I had settled down to a relaxed question-and-answer session and I was hoping that my old professor Dr. G. S. Mahajani would throw some questions at me which would help me to really impress the Chairman. Unfortunately, when the Chairman looked at him, Mahajani said, 'I do not wish to question the candidate because he is my ex-student. I would, however, like the Board to know that he was a good student'. I felt somewhat let down. When the results were out and I found that I had got the minimum 105 out of 400 marks to be eligible for selection. I often wondered whether it was Mahajani's remarks that secured for me the minimum marks and a place in the IAS. I also realized that as advised by my friends I indeed have a poor 'Poona Personality'.

While awaiting result, I had resumed my work with the Gokhale Institute, I enjoyed working with Prof. V. N. Dandekar, who was directly in charge of the NSS project. I occasionally met Prof. Dhanjayrao Gadgil, who had built up a formidable reputation as an economist and the Director of the Institute.

By the time I appeared for the viva-voce, four months after the written examination, both Sir Raghunathrao and S. B. Dhavale, who was perhaps the oldest living member of the ICS (1908), had grown fond of me. I soon started visiting them at their homes and spending hours in their company. Justice Dhavale was the son-in-law of the great Gopal

Krishna Gokhale, whom Mahatma Gandhi regarded as his Guru. Dhavale lived in Gokhale's sprawling house and met me in his Library with cupboards all along the walls lined with books bound in leather. Sir Raghunathrao lived in a attractive modern bungalow near the Fergusson College. He grew very fond of me. The day I got selected for the IAS, I was greatly touched when Sir Raghunathrao told me that my success had given him as much pleasure as the selection of his own son. I felt gratified because he had no son.

Soon I had to start getting ready to report to the IAS Training School in Delhi, but not before a determined effort was made to dissuade me from joining the government service. That was typical of Poona mentality of that era. Along with me Madhukar Namjoshi, who had done his post-graduation in Economics and who was also working in the Gokhale Institute had also appeared for the competitive examination. His was the most unusual case, perhaps in the history of the All India Services examination. He got the lowest aggregate marks in the written examination and the highest marks in the viva-voce : 400 out of 400. He was amongst the top ten to be considered for the Indian Foreign Service. For that he was interviewed first by Sir Girja Shanker Bajpai ICS, the Secretary General of the External Affairs Ministry and later by the Prime Minister, as the Foreign Minister. Namjoshi had impressed them and he was selected for the Foreign Service. It was a great achievement. When he got his letter of appointment, he went to see Prof. D. R. Gadgil, the Director, who advised him not to join the Foreign Service and held out for him a brilliant future in the Gokhale Institute. Madhukar's late father had been a members of the ICS and it was natural for him to have joined either the IAS or IFS. However, he was influenced by Prof. Gadgil and he decided not to join despite advice by his family and friends.

Knowing the over bearing personality of Prof. D. R. Gadgil, the Director, I did not want to be subjected to a similar persuasion. The very next day, I met Prof. V. N. Dandekar asked for salary due to me to be settled immediately so that I could quit the Institute. Despite messages from Prof. Gadgil to see him, I avoided meeting him.

Madhukar Namjoshi's case did not end there. I later learnt that the Prime Minister, who had been greatly impressed in the interview, mentioned to his elder brother, Capt. Namjoshi, who used to pilot the Prime Minister's plane to persuade his younger brother to join the IFS. PM was reported to have remarked, 'Why is your brother being foolish?' However, having made up his mind, Madhukar Namjoshi stood his ground and by doing so, I believe, India lost a great name in the international economic field.

I was asked to report to the Principal of the IAS Training School on 1st April 1952. After equipping myself with the minimum necessities I left for Delhi. It was emotionally hard for me to leave my father behind to take care of my two younger brothers and two younger sisters. They were too young to understand what their brother had achieved. They only knew that I was going to a far away place.

I was not a stranger in Delhi. I was educated there between 1935-41 when my father was posted there in the Military Accounts Department. We had lived in different areas including the Timarpur, a new government colony on the bank of Yamuna river. From there we went by a tonga (one horse light carriage) to the Hartcourt Butler high School located beyond the Gol market. Everyday we passed the Metcalfe House without knowing that one day my future would be shaped on the grounds of that historic building. That was where I headed after bidding good-bye to my father and my siblings to be shaped from a probationer into an IAS officer.

Table of Contents

Dedication

Preface

Foreword

Prologue

PART I : Making of an IAS Officer in 50's

1. Metcalfe House 3
2. The Making of an IAS Officer 9
3. With the Army 23
4. Tourism 34
5. Transformation 39
6. Changing Times 46

PART II : In Bombay State (1953-62)

7. Reporting to the Secretariat 55
8. First Encounter with an Ascetic 61
9. Initiation into District Life 64
10. Some Soft Lessons 69
11. First Lessons in Governance 80

12. The Style and Pomp of RAJ 103
13. To the Western Ghats 118
14. Disastrous Beginning 123
15. A District Collector's Life 129
16. Dealing with the Feudal India............................. 137
17. Earning Chavan's Trust 145
18. Transition to Bombay Secretariat 152
19. With Y. B. Chavan.. 156
20. Lessons in India's Democracy............................. 168

PART III : In Defence Ministry
21. India – China War.. 179
22. Some Memorable Visits 185
23. The Henderson- Brook Reports 192
24. Laying Witch - Hunt to Rest 198
25. Three Foreign Visits 201
26. My Decision to Quit 215

PART IV : International Trade & Diplomacy
27. Launch into Economic Field............................... 221
28. Tripartite Negotiations 235
29. UNCTAD- II in Delhi 240
30. Into Diplomacy 247
31. All Purpose Task-man 259
32. Into International Civil Service........................... 267
33. Memories of Places 274

34. Treasured Personalities 290
35. Good-bye to International Career 300

PART V : Back to the State
36. Return of the Native 309
37. Between Two Power Centers 320
38. Renaming of a University 326

PART VI : The Director General of Shipping
39. A New Area of Work.. 333
40. On a Diplomatic Assignment 341
41. Coastal Shipping.. 348

PART VII : On International Assignment
42. On a Globe Trotting Assignment for UN 355
43. Again to United Nations..................................... 358

PART VIII : Chief Secretary Maharashtra
44. Unexpected Recall 367
45. To Bombay as Chief Secretary............................ 371
46. The Assembly Session in Nagpur........................ 381
47. Vasandata Patil as the CM 385
48. The Longest Textile Strike 390
49. Testing Times 395
50. All for Bombay/Mumbai..................................... 398
51. More Opportunities to Serve 404
52. Unearthing FSI Scandal...................................... 408

53. Differences with Chief Minister 414
54. Environment Matters 420
55. Reforming District Administration 428
56. Setting up MIDA 434
57. Modern Art Gallery, Mumbai 439
58. Raja Dinkar Kelkar Museum 445
59. Bhiwandi Riots 448
60. Post Mrs. Indira Gandhi's Assassination 453
61. Meeting Mrs. Margaret Thacher 457
62. Meeting Young PM of India 460

PART IX : Union Home Secretary
63. In the North Block 467
64. Conflicts in the Northeast 474
65. Nagaland 480
66. Farewell to Arms 487
67. Dealing with Conflicts 497
68. To Arunachal Raj Bhawan 501

PART X : Epilogue
69. End of Civil Service Career 511

PART I :

IAS Probationer's Training in 50's

Chapter 1

The Metcalfe House
- IAS Training School

With a twinge of sorrow at leaving father and the family behind, but looking forward excitedly to a new career, I left Poona. We were asked to report to the Principal of the IAS Training School on 1st April. Some one mentioned that 1st April being the 'All Fool's Day', that was designated to make a fool of us and it would be wiser to join on 2nd April.

The IAS Training School was situated in one corner of the vast estate of the Metcalfe House. Hostel blocks were constructed to accommodate army officers during war time. These hutments were laid out as two-room units; outer room served as a living-cum-bedroom, while the inner one combined in itself the function of an ante-room, a tub bath and toilet. There being no water-closets, toilets were enamel pots mounted on wooden stools. These were known as 'thunder boxes' that served British Officers for over a century.

One bearer was attached to four of us. He looked after all our requirements including serving bed-tea, evening-tea, cleaning of rooms, delivering and receiving our clothes from the laundryman and rendered all petty services. The one attached to me was called 'Jeeves', looked as sharp and crafty as the famous Wodehouse character.

A building adjoining the hutments had been converted to provide a class-room, offices for the Principal and the Vice-Principal and a lounge. Adjacent to it was a fairly large size hall that served as the mess. We found that the mess was not like any other eating place, but an institution by itself, around which would center our social and cultural life.

I vividly remember that the first person I met in the Superintendent's office was A. P. Venkatashwaran, who had been selected for the Indian Foreign Service. We introduced ourselves, and in his inimitable style, he congratulated me for having proved myself another wise person, by refusing to join on 1 April. He showed a rare sense of humour. He retained it throughout his career, which led him up to the Foreign Secretary's post. One day he voluntarily retired from the service in a blaze of publicity because of some statement he made in Islamabad that was resented by the Prime Minister Rajiv Gandhi. AP has remained a lifelong friend.

It was a novel experience to meet persons from different parts of the country. All of us had come there on our merit through a grueling competitive examination. Most outstanding was Shankar Prasad Mukherjee from Delhi, who had stood first in the competitive examination. He had a record of standing first in all the examinations that he had appeared. Dileep Kamtekar from Baroda who had been selected for the Indian Foreign Service (IFS) and myself were the only two from the Bombay State. Many wondered why an advanced state like Bombay could not send more probationers. Most could not believe that Madhukar Namjoshi, who had been ranked in the first five had refused to join the IFS. Perhaps young persons from the Bombay were not keen on joining the government service, as there were several more lucrative careers available. But the truth was that the 'Poona Mentality' prevailed all over the state. That explained why in the ICS there were hardly six or seven officers, mainly from poor Konkan region where young Brahmins had brilliant brains but no employment opportunities. Others were from Gujarat area Although times have changed, even now one finds that compared to other states, not many Maharashtrians get selected at the competitive examination.

In the batch of 38 probationers there were 14 from the South India, 15 from the North, 5 Bengali speaking and 3 Marathi speaking besides Kamtekar and myself, we had B. K. Halve from the Central Provinces Among the three from Punjab, there was a lady probationer - Miss Sarla Khanna. She was the second woman to joint the IAS. Bihar, Madras Presidency and even Kerala were well represented.

S. B. Bapat, ICS and our Principal, was a Joint Secretary in the Ministry of Home Affairs and also occupied a high sounding post of the Establishment Officer to the Government of India. J. D. Shukla, ICS of the U.P. Cadre, was the Vice-Principal. Bapat, as befitted his designation and rank, worked at a higher level and except for delivering a few talks did not spend much time at the School. Task of shaping students to officers of the IAS was left to J. D. Shukla. He apparently relished the task.

Our training programme included study of Law, especially the Indian Penal Code, the Criminal Procedure Code and the Evidence Act, and the pattern of District Administration in India. The more important aspect of our training was widening our minds and intellect by getting acquainted with a variety of subjects, including art, architecture, religious teachings and panorama of Indian history. Teaching through lectures and discussions was supplemented by visits to institutions and organisations in the field, including a two week attachment with the Army. The training would also provide us enough opportunity to see a great deal about our own country through visits to Jammu and Kashmir, Assam, some parts of U.P., and Rajasthan. We would also have opportunities of meeting a large number of senior civilians, defence officers and intelligentsia of Delhi. It was exciting to be suddenly treated as officers with a great future ahead. Transition from being mere students was sudden, and some would not adjust easily to the new role. Some probationers had already worked as lecturers in colleges and appeared to be more mature. They were also cynical about the value of the training in the School and were convinced that it was waste of one year of one's service career! As we went up the ladder, we found that in the IAS, as also in IFS and IPS, a batch mate has some significance, what is now called net working.

The elite of the School were the five IFS Probationers: Dileep Kamtekar from Baroda, A. P. Venkateswaran from Madras, Thomas Abraham from Kerala, K. S. Bajpai called generally as Shanker - son of the great Sir Girija Shanker Bajpai - and Ajamani, whose elder brother Khub Chand was already in the IFS. They would be with us for four months or so and leave for the United Kingdom to study for one year either at Oxford or Cambridge.

It was a new and refreshing experience to meet Shanker Bajpai and A. P. Venkateswaran. Girija Shanker was then the Governor of Bombay. His was the most outstanding career in the ICS during the British rule. Shanker had been educated at Berkeley in the US and Oxford. He had seen a great deal of the world during his father's postings in Paris and Washington and was earmarked for a great career in the Foreign service. He would go on become our Ambassador to China, Pakistan and the United States. At a personal level, despite all the awe surrounding his pedigree at the School, he would remain the most gentle, unassuming and friendly. A. P. Venkateswaran's father was also an ICS from Madras, who became a Judge of the Madras High Court. I have not come across any one with a sharper mind and a rare sense of humour. Perhaps too much of the latter.

On the first day, as I was settling down in my modest room, I reflected on my past and my surroundings. The river Jamuna (in Marathi, Yamuna) was hardly hundred yards away. The site of our school was very pleasant and that night in my first letter to my father, I wrote : *The moods of this mighty river of India will be seasonally changing and these should add colour and new rhythm to our strenuous life here. Indeed, if one casts one's mind along the flow of Yamuna, one should get a reflection of the vastness, greatness and variety of Indian life and culture. It will illustrate the dictum of 'Unity in diversity' - the same that we are experiencing here in the School.*

I did not know then that what I had felt about the Jamuna was almost the same as expressed by Jawaharlal Nehru about the Ganges in the Discovery of India.

ಬಂಡಬಂಡ

Chapter 2

The Making of an IAS Officer

Training

The task of shaping the probationers was taken in hand by J. D. Shukla with his characteristic zeal. Of a medium stature and stocky build, he had a sharp eye and a ready wit. He would notice everything, however minor, especially our defects. In the beginning, he delivered a series of talks on the district administration. Shukla, with his prodigious memory, would quote scores of Sanskrit shlokas as well as Urdu couplets from Mirza Ghalib. He copiously quoted from the notes of British administrations describing the multifarious duties of Assistant Collectors and Collectors. He encouraged us to read memoirs of empire builders like Metcalfe and Darling. Darling was an ICS from the Punjab Commission and he was the first to undertake developmental activities in his district. We found Darling's memoirs interesting because just then some ideas of community development were being aired by S. K. Dey.

J. D. Shukla drove home to us as to how much the foreign administrators had tried to study and learn about village life in India. They had taken deep interest in every aspect of administration at the grassroots and left behind copious notes. They had not only described in detail the nature of work of an Assistant Collector, his duties, powers, but had gone at length to explain, how to behave towards superiors, how to handle inferiors how to deal with farmers and villagers, how to take best out of Tehsildars and other subordinates. These foreigners had shown remarkable insight into lives of the real Indians.

Shukla's lectures left us wondering as to how we could perform all the multifarious duties expected of an Assistant Collector. Some of us were greatly worried as to how one could tour for 240 days in a year in villages and forests. Whenever we asked Shukla any questions about what kind of life we were embarking upon as Assistant Collectors, he quoted to us a judgment passed by an eminent British administrator who said: "An Assistant Collector's life is worse than a mad dog's!" Further, the Administrator advised the Assistant Collectors to compare their life with that of an outcast: "Is not a mad dog's life preferable to that of a Mahar or an outcast!" These words were written in 1910 A. D. and according to Shukla, the life of outcasts, then called Harijans (now Dalits), had not changed. When we went to our districts, we found how correct that British administrator was.

Shukla's talks and our visits to villages had one good effect. Most of us, being, city bred had not realized the importance of seasons, especially the rains for the farmer. Not only the life of his Ryot but the Collector's life and comfort depended on that. We also learnt that as Collectors of land revenue, first ten and fifteen years of service will be intimately associated with the land and the people who till the soil. This was indeed the grandeur of the Indian Civil Service. People might call ICS men (now IAS as well) armchair bureaucrats or many other names, but no one comes more intimately in contact with the villagers and looks after them in case of famine and natural disasters than these bureaucrats. We thus learnt how the civil service could handle non-challantly any department of the State activity. They would know the people in villages - the real Indians - and get involved with the life of a farmer more intimately than anyone else. That experience, in the first decade of one's service would be lay the foundations of further career. Unfortunately, things have changed rapidly.

Our Vice-Principal, popularly called VP, was very particular about our behaviour, manners and dress. On the very first day, he pulled up a probationer for not buttoning up his coat properly and another one for walking about sloppily. He impressed on us that as members of a superior Service, we must maintain the best standards of behaviour and show ourselves as energetic individuals since other would certainly try to emulate us.

After a series of class-room lectures, we were taken to near about villages to see the situation in the field and add to our knowledge through observation. For many of us, it was a great experience to meet farmers and village folk whom we could identify as the 'real Indians'. One day, we were taken to a village named Kajauli, about 16 miles from Delhi. On reaching there, we first discussed with the local officers their problems in the field of Co-operation, Rural Banking, Panchayats and Cottage Industries. We were suitably impressed. After lunch, we went to the village site to discuss these matters with the villagers. We very soon found that they were total strangers to all those fields and schemes, which were meant for their benefit.

On another occasion, we visited Nangoli, a village about 12 miles from Delhi. We were introduced to the duties and functions of several village level officials such as the Patwari, the Lambardar, the Tehesildar etc. We were shown how the various village and tehsil accounts and other books of land revenue are inspected. Then we went round the village and discussed with the villagers their problems. We learnt that they may be uneducated and mostly illiterate, but so far as their problems were concerned they were very much aware and knowledgeable - also shrewd.

One morning, we were taken to Bulundshar, a district head-quarters. In the evening, we were invited to the Police Lines for a tea party. We got a surprise when the Police band came out and gave us a ceremonial salute. One did feel a bit puffed up on such occasions!

Lectures on Law were interesting and made more enjoyable by Munir, a retired District and Sessions Judge from Allhabad. He was very popular with the probationers. I found the study of law very fascinating. As a student of mathematics, both applied and pure, I found that law was governed by logic. That helped me top in that subject and I became Munir's favorite pupil.

The most enjoyable part of our training was the non-formal education in several diverse fields imparted through visits and talks by eminent personalities.

The Prime Minister had been taking a great deal of interest to introduce scientific ideas and temper. Our very first visit therefore was to the National Physical Laboratory in Delhi. Dr. Krishnan, the Director of NPL, personally took us round and explained work and organisation of the NPL.

On another occasion, we visited an art exhibition at the Hyderabad House to see a very good collection of rare manuscripts, jewelery and art-pieces. We had an opportunity to see the hand-writings of almost all the former Governor-Generals of India, Quran of Aurangzeb written in his own hand writing, ancient Indian scriptures on palm-leaves, on copper plates and on stones; art-pieces from the famous Salar-Jung's collection, including Jehangir's sword, Aurangzeb's dagger and many medieval armaments.

We could enjoy our visit greatly because Dr. Srinivas Chari, the Director of Archaeology (Hyderabad), a well-known scholar had specially come to explain to us the exhibits and how to handle, preserve and collect such pieces. According to him, many of these objects were collected by the civil service officers while touring in districts. He appealed to us to be always on the lookout for such objects during tours. He delivered a long lecture on Indian Paintings, showed us copies of the masterpieces of Ajanta and Ellora and explained the trend in modern art. We spent six pleasant hours in his company.

Those days, Malaria was rampant everywhere. We were therefore taken to the Indian Malaria Institute situated very near the Metcalfe House. We were taught to distinguish the various types of mosquitoes, to analyse their blood, to study malaria fever in all its stages and control of this scourge in districts. Col. Jaswant Singh, the Director, made the visit very interesting.

Then there was a course of lectures on Indian History by Pandit Bhagwat Dutta. He took two topics at the beginning, viz. 'Home of the Aryans' and 'The Vedas'. A renowned historian and Sanskrit scholar, his approach to history was purely Indian in spirit and he had challenged many theories of the Western historians. His approach being novel and refreshing, we heard him with rapt attention, though some were skeptical of his conclusions.

Another memorable visit was to the Central Asian Antiquities Museum on the Jan path. Many objects there were the collection of an Englishman named Sir Auriel Stein. In the beginning of the last century, he explored Tibet, Central Asia, Gobi desert and brought a vast collection of relics to Delhi. These include large size painting on walls. Today, it is difficult to imagine as to how he could manage to transport such walls over high altitude Himalayas over backs of mules. From artistic point of view, these paintings have strange admixture of the Chinese and the Indian features: figures with distinct Mongoloid features and eyes and fingers as are found in Ajanta Caves. At the museum, we were shown the Babar Nama - autobiography of Babar - in original.

We also spent four days at the Agricultural Research Institute, Pusa. Originally the Imperial (now Indian) Agricultural Institute was situated at Pusa, a town in Bihar. It was destroyed in an earthquake in 1936 and the Institute was moved to a township about 11 miles from

Delhi that was renamed Pusa. In this Institute, research work on agricultural problems is carried out. There are various divisions, such as Dairy, Agronomy, Agricultural Engineering, Soil Conservation, Mycology, Chemistry etc. Our stay at the Institute was a pleasant one, except that we had to work for long hours in strong sunshine and walk for miles. Our VP did not fail to tell us every now and then that this kind of life was going to be our lot for at least 8/9 years of our initial career.

Meeting Personalities

The most interesting aspect of our training was the talks by some eminent personalities. We looked forward to these opportunities.

Sardar K. M. Pannikar, India's former Ambassador to the People's Republic of China, visited the School one evening. He delivered a delightful talk on the communist revolution in China and new administrative set-up there. We had an opportunity to discuss many political problems relating to the Far East.

Bhootlingam, ICS, a Secretary in the Commerce Ministry gave us a lucid talk on 'India's Foreign Trade'. On another evening G. L. Mehta, a member of the Planning Commission and our Ambassador-designate to the USA gave us a talk on the 'Place of Industry in the Five Year Plan'. On yet another occassion, K. P. S. Menon, ICS, the Foreign Secretary, who had one of the most exciting career, talked about life of a Political Officer in the North West Frontier of pre-partition India. He also spoke about his travels across the Himalayas and kept us spellbound with his brilliant presentation and his wit.

Another speaker we enjoyed very much listening to was Vardachar, the Secretary of the States Ministry who explained to us the principles and policies adopted by late Sardar Patel in the integration of States. He briefed us on the nature of the work we shall have to do in Part B or C States and merged States. Coming straight from a man who was intimately associated with Sardar Patel in evolving the administrative set-up in those feudal and princely ruled areas, his talk was very instructive. In my very first posting as the Assistant Collector of Ahemdabad district, I had a first hand experience of dealing with these relics of per-independence India.

One of the popular visitor was Shri Anantha Sayanam Ayyangar, the Deputy Speaker of the Lok Sabha. A jovial personality and a brilliant conversationalist, he regaled us for hours with his wit, but at the same time impressed us with his erudite knowledge and learning. He spoke on 'India as a Secular State'.

A. A. A. Fyzee, former Indian Ambassador to Egypt, who was then a member of the UPSC, briefed us about the new format of interview that the UPSC would be introducing for IAS and IFS that year. After my unfortunate experience, I felt that such a reform was very much called for, because the interview board ought to find out what the candidate knew - and how well - rather than trying to expose his ignorance! I am glad to find that this is now accepted.

By common consent, the most impressive speakers were Jaipal Singh, M. P. Dewan Chaman Lall (M. P.), and Dr. R. K. Patil, a Member of the newly constituted Planning Commission. Jaipal Singh has had one of the most colourful and unusual career. An adivasi by birth, born in Bihar's tribal area, he captained the Indian Hockey team in the Amsterdam Olympics in 1928. It was the first time that India won Olympic title and had kept it till then. Later he joined the ICS. He resigned to join the national movement. He was the acknowledged leader of the then twenty-two million Advasis in India. He could be called the father of present day Jharkand and Chattisgarh states. In most simple language, he explained to us the problems of Adivasis and the attitude of the present Government. It was a highly polished and lucid analysis and had a great impact on our young minds. We learnt that from the point of view of civilization, the Advasis may be primitive people, but culturally they are far more advanced than us. In our march towards prosperity and more economic well-being, we have to carry these people with us without altering their happy way of life. The problem of Nagas in Assam had already assumed international importance. His lucid exposition of the Advasi and their problems had a deep impact on me. Later in my career, I was to handle the Mizo problem and succeed in restoring peace after over thirty years of militancy. Unconsciously, what I had heard from Jaipal Singh must have guided me in dealing with tribals.

Dewan Chaman Lal, an intellectual in Congress, was formerly India's Ambassador in Turkey. As an eminent barrister, he had a knack of putting across his arguments most convincingly. He represented the Congress Party's point of view regarding the present administration. He reminded us that the times are revolutionary and the administration must keep pace with the time. The role of the Service is now not in cloistered offices, but in public.

R. K. Patil, a member of the newly constituted Planning Commission, was a modest looking man, who had shown immense administrative and organizing capabilities. He was formerly in the ICS. He resigned to participate in the Freedom movement. Later he was to become a minister in the Central Provinces and appointed as the Food Commissioner to handle the India-wide 'Grow more food campaign'. We were greatly impressed with his humility and his grasp of the economic and other administrative problems involved in the implementation of the First Five Year Plan.

In addition to these class-room activities, we were kept busy with Physical Training or Tennis in the morning; weapon's training in the afternoon or classes in motor mechanics. In the Weapon's Training class we were taught to handle and fire all Police weapons.

Soon it was the month of August and our IFS colleagues were to leave for the United Kingdom. We had number of farewell parties. It was during one of these dinners that I was persuaded by one of these colleagues to taste beer. As part of their duty, the IFS colleagues had already been initiated into drinking stronger alcoholic beverages as well as various kinds of wines. That night I felt guilty that I had sipped an alcoholic drink - I had never tasted one and knowing that I was to work in the Bombay State, where total prohibition prevailed, I was very uncomfortable for a few days. Fifteen years later, when I started visiting Geneva for trade negotiations, I started enjoying wines without a guilty conscience. Later I would graduate as a connoisseur amongst my colleagues.

Our Guest-Nights - and other Nights :

An institution in itself, our mess was to play an important role in our training. Apart from social activities, we would have our Guest-Nights. We were to meet the high and mighty of the land and talk to them with assumed airs of future rulers of the country.

Before we had our first Guest-Night, our V. P. spent an evening with us teaching us correct manners in greeting seniors and their spouses, in table manners and how to propose toasts. Also how to use the cutlery. How one must mix with guests and not monopolize conversations, especially with the fair-sex. Our first Guest-Night was in the third week of April 1. I had been nominated on the mess-committee and we had the responsibility to ensure that everything went off smoothly. Our chief-guest for the evening was H. V. Iyengar, ICS, the Union Home Secretary. He belonged to the Bombay cadre and was regarded as one of the most distinguished civilians. He had been a Private Secretary of Pandit Nehru, and had also served as the Defence secretary.

That night we had a delightful gathering consisting of nine ICS officers and other officials with their spouses. That included Dr. K. Raj, Director General of Health Services, Maj. Gen. J. N. Chaudhuri of Hyderabad fame and his wife, Dr. Krishnan, Director of the National Physical Laboratory and several officials of the Union Home Ministry. We had opportunity to meet V. P. Menon and several others who had delivered lectures at the School. It was interesting to find how all these men with vast experience and practical outlook engaged us in conversation regaling with anecdotes of their experiences and impressed us with their profound observations. It was no less pleasant to listen to the wives of these high officials talking about their role. Many a time, they showed refreshingly novel outlook and brought their husbands down from high pedestal to human level. Moreover, as many of us were bachelors, they were keen on giving us advice on marriage. We had been warned by our mentor the VP to be careful, as some of them will be looking for prospective son-in-laws.

We had at least one Guest-Night each month and we looked forward to the occasion. Some of these were truly memorable. One night we had K. P. S. Menon, the Foreign Secretary as the Chief Guest. He was a delightful conversationalist, with a rare sense of humour. Along with him, we had invited many of the senior officers of the External Affairs Ministry. I had an opportunity to meet Harishwar Dayal ICS, Joint Secretary, External Affairs Ministry. He was a member of the UPSC Interview Board, before which I had appeared. After the mauling I had received at the hands of R. N. Banerjee, the Chairman, I could never forget the gentle and suave H. Dayal. To my surprise, I found that Mrs. Dayal was a Maharashtrian, nee Miss Leela Rao, before here marraige. At one time, her name was well known in India. She was the All-India Tennis Champion three years in succession (pre-war years) and also played at Wimbledon - a very great achievement for any tennis player. She insisted on talking to me in Marathi and we had a good time recalling some old Marathi dramas and artists.

The Making of an IAS Officer

One of the most popular guest was Gen. K. C. Cariappa, the Commanding-in-Chief of the Indian Army. Immaculately dressed in his mess-kit, with his clipped English and perfect manners, he was a great attraction. He came over twice - a great honour to us. In return, he invited one evening the members of the Mess-Committee, that included me. That evening Maj. Gen. J. N. Chaudhuri had come to our School to give us a talk on the military-cum-civil liaison in the Hyderabad operations. Hyderabad Police Action remains one of the best examples of an integrated military and civil operation. After the talk, he escorted us to Gen. Cariappa's residence for dinner. There were six of us: four members of the Mess Committee, Gen. Chaudhari and our host. The dinner was spread over three hours, with seven courses in true military order. After dinner, we had a frank and interesting discussion on various topics. Gen. Cariappa - a very straight forward man- did not mince words in expressing his opinion on men and matters. Altogether, we had a very pleasant evening.

One evening, by coincidence, we had a number of Maharashtrian ICS Officers. Mr. Ambegaonkar, ICS, Secretary of the Finance Ministry; Mrs. and Mr. A. V. Pai, ICS, who was soon going to take over as the Home Secretary; Mrs. and Mr. Nagarkar, ICS, Member of the UPSC. On that occasion, I also met Mrs. and Mr. G. R. Kamat, ICS who was a Joint Secretary in the Finance Ministry and whose younger brother A. R. Kamat was my favourite professor of mathematics at the Fergusson College. Once we had at dinner V. V. Giri, a prominent labour leader who was destined to become India's President one day.

S. G. Barve, ICS, a Joint Secretary in the Economic Affairs Department, had also come as my guest. His name was well known to me as the first Municipal Commissioner of Poona. He had transformed the infrastructure of the city. In turn, he invited me to visit the Ministry of Finance in the North Block and acquainted me with the various activities of that important Ministry.

I met there for the first time P. D. Kasbekar, IAS, who was than Private Secretary to C. D. Deshmukh, the Finance Minister. Kasbekar had broken Sir Chintaman's - as he was known those days - record in the matriculation examination and that's how the Finance Minister had chosen him to work as his Private Secretary. Several years later I would work with P. D. Kasbekar, when he was the chief secretary and I was the Home Secretary in Maharashtra.

We had also the great R. N. Banerjee, ICS, Chairman of the UPSC. It was a fun to meet him outside viva-voce room. He was in a very gay and sporting mood and did not fail to tell us that if we made our career a success, credit would be his, and if any one of us did not live up to the "Service Standards", he would own the mistake! A very fair man indeed - but strictly outside the interview room.

Chapter 3

With The Army

A close co-ordination between civilian and army authorities was an important feature of colonial administration that we inherited. In a vast sub-continent, a small number of civil officers could not administer without visible and not-too-visible support of army. It was important for the civil administration and the army to get to know each others' administrative and field structures so that in any emergency or serious law-and-order situation these authorities could function as a team, knowing well the respective roles and the limitations in the use of force. For that purpose, the IAS officers were sent for two week attachment with units of army.

Our batch was given an option to either go to Kashmir or Assam for the army attachment. Only eight opted for Assam. The main aim of our military training was to study the organization of the army, its discipline, role of the army in aid of the civil administration to deal with law and order situations, troop formations on the front lines, use of automatic-weapons etc. After fifteen days of army attachment, we were allowed to tour Kashmir for ten days on our own.

Gen. Cariappa, the Commanding-in-Chief, had taken a great deal of interest in our attachment with the Army. Maj. Gen. J. N. Choudhuri, who was the Adjutant-General, briefed us on the organization of the Indian Army, its peace and war time formations, officers mess, life in Kashmir, security measures and scores of other subjects.

We left Delhi by the Kashmir Mail and when we arrived at the Pathankot railway station next morning, we were given a warm reception by the army authorities and escorted to the Officers Transit Camp. After lunch, we started on our journey to Jammu in army trucks. By that time, in the month of June, temperature had soared to 110 degree. It was a grueling experience to travel in an army truck in such heat. The only consolation was the sight of the roaring river Chenab.

R. Krishnamurti, Sivagnanam, B. S. Raghavan and self went for sightseeing in the Jammu city. We visited the famous temple of Raghunath, and had meals in the Hotel Cosmos, where South Indian friends were surprised to get their favourite masala dosa. For them, it was a great triumph of the South Indian cuisine. Next day we started very early for the Bannihal Valley.

Late in the afternoon, we started climbing up to Kurd and the temperature began to fall very rapidly. It was late in the evening when we reached Bannihal town. It was very cold and we had to take out our winter clothing. The place for our night halt was very beautiful and moonlight added a charm and mystery to the atmosphere. A stream of ice-cold water was roaring behind the room where I slept with a friend. It was only in the morning that we learnt that the room was the mortuary room of the adjoining hospital.

Those days one had to drive to the Bannihal Pass at the top up to over nine thousand feet. It was a very arduous drive on narrow road with innumerable bends. Accidents were frequent and many a truck had gone hurtling down into the valley. Slowly climbing up, one saw one of the most beautiful sights. There were terraces of rice fields, one rising above other on mountain slopes. Streams were trickling everywhere and the fields were green. As we went higher, the rice fields became smaller and smaller until the whole valley looked like a huge chess board. On reaching the Bannihal Pass, we drove through a small tunnel to enter the Jhelum valley. The pass was generally snow-covered in winter and was the only entry to the Kashmir valley. This is where the Jammu region ends and the vale of Kashmir begins.

We motored down the Jhelum valley to race towards Srinagar forty miles away. We were accommodated in the Holiday Home, a mess for the officers on holiday from operational areas. Next day, we reached Baramulla where we were received by Maj. Gen. Thakur Mahadev Singh, Divisional Commander, who briefed us in a scholarly manner about our attachment. We were divided into eight batches of four each. Three were attached to Uri, three to Tithwal and two to Baramulla sectors. My batch was attached to the 1st Jat located on a mountain slope in the Uri sector.

On arrival, we were received by Major Prithvi Pal Sigh, called P P, who introduced us to Lt Col. Ujjal Singh, the battalion commander. We were accommodated in tents put up along side of the mess. In the afternoon, we were ceremoniously received at a parade with all officers and

400 troops present. Only then we realized that we were to spend next few days with one of the most celebrated battalions formed in 1803. In 1861, the 1st Jat marched from Delhi to Kabul in a record time and thus earned the title of the Light Infantry.

Thereafter, we were taken to a sand model of the area. Uri sector was the place where a fierce battle had been fought between India's army and the Pak army intruders in1947. The cease-fire line was about ten miles away.

Next day, the C. O., addressed as Tiger, drove us to the Uri town where before the conflict in 1947, 4000 houses existed. Now only 4 remained, of that one was the guest-house of the Kashmir state. In 1946, it became famous, as the then prime- minister of the State, Ramchandra Kak, arrested Pandit Nehru and interned him in that guest-house.

In the afternoon, we were driven to the Mile-Stone 58. Prior to the partition, the route to the Kashmir valley was via Rawalpindi/Murry and one crossed the bridge at Kohala. All distances in the valley were measured from that mile- stone. Now the Mile-Stone is on the cease-fire line (CFL).

Our journey to visit the CFL was an adventure. The road was in a very bad shape as the UN Observers would not allow repairs because that may facilitate movement of troops. Moreover, it was a narrow road with high mountain on one side and the roaring Jhelum 200 ft on the other. Somewhere, the driver lost his nerve and the truck landed in a ditch by the mountain side. We escaped

With The Army

with scratches and bruises on bodies. We were rushed to a military Field Ambulance and given first-aid. The C. O. of 1st Jat rushed there and Gen Mahadev Singh sent his ADC to enquire about us. With all that fussing, we had a comfortable stay and reached our unit late at night.

Next two days were full of several activities such as the weapon training, map reading, and witnessing how discipline was administered in the army. 'Orderly-Room' was an unforgettable experience. Once a week, the CO examined cases of breach of discipline committed in his battalion, passed orders and awarded punishments. In fact, his room was then an 'Order-Room', but over a period it has come to be called Orderly-Room.

We witnessed an interesting case of what is an act of indiscipline. On the previous day, a Lt. Colonel from the Western Command had come to inspect the unit. He went to the jawans' langar (Kitchen) and asked the jawan X, 'How is the food here? Instead of X replying, Y said 'The food is very good'. Replying, when the question asked was addressed to some other jawan was considered an offence. Y was sentenced to three days R. I. After that Orderly-Room experience, we had a heated discussion with the CO on the procedure of military trials. We were told that all that was necessary in the interest of military discipline. We unconsciously learnt what not to do.

One afternoon, a demonstration of the role of the army in times of internal disturbances was held. It started with a riot in a town – the District Magistrate calls upon nearest battalion commander, entry of the military, and all other official formalities in great details. It was presented in an excellent way – with all the dramatic effects – including mock killing of a couple of civilians.

The most enjoyable part of our training was to learn the use of different weapons, such as revolver, sten, rifle and machine gun. There was no restriction on the use of ammunition and we fired to our heart's content. Bayonet training was interesting but thoroughly exhausting. It called for tremendous animal-energy, both physical and mental. At the end of the two hours, we would lie flat on the ground, with as much emotional fatigue as the physical exhaustion. For us, it was not easy to thrust a bayonet into someone – although the enemy was only a saw-dust dummy!

We had our quota of excitement and narrow escapes from the jaws of death. We had already had one accident on the way to see the cease-fire line.

One evening Man Mohan Kohili and I went for a walk. We crossed a suspension bridge near our camp and went on the other side of the Jhelum. We walked in fields and meadows for about one-and-half hours and reached a village named Ta-th-da Kanal. Everywhere we were greeted by young and old ones with shouts of 'Jai Hind'. We ate some aluchas and mulberrys. While returning, we were charged at by a bull, who came straight at us furiously and almost trampled us down! It was a miracle how both of us side-stepped at the nick-time – only to find that a young, fragile and very beautiful girl had taken hold of the bull and led him away by the rope. Being city born and city bred we obviously did not know how to handle such a situation.

On the way back, we took the famous Moghul track. It was quite thrilling; on one side were the mountains on the other, a sheer drop of hundreds of feet down into the roaring Jhelum. We were walking on a foot track hardly a couple of feet wide which the Mogul emperors and their zenanas used to travel from Lahore to Srinagar via Rawalpindi. We walked on the narrow path taking a long breath of relief after each step. At the end of the adventure, we laughed over the whole thing – as all this exposure to danger was wholly unnecessary and uncalled for.

One morning, we were woken up very early to go up to '8416'. This was the tactical headquarters of our battalion, and for security considerations, described according to altitude of its location. At 'mile 73' we got off the truck and started a steep climb of about 4000 ft. It was a painful ordeal. However, the sight of Jhelum, which looked like a small stream from that height and the sight of other mountain tops closing on us, were exhilarating. After six hours, we reached the top of '8416' and were received by Major Ganpat Singh with a hearty handshake. He had come over there two days earlier to make arrangements for our visit.

It was indeed an exhilarating sight to stand on the top of '8416' and see on all sides mountain tops glistening in the early morning sun. Chota-Kazinag was covered with snow and Nanda Devi (in Pak occupied area) was towering majestically in the sky. We were standing at a point, that would be most strategic if the hostilities started. Through binoculars, we could even see the movement of Pak troops. Standing there, we realized the value of mountain tops in case of combat.

All of a sudden at 8.30 p.m. we were asked to go with a Patrol Party for night duty. Those were dark nights and the mountain slopes looked dangerous. Death was certain in case one slipped from the narrow one-and-half feet path.

We started at 9 p.m. We were warned while on these patrols, one has to speak in low tone; one cannot use battery torch or any other light. One could not even light a cigarette, because a cigarette - end can be seen from miles away and the enemy line was only three miles away. We entered a small village (about 50 houses) and kept a watch on the inmates. It was known that at those hours Pakistani agents visited the territory to spy on our troops. We were there till 3.30 a.m. silently watching. However, nothing exciting happened. Then we started to climb up by another route. On reaching a picket a young Lieutenant offered us tea. We had not imagined the physical strain in climbing each step called for an extra effort. Danger was also ever present. At last at 6.45 a.m. we reached 'our top'. At that hour in the morning sunshine, the valleys appeared very beautiful and inviting but at night they seemed like jaws of death.

One day, we visited nearby installations and the famous Serr Bridge – place of bitter fighting. It was at this spot that Nandu Singh, Vir Chakra, was killed in action. That day we had one more thrilling experience, while returning, we saw a bridge across the Jhelum, constructed by the army. It was a simple suspension foot-bridge with steel girders on both sides and strong steel ropes hung across the river, which supported wooden planks. Mighty Jhelum roared under the bridge with its crystal clear water glistering jade-like in the sun. We expressed a desire to cross the bridge. However, on second thought seeing its precarious condition, and the sight of the bridge swaying in the wind, nobody dared to step on it. After some discussion, I agreed to lead the party and walked steadily for about sixty feet with somewhat heavy Ramesh Chandra, following me. Accidentally, he looked down and felt giddy. A few feet below our feet the water was making such a turmoil that Ramesh Chandra took hold of the wire by hand on one side. With his heavy build, as soon as he moved away from the center of the bridge, the suspention- bridge began to swing sideways in the air.

Capt. Harminder Singh who was following Ramesh Chandra acted quickly. He took hold of his collar and pulled him down, and shouted that I should lie down. By then due to all the activity the whole bridge was swaying dangerously. Four of us lay on the bridge for ten minutes, which seemed like eternity. After the bridge had steadied, we started slowly creeping back to safety. Thus ended another escapade from the jaws of certain death. That was however not the last one.

On the last day of our stay, we moved about in the unit. We met jawans, talked to them and ate food in their Langar (mess). Later we were requested by the Junior Commissioned Officers (JCO's) and the Subhedar Major to visit their mess. We found the jats, simple sturdy and very gentle except when they get worked-up or fight. They liked the way we met them informally.

A farewell-dinner was arranged in our honour. After dinner, a toast was proposed to the President's health and I gave a suitable reply on behalf of the Probationers. Thus ended the last day of our stay with the army – a memorable experience.

Before leaving the 1st Jats, we called on Lt. Col. Ujjal Singh. He spoke very feelingly about our stay. We were deeply moved and reciprocated his feelings. Our stay had been very pleasant. There was hard work, plenty of it; but there was a child-like delight in seeing and learning new things. There was danger – but what else could we expect on a battle front. We came intimately in contact with the jawans, the JCOs and the senior officers. They greeted us with open arms everywhere. Our every single word of sympathy was appreciated and during these fifteen days, they almost came to love us. We were no longer strangers – their own kith and kin. They gave us a peep into a fighting man's life and his psyche.

As our jeep was racing towards Baramula, a thousand thoughts raced through my mind… I had made new friends. Capt. Harminder Singh was unusual army officer. He was intelligent, suave and very well read. No doubt he had been selected by Lt. Gen. S. P. Thorat to work as his ADC, when Thorat was the Corps Commander. Harminder told me a lot about this General, whom I was destined to meet in different capacities much later in Bombay. A few years later, Capt. Harminder Singh took early retirement from the army and joined the Indian Frontier Administrative Service. He served in the North East-Frontier Agency (NEFA). One day his name flashed in the newspaper, as the Political Officer who escorted His Holiness the Dalai Lama when the latter crossed over one night from Tibet into India in the Tawang sector of the present Arunachal Pradesh.

Another name that I would come across in my future career was that of Captain Hayde, the Adjutant, an

Englishman by birth, he became an Indian by choice. In the course of a lecture on 'Admin', one of us made a casual remark that he felt 'let-down'. That was enough to set up a volcanic reaction. Capt Hayde explained that in company of a military officer never to use that expression. That was the ultimate abuse and aspersion on the uniform. An important lesson!

During the 1965 war with Pakistan, Capt Hayde, who was then a Lt. Colonel commanded the 1st Jat in the famous battle of Dograi in the Lahore sector. He was awarded the Mahavir Chakra (MVC). He would earn another MVC in a battle in the Sialkot sector.

Our quota of adventures was not yet over. After four days stay in Srinagar, we were to fly back to Delhi. Flying from Srinagar to Jammu we had to cross the Bannihal range. With mountains on both sides at an average height of 10,000 ft, our plane, a Dakota, had to fly over 12,000 ft. high. The weather conditions that afternoon were very bad. Flying at a height of over 12,000 ft, the wing tips of our plane were soon covered with snow and the plane was being tossed about in the strong monsoon gale. We hovered over Jammu for over two hours. As soon as the weather conditions became somewhat normal, the pilot attempted a successful landing. That was a thrilling end to the tour of the Kashmir valley.

Chapter 4

Tourism
- Summer 1952

We had a memorable holiday in the valley. We visited Gulmarg, Sonmarg, Martand, Anantnag and Pahelgam. Nature was in full bloom and fruits were plenty. On my birthday on the 27th June, I got up early in the morning and along with two friends climbed 3,000 ft. height, to the famous temple of Shiva, put up there by Sri Adi Shankaracharya when he came to the valley to revive Hinduism.

Other memorable visits were to Dehradun, Mussoorie, Hardwar and Rishikesh. We left Delhi one evening by train and reached Dehradun early morning. The Registrar of the Forest Research Institute (FRI) greeted us at the station. We were accommodated in the Hostel of the FRI, which was beautifully located and tastefully furnished. Since we had carried our mess-staff, we were very comfortable. The place where we stayed was the Training School of ICS Officers during the Second World War- years (1941-44).

We also visited the Surveyor General of India's office, where we were shown all the stages through which maps have to go before they appear in print. Unless one sees it, one cannot realize how very painstaking and complicated work it is. In the main Survey Office, we were shown the instruments used for survey work and methods of surveying. One is indeed overwhelmed to learn of the silent work done by the surveyors in India over past two centuries. It is a stupendous task to measure and map every inch of our land.

We were greatly fascinated with this introduction to survey work. We were told that very soon, on getting charge of the respective sub-divisions, we would have to undergo an examination in surveying and that survey being the back bone of revenue settlement and land records had great implications for the rights of individual land owner.

One day we visited the National Defence Academy. As the Commandant, Maj. Gen. M. S. Wadalia had gone to Khadakvasla, at Poona, we were received by the Deputy Commandant Col. Niranjan Prasad. He gave a short historical preview and then we were escorted in batches to see the Gentlemen Cadets at work. We saw them at parade, attended their lectures and informally chatted with them.

Another day we visited the Joint Services Wing, where boys between 15-17½ years are taken up for commissions in Navy, Army and the Air-force. We studied its organization and methods of instruction. I was glad to meet there Cadet Namjoshi, the younger brother of Madhukar Namjoshi of Poona who had refused to join the IFS.

Next, we reached Mussoorie at around 9 a.m. It was bright and sunny and everything was fresh and we realized why, Mussoorie, called the 'Queen' of hill-stations in India, continues to be known so even today. At that time, it was reputed to be one of the cleanest town in India. Alas, no longer!

Before going up, we had arranged through the District Collector of Dehradun, V. C. Sharma, IAS about our stay at the Savoy, the biggest hotel in Mussoorie. We found it palatial and its owner Kirpa Ram was waiting to greet us. A good old man, he took great interest in organizing trips of IAS Probationers to Mussoorie each year. Normally the rooms at Savoy would cost Rs 50/- per day. But he had granted concession to us and we were to pay only Rs 15/-.

As soon as we entered the hotel gate, the old man came out and asked, "Are these my young Collectors?" He was visibly happy to receive us and expressed great pride for the new Indian Administrative Service breed of officers. Obviously, for several decades he had been playing a host to the ICS and recognized the change of times. It struck us that for him knowing an IAS officer, especially one who was going to work in U.P. and who was on the threshold of his career was good business!

Next day we left for Rishikesh, from where we went to visit the Lakshman-Jhoola the suspension bridge over the Ganges, about seven miles upstream. When we reached Lakshman-Jhoola, standing there, I realized why Indians have been worshipping this river: not only because it is regarded holy, but the Ganges stands for the life and happiness of the millions of Indian habiting north India. The very next day, I was to experience that.

Next day, we visited Hari-Ki-Pavadi the bathing ghat at Hardwar. I enjoyed the dip in the Ganges and we took

Tourism

some photographs. At Hari-Ki-Pavadi the Ganges has been diverted for benefit of the pilgrims. We crossed a bridge and went over to the other side, where a large barrage has been constructed. We introduced ourselves to the officer-in-charge who was every pleased to receive us and showed us round the place. The Upper Ganges canal has been taken out at Hardwar. This canal carries very large volume of water – we were told one of the largest in the world. The canal runs for about 120 miles and is responsible for the prosperity of Western U.P. It is also remarkable in many other respects : sometimes it goes over some rivers, sometimes rivers go under it and sometimes it is difficult to distinguish between a river and the canal. At places, the whole scene looks like an optical illusion – a great engineering feat. There are eight hydro-electric works constructed on it and they supply power to western U.P. This was a golden opportunity for us to see the benefits of irrigation works. During the journey, I saw one of the richest and high yielding lands of India.

We drove towards Delhi via Roorkee, Muzaffar Nagar, Meerut and arrived at the Metcalfe House late in the evening. In three days we had covered a vast stretch of our country. We had lived comfortably, with our Jeeves looking after us. Our expenses per head were Rs 87/- might appear insignificant today, but that was higher than the allowance sanctioned by the Government.

Our next sojourn was to Mt. Abu, where we were to spend ten days at the Indian Police Service Academy. On way from Delhi, we visited Udaipur, Chittorgadh and Ajmer. Everywhere we were looked after well. At Udaipur, we even spent an hour with the old Maharaja, the symbol of

Hindu supremacy, whose ancestors had refused to go to Delhi to bow to the Mugal Durbar. In 1911, he had even refused to go to Delhi to pay homage to His Majesty, the King George V. It was a moving experience, just to see this 'Sun-God'. He was old and semi-invalid.

Our stay in Mt. Abu was very enjoyable. There were 36 IPS officers under training and I got to know several of them well. Some of them, I would meet again after 33 years, when I became the Union Home Secretary. I fell in love with the tiny hill station, situated in the plains surrounded by desert. Three year later, I was posted at Mt. Abu as the Sub-Divisional Officer and spent over two delightful years there.

On the return to Delhi, I had decided to visit Mahajanis in Jaipur. Dr. Mahajani was then Vice-Chancellor of the newly established Rajputana University. During that one day, they overwhelmed me with affection and hospitality. It remains for me an unforgettable experience.

෩ඥ෩ඥ

Chapter 5

Transformation
- From Students into Officers

Days and months were passing by – in fact too rapidly. We were to call on the Prime Minister and the President in the last month of our training.

IAS probationers were asked to work on several committees set up in the Defence Ministry to organize the flag-hoisting at the Red Fort on the 15th August and the Republic Day Parade on the 26th January. Arrangements for these occasions were complex and we learnt in what great detail everything had to be worked out, discussed and efficiently carried out. We worked with the Army, Navy and the IAF officers and learnt by observation their ways of working. We also worked with the District Magistrate of Delhi to work out Police arrangements for crowd control. That experience would be very useful in our districts.

Earlier we got opportunity to see the Prime Minister and the President at close quarters. After India was declared a Republic and first General elections held in 1952, the first session of the House of People was convened in January 1953. There was shortage of ushers. Probationers were drafted to undertake that task. As ushers, we witnessed the historic opening of the First session by the President of the Republic of India, when Dr Rajendra Prasad addressed a joint session of both the Houses of the Parliament. For us it was exciting to receive and escort great leaders of our Freedom movement, including Pandit Nehru, Abul Kalam Azad, S. K. Kriplani etc.

Later we were invited to observe the working of democracy and seated in the galleries to see the great leaders of India's freedom movement. Prime Minister was the focus of everyone's attention. I found that by merely sitting in the lobbies of the Lok Sabha one received education in the working of the Parliamentary democracy, which no university can aspire to impart. Later in my career, as private secretary to the defence minister of India, I would spend several days in the lobby for officials observing the prime minister Nehru facing criticism for his mishandling the China's claims on India's border and for the debacle of the army in the north-east. That was in 1962-63.

It was already month of February. Our training was coming to an end. As young bachelors, we were in demand—as prospective grooms.

One day Halve and I were invited to tea by Mrs. & Mr. N. M. Buch, ICS at 1, Akbar Road.

He belonged to the Punjab cadre and after partition opted for Bombay cadre of the ICS. He was then the Director General of Disposals in Delhi. Earlier he had been a joint secretary in the States Ministry and worked closely with Sardar Vallabhbhai Patel. He regaled us with stories of integration of Saurashtra.

Transformation

At his residence, I met Mrs. and Mr. S. A. Gadkari. He was a member of the Central Board of Irrigation and Navigation. A well known hydro-electric engineer from undivided Punjab, he was then associated with several big multi-purpose projects under construction, including the Bhakra-Nangal and the Damodar Valley Project. He was the brother of the famous Gadkari Pleader of Poona. I spent a couple of hours in very pleasant company.

I was greatly impressed by Mrs. Gadkary. For her age she was not only attractive but remarkably well preserved. She was a post graduate (M.A.) in English, of a generation when not many girls received even high school education. She was Morarjibhai Desai's contemporary at the Wilson College in Bombay 1920's.

S. A. Gadkary had graduated with an engineering degree from the Engineering College Poona in 1919 and got post-graduate degree from the Indian Institute of Science in Bangalore. He had stood first-class-first in all examinations and was selected by the General Motors Co. He worked there for over five years before joining the Punjab Government in 1929. I was greatly fascinated meeting this highly educated and polished couple. The very next day Mrs. Gadkary rang up to ask me over for dinner. On some excuse, I politely declined. Instead, I had invited them for dinner to our next Guest Night.

A couple of weeks later, the probationers were invited to the President's reception at the Rashtrapati Bhavan on the Republic Day, the Mughal garden. With flowers in full bloom and the gay atmosphere of the Republic Day, there was festive atmosphere all round. The whole

Rashtrapati Bhavan and the two blocks of the Secretariat were illuminated and it was a splendid sight. In the night, there was a display of fire works near the Turkman Gate. That Republic Day reception would be memorable for me, because I would 'see' my would be wife for the first time in the Moghul Garden.

At the Reception, Gadkarys accosted me. I was happy to meet them again and did not fail to notice their daughter standing at some distance with some friends. A few days later, they invited me to dinner. I gladly accepted – although the thought of getting engaged to any girl was far from my mind. In fact, our VP had repeatedly warned us that for a successful career it was important that we remain as bachelors for at least first five-six years. But perhaps fate – and emotions – prevailed and very soon I was engaged to their daughter.

It was fortuitous that it would all begin in Buch's house at 1, Akbar Road, which one day would find place in the history books. Smt. Indira Gandhi used the house as an attached office to here residence at 1, Safdarjung Road. It was while walking over to the 1, Akbar Road that she was brutally assassinated by her police guards.

I was to enter that house again only when I became the Union Home Secretary in January' 85 and attended late night meetings with the young Prime Minister Rajiv Gandhi. The lively drawing room where my future personal life had perhaps been determined was now a waiting room. It was cold and an electric heater warmed the room. I recollect that when I visited Buches' it was also the month of January and wooden logs burning in the fire place kept us warm.

Transformation

By the beginning of February, we were all conscious that the final examination was drawing near and we had again become students burning mid-night oil. After the examination in March' 53, we were to leave the School in the third week and after availing of a two-week holiday we were to report to the respective state Governments.

These last few weeks were also the most crowded. The Prime Minister had invited us to the Teen Murti House for a talk after which he hosted an evening party. We would also pay our respects to the President. There were also a number of invitations from senior officers as well as some foreign embassies. A number of distinguished persons visited the School. Home Minister Kailas Nath Katju came over and gave us advice how to be good public servants. At long last, Sir Chintaman Deshmukh also came over. We had been waiting to meet him for a long time. He was the ideal of a civil servant and his career was a great inspiration for us of what a brilliant and a conscientious civil servant could achieve.

I had also started taking lessons in motor-car driving and was determined to get my driving- license before leaving the Metcalfe House. It was also a good excuse for taking my fiancée on drives around the town. For me, the last few weeks of stay in Delhi were very pleasant. I had enjoyed my training at the School. I had made new friends. I had got myself engaged to a nice girl of my choice. Life was gay but at the back of the mind was always the anxiety about the responsibilities of the office I would soon assume. Also to go and live in villages seemed to be a daunting challenge.

In the written examination, I did reasonably well. However, again in viva-voce I got poor marks. My friends were right that I had a poor 'Poona-Personality's. It was perhaps unfair -more to Poona than to me. Soon I got the confirmation of my allotment to the Bombay State and posting to Ahmedabad for the training period. I was happy because Ahmedabad had a long tradition of Supernumerary Assistant Collectors going back to the beginning of this century. Also, next to Bombay and Poona, it was the most important city in the erstwhile Bombay State.

We had our last farewell Guest-Night. All the ICS officers posted in Delhi had been invited and most of them turned up. At the dinner, C. S. Venkatachar ICS, the senior most officer proposed toast to the Service and to the young IAS and wished us for as good career as they had. Times had changed and everyone was acutely aware of that. K. L. Mehta, IAS, proposed to the passing out batch and Man Mohan Kohli replied on our behalf. We missed meeting Sir Raghavan Pillai, the Cabinet Secretary. He was too busy those days. I was destined to meet him several years later in London and spend some very pleasant evenings in his company in his apartment in the St James Courts.

Soon it was time to say goodbyes. Mr. and Mrs. Gadkary hosted a cocktail to announce my engagement to their daughter and also to say goodbye. I met a lot of ICS officers and engineers from the Punjab who had been Gadkary's life long colleagues in that state. Before the party, I had informed my father about the engagement and he sent a telegram conveying his blessings to me.

Transformation

I had conveyed to my father that I would be reaching Poona on 20th March by the Deccan Queen. I was to report to the Chief Secretary on 2nd April – the anniversary of my joining the Service.

෴෴

Chapter 6

Changing Times
- And Changing costs

Before leaving Delhi I wrote two letters to my father, analyzing changes that had taken place within me, aims and ideals that would guide me and some advice that I wanted to tender for the benefit of my brothers. These perhaps contained some profound thoughts penned by me, as well as some trivial information. My father would carefully preserve those letters and hand then over a few months before his death in 1972. Thirty five years after I had joined the Service, I would thus have my own yard-stick to judge, how well I had lived up to my own expectations.

Let me first recall the trivial. We had started on an initial salary of Rs 350 per month. In my case, how rich I found myself, could be seen from the account that I rendered to my father. Following is briefly my financial position:

	Rs	As	Ps
Pay :	350	0	0
Dearness Allowance	40	0	0
Total	390	0	0

Deduction on a/c of Provident Fund (-)	33 - 0 - 0
Deduction on a/c of Income Tax (-)	5 - 0 - 0
Net Pay	352 - 0 - 0
Expenses :	
To Mess (for morning tea, breakfast, lunch, tea, dinner) @ Rs 5 per day	150 - 0 - 0
Room rent (Furniture, electricity, service of sweeper & bhisti *)	20 - 0 - 0
Dhobi (laundry)	12 - 0 - 0
Room Bearer	12 - 8 - 0
Canteen bill (small necessaries such as soap, oil etc.)	15 - 0 - 0
Total	242 - 8 - 0

*One who filled pots/ buckets with water in our rooms.

Savings : Rs 110/-

As regards clothing, as soon as joined the Metcalfe House I had to get formal dresses stitched viz. a silk Achkan and chudidar pyjamas; one dinner suit, i.e., a black woolen pant and a white dinner jacket or a jodhpuri (a coat buttoned up to neck). Those were absolutely essential to attend formal functions and dinners. Today it would appear unbelievable that these clothes cost about Rs 175 and the black leather shoes Rs 16.

Later in the year, I would have to make a woolen dark suit for formal dinners. I got an imported black Vacuna trousers and a closed collar coat made for about Rs 150. Till a few years back, that coat was still in a good condition and I occasionally wore it for formal dinners when I became the chief secretary thirty years later. That showed both the purchasing power of the rupee in 1952 and also the quality of the material.

I recollect that as a Supernumerary Assistant Collector, in my first posting salary was Rs 450, including dearness allowance. When I got a horse for touring, government gave an allowance of Rs 75 per month. On marriage, I received allowance of Rs 60 only. This cause much amusement to my wife and her friends. Money-wise, maintaining a horse was preferable to acquiring a wife. I used to counter that by saying that perhaps that's because their friend ate much less than my horse.

In other letter, there was some gratuitous advice to my brothers. This was provoked because of some family problems – nothing unusual in any family. I do not recollect the exact provocation, but apparently my elder brother and my younger brother were staying away from the 'middle class' values, and I must have been upset enough to pen my thoughts on what I thought should be the correct behavior for an IAS officer's family members. Perhaps I was wrong. I am reproducing these words of wisdom.

I wrote :

"Firstly, it should be noted that I have to work as a District Officer, a man who will be looked up to by the people as an ideal.

Secondly, I have to be a Magistrate and after some years a District Magistrate. And for this job nothing pays like character and spotless reputation.

Now it is admitted that the above will depend on my character and my performance – but not on me alone. My job cannot be done singly. It is a co-operative effort in which every member of the family will have his share. Whatever they do, what kind of reputation or notoriety they gain will immediately reflect on my life. A man cannot hold a responsible post or nobly discharge his duties unless everyone in his home helps him.

In a way I think that in a service like mine, it is better to be outside one's province, away from one's relatives. It makes the job much easier. But as I am, fortunately or unfortunately, coming to my home State, I hope I shall get the best of help and co-operation from my brothers and sisters. By this I do not, in the least, mean that they should obey my wishes or be under my obligation. What I want is character and absolute character. After that everyone has his destiny, fortune and luck."

It may be amusing to recall my first response to what I considered as correct behaviour.

Before leaving Delhi, I received an invitation from an educational society formed by the CKP (Chandraseniya Kyastha Prabhu) community, the one in which I was born, to host a function to honour me. I wrote to my father that:

"I had sent them a telegram informing them of my inability to accept. Our's is a silent service and our job is to 'get things done'. At least the members of the IAS are not expected to succumb to adoration or praise nor to adverse public criticism.

Our ideal is to work, more work and go on working. No leisure, no comforts nor any outside things that touch human vanity. I am convinced of this, and I am going to strictly follow this rule.

Today this may appear strange. A community in which one is born has a right to honour and give public recognition to one who has achieved something exceptional. It also serves as inspiration to young. But I was perhaps too much under influence of what had been dinned into probationers at the Metcalfe House. In a way, our batch of 1952 was a kind of bridge between the era of the RAJ gone by and new era of the REPUBLIC born that year.

But it is a fact that during my service career I declined all such invitations. Only after becoming a Governor, I accepted one in 1987.

We bid good bye to each other on the night of 18th March, 1953. It was very poignant parting. We were young and looking forward to our future. We were no longer competing against each other. Our seniority had been determined on the basis of our performance at the School. Because of my good performance in written papers, especially law, I had gone up several notches in seniority. When we parted we never imagined that some of us will never meet again. We were too young to think of death, but some would die during next thirty years.

Before I boarded the Frontier Mail, I wrote to my father somewhat pompously as to how I saw my future. Yet at the end I wrote philosophically and quoted Khalil Gibran:

Changing Times

> "The first morning of creation wrote,
> What the last dawn of reckoning,
> Shall read."

Perhaps in writing that I gave an expression to a fatalistic feeling. It would be mid-career that I came to realize that mere seniority did not determine how ones' career would shape. My started with a little bit of luck and some pluck. It ended thirty four years later the same way. I would describe it as "Never a Dull Moment."

༺༻༺༻

PART II :

In Bombay State (1953-1962)

Chapter 7

Reporting to the Secretariat
- Non Formal Training

I spent ten days in Poona with the family. I also met my old mentors Sir Raghunathrao Paranjpye and Justice S. B. Dhavle. They were delighted to meet me. I also called on my professors in the Fergusson College. I scrupulously avoided meeting Prof. D. R. Gadgil. I was afraid that even at that stage he might attempt to talk me out of continuing in the Service.

On the morning of 2nd April 1953, all of us who had been allotted to the Bombay State, met at 10 a.m. sharp P. J. Fernandes, IAS (1948). Popularly known as Praxy, Resident Under Secretary (RUS) to the Government. That was our formal reporting to the State Government. We were five: M. Venkatesan, S. Ramanathan, K. N. Zutshi, S. Sivagnanam and myself. Later, when the States would be reorganized, the first two would go to Karnataka and the other two to Gujarat, and I alone would be left in Maharashtra.

Praxy Fernandes, who had already put in over four years service, was to look after us during our two-week stay in Bombay. He had a very pleasant personality and with his polished manners and the Goan verve, we could not have had a more pleasant senior to guide us. As Resident Under Secretary, briefly called RUS, he had a spacious apartment on the top of the old Secretariat building (now the Sessions Court of Mumbai), which was then the seat of the State Government. The present Mantralaya building was to come later in 1958, after the formation of the Bilingual State. He also acted as Protocol Officer and in that capacity rubbed shoulders with important dignitaries. It appeared to be a very attractive post. No wonder some of us decided in our minds to make a bid for it when our time came.

Praxy arranged for our calls on all the senior officers. The chief secretary, M. D. Bhasali, ICS, tall, dignified with silver gray hair neatly combed and with impeccable buttoned up coat, received us with great courtesy. His old world charm and polish commanded affection and respect. On the other hand Dehejia, ICS, the Finance Secretary, was brilliant but sharp and would not mince words, he called a spade-a-spade. Later he was to be the Finance Secretary in the Union Government for several years and greatly feared by his colleagues for his incisive mind and blunt mannerisms. D. S. Bhakle, ICS, was the Revenue Secretary and as such was the immediate superior of all the Collectors in the State. With a goatee, he looked a philosopher and we found him a polite, but a somewhat remote and cynical person. His apparent lack of social grace was made up by his wife, who was very kind and considerate to us. Later when I worked with Y. B. Chavan, I would come to know her well as she was involved with several social and cultural activities. By then D. S. Bhakle would have withdrawn himself to his neat little house near Alibag, on a lonely beach across the Bombay harbour.

After retiring he spent years as a recluse in a monastery in Spain.

We also met some younger officers. M. R. Yardi ICS, deputy secretary in the Revenue department was busy looking after perennial famine conditions that prevailed in some parts of the sprawling State. A scholar of Sanskrit language and serious student of Bhagwat Gita, with clear perception of self and courage to note on the files what he thought was right, he acquired a formidable reputation and served for several years as the Finance Secretary in the central government, where his qualities were very much respected. M. G. Pimputkar, ICS, was another officer whom we were eagerly looking forward to meeting. He was relatively junior civilian, but had already acquired a name for a certain degree of dash and as a ruthless disciplinarian. Soon, I would learn more about his way of working, where I was posted as the supernumerary Assistant Collector in Ahmedabad.

Our four days in Bombay passed very quickly. A few senior officers were good enough to invite us for meals. Their wives gave us useful tips on what to carry from Bombay for the kind of nomadic life that we would very soon lead. A folding-cot, a few utensils, a primus-stove and a solar hat was a must; also a wooden box to carry the stuff from camp to camp. I equipped myself accordingly and got ready to leave for Ahmedabad.

I did not know then that I would not again visit that Secretariat building for another four years. That building in stone, built in the last century, had a charm and a beauty of its own. Secretaries' rooms, which were cubicles, arranged around a common reception halls, overlooked the Oval grounds. Its entrance was from the back through a lane opposite the traffic island known as 'Kala Ghoda' --- in 1952, there was a majestic statue of King Edward on horse back. From the widows of the cubicles, one could see the Arabian sea. A few years later the new Secretariat building on other side of the Oval and the, reclamation would trigger multi-storied development on the land adjoining the Nariman Point. That changed not only the skyline of the city, but the beauty of it's shoreline along the Cuffe Parade.

෴

We formed an impression that the senior officers in the State Secretariat, as befitted the reputation of the Bombay State, were all a serious-minded lot. We were, however, very soon to meet some others whom we found more interesting and entertaining.

In contrast to what we had experienced the first two days, we were to meet someone whom one would call a 'Resident Eccentric'. It is not necessary to name the person. He was then the secretary to the government in one of the departments. As soon as we entered the room, we saw a strange sight of a gentleman standing in the middle of the room throwing something in the air and smartly catching it in his open mouth. After introduction, he offered us groundnuts and very soon under his able guidance we were also doing likewise. Anyone entering the room at that time would have witnessed a hilarious scene of five young probationers being trained as circus clowns by no less a person than a secretary to the State Government. We were not surprised to learn that he was a brilliant officer, but a genuine eccentric. We also learnt it was a tradition in the old ICS to develop one's personality as one wished. That also included being eccentric!

There was another senior officer, who would greatly impress us for a somewhat different reason. He was J. D. Kapadia, ICS, who was then the Collector of Bombay. We were required to work with him for a couple of days to get acquainted with complex problems of the Bombay city and the district of which the city formed a part. He was also expected to initiate our training in surveying and mapping. One morning we were picked up by the Collector from the hotel and driven to the Madh Island. Those days that part of Bombay was mostly uninhabited, densely forested with coconut groves; sprawling beaches were clean and the sylvan beauty was enchanting.

We were driven to a small Inspection Bungalow, where the local Tehsildar and other staff awaited our arrival. After sumptuous breakfast, the collector asked us to follow him for some survey training. He obviously meant business, because he was dressed in khaki shirt and shorts, with a solar hat on his head. We enthusiastically followed him a few hundred yards down the beach where a tripod with a survey telescope mounted on it and other familiar instruments such as the measuring-chain and flags of different colour were neatly arranged on a table. Very gravely the Collector showed us the various instruments and asked us to see through the telescope a survey flag that had been mounted a hundred yards away. Having done that, presuming that our appetite for surveying had been whetted, Kapadia said, 'Gentlemen, I am now in a position to certify that you have undergone the necessary survey training'.

Before we could realize what was meant, with a very grave look on his face he added, 'Now we will indulge in some serious business of enjoying this beautiful place'. Very soon we were asked to shed our clothes and don the swimming trunks, which he had already arranged for us and we were frolicking on the beach. We had a very pleasant picnic indeed. Strictly all male affair.

We found that the State Government was obviously not as ascetic and austere as we had been made to believe. There were senior officers, who were real human beings with an appetite for work, but also with a flair for enjoying life. Kapadia as a collector knew that very soon we would be sent on one month's course in Survey and Settlement Training in Poona and it was not desirable to deny us pleasures of a well known picnic spot of Bombay. Some years later when I came to the secretariat to work as chief minister's secretary I got to know him well. J. D. Kapadia was then the Secretary in charge of Public Health Department. While unlike other Bombay civilians, he looked non-serious, when occasion demanded, he was refreshingly candid in putting across his views. With his unorthodox views and the ability to cut through the usual verbiage, Y. B. Chavan, the Chief Minister, found Kapadia interesting. In Dr. Subramaniam Swamy, he got an equally unorthodox intellectually gifted son-in-law. Unfortunately, I have not had the pleasure of knowing the latter.

Chapter 8

First Encounter with an Ascetic
- Morarji Desai

The chief minister Morarji Desai, who had succeeded Balasaheb Kher, was the second chief minister of the Bombay state. He had a formidable reputation as an administrator and as a no-nonsense man. He was equally ruthless and rude to officers and his colleagues. He was a deputy collector in the Raj. He resigned and joined Gandhi's first Satyagrah movement. In the footsteps of the Mahatma, Desai outwardly adopted all his symbols : non-violence, simple living and use of hand made cotton (Khadi).

RUS had fixed our call on the CM at his residence at Sayhadri* on the Ridge Road on the top of Malbar Hill for 3 April, at 5 p.m. That morning, we heard some talk that one of his young daughters had committed suicide. No one knew exactly the facts but it was rumored that she wanted to marry someone, whom Morarjibhai Desai did not approve of. Since our appointment was fixed for that very evening, we checked up with the RUS, who told us that we must go unless it was cancelled by the chief minister's secretary.

*Then known as 'Sahyadri'-- it was pulled down; now a five star government guest-house has been built on that site.

Accordingly, we went to his residence, with a certain degree of hesitancy whether it was proper on our part to go on an official call, when it would be more appropriate to pay a condolence visit. While we were exchanging such doubts amongst ourselves, we were ushered into his presence and greeted him with a polite 'Namaste', but without any sign of even faint smile on our faces, as befitted the occasion.

After introducing ourselves, one of us said, 'We are sorry to learn…..'. Even before he had completed the sentence, the CM curtly said, 'Why should you be sorry?' Before we could realize what he meant, he said, 'You have no business to talk about personal matters. As officers, you are concerned only with public affairs. Moreover, life and death are inevitable. Every human being brings his or her own destiny, etc. etc'. After that we behaved as if we did not know anything about the tragedy. Later when I came to know him better and got to understand his mental makeup, I found that he was not trying to hide his emotions by putting up a show of stoic attitude. He had disciplined his mind that way.

But I also found that there was a lot of hum bug in him. He wore Khadi – but only the best and the costliest. Unlike other congressman, he did not believe in wearing hand washed clothes. His were washed, starched and well ironed, at any time. any where. His rude behaviour was a put up show, perhaps a relic of his past as a deputy collector.

He was specially rude to senior ICS officers, probably because he had suffered their rude behaviour.

First Encounter with an Ascetic

Later in my career, I would come to know him intimately as extremely kind and human. But that was much later. Always much feared, but always admired for fearlessness.

Chapter 9

Initiation into District Life
- Lesson in Dignity of Office?

On 19th April 1953, as the Gujarat Mail steamed into the Ahmedabad Railway Station, I saw a couple of peons in white uniform, with a red sash across their chest, along with some police officers standing on the platform. Apparently the party was there to receive some important dignitary, perhaps a minister from Bombay.

As soon as I got down, they moved towards me. I was greeted by a tall gentleman, with graying hair, wearing a white full-sleeved shirt and white pants. He was my Collector, Rajpal IAS. At 5 O'clock, he had come to receive his Supernumerary Assistant Collector. I cherish that gesture even today.

He drove me to the Circuit House located in an area named the Shahi Bagh, so named because the Mugal governors of Gujarat, normally princes of the royal blood, used to reside in a palace just across the road from the Circuit House. It was then very well-maintained with six suites of room on the first floor. Since I would be staying in the

Initiation into District Life

city for the next four-five months for my training with the various officers in the city, Rajpal had arranged for me to stay at the Circuit House on payment of ten percent of my salary, i.e., rupees forty per month as rent. The location was ideal, being only five minutes distance from the Collector's residence as well as of the Superintendent of Police. Several other officers also resided nearabout.

Shahi Bagh palace on the banks of the Sabarmati river was then occupied by U. M. Mirchandani, a very senior ICS Officer, appointed as Director of Local Authorities, who supervised working of all municipalities and local authorities in the Ahemdabad revenue division, but without any responsibility for the Revenue Administration. He was soon replaced by K. L. Panjabi, ICS who a few years later would be the chief secretary. It was a huge sprawling palace in bricks with doorways big enough for an elephant to pass through. Built for the governor of Gujrath, generally a prince of royal blood it was a majestic structure. At the rear, there was a wide terrace along the embankment of the Sabarmati river. I would spend there several happy evenings in the company of K. L. Panjabi and his wife.

Rajpal, who had joined the IAS a few years earlier through the Special Recruitment, had formerly worked in the Defence Accounts Department. He and his charming family welcomed me and helped to quickly settle down. Other officers were equally kind. Among them most popular being Dr. Miller, an Englishman who was the Civil Surgeon, married to a South Indian lady. Traditionally the couple used to act as guardians to all Supernumerary Assistant Collectors posted at Ahmedabad. Their house was always open to me for tea or dinner.

Equally pleasant was K. J. Nanavati, DIG of Police and his wife. Nanavati, an officer of the Indian Police (I.P.) was a strong, silent type Parsi, with easy manners. A sportsman fond of hunting by tracking wild life he was a no nonsense man feared by his subordinates and criminals. Their home was also an open house for me. I was also happy to meet the Superintendent for Rural areas, Kagal. His wife was the sister of my good friend Vitthal Mavinkurve from Poona, who very soon would come over to Ahmedabad to work with the Times of India as local Representative.

For the first few days, the Collector made it a point to pick me up in his car and take me to the office. He had put a small table and a chair for me by the side of his large size table. Every file or piece of paper that he dealt with, would return to the office via my table. Thus, in a few days, I got to know variety of subjects that the Collector had to deal with and also how incisively he went into each matter. I also found that he paid special attention to work of his Sub-divisional Officers (SDO) and would not hesitate to tell them off in writing, if he was not satisfied. That was something for me to take note of, as I would soon be his SDO.

For the first few weeks, I would spend the morning hours with the Collector and the afternoon with the local Sub-divisional Officer, called Prant Officer in Gujarat. While I was with the Collector, the Collector would be addressed by his personal staff as Saheb Bahadurji and I would be addressed as Chota Sahebji. In the afternoon, the Prant Officer would be addressed as Rao Bahadurji and I would get one degree of promotion and become Sahebji. It would take me some time to get familiar with these honorifics that were used to addressed officers in Gujarat from the Patwari upwards to the Collector.

I had also got a lesson connected with the dignity of my office! On the first day, after lunch with the Collector, I decided to walk over to the office of the Prant Officer, which was hardly ten minutes away. As soon as I started marching, I found that not only there was a peon in his ceremonial uniform walking five paces in front of me, but there was another peon in uniform behind me as if we were we were walking in a procession. To me it appeared somewhat ludicrous. I tried to persuade my head peon, named Manilal, not to escort me in that manner. He would not agree, because that is how it was done for the past several decades. Ahmedabad had a long tradition of having supernumeraries and Manilal had 'trained' several of them. He knew how to handle them and look after their dignity. After all, how could people know who was walking? I had to appreciate that argument since it was Manilal who wore a big size brass plate on the red sash across his chest announcing 'Assistant Collector, Ahmedabad'. I had no insignia to show my rank or my office.

One day, to get out of this incongruous looking spectacle on the crowded main street of the bazaar, I announced that I would like to ride a bicycle to the Prant Office. Manilal protested, 'Sahebji may walk, but if he has to ride anything it must be either a horse or a motor-car.' I could not be expected to ride a bicycle like clerks in the office.

Till I left the district one year later, Manilal continued to guide me with his 'dos' and 'don't'. For him, it was a matter of pride that he had trained another Supernumerary Collector. He would soon take a fresh one in hand that was his prerogative.

Chapter 10

Some Soft Lessons
- A Rolls Royce and Other

On Manilal's advice, I had started thinking of buying a car. I consulted Rajpal and he advised me to buy a good second-hand car from the Bombay Garage. Mr Bharucha, the Parsi owner, was personally known to him and he would offer a good car for a reasonable price. One morning, I met Mr. Bharucha. He was very kind, and the collector having spoken to him, showed me several sturdy Fords, including some very good T-Models, which were suited for sandy tracts surrounding Ahmedabad. I, however, got attracted to a big beautiful red coloured one, with foot-boards on sides and chromium plating all over. It's engine was remarkably silent one and I found it very easy to drive. I closed the deal for Rs 6,000/-, subject to the collector sanctioning loan for the purchase of the car.

That evening I went over to Rajpal and excitedly told him about the car He asked me, 'What make is it?' I said, 'Rolls Royce 1940'. He looked at me incredulously and asked 'Are you buying a car or an immovable property?' He told me to go and find out how many miles to a gallon the car would make. Since I was hesitant to go and ask Bharucha such a mundane question, he picked up the telephone and found that car would make five miles to a gallon.

Rajpal was firm that he would not recommend my buying a car that I could not maintain on my monthly salary of rupees four hundred. As a protest, I decided not to buy any car and instead I bought a horse. Even today I regret for not acquiring that Rolls for Rs 6,000/-, which unfortunately, I didn't have. As an immovable property, it would have been a good investment and should be worth several million rupees at current prices.

In Ahmedabad, I went through the prescribed training, spending a few weeks each in the Tehsil and Prant Offices and in the Court of a First Class Magistrate. I also sat in the Sessions Court on two murder cases, where I found that the District Judge, a very fine gentleman otherwise, was more vociferous and argumentative than the Public Prosecutor. He had been a Government Pleader and had not adjusted to his new role of playing a Judge.

I had also to work in the District Treasury Office for four weeks. During that period, the Treasury Officer had to proceed on two weeks' leave for the marriage of his daughter and I was to act as the Treasury Officer. While taking over charge, I learnt that Ahemdabad being an highly industrial city, how much cash reserves the treasury had to hold in its strong-room. It would take me almost fourteen-fifteen hours to count the cash balance, stocks of revenue stamps and of opium kept for the benefit of addicts.

Some Lessons

During that brief period, I also spent some sleepless nights. In one case, Bombay High Court had ordered to refund twenty million rupees wrongly recovered in by the Income tax authorities from a prominent mill-owner. I went over the judgment several times, though it was not for me to decide whether refund was justified or not. For three nights, I kept the cheque locked in office safe, despite several gentle reminders by my staff as agents of mill-owner were pestering them. How could they know that I had lost my sleep imagining in case I committed mistake in authorizing the payment, how many generations of Pradhans' I would be mortgaging. Ultimately, the threat of the party going to the High Court for contempt of the Court persuaded me to affix my signature after carefully counting seven zeroes ten times over and praying to all gods and goddesses to protect me. Fortunately, there was no mistake – nor was there any possibility of committing one.

I was soon to receive some more lessons of different kind. One morning Morarji Desai, the Chief Minister arrived by Gujarat Mail. Since the collector could not return from his tour in time to receive him, I went to the railway station. Chief minister got down, as usual immaculately dressed in starched white clothes, a buttoned up Nehru jacket and dhoti. After exchanging words for a few minutes with the Congress party leaders who had come to receive him, we got into the car. I was flattered that he asked me to sit alongside on the back seat. Having experienced his penchant for retorts, I sat silently not even daring to say innocuous 'How do you do', lest he took offence at any personal enquiries about his well being.

After a few minutes, he suddenly turned towards me and said "I do not expect young officers to stifle themselves with shackles of foreign rule. Why must you wear a neck tie?" He would prefer a buttoned up coat or even an open shirt, but not a necktie. Also clothes must be of hand woven cotton cloth - Khadi. Although I was expected to say 'Yes Sir' I kept quiet.

When he asked me whether I had noted his advice, I told him that I had as yet to receive my first pay cheque and how could I discard all clothing that we were told to wear at the training school, when I had no cash to buy my daily necessities? He was apparently satisfied with my straightforward response. However, he advised that in future I should tailor only khadi clothes and not wear a neck tie. I found that eminently sensible and despite his reputation as a hard and harsh person, I built up a very cordial relationship that lasted until his death. I found that my collector and other district officers always kept handy one buttoned up khadi coat in their offices. Moarji Desai and some Gujarat ministers were touchy about that. It would take me six months to save enough money to buy one khadi raw –silk coat. That would last me for next ten years.

I also learnt that senior officers in the Secretariat would come in coat and tie but when summoned by CM would hurriedly put on a buttoned-up jacket. It was funny when the tie knot protruded. This practice was given up when full sleeve bush shirts replaced suits.

ॐ

Some Lessons

For me, social life in Ahmedabad was somewhat hectic one. Being a bachelor, I was always on demand to join a table whenever at the last minute a guest or someone's wife would not turn up. It was understood that a supernumerary should not take offence to a last minute call from a hostess, if she happened to be the wife of the Collector, SP, DIG or the Civil Surgeon.

My friend Vitthal Mavinkurve had joined as the Times of India's correspondent. We spent several hours at his brother-in-law's place or occasionally on long walks in the cantonment area. Knowing that I used to spend some hours every day sitting by the side of the Collector, he used that to pump some juicy news out of me. It was professionally important for him to establish his credibility with bosses at the headquarters in Bombay. He used to ask me all kinds of questions to elicit news worthy information.

I was happy that I could give him one day, his first "Box-item" on the front page. That day my collector asked me at a short notice to accompany him for one night - halt. We drove in his jeep thirty miles out in desert, upstream of the Sabarmati river. Collector had taken me to the ex-Residency of Sadra*, where an old fortress was to be auctioned. It was situated on a bluff overlooking the river. There were a few merchants who had come to see and find whether it was worth bidding. Obviously it was not worth acquiring. The only bid was grand sum of Rs 3,251. It was great news and Vithal Mavinkurve got his first Box-item. As tribute to old time friendship I quote that :

"A fifteenth-century castle at Sadra, 27 miles from here was recently auctioned for Rs 3,251."

The commoner who bought it does not propose to live in the imposing edifice which had housed kings, potentates, chieftains- and recently - Political Agents of the British Government of India.

"I will pull down the castle and sell it brick by brick", he told an inquisitive friend"

I made another friendship at Ahmedabad. Sharad Rege, IPS, was the Assistant Superintendent of Police (ASP) posted for the city. He was son of D. S. Rege, a very senior ICS Officer of the Central Province. My fiancée had known the family. We soon became very good friends and both being bachelors, spent a lot of time together in his small bungalow, situated just across the railway lines. Coming from the ICS stock, he knew how to keep a good table with a proper bearer in white uniform with red- waist band and a smart cap. I enjoyed his company. When after a few months both of us got married, almost in the same month, our wives also became very friendly.

It was interesting to find that Sharad enjoyed long siesta in the afternoon. Our VP in the Metcalfe House had dinned into us not to get into the habit of siesta, except on Sundays. I used to make fun of his habit. Two decades later when I became the Home Secretary in the State, I found that he had earned a reputation for being easy-going and his afternoon siesta was talk of the town wherever he served. When I, as the Home Secretary, evaluated his work, I found that he had followed the

- **Footnote :** Some years later I read in memoirs of Charles Chenevix Trench in book titled, 'Viceroy's Agent' an interesting description of Sadra and his stay there. He wrote : During the monsoon the humid heat was utterly depressing, and the boredom even worse.... For eight weeks Lalge (his wife) and I did not live in Sultan Mahmud's fort except to take walks in surrounding countryside. We felt like prisoners taking their permitted quota of exercise......' It was a god forsaken Fort.)

traditions of old time police officers, namely relaxed lifestyle, delegation of power, leaving subordinates to do their job without breathing down their neck all the time and to go plodding methodically after the criminals. In fact, the crime detection record of his Police Range was the best in the State. I was, therefore, happy to get him cleared for his next promotion, which had become overdue, but denied to him because of his 'easy-going' reputation.

With Rajpal taking interest in my work, I soon completed the prescribed training. I also learnt something on my own. Since I had heard so much about M. G. Pimputkar and his work – Pimputkar was the Collector of Poona when I was in Ahmedabad – I very systematically went through all the reports of village inspections filed by him as the Collector of Ahmedabad. These were masterpieces in thoroughness and I was greatly impressed by the way in which, by cross-checking certain village records, Pimputkar would catch the culprit, who had either made a false entry or committed mistakes in making entry in the Record of Rights that recorded ownership as well as encumbrances, if any, on that piece of land. Almost each and every inspection report ended with not only a warning or a more deterrent punishment for village official, known as patwari, but also certain amount of fine. I thought I learnt a great deal by studying those inspection reports.

I also came across reports of how Pimputkar wearing false moustaches and dressed as a truck driver drove around in search of trucks transporting illegally essential commodities acroos the border, or to catch hold of policemen at check posts who would connive with illegal activities. As a greenhorn, I found all that very exciting, but later, after a little bit of seasoning I found that such action by the collector was uncalled for, when there were so many other professionals who could be deployed to perform those task.

Rajpal would often take me with him on his tours. Very soon the chief secretary had noted that I was spending too many night-halts outside the city. He gently advised the collector to ensure that my 'prescribed training programme was not disrupted by his taking me out on tours with him too often'. I was somewhat disappointed because I had started enjoying these tours. My friend Mavinkurve had also benefited from the very first outing I had with Rajpal.

Learning on the job was the greatest virtue of the civil service. There were no books or management studies to guide us how to perform our tasks. There was a Manual for Assistant Collectors, a copy of that was handed over to us at the Secretariat. But that was more to guide us in manners and what not to do. It is interesting to recall some gems from that written by Honourable Sir Fredric S. P. Lely, K.C.I .E, CSI, ICS., in April 1905. It was revised in 1937 First edition began with the words :

"This handbook is designed to aid the Assistant Collector in his revenue work by giving in a practical form the principles and rules according to which he has to perform some of his more important duties."

- *"From first to last the District Officer should remember that though he can by study of books gain much side-light on the problems that will confront him, his main business is to get a knowledge of, and deal with, men and things as they are in the village, the field and the bazaar."*

Some Lessons

- *He should begin by reading over the volume for his district of Campbell's Gazetteer especially those parts which relate to his charge.*

- *"In a discussion of any point with the average man, a homely and apposite proverb, will move him more 'Than all the ranged reasons of the world."*

- *"He should resist the tendency of all about him in these days to speak only in English. It makes the common people think him aloof from them, and only to be approached by a privileged class. For obvious reasons his English-knowing subordinates will foster this notion by speaking nothing else, at least before others, unless resolutely checked."*

- *'To be just and fear not' is a tradition which every District Officer is proud to maintain. Especially cultivate; Accessibility – The 'open cutcherry' is the palladium of the Indian ryot.*

- *Insight – The man who 'all ear and no eye', is not of a type that wins popular respects.*

- *Knowledge of common lore - The countryman, everywhere in the world, thinks the man a fool who does not know the things he is himself familiar with.*

- *Sympathy*

- *An even temper*

- *Thoroughness*

- *Dignity – Nothing is gained by forgetting his position as representative of Government, or allowing others to forget it.*

"Lastly, let it be realized that in this country every man of official position lives in the open, in the midst of prying eyes from which nothing is secret.

Never be unwilling to ask questions on any matters of which you are ignorant, whether from your superior officers, or from subordinates, or from the public. If you pretend knowledge, which you have not, of rules and regulations, your subordinates will certainly spot it at once, and it is better to admit that you do not know, and to see if they know; but verify afterwards the information they give you."

There was special advice for a probationary Assistant Collector :

- *Assistant Collector carries in his hands the honour of his Government and let him never suppose that he can do anything to sully it which is not speedily known and talked about in the kitchen, the cutcherry, the village and the bazaar.*

- *The Office of an Assistant Collector in charge of a Prant consists usually of a Sheristedar and two to four clerks. The Sheristedar is an upper-grade man with ambitions to become a Mamlatdar, and he and his clerks know very much more about the running of an office than any new Assistant Collector can.*

- *The public presume that an Officer, especially a young one, is under the influence of his Sheristedar, and the average Sheristedar, being human, does not discourage the idea.*

The Assistant Collector should be careful not to accept and sign papers merely on the word of the Sheristedar, also not to disregard the opinion of a trustworthy Mamlatdar as against that of the Sheristedar.

I carefully read again the Manual that had advice on several other matters. For example, whom to offer chair, who should be received by standing up, whom by merely lifting your bottom, what to accept as gift, from whom flowers and whom fruits etc, etc.

Over a period, each one would have his own style. Some also cultivated eccentricities. I was told that one of my batchmates in Indore used to get massage on Sundays, lying on a charpoy in the court yard. Once the Commissisoner came to the Inspection bunglow for some urgent inquiry. He sent word to the assistant collector to come and see him. When he did not report, after half an later the commissioner sent a word 'to report as he is'. Knowing temper of the superior, my batchmate asked four peons to lift his charpoy and carry him, as is where as, condition. His boss did appreciate his sense of duty. But did not give him good report. There were others of this type. None of them progressed far.

During my years in districts, I found that so far as life of a collector or an assistant collector, the advice was sound and of much practical use. Ultimately it would depend on individual how he would adapt himself to life with the ryot—the people whom he was expected to serve. I learnt what was meant by the word 'Service' in the ICS and the IAS.

Chapter 11

First Lessons in Governance
- Camping adventures

After six months in Ahmedabad, on passing the prescribed departmental examinations, I was due to be placed in charge of one tehsil, called taluka in Maharashtra. I was posted at Dholka situated about thirty-five miles, by narrow-gauge rail from Ahmedabad. On reaching there I a two "one horse driven" town, with neither electricity nor piped water supply.

R. A. Naik, IAS, who was two years senior to me, was the Assistant Collector of the sub-division of which Dholka was one of the tehsils. He was married. He had taken on lease the only private house in Dholka which was considered fit for the residence of the Assistant Collector. I had, therefore, to live in one of the two suites on the top of the old style office building, with ceiling as high as thirty feet with ten feet high doors and wooden beams supporting the roof.

Traditionally, Supernumerary Assistant Collectors were posted to Dholka for training. The staff there, led by the office Superintendent, called the Shirestedar and addressed by every one as Rao Saheb, had shaped several

First Lessons in Governance

supernumeraries. He immediately took in hand the new one.

Since I had no car, very soon a horse of a local breed was procured for Rs 300/-. It was a sturdy animal of medium height, with a powerful chest, necessary for galloping in the sandy tract. My personal man servant Ganpat, whom I had brought from Poona, looked after me. The horse was looked after by the numerous peons who were too happy to find in me an Assistant Collector, who would maintain a horse, instead of the usual old Ford or a Dodge. My horse also heightened their dignity in villages, mainly habited by warrior class Rajputs and high cast peasantry. They had not met an Assistant collector on horse back after the British had left. In fact I later found that I was the last breed to buy and ride a horse, in the good old Bombay state.

It was already the middle of month of May and temperature had started soaring to around 115 degrees Fahrenheit. Very soon that would be the temperature in shade. I would leave for my village inspections very early in the morning on my horse and try to return to my camp by mid-day. At that hour, despite the sola hat, one could feel the blood boiling in one's temple.

Once, while returning from a village on my horse back, I saw on the horizon domes and minarets of mosques and tall poplar trees. The skyline of the town had a distinct Islamic features. I was disappointed to learn that it was a mirage, a very common feature in the summer days. I was warned not to move about without an experienced guide or a compass, because the mirages could lead one, on and on in the wrong direction!

Being in-charge of only one Tehsil my touring was restricted to 10-12 days in a month as against the normal touring of 20 days for a Prant Officer. File work was not much and most of the time was taken up in hearing appeals in revenue and tenancy matters and also in conducting criminal trials. The Judiciary had not been separated from the Executive and I had also been conferred with the powers of the First Class Magistrate to try criminal offences that attracted maximum imprisonment of two years. Other cases, I had to hear but commit to the Sessions court for trial and punishment.

Very soon I learnt that while the offences were simple enough, they were committed in a heinous manner on account of either land or woman. Perhaps the heat and the desert made an individual mad and he lost all senses while committing the crime. However, in the Court room, it was a maddening experience to tolerate antics of lawyers. They would not only put irrelevant questions to witnesses but try to argue with the Magistrate as well. In the beginning I tried to explain that all that was unnecessary since the facts were fairly clear, but soon got used to their style. The country lawyer had to follow, what the Goldsmith had said about the Village Teacher : "Though vanquished, he would argue still"

My Shirestedar persuaded me to learn patience and allow the lawyers their say, because their fees would depend upon the vehemence with which they could argue the brief and impress their client. I could very well appreciate that point but one day I really lost my patience when I found a lawyer addressing me as 'My honour'. I explained to him that the correct form would be 'Your honour', but he opened the High Court Reporter and showed me that in the High Court the Judges were always addressed as 'My lord' and therefore the correct form of address in this Court should be 'My honour'!

Finally, I had to give up and advise the lawyers to simply address me as 'Sir'. Having won his point he saw no difficulty in accepting the suggestion.

During my one year stay in Dholka I would experience what a family feud meant. There were two prominent Muslim families. Nobody remembered how the feud had started, but every other month, alternatively, a member of the either family was hacked to death. It was understood that the murder must take place in the town square in the presence of a large crowd. The job would be done quickly and with such ferocity that no one would dare to apprehend the culprits nor come forward as witness. During those twelve months six murders were committed. After each incident the police rounded up about twenty odd members from both the families and produced them before me for obtaining their Bond under section 107 of the Criminal Procedure Code to maintain peace. It was like locking the stable after the horse had bolted, but the execution of the bond -and- bail was carried out in due solemnity. I would then call the elders of the two families, first separately, and then together to advise them to stop uncalled for blood shedding. Both the parties would agree in my presence on the understanding that the other party would behave itself. However as they could not decide who should have the last word in the family feud, the ritual murders would continue.

My Shirestedar, who had been there for a decade, had already warned me not to waste my good advice, especially since the feud did not affect anyone else in the town. According to him there was no danger of breach of peace, except of course, occasional loss of life on either side!

This was a period of my learning on the job and putting to test what I had already learnt from the manuals and the field inspection reports that I had studied in the Collector's office. In revenue matters my field training was taken in hand by one Shaikh, the Circle Officer (CO). A tehsil had three or four Circles depending on geographical area and number of villages. CO supervised work of patwari, village officer in-charge of revenue records who continues to be government's presence at village level and foundation of Revenue administration set up by one Mr. Anderson, an ICS officer in 1880's. It may appear strange to city - bred that the system is still in operation and a document named 7/12 is basic to holding or owning agricultural land even today. Anderson's Manual is the first reading for any revenue officer, whether a patwari, circle officer, tehsildar or an IAS assistant collector.

Shaikh was a seasoned revenue officer who knew all the tricks that the patwaris played and also knew how to handle young Prant Officers. He taught me something which I could have never learnt sitting in the office. When he found that I had acquired a horse, he also 'borrowed' a horse from a village Patel, a functionary appointed by government in an honorary capacity who was highly respected by the villagers and worked in tandem with patwari on all village matters. He had made sure that his horse was at least one foot shorter in height so that he would not compete with the dignity of the Prant on horseback, when riding along-side. He also made certain that the Prant's horse was very well looked after by villagers. That ensured that his horse would also be properly looked after. The Government allowance for horse keeping was Rs 65/- per month, which I would hand over to the Shirestedar to make the necessary arrangements. However, I never found my horse either short of good grass or the usual feed, without much efforts. I suspected that my horse allowance was being shared by the Circle Officer and the Shirtesdar.

This was a period of my learning on the job. Shaikh was my tutor and mentor. Shaikh showed me how the Prant could be fooled by the villagers. One important duty of a revenue officer in those days was to check that the Taccavi - loans at concession rate of interest - given by the government to dig new wells or buying bullocks for farming were properly utilized or not. I had to visit sites of wells in far off fields for verifying that money was properly utilized. That was simple, although one had to ensure by studying survey maps that the well was located in the land owned by the farmer who had taken taccavi. I learnt that farmer, who appeared poor and uneducated, had learnt all tricks of trade to fool a young officer. My CO was an excellent teacher.

In case of oxen it was more complicated. Unless one was careful one might be shown the same oxen twice over. He therefore carried with him generous quantities of dhobi's (laundryman's) marking ink and soon as an ox was brought for inspection Shaikh would mark the animals behind. This would ensure that the same animal was not produced by five different owners the same morning for inspection.

Beyond Expectations

But what about the age? The money was given to buy a young ox. Shaikh would show how to open the mouth of the animal and examine the teeth to ascertain the correct age. Soon the villagers were talking about the new Prant Officer's extra-ordinary abilities to tell age of the cattle. As it happens in villages these stories spread rapidly, and I found that all newly acquired oxen were lined up for my inspection and for certifying their age. Shaikh was clever. He asked villagers wishing to take their oxen to weekly cattle-market for sale would ask them to get a certificate that the age had been verified by the Prant officer. He charged a small fee for that service.

Shaikh's best lesson was however to persuade me to unlearn something which I had learnt. While working in the Collector's office I had carefully studied the Village Inspection Notes of M. G. Pimputkar who had served as collector a few years ago. Those notes were model for any young officer, to learn how to thoroughly inspect the daftar (records) of a patwari. Unfortunately, I also learnt that the village inspection must result in not only finding out defects in the records, but also meting out on-the-spot punishment. In true Pimputkar style, I would record adverse comments to be transcribed later in the annuals confidential record of the patwari (also called Talati), but imposed fine, varying from Rs 10 to Rs 30. It was quite a substantial amount, in relation to the emoluments then prevailing.

For the first three-four months Shaikh did not correct me. One evening while I was sitting in my camp he came over for the usual evening walk in the village and said, "Sir, may I bring one thing to your honour's attention?" When

I asked him to go ahead, Shaikh explained that whenever I imposed fine, it was like imposing a collective fine on the village. My reputation had already spread and just as in the days of Pimputkar Bahadur, the Patwari would tell the village Patel to make sure that the 'collection' was ready before the Prant Officer arrived. After all the Patwari was serving the village and if he did something wrong it was under the influence of the Patel and why must Patwari suffer on that score. Consequently, Rs 25-30 would be collected in advance and as soon as I had recorded the order the Patwari would pay the fine to the Circle Officer on the spot. On most occasions as the amount of fine was less than the collection, the Patwari was richer by the balance amount. Thus, it was a fine on the village.

Shaikh further explained that imposing fine did not improve the performance because the Patwari knew that the Prant Officer would not visit that village for at least two years. As a result the village records would get from bad to worse. I found Shaikh's logic unassailable and his advice very sensible. I unlearnt Pimputkar's lesson and instead concentrated on educating the Patwari by correcting his mistake in the Chavadi (public place) in the presence of all the villagers. I soon learnt that kind of admonition put him to greater shame compared to the fine, and regarded as more severe punishment. After all in villages one's 'face' was the most important asset. Sir Fredrick Leyle's advice was sound and practical.

౸౿

My favourite camping place was a small Inspection Bungalow at a place called Bavala, a rail station midway between Dholka and Ahmedabad. With an oil-mill and a ginning factory, the place was already showing the first signs of industrialization. Patidar Patels, a community of highly developed agriculturalists who habited Bavala, took great pride in their cotton, maize and groundnut crops. The place had an added attraction. One Patel whom I had come to know in the Gokhale Institute in Poona and who had already done his post-graduation, belonged to Bavala. He had returned to work in his family business. Thus, at least I had some highly educated and decent company to while away my evenings.

There was an added attraction. The Inspection Bungalow at Dholka was constructed over a century ago, about two km away from the railway station. Surrounded by green irrigated fields it was very attractive. Constructed with thick mud and lime walls, with high ceiling, it was relatively cool in summer, a more habitable place compared to my residence in Dholka. I liked the place. I also had my work cut out there.

Government's Town Planning Directorate had carried out a survey, mapping of Bavala and I had been appointed to hear disputes and finalise the draft plan. Town planning is undertaken when a town starts developing and it is considered desirable to prepare a long-term layout to plan for its future development. The whole exercise begins by first measuring and plotting on a map each piece of immovable property and recording the rights of individuals. As it happens in such cases, most of the disputes were relating to what had been identified by the surveyors as encroachments on government land. A number of these encroachments were in the form of steps alongside streets for entering a house-hold, because the tendency of the people was to construct houses right up to the boundary of their land. Naturally the steps would be abutting on a public road or on the government land, in most cases over a drain flowing by the side of the property. For hearing these disputes I had, therefore, to visit not only the main roads in front of the houses but back lanes where gutters and all the dirt lay. I had thus become familiar with the nook and corner of the town. Very soon my visits had become a great source of entertainment for the ladies and the youth. They used to enjoy my speaking fluently in Gujarati and banter with villagers while wading through filth, where normally only pigs were to be found.

Since I had been given a period of three months in which to complete my task I had worked out a time table for inspecting a certain number of properties on the site in the morning and hearing the parties in the afternoon. I soon discovered that disputes between the parties could be sorted out by some amount of give-and-take, but it was impossible to find any one admitting that they had encroached on the government land. The Patels of Bavala were known for litigation and the parties would engage eminent lawyers from Ahmedabad to argue their cases who would come to Bavala in the morning and leave or Ahmedabad by the evening train. I found that they charged exorbitant fees and that a piece of land where encroachment could be regularized by paying as little as Rs 100/- to the government, the party would be willing to spend Rs 500/- per day, on the lawyers fees alone.

I had taken great deal of trouble to learn the old Gujarati script, akin to the Modi in Marathi, and made it a practice to laboriously go through several documents, some three/four centuries old, that parties would produce to assert their claim. But whenever out of practical considerations, I suggested that instead of wasting time and too much money, they should agree to accept the Government's case that it was an encroachment and get the same regularized by paying a nominal amount of fine, there were loud protests. How can we concede that our ancestors had committed encroachment on Government land? That was just not possible.

It would be explained to me at great length that such and such a Saheb Bahadur, a high government functionary, in the good old British days had visited their abode. How could he have entered the house, if the steps had been an encroachment on the Government land? Often records were produced to show that some parties had challenged such allegations in the past, not only in the Federal Court, but had gone up to the Privy Council of the House of Lords, in London.

I had to finally give up efforts to persuade them when I found that lawyers from Ahmedabad would also not let their clients give up their stand. So, day after day, I had to hear cases at length and sit down in the evening for several hours to write judgments in detail, since the parties had already threatened that they would go right up to the Supreme Court.

The office would send every day's dak (postal mail) and other papers to the camp. These would be attended late in the evening and returned next morning. The relay system worked very efficiently. My day would be fully occupied with village and field inspections in the morning and hearing of criminal and revenue cases in the afternoon. Evenings would be spent in the village chatting with the villagers. It was surprising to find how relaxed they were in the evenings after having worked all day in their fields.

While carrying out that work in Bavala, I got a lesson, how old-time officers could live and work in remote areas without strain and stress. On one occasion, I was traveling by train from Dholka to Bavala to hear the usual city survey and some revenue cases. These were mostly appeals and I had decided to hear about twenty cases during the day and return the same night. On reaching the Inspection Bungalow I found that my office peon had forgotten the bundle of papers in the train, which was already on way to Ahmedabad. I was deeply agitated since the parties with their lawyers would come very soon and in the absence of papers I could not do any work. Also the loss of papers would be known and the lawyers could play havoc. I imagined all kinds of scenarios, including losing my job for having lost the original case papers or at least being administered strictures by the High Court.

Without revealing to the parties the real cause, along with my peon, I went back to the Station and asked the Station Master to send a message on the Railway telephone network to look for the papers in the compartment in which I was traveling. I caught the next goods train going to Ahmedabad. On reaching the main station there, I learnt that the train had been thoroughly searched at Ahmedabad by the railway police, but there were no papers. In a greatly agitated mood I went to see the District Magistrate (one Suradkar, who had succeeded Rajpal) at his residence and confessed to him about the grave blunder committed by my staff, for which I was ready to accept the punishment since I was responsible for the custody of papers. Without uttering a word the DM offered me a cup of tea and went on quietly munching the betel-nut in his mouth. I thought he had not realized the gravity of what had happened. So, I repeated the story. He looked at me and said "What is so great about it?"

I was utterly taken aback. I again explained that the papers were the original case papers and their loss meant all the hearings would have to take place again, etc. He looked me in the eye and said, "Do you know how many hundreds of files are lost in government offices each year?" After deliberately munching the nut for a minute, he added "What difference would it make, if your papers are also lost?"

Then he had a word of advice. I should call one by one the party in whose favour the original decision had been delivered. That party being interested was bound to produce the copies of the original. On the other hand the party which had lost in the lower Court would be interested in the papers getting lost and both would argue for years which were original and which were 'true copies' of the original. I looked at him incredulously. What he said made sense. I was completely bowled over!

Fortunately, for me when I walked over to the house of the Superintendent of Police, I got the good news that the police had apprehended a chap who had got down at a station just before the Ahmedabad railway station and was seen carrying a bundle. When he was accosted, he readily handed over the bundle to the police. He was greatly relieved to find that the bundle contained only useless government records that would have only brought him trouble.

Who could have given such good advice-How not to lose sleep on trivial matters? That came useful when I occupied higher and responsible posts.

ഔര

After six months in the district I duly appeared for the Lower Departmental examination in Bombay and beginning of October, went to Delhi to visit my fiancée. It was a pleasant holiday, where I also met here other young relations who became my life-long friends. It was at that time that her parents told me that the date of the wedding may have to be advanced-I had earlier indicated at least eighteen month wait - because they were likely to go on a posting to Bangkok from where they may not return for a couple of years. I promised to consult my father and on return to Dholka pondered on my situation. While I had passed the Lower Departmental examination, I would complete my probationary period only on passing the Higher Departmental, to be held six months later.

I did not tell that I was without a 'home' for my bride. I was expected to tour a great deal in the winter months and the touring season had already set in. She may have to either trudge along or remain alone at Dholka and that my movable property consisted of two trunk-full of clothes and books and a medium size wooden box to carry my kitchen. I possessed no furniture, no crockery or cutlery or table linen. My salary in hand was still less than Rs 400 per month. How could I get married and try to settle in the desert like area with a girl who was mostly city bred or brought up in the districts of Punjab where there was always plenty of water as well as electricity. All this on the negative side. On the positive side : my fiancée wanted to get married and come to share my life!

The family pressures worked and I agreed to get married in the middle of January 1954. Because I had no 'earned leave' to my credit, I had made it clear that I could only avail of ten days of "casual leave". My father-in-law, by profession an engineer, arranged the whole programme meticulously. The wedding took place in Bombay, on 17 January at the Radio Club.

The very next day we left for Matheran for our honeymoon and three/four days later to Poona to visit the family. We returned to Bombay on the evening of 25th January to be welcomed by my wife's relations living on the Altamount road. Next day being the Republic Day and a holiday I had decided to leave for Ahmedabad that night, by the Gujarat Mail. That evening we had accepted an invitation for tea to some friends of my wife, not realizing what Bombay could be on the evening of Republic Day, with lakhs of people streaming into the city to see the lights on public buildings. After the tea, when we inched forward in that traffic we realized that we might miss the train. Luckily we managed to reach the Cumballa hill, collect our baggage, say good-byes and leave for the Bombay Central Station. With my bags and my brides ten trunks of trousseaux we checked in and boarded the Gujarat Mail. Being young and full of excitement, we took everything in our stride. My young wife was eagerly looking forward to the district life – not knowing what awaited her.

First Lessons in Governance

Next morning on reaching Ahmedabad we were duly received by some friends. Rajpal was good enough to send his car with driver to pick us up. During the course of the day we called on him and his wife and we met some of the younger friends at Sharad Rege's place. Since he had also got married less than a month earlier it was great fun getting introduced to each other's wives. In the evening we left by train for Dholka.

Finally, when we got into the train I told my wife that instead of going to Dholka we shall be de-training at Bavala, from where I had 'broken the camp' to get married with her and I must return to complete the work before returning to my headquarters. At Bavala we were received by the local officers, few gentry including the Patel of the Gokhale Institute days. He had thoughtfully brought his car to drive us to the Inspection Bungalow.

She very quickly adjusted to life in the I. B. She also enjoyed meeting village belles, who started hovering near the bungalow, to see the bride of the Prant Officer. After a week's stay there, with some trepidation in my heart I decided to take her to Dholka. Our train steamed into Dholka Station at around 8 p.m. She was greatly impressed the way the Station Master in full formal uniform greeted us and how Manilal had organized our arrival. One of the two village 'tongas' (one horse carriage) was waiting in the porch of the station for us. Only after we had arrived at my residence – one room at the top of the office – did she realize that there was no house to stay in. There was neither electricity nor piped water supply. Of course there was no fridge. The only water- cooling equipment was a earthen jar. It came as a shock to her – but she took all that sportingly. Very soon she got adjusted to the new environment.

We deposited ten steel trunks carrying her trousseau in my office and left on an extended tour of my charge. Shaikh was good enough to make available his horse for her use. Very soon she had mastered the peculiar 'Rabadi gait' of the horse, which was in-between a canter and a gallop.

We had worked out a programme of camping ten days in a tent followed by eight days stay in an Inspection Bungalow. She was fascinated with the tent camping. A day prior to our arrival at the camp. Manilal would get the tent pitched on a site which had been traditionally earmarked for the Prant Officer's camping. Normally it used to be outside the village, but close to a water source and preferably near some grove of trees. We would follow on horseback to be greeted with great deal of excitement on our arrival at the camp. All the village servants called the 'Twelve Balutedars', including the revenue patel, the police patel, the patwari, the barber, the musicians, going down the ladder to the one responsible for the meanest task of clearing human waste and those for removing carcasses of dead animals etc. would be present. After the British left, they had not seen a Prant Officer's wife riding on a horse accompanying the Saheb Bahadur. They were therefore greatly impressed with my wife's arriving at the camp and smartly getting off the back of the horse.

Our tent was called 'Swiss Cottage'. It was very presentable and quite commodious with a living room in front, a bedroom in the middle and a place for bath at the back. It was tastefully furnished with thickly woven cotton carpets called daris, tables and chairs of folding type. Manilal took great pride in ensuring that every thing was spic-and-span and the table linen and the bed linen duly starched. In the night the Swiss Cottage would be lighted by a petromax - a lamp that worked on kerosene and shed bright light by burning of gas - that would occasionally throw its flame leaping upwards. It took some time for my wife to get over the fright of seeing flames almost licking the canvas top of the Swiss Cottage.

In the month of February/ March the weather was very pleasant and the rabbi (summer) crop of maize sprouting all around the Swiss Cottage made it all the more enjoyable. While my wife had adjusted to camping, for a city-bred girl the greatest challenge was to walk fifteen yards to a small tent pitched to serve the usual facility in full gaze of the Police guard and the village servants. That was the ultimate in shedding one's modesty however, human needs prevailed over inhibitions and she got used to that walking all the way looking down and pretending that no one looked at her.

Soon she started enjoying the horse riding and meeting village women. For her it was wonderful to experience the carefree life, especially of the Rabadi women. Traditionally, Rabadis are nomadic who move about with their cattle from place to place in search of grazing. However, many Rabadis had started settling down in villages and their main profession was to supply milk to the villagers. My wife was fascinated looking at the tall and beautiful Rabadi woman, with their bright red and green colourful skirt and a top, embedded with dozens of small circular mirrors, walking down a path, carrying as many as three vessels on her head. They walked in a line, with their backs straight and their arms swinging in the air, with carefree smiles on their faces. Perhaps they were equally fascinated to see the young city-bred bride in a finery sitting on the verandah of the I. B. or moving about near the Swish Cottage. Very soon she also started visiting villages late in the afternoon to have a chat with the ladies. Once the initial barriers of language and shyness had been overcome, one could notice that the village women would expectantly wait for her visit.

As we had no house to live in, there was no compulsion to return to Dholka. On return we would expectantly look to the mail and the newspapers. After dinner I would attend to my papers. By 10 p.m., we would call it a day to begin next morning at 6 a.m. It was great having company of an educated young girl. Life was marching forward.

ೲಌ

In the month of April I had to appear for my higher departmental examination and that gave us an opportunity to visit Bombay for a week. It was exciting for both of us to meet several new relations and old friends.

After passing the examination, I was appointed the regular Assistant Collector for the Dholka Sub-division, which consisted of three Tehsils: Dholka, Dhanduka and Sanand Mahal. Dhanduka sprawled westwards towards Limbdi State in Saurashtra and the so-called rivers in the area were really big rain-water drains. Except for the monsoon the area was dry, sandy and the water was brackish. In some places nearer the Limbdi State the ground water was so salty that one did not have to add any salt to the cooking.

First Lessons in Governance

Towards Sanand, which was near Ahmedabad, it was greener with mango groves and the peasantry, called Girasdars, were very rich. Most of the area was habited by jagirdars and inamdars and as Rajput thakurs who wielded great of influence over the peasantry. Now Sanand is in news as Tata's have set NANO, small car project there.

We were soon comfortably settled in the house vacated by the Naik's. Situated in the residential area it had an old style big doorway opening on the main street. One entered a courtyard, on the left was a two-storied structure, which served as our living quarter and on the right a one-storied structure, which was our kitchen-cum-dining, beyond which was the facility. At one end of the courtyard was a well to collect rain water. This was the usual insurance against failure of rain. Water remained surprisingly clean and cool, although not very potable, except for emergencies. A few minutes away from the house was a public well where recently a hand pump had been installed and every one collected water from a nearby water tap.

We were well served by Ganpat, who was first excited to find a mistress in the house but progressively became somewhat sullen, when he found that he was losing the freedom that he enjoyed while working with a bachelor. We had a maid servant who brought water and helped with the cleaning of the house. A strong and handsome Rabadi woman, we did not realize that she was carrying till one day she absented herself, delivered the baby and came to work the next day. It was all very natural and looked surprisingly swift. My wife was astonished to learn that the birth of a baby could be that easy. While moving around as nomadic, we were learning many new facts of life.

During the next couple of months, since there were not much rainfall in that area, we moved extensively in all the nooks and corners of Dhanduka. Some of the I.B.'s in that area were more than 100 years old and the one at Barvala bore an inscription in stone announcing : '1846'. The chowkidars in charge of these I.B.'s took great pride in keeping them clean and could produce a decent meal at short notice. In the summer months, there being no fans, one slept under a punkha,- an apparatus hanging from the ceiling with wide cotton flaps --which moved like a swing by a rope drawn by a young chap sitting outside, who would appear to be asleep but nonetheless would be drawing the rope rhythmically.

In rural areas, there being no source of entertainment nor any company one tried to make the best of the day light hours by mixing with local village folk. In the desert like conditions evenings would get progressively cooler. One always slept 'charpoys' (cots) under the sky with a mosquito net to keep the insects and undesirable crawling creatures out. With unexpected always around the corner, life was never dull.

Once while sleeping outside the I.B. of Dhanduka, suddenly in the early hours of the morning we were woken up by a number of cattle running down the river bed. Soon there was a lot of gurgling and gushing of water and before we realized what was happening our wooden cots were floating in water. It was a flash flood. Fortunately, being on the edge of the river – bed, we could scramble to safety. However, our bedding and linen was washed away, literally down the drain.

My first Collector, Rajpal had been transferred to Bombay and his place was taken up by another old time deputy collector who had been promoted from the state civil service into the IAS. Mr. Suradkar was very much different to Rajpal. He had three/four years left before retirement. Having experienced life and administration, he had a certain detached look about everything. He worked quietly and efficiently and never volunteered to tender advice. He was down-to-earth and I have already recounted advice given by him to take life calmly and not get hassled. I was therefore left alone to administer my charge. I did not really mind that, because that would give me greater freedom and help to build up my confidence in dealing with men and matters.

The very first time he visited Dholka, since we were not equipped for hosting a decent meal, we invited him for High Tea. My wife was greatly excited to welcome my collector for the very first time to our home. With Ganpat's help she got a sumptuous menu ready and laid out Tea in the new crockery brought by her from Delhi. Mr. S. came. He was very polite and talked to her about her parents and education. All the preparations were duly served in his presence in a plate and offered personally by my wife. He looked at the plate and said, 'I am sorry, today is my fast day.'

It was typical of him, but that evening I had to face my wife's wrath for not having found out earlier whether it was the collector's fast day or otherwise. My explanation that it was for the guest to inform to the host in advance, was not found acceptable. For the next few days, I had to survive on those preparations which, of course, I did not mind. However, we made up and decided to call Mr. S, 'Dev Manus', God's good man. Conveniently it also abbreviated to D.M. i. e. District Magistrate. I also found that the Dev Manus was not as innocent as he appeared. He could be ruthless when occasion demanded, but generally helpful. One could learn a great deal of practical administration from him.

My wife and I occasionally visited Ahmedabad, generally to attend a one-day monthly meeting of all the district officers. It was a great pleasure to meet our friends, the Reges' and occasionally Mavinkurves', Vitthal having got married in the meantime. Our greatest pleasure was to have dinner in the newly opened Kwality Restaurant and see a picture in the Relief Cinema. Thirty years later when we visited Ahmedabad we patronized both the places.

By the middle of the year we decided to go on a two-week leave to Delhi. While there I received the pleasant news of my transfer to Abu Road Sub-division of the Banaskanta district. The most attractive part of the posting was Mount Abu where the headquarters of the sub-division had been recently shifted. Having visited Mount Abu while I was in the IAS Training School, I knew what a beautiful change it would be, after our stay at Dholka.

That is where foundations of my future career would be laid.

Chapter 12

Style and Pomp of Raj
- V. Shankar, ICS

Banaskantha was the northern-most district of the Bombay State. It was considered a punishment posting, because most of the area was desert-like and the Great Thar desert to the west was hardly a couple of hundred miles away. It was formerly Palanpur State and the Nawab was highly regarded by all the Princes. He was an educated, polished gentleman married to an European lady. He had a reputation for moderation and good relations with the Viceroys. In 1947 while some of the neighboring States, including a Hindu ruled one were toying with the idea of accession to Pakistan, the Nawab not only took the initiative to accede his State to India, but persuaded others also to do so. He was therefore highly regarded by the post-independence regime as well.

After a couple of hours rail journey on Ahmedabad-Delhi rail route en route to Abu Road, we reached Palanpur. At the rail station we were met by some officers from the collector's office. They had come to greet us on behalf of the collector, V. Shankar ICS and also to convey a message that I should not bother to come to Palanpur for the customary call on the collector, till I was specially asked to do so. I was a little puzzled to get that kind of message.

On arrival at Abu Road, we were received by the local Tehsildar and the President of the Municipality, a venerable old Parsi gentleman, who was good enough to provide a car for us to go up to Mt. Abu. In about an hour's time, we were on the top to find ourselves surrounded by trees and greenery in contrast with what we had got used to at Dholka.

I excitedly took charge of my several offices. I was to be the Assistant Collector and Sub-divisional Magistrate for Abu Road and Danta tehsils. I would also be the Forest Officer, the President of the Mt. Abu Municipality and over-all in-charge of all the local offices in my capacity as the Superintendent of the Hill Station. The post of the Superintendent had been first created by the British first for Mahabaleshwar, in order to have an orderly development of the hill station with one officer overseeing and performing a variety of tasks and thus avoid waste of time on co-ordination with others.

For me greatest attraction of the place was the IPS Officers' Academy, which was then commanded by Sardar Waryam Singh of the Indian Police(IP). He was a Punjab cadre officer and knew my parents-in-law. He and his wife greeted us most affectionately and during our two-and-half years' stay there we were to enjoy the warmth of their hospitality. We also made friends with their elder daughter and the son-in-law, Col Arjun Singh of the Engineers, who rose to become a Lt. General. Their younger daughter Amrit Kaur was then hardly nine-ten years old. She married Inderjeet Chaddha of the Indian Foreign Service, who would succeed me in Geneva as India's Resident Representative to GATT and UNCTAD and distinguish himself in international economic diplomacy. He worked for several years in the UNCTAD Secretariat and later became India's Ambassador to Bangladesh.

For the first few months, we lived in a rented house. After a few months a bungalow, named, The Carrick Cottage, situated across the road and opposite the gate of the IPS Officers' Mess, named the Rajputana Mess, was officially designated as the Assistant Collector and SDM's residence. Earlier there was no such accommodation, as Abu Road was the sub-divisional headquarters, until a few weeks prior to my arrival there. We were soon settled in our cottage with the usual complement of servants, a cook and a bearer. Later when our son arrived an Ayha would be added. Life was not only interesting, but enjoyable.

Mt. Abu had been developed as a hill station for the Gujarat and Rajasthan and most of the princes had built palatial houses or country cottages for their occasional visits in summer, because the Resident for the Rajputana State had made Mt Abu his headquarters for summer months. Building of the Residency was perched on the highest point on the hill and was maintained by the Government of India for occasional visit by the Home Minister and other dignitaries. There was a good Club; a lively place to spend our evenings. It was then maintained in very good condition and the presence of the Commandant of the Academy and the Colonel commanding the battalion located there, almost every evening, ensured at the Club that the old standards were maintained. I was comparatively a very junior officer, but being in-charge of the sub-division, I was asked to become the President of the Club. Those were still good old days when traditions prevailed and rank consciousness did not supercede good manners.

Dilwara temples, a few miles beyond Mt. Abu, provided an attractive tourist spot. There were several other good 'Walks' and 'Points' for the tourists. During my three year stay, I would develop the lake and its surroundings by providing a path round the lake and tastefully electrifying the whole area. Location of Mt. Abu had only one disadvantage: for touring my charge. I had to motor down to Abu Road for visiting any part of my charge. The tehsil, formerly part of Sirohi, a small princely state was mostly habited by the Bhils and ruled by a Rajput prince. On the border of the Abu Road and Danta tehsils was situated the famous Ambaji temple, venerated by the people of Gujarat and Rajasthan. I made several visits and camped in tent in that forested area, where occasionally one would come across tigers. The Inspection Bungalow or the tent would always be surrounded in night by the Bhils with a number of fires lit all around the place.

Within Abu Road tehsil and in the adjoining areas of Sirohi, we were soon to face another type of desperadoes. A woman dacoit named Putli and her gang was very active at that time and government officials, especially magistrates had become targets of her wrath. Once I had a narrow escape. I had decided to camp at a place about 10-12 kms from Abu Road. I was to leave for the camp for night-halt after finishing hearing of criminal cases in Abu Road. My baggage had already reached the camp along with my Jemadar- the head peon. At the end of the day, I do not know why but I did not feel like leaving Abu Road for the camp. Instead, I decided to leave early next morning. Next day when I arrived at the camp, I found a great deal of commotion. Putli and her gang had attacked the camp in the night and looked for me, but not having been able to find me there, had severely beaten my Jemadar and the Chowkidar at the Inspection Bungalow. That was indeed a narrow escape.

My Collector, V. Shanker, ICS, had sent a word that instead of my going down to meet him, he would come up to meet me. He had already built a formidable reputation in the Service. He had worked for several years with Sardar Vallabhbhai Patel, as a private secretary to India's first Deputy Prime Minister. V. Shankar was known for his shrewd and astute mind. In the Princely India, his name was well known, perhaps next only to that of V. P. Menon the Secretary to the Ministry of States. He had already gone up the ladder to the level of a Joint Secretary in the Government of India and would have continued there, had he not married a young lady well known in high society. His first wife, daughter of a very senior ICS of the United Provinces (now Uttar Pradesh) was alive and he had two grown-up daughters. His second marriage was the talk of the town at a time when social mores were strict. Moreover he had done so despite advice from the Prime Minister. On marriage he was ordered go to the Bombay State. The chief minister Morarji Desai, who liked Shanker and had great admiration for his administrative and diplomatic abilities, knowing the PM's attitude, as a punishment sent him as the Collector and the District Magistrate of Banaskantha, the remotest and most backward district of the State.

V. Shanker took that in his stride. He and his young wife had soon settled down in Palanpur where instead of bemoaning his punishment posting, he had decided to launch extensive programmes for the development of the backward area. For undertaking the task, he asked the chief minister to post under him two young IAS officers. This was agreed to and he was given the choice to select from a panel of young officers. He selected B. G. Deshumkh, IAS, who was then in Thane district and myself. Deshmukh who was one year senior to me was put in charge of Thar sub-division bordering Pakistan. It was mostly sandy and desert-like, and he had to travel mostly on camel. Since my sub-division had some roads, Deshmukh offered me his old Dodge for my use, which greatly facilitated my journeys, at least on the main road between Mt. Abu – Abu Road and Ambaji. Otherwise, I was using a horse.

Corresponding to the two Revenue Sub-divisions, there were two Police Sub-divisions: one headed by R. N. Haldipur, IPS. Later he would join the Indian Frontier Administrative Service and distinguish himself in the Northeast and would become the Lt. Governor of the Union Territory of Arunachal. In the other sub-division, we had Kalyanpurkar, IPS. He and his wife, who was a doctor, were very nice to us. However, very soon they would leave for Delhi, as he was seconded to the Foreign Service. I lost track of him till on 20th November 1962, I saw his picture flashed in all the newspapers. P. K. Banerjee, India's Charge d'affairs in Peking and he were shown on a mid-night call with Chou-En-Lai the Prime Miniser of the Peoples Republic of China For cover, he had adopted his family name Row.

For me, V. Shanker's first visit to Mt. Abu was a memorable one. Having heard of his princes-like life style, I was eager to see him in person. He did not disappoint. A portly figure with a twinkle in eyes and smile on his lips, he appeared to be an easy going persons. Soon I was to find that only a social façade. On that occasion, instead of staying in the Circuit House that had been specially got ready for his stay, he opted to live in a secluded cottage belonging to a Rajputana Prince, where his all comforts were taken care of. I received him on arrival and his young and beautiful wife Krishna was particularly kind to me. I was young and probably of her age. After I had a cup of tea with them, V. Shanker told me to disappear for three days and to see him an hour before his departure for Abu Road. I was little puzzled, but since his instructions were specific, I did not go to see him, nor did I have the occasion to see him or his wife anywhere in the hill station. On the last day, I went to the cottage at the appointed time. I found him relaxed lounging comfortably on a sofa. He had obviously enjoyed his holiday. Apparently some old friends of his from princely families had taken care of the couple. I noticed that the reception room was crowded with bouquets of flowers and several boxes of jewelry and a few costly articles presented to him were spread on tables. These were obviously given by ex-maharajas, who had come to pay court to him. He made a few desultory enquiries about me and how I was settling down to my job, while his young wife offered me tea.

Before leaving he said, 'Have you anything to ask in the nature of guidance?' All that time I had been carefully watching the lordly style in which he and his wife had been entertained for three days and also presented with several silver articles and costly jewelry. To my young mind that was against everything that had been told to us by our at the Metcalfe House. It was dinned into us that a Service officer must not accept any costly presents. With those lessons still fresh in mind and not suffering from any inhibition, pointing to all the articles lying about, I asked 'How all this is consistent with what we were told at the School about not accepting presents?' Without any elaboration on my part, he understood what I had in mind. He looked at me and said, 'Pradhan, these are for services rendered. One should not accept anything for services to be rendered.' No further explaining was necessary. I learnt, why V. Shanker was already regarded as one of the empire builders in the ICS; he had style and also courage to do what he wanted.

ಶಿಂಡಿ

That was a very brief meeting with the collector and I was asked to should meet him in Palanpur on the day Morarjibhai Desai, the chief minister would be visiting there. Both Deshmukh and myself were called for the occasion.

I had already met Morarji Dsesai a couple of times in Ahmedabad. He was kind and asked me a few questions about the agitation for merger of Abu Road with Rajasthan, which used to erupt from time to time. He had no doubt that it must be handle firmly, even if I had to resort to firing, which unfortunately I had to do twice during my stay there. Then we talked a little about the development of Mt. Abu, for which the State Government was liberally releasing funds hoping to win over the Princes and the gentry who mattered. Noticing that the chief minister had been taking personal interest in the various development schemes, I requested him to visit Mt. Abu to inaugurate the water supply scheme, which was then under execution. It was an important project, costing over a million rupees. He gladly accepted and I thanked him for the same. However, that was not going to be the end for me.

In the evening, V. Shanker called me over to see him. When I was ushered into his room, he said : 'It was foolish on your part to have invited the Chief Minister'. I did not understand what he meant. I also felt offended and asked him, 'What was wrong in inviting him. I had done so in my capacity as the President of the Municipality.'

V. Shanker told me off that, in any case that capacity was ex-officio and subject to over-all control of the collector. He was right, but I didn't like the way he had talked to me. Perhaps he also realized it. That night around 9 p.m. he sent his car with a message with the driver asking both me and my wife to come over and have coffee with them. I declined the invitation. The driver, belonging to old princely state, was shocked at my defiance.

Next morning, when I went to see V. Shankar, he was good enough to say, 'I am sorry, if you feel offended'. That was great about him. From that moment he became my real mentor. He took interest in everything I did and next time when he came to Mt. Abu he made it a point to introduce me to his several friends, the Princes. He gave me so much latitude in my work that it was known that whatever I did, it had the support of the collector. This helped me to settle a score between the Municipality and the high and mighty

Mahant of the Raghunathji temple who was considered a bully. That made me popular with the local population.

V Shankar imbibed in me the habit of never taking a decision on land related dispute without seeing the land. I had learnt that the hard way in Bavala during city survey. By one visit one can resolve a dispute that might take years on paper. As V. Shankar put it, 'Pradhan, remember that behind a file is a human or a family'.

For me the work and pleasure went hand in hand. In the morning when I went for horse riding, I was also doing my duty of inspecting the municipal works; when I cantered through the forest, I was a Forest Officer and often apprehended culprits cutting trees. In the afternoon, I would sit in the Court as a Sub-divisional Magistrate and sentence the culprits. As an Assistant Collector, I used to send out stinking notes to the Chief Executive of the Municipality, which he would dutifully submit to me with draft replies to be approved by me in my capacity as the President. When some matters had to be dealt with, which did not fall under the jurisdiction of any of the several offices that I occupied, I would assume powers of the Superintendent of the Hill Stations, since those were undefined.

At Mt. Abu, I was still in the process of learning on the job and in doing so, since there was no one to guide me on the spot, I had to ensure that I did not make a fool of myself. Once I almost did it. I had been appointed by the High Court as the sole 'Arbitrator' in a dispute between Abu Road Electricity Company and the Abu Road Municipality on the rate of electricity and the huge amount of arrears that the Municipality owed to the

Electricity Company. I studied all the papers thoroughly and when sat for arbitration, I was so much disgusted with the incompetence of the lawyers on both the sides that I started arguing the case myself, unfortunately for both the parties. In fact, I did it so successfully that both the parties lost faith in the Arbitrator and approached the High Court to get me changed. I did not mind.

Those days High Court had a style to deal with such matters. Most judges were from the ICS and had gone through the mill. In my case, instead of being admonished in court premises, I was invited for breakfast by Justice Bhagwati at his residence. He asked me as to how I had proceeded. With a gentle smile he explained role of an arbitrator. He was supposed to function as an impartial judge, who after hearing both the parties should frame issues and see how a mutually acceptable solution could be found. An Arbitrator was a friend to both sides. In my case, I had not only acted as an advocate for both and forgotten my neutral role. However as he was satisfied that there was no mala fide in my behaviour, he had thought of talking over the matter with me.

That was a lesson for me, how to deal with erring young officers. I followed that when I became chief secretary. In return I got respect and affection. Learning on the job, I also made abiding friendships with some IPS officers in Mt Abu.

The Carrick Cottage, situated in front of the Mess, which was formerly Rajputana Hotel, was soon a great attraction for young IPS probationers. On Sunday morning, it was open house and several of them would stream in for a cup of coffee. We made several friends and saw as many as three batches passing out of the Academy. I would meet several of these young officers when I become Union Home Secretary. We became very fond of M. K. Narayanan*, one of the most brilliant probationers, who rose the highest position of the Director of Intelligence Bureau and later as the National Security Advisor Prime Minister.

Several other brilliant officers, whom we knew, rose very high in their career. Julio Rebiero and Mohan Katre were in police. Julio, three decades later, became Director of Police in the Punjab and earned high reputation for handling militancy in the Punjab and came to be known as the 'Super Cop'. Katre retired as the Director of the Central Bureau of Investigation (CBI) and earned a great deal of publicity (some say notoriety) for his handling of the Bofors Gun deal scandal. B. P. Singhal, worked with me as Additional Home Secretary and on retirement joined the BJP and became a Member of Parliament. S. Swaminathan, rose to high position in the intelligence set up the RAW (Research and Analysis Wing). He was actively involved in my negotiation with Laldenga in settling the insurgency in Mizoram. Those were score of others like them, who formed my 'network' when I became the Union Home Secretary. I was fortunate to have met them when we were all young officers and about to begin our careers. All of them rose to high positions and remain my life-long well wishers.

Carrick cottage and the gate of the Rajputana IPS Officers Mess played an important role in shaping my future, both career wise and family wise. My eldest so Rajiv, born a few months after our posting was a great attraction to young probationers, who apparently were missing their younger brothers and sisters. My wife, hardly twenty three years old then, became a life long sister to some, especially to M. K. Narayan, who is currently the Governor of West Bengal.

∞⌘

The highlight of my work in Mt. Abu was to appear before the States Reorganisation Commission (SRC) consisting of the Chairman, Justice Fazal Ali, and Dr. K. N. Kunzru and Sardar K. M. Panikkar as members.

Mt Abu was part of the Sirohi state of Rajputana. At the time of the merger of the State with the Indian Union, one tehsil of that state had been detached and merged with the Banaskantha district. It was not clear for what reasons that was done. V. P. Menon was perhaps influenced by the consideration that Sardar Patel was from Gujarat and that region of the erstwhile Bombay state had no hill station for summer season.

V. Shanker, who had become the Revenue Secretary in Bombay, wanted me to place the case for the Bombay State before the Commission, as best as I could. The brief that was sent to me by the Genaral Administration Department was weak. There was no justification as to how only one tehsil was detached and merged with the Bombay state. I carried out a great deal of research on my own The Residency had a good library and the place from where the British Residents kept an eye on the Rajput states. Almost all those States had palatial summer residences spread over Mount Abu and had to attend on the Resident during summer months. I carefully went through all old records and maps and prepared a case based on history and concepts of geographical contiguity, as well as the fact that of the economy of the Hill Station depended mainly on the tourists from Gujarat region of the Bombay state and from Saurashtra--- then a Part B state.

The three member commission was put up at the Residency and as instructed by V Shankar their comforts were taken care. On the appointed day, I presented myself before the Commission and argued the case with a great deal of vehemence. I thought, the Commission was greatly impressed with my presentation with several charts and maps that I had got specially prepared. My case was unassailable. I looked expectantly for some reaction.

Sardar Pannikar looked at me with a twinkle in his eyes and a smile. Fondling his goatee, he said, 'Well, Mr. Pradhan, the Commission is impressed that you have performed your duty brilliantly.' After a pause, he added, 'Unfortunately, the geography is against you.' When I looked at them somewhat puzzled, he said, 'In mountain areas, we must follow the internationally accepted principle of the watershed.'

He added gravely, 'Unfortunately, Mt. Abu is situated on a slope with watershed towards Rajasthan. Therefore, geography is against you.' He paused for a few moments to ensure that the logic of his argument would be appreciated and added, 'The history is also against you. If Sardar Vallabhbhai Patel wanted Mt Abu to be a part of the Gujarat region, he should have merged the whole of State in the Bombay State. It was a historical blunder, not to do so.'

I could not argue with his logic. The Chairman was good enough to assure me that they would tell the Chief Minister, how well I had argued the case for the State. Very soon, I received a letter of appreciation from the Chief Secretary. I was gratified that I had done my duty and that the government had noted my performance.

On 1st November 1956 I handed over Abu Road tehsil, including Mt. Abu to Rajasthan. The Chief Secretary of Rajasthan, one Mr. Mehta came over personally to take charge, along with an officer who would replace me as their sub-divisional Officer. The high and mighty Bombay Government did not think it worthwhile to send any senior officer on their behalf. I had been given all the plenipotentiary powers of the State Government to do the needful. I signed the necessary documents and left in the Dodge for Abu Road en-route to Palanpur.

I worked for three-four months in the Collector's Office as SDM. One day, most unexpectedly, I received orders to proceed to Poona to take over in the newly created post of the Additional Collector. I did not know then that my posting to the western Maharashtra was to change not only the course of my career, but the course of my life!

Chapter 13

To the Western Ghats
- Learning Maratha History and my Roots

My transfer to Poona came as a great surprise for everyone because normally at the level of assistant collectors, officers were not transferred from one region of the state to the other. However, that was the first time that the government had created post of Additional Collectors for Ahmedabad, Poona and Bombay, and since Shivagnam, my batchmate who was in Baroda, was posted in Ahmedabad, I was to be sent out of Gujarat.

I was happy to go to Poona. I had not spent much time with my father since I joined the service. Also, I was looking forward to get to know my younger brothers and sisters. They were equally excited that we would be coming there with our son Rajiv, who was born on 11th June 1955.

We had a very enjoyable stay in Mt Abu and it was with some regret that we left Banaskantha district. We had also to say goodbyes to our cook-cum-bearer and the ayah, who had looked after Rajiv well. For them going to Maharashtra was like going to a foreign country. Fortunately, very soon we would find an equally good set of servants in Poona. Being an old established district, even before we had arrived at Poona, our accommodation had been arranged and a part of the Collector's office had been specially got ready for the Additional Collector.

26 Queen's Garden was beautiful old style bungalow in stone with Mangalore tiled roof. We were to stay on the first floor and since the house was too large for us, the ground floor was allotted to P. Chandrakant Nayak, IAS, who was the Supernumerary there. He was then a bachelor and we lived as one family.

As soon as we shifted over modest belongings to the huge first floor allotted to us, I could see anxiety on my wife's face; with the baby on hands, her priority was to set up the kitchen. However, not having had the opportunity to do any cooking till then, she was quite anxious about what she could produce for the meal. As luck would have it, a middle-aged couple walked into the bungalow. Shri Ram was the cook of Brig Moti Sagar, who had left Poona on transfer, a couple of days back. He produced the necessary certificates and we employed him straightaway. His wife Lakshmi was willing to work as an ayah. The couple was very happy to find employment for both. They would work with us for several years, very faithfully.

Dr. A. U. Shaikh was the collector of Poona. He had already earned considerable reputation as a development oriented officer and one whose work was very much well publicized in the newspapers. The State Government wisely anticipated that the creation of an additional collector's post might create some problems between the two officers of equal status and therefore had done the distribution of work between the two through a gazette notification.

Thus, there was no occasion for us to have any friction in working relationship. I also made it known to the staff that being much younger, I was the junior between the two of us and the Collector and the District Magistrate of Poona Shaikh was also my boss. That scotched efforts on the part of some subordinates, who were always on the look out for creating mischief in such situations. Shaikh had been inducted into IAS from the State civil service and we built up a healthy relationship. I learnt later that some of the other additional collectors had to face difficult problems in relationship with their seniors.

Poona also gave us an opportunity to meet a large number of senior army and civilian officers, as well as a number of distinguished non-officials. Among the senior officers, we were very well received by B. B. Paymaster, ICS and his wife. He was an unusual Parsi gentleman. Somewhat unorthodox in his views, I found that he could approach a problem in a refreshingly different manner. He was then the Director of Local Authorities. He would end his career as the Chief Secretary to the Government of Maharashtra. He and his wife remained our life long well-wishers.

Within a few months of my posting there, the old posts of the Commissioners were revived because it was not found feasible to administer the Bilingual State consisting of almost fifty districts, directly from the Secretariat. G. L. Sheth, ICS, was appointed the Commissioner. We found that he was his wife were so much different from other officials. Belonging to affluent Gujarati families, they maintained a very high standard of living. They extended us hospitality and affectionate welcome and were very kind to us. Soon my wife and I were regarded as members of their family and remained to throughout their life. Their son Nanak and daughter Kanan were very fond of us. I regarded Kanan as daughter and she gave us much affection. Unfortunately, she passed away a few years back at an early age.

The most important part of my work was to deal with the implementation of the Tenancy legislation and the abolition of Inams and Jagirs. The latter gave me a great deal of insight into the Maratha administration set by Shivaji the Great. These jagirs and inams were granted to win over the loyalty of important families and for performing official duties. In order to facilitate enquires into these grants, I undertook extensive tour of the remote areas of the district. Fortunately, most of the areas were around the old forts and that gave us opportunities to visit a number of forts around Poona.

We also met some old families, who had for generations served Shivaji and his successors. Luckily these areas, particularly the Maval, Junnar, Bhor, Bhatghar etc. abounded in forests and several water reservoirs. Thus, camping and touring with the family, including the cook and the ayah, helped us not only to enjoy the rugged beauty, but also to learn a lot about the people. There, for the first time, I came across several families, who belonged to the small community, the Chandraseniya Kayastha Prabhu, popularly referred to as the CKPs, to which I belong. Many of these families produced the Sanads, bearing Shivaji's signature and seal to attest their original grants. Since I had already learnt old style Marathi alphabet, called Modi, I read with great fascination valours for which the families had been granted inams and jagirs. I also found that in all these documents, there was one common denominator: 'The Loyalty'. CKP as a community had earned high reputation for the great sense of loyalty with which they served their masters. There were several who worked for Shivaji and laid down their lives. Because of this unique quality, which is in their blood, the CKPs were always deployed by the Maratha Princes as well as the Peshwas to handle their most confidential work and correspondence. In turn, they received loyalty, which has become a legend.

The community was well known for another quality, that of penmanship. They were good scribes and with their ingrained sense of loyalty, the CKP's distinguished themselves as keepers of records and confidential advisers to rulers. A tradition for integrity and loyalty was thus built up over the centuries.

I did not know that my posting in Poona would very soon lead me to work with Maratha leader, where my latent and inherited qualities would be called into play. Again, at the tail-end of my career, I would have the honour of serving a young Prime Minister of India in a similar manner.

Chapter 14

Disastrous Beginning
- Y. B. Chavan

It is strange, but true, that one does not realize how exactly and when human bonds are established. This was equally true in case of my relationship with Yashwantrao Balwantrao Chavan.

Mt Abu was a favourite place for holding conferences and meetings, especially during the spring and summer months. In the summer of 1955, Government of Bombay decided to hold at Mt Abu a conference to consider various aspects of the Community Development projects and specially the National Extension Services (NES) schemes. As the Sub-Divisional Officer at Mt Abu, I was made responsible for making all the arrangements for the conference. My collector, V. Shanker told me to take all the decisions on the spot and not to refer any matter to him. Obviously he wanted to test my organizing ability. Fortunately, thanks to several former Rajas and Maharajas who had made available their houses and the excellent support, I received from the IPS Officers' Mess and their Commandant Sardar Waryam Singh, I. P., everything worked very smoothly. It was no mean achievement.

The conference was attended by over 200 dignitaries including the entire Cabinet, the chief Secretary, most of the secretaries to the government and senior officers, collectors of all the districts of the state. They were greatly impressed with the physical and other arrangements made for the Conference. Yashwantrao Chavan who was at that time the Minister for Civil Supplies and also the Minister in-charge of Community Development Programme must have been also suitably impressed. On the last day of the three day conference, my Collector, V. Shankar called and told me that Y. B. Chavan had asked for my services to be appointed as the Project Officer for the first National Extension Block at Karad, his home town in Satara district. Shanker told me firmly that he was going to tell the Chief Minister that my transfer at that stage was not in my interest, nor would he agree to my shifting from Mt Abu as long as he was the collector of Banaskatha. Since I did not know anything about the background, I did not react either way to the suggestion, but told my Collector to do what he thought was best. Later I learnt that there was a discussion between the chief secretary, K. L. Panjabi, V. Shankar and Capt. Shankar rao Mohite, who was the Development Commissioner, and Chavan about me. Just before he left Mt Abu, Chavan called me over to meet him and thanked me all arrangements and told me that he wanted me to work as the first Project Officer for the Community Development Programme at Karad. Unfortunately, his suggestion had not been accepted.

In his inimitable manner, with a smile, he said, 'Perhaps, one day, we shall have an opportunity of working together.'

Disastrous Beginning

Frankly, I did not take these words very seriously. I was still under the influence of advice that we had received at the IAS Training School from many senior ICS Officers to not get involved too closely with individual politicians. They had always an ulterior motive to establish links with civil servants! I therefore did not give a second thought to the matter.

After over three years of stay in Banaskantha district, I was hoping to get posted to a better Gujarat district, such as Surat or Baroda. I was therefore surprised to be posed at Poona. Later I learnt that Y. B. Chavan, who had become the chief minister of the bigger Bilingual Bombay State, had not forgotten me. My posting to Poona was the beginning of a relationship – on a purely professional basis. It however, started on a disastrous note.

At the beginning of 1957, I was holding charge of the post of Collector, as Dr Shaikh had been transferred. One day, I was informed that the President of India, Dr. Rajendra Prasad, will visit Poona for the inauguration of the National Defence Academy at Khadakvasla. Poona was an important district. It was also the capital of the state during monsoon when the government and the governor shifted there for four months. It was also the Headquarters of the Army's Southern Command. A large number of senior service officers were posted there. Also, a number of senior officers had settled down after their retirement. Presence of all these big wigs made protocol arrangements all the more difficult. The President's visit was therefore a nightmare for the collector.

In the early hours of the morning, the President arrived by his special train. Unfortunately, when the President's coach came to a halt at the Poona Railway Station, there was breach of protocol because of over-eagerness on the part of the then Southern Army Commander to greet the President. This was clearly noted by everyone. But once breach had taken place, there was hardly anything that could be done at the moment. G. L. Sheth, the Commissioner of Poona Division, told me that he will take up the matter appropriately after the visit was over. We, however, did not realize that the young Chief Minister had taken great offence to the breach of protocol for which I was in no way responsible. The day had not augured well for me.

An hour later, when I escorted the chief minister to the circuit house, I was to attract Yashwantrao's wrath for another protocol lapse. The chief minister's programme showed that he was expected to accompany the President to the National Defence Academy and have lunch with the Cadets. As soon as we reached the circuit house, he asked G. L. Seth as to how he was expected to visit the NDA without any formal invitation. When Seth asked me I told him that the formal invitations for the chief minister had been delivered to my office and I had arranged the same to be placed in his suite. Chavan's was already seething with anger over the morning incident and when he was told that the invitation had been delivered in collector's office, he bluntly asked G. L. Seth : 'Since when the Chief Minister of Bombay has become care of the Collector of Poona?'

He told Seth that since the invitations had neither been properly addressed, nor delivered to him by the NDA authorities, he would refuse to accompany the President. He was, of course, very angry and annoyed that I had taken delivery of the invitation on his behalf. I unwittingly became a target of his anger. G. L. Seth tried to explain but found that it was impossible to smoothen Chavan's ruffled feelings. With great difficulty, he persuaded him to at least see me and give a hearing to me.

For a young officer with hardly four years of service, to face the volcanic anger of the chief minister was the most unpleasant prospect. I knew that no amount of explanation would help. At the same time, I was convinced in my own mind that Chavan's anger was somewhat irrational. I instinctively felt that arguments would not serve any purpose, nor did he appear to be in a mood to accept explanation. I took a piece of paper and wrote : 'I apologies for the unintentional slight. If you think I am responsible, I would unhesitatingly offer to resign from the IAS'.

As soon as I entered the room I said, 'Sir, you are the Chief Minister. If you feel that I am responsible, I am ready to resign'. So saying, with tears in my eyes I offered him that piece of paper. He looked at it and most unexpectedly asked me to come over and sit by his side on the sofa. He put his arm around my shoulder and said, 'Please forget the whole thing and don't talk about it to anyone. Perhaps I was over-reacting so far as you are concerned. However, so far as the Army is concerned, both the Army Commander and the head of the NDA owe an apology to the Chief Minister'.

I did not utter a single word. Later when I met the Army Commander, Lt. General P. N. Thapar and told him about the unhappiness of the Chief Minister on the breach of protocol at the Railway Station, as a gentleman soldier, he immediately went over to see him and conveyed his regret. Likewise, the Commander of the NDA immediately sent a senior officer with a personal invitation to the Chief Minister.

Chavan accompanied the President – but I did not think he unreservedly accepted the army's gestures. Anyone looking at the photographs of his visit accompanying the President of India to NDA, will notice sense of hurt pride clearly visible on his face. I later found that it was impossible for him to hide his emotions. His face was always a mirror of what went on within his mind.

Chapter 15

A District Collector's Life

After hardly eight months' stay in Poona, I was sent as officiating collector at Kolhapur. It was known that Y. B. Chavan took great interest in Kolhapur district. He and many of his colleagues from the western Maharashtra had received their educated there, thanks to progressive policies of the former ruler, the late Shahu Maharaj. Chavan regarded Kolhapur as his 'Karma-bhumi' and he was deeply interested in promoting the economic and social development of that district.

It was known that he was not very happy with the then collector there, who was an elderly person promoted from the Baroda State civil service. When he asked for leave, Chavan decided to appoint a younger person. Kolhapur was regarded as a prize district in western Maharashtra. I later learnt that although my appointment was in the officiating capacity, that was not liked by the then chief secretary and by my former collector, V. Shankar, who was by then the secretary of the Revenue Department. They felt that having regard to its importance of the place and problems there, a senior officer should have been sent there. I was sure that both of them were thinking of my interest, because, if I were to blunder in handling my charge, my future career would suffer.

Those days Kolhapur district was seething with law and order problems. Kolhapur city was the headquarters of the Samyukta Maharashtra Movement (SMM), a joint front of several political parties formed to agitate for the formation of a State of Marathi speaking people. It was a powerful combination and in the previous election, the Congress Party had been swept away. All the thirteen members of the State legislatures (MLAs) as well as all the Members of Parliament (MPs) belonged to the opposition parties. The city had become notorious for constant outbursts of violence and one of my predecessors – a very senior ICS officer – had been peremptorily transferred out of Kolhapur because he had failed to handle the law and order following violent agitation by the SM movement. I therefore went to Kolhapur with a certain sense of trepidation. At the same time, being young, I was determined to face the challenge – with a little bit of luck!

My entry into Kolhapur made news of a most unexpected kind. I and my family, including wife, Rajiv, cook and ayaha were traveling in my big black 1947 model Chevrolet car. Around 6 p.m., we entered Kolhapur district after crossing the bridge over the river Warna. By that time, it was already getting dark and appeared dismal because of overcast sky and drizzle. Since it was getting late, I was trying to speed up to reach Kolhapur – another twenty miles away. The collector, G. R. Reddy, IAS, was waiting for me to hand over the charge on my arrival. Suddenly, on a bend, I saw some dark shape crossing the road. Before I knew what the object was, I had hit a buffalo crossing the road, on either side of which were deep ditches. Chevrolet being a sturdy car, took the impact well and I managed to bring it to a halt on the edge of the road.

No one within the car was injured. However, we were badly shaken up. Very soon villagers, who had watched the accident, came running and surrounded the car. They were wielding lathis (bamboo sticks). I got out and tried to explain that it was an accident and I was ready to compensate the owner of the buffalo. They were in no mood to talk business because they could see at that hour by threats they could get away with anything they wanted. That area of Kolhapur was well known for hot-heads.

Just as the situation appeared to be getting desperate, a car which we had overtaken near Satara came to a halt and out stepped P. D. Kasbekar, IAS, who was then Director for Sugar Co-operatives. He had with him a couple of khadi clad persons. One of them was Ratnappa Kumbhar, a top leader of the Congress in Kolhapur district. At that time, he was involved in setting up of a co-operative sugar factory and that is how he was traveling with Kasbekar.

When they told the villagers that I was the new Collector, the whole scenario suddenly changed. They started asking, 'Sir, why didn't you tell us earlier?' One or two elderly persons came forward and told, 'Please don't worry about the buffalo. It was already old and had stopped milking long back. You do not have to pay any compensation.' On my insisting, they gave the name of the owner. I assured him that my insurance company will take care of his claim. I also told him not to hesitate in putting proper claim only because his buffalo had been killed by the new collector's car!

After that, with Kasbekar following our car, we reached the collector's residence where Reddy was anxiously waiting. We began the formalities of handing over and taking over and it was late in the night I completed the counting of the cash in District Treasury and verified the number of prisoners in the magisterial custody.

Next morning my entry into Kolhapur was heralded by the two local language newspapers, boldly on the front page : 'Providential Escape for the New Collector of Kolhapur'. There was no mention of the poor buffalo which had lost its life. I greatly appreciated their gesture in saving me from an embarrassment and the insurance company's agent was good enough to settle generously the claim of the buffalo owner and also my claim for the repairs of the vehicle.

That entry proved fortuitous for me. Kolhapur has a high literacy and alert ryot (peasantry). I did not know that before arrival there. A former Maratha kingdom, I had imagined a backward place and people bound by traditions – unlike liberated Poona. I was soon to learn how wrong I was!

ೞಡಾ

I knew that my officiating tenure was exactly for sixty days, and if I was to prove myself capable of handling such a major district, I had to do so in the next one month. Thanks to the accident, I had already met Ratnappa Kumbhar, in whom I found a very well-informed and helpful political leader. I quickly arranged to meet other political personalities. Since all the Members of the Legislative Assembly (MLAs) and Members of India's Parliament (MPs) of the district were from the opposition, they were greatly impressed that the new Collector had taken the initiative to meet them. On the law and order front, I assured them that I would come down heavily in case there was any attempt to breach the peace. On development matters, I told them that my doors were open and I would take the initiative to help them to carry out projects in their constituencies.

To prove my bona-fide, I fished out a few schemes still in gestation and launched them. That also gave me an opportunity to visit far-flung tehsils and meet the people. Very soon there was a talk that the young Collector was in tune with the 'Kolhapur -spirit'. That spirit was, and even today is, a combination of grit, determination and hard-work, and that is why Kolhapur district is now reported to have the higher per capita income in India.

Fortunately for me, all that I was trying to do was being reported to the Chief Minister who, I was told, was also keeping himself closely informed through his own political network. He had also deputed his Parliamentary Secretary Homi J. H. Talyarkhan to visit the district. Homi who was then bubbling with enthusiasm very soon struck good friendship with me. We developed admiration for each other and he must have told in glowing terms to the Chief Minister of my involvement with the people and development activities in Kolhapur.

Soon Reddy's leave was getting over and one day I received orders for my transfer as collector of Osmanabad a relatively backward district from Marathawada, an area from the old Hyderabad State of the Nizam that had been merged with the Bombay State. Since my wife and I knew that we would leave Kolhapur soon, we started saying our farewells to a few families we got to know and prepared ourselves to depart for Osmanabad. As usual, our truck carrying our baggage left one day prior to our departure. On the morning of our departure, we got our Chevrolet loaded and I was about to leave for the collector's office to find out whether there was any information about Reddy's arrival. I was pleasantly surprised, when the chief secretary rang up to say that the government had decided to post Reddy elsewhere and, I should continue at Kolhapur. That is how I became the collector of an important and politically sensitive district. That also brought me personally closer to Y. B. Chavan.

My wife and I were overjoyed to learn that we would stay in Kolhapur. In the short period that we were there we had made friends with some young persons of our age. We had also been well received by the Jagirdars and Inamdars of ex-Kolhapur State, who formed the social milieu. They were not highly educated, but very well brought up with western manners and educated in private schools set up in the days of the Raj. They were all enthusiastic sportsmen, fond of tennis and shikar - hunting. Their ladies, most coming from princely Maratha families, were charming and some outstandingly beautiful. They were all good companions for us. We made it a practice of visiting the District Club in the evenings and that encouraged more and more ladies and men from these families to start coming to the Club regularly. Every one was happy that the new collector and his wife were trying to revive the Club. Many of them had withdrawn from club-life because of somewhat antagonistic attitude of my predecessors to princely families.

We were to spend next three and half years happily. Our second son Vivek was born there on 19th June 1959. I was happy in my work enthused by the 'Kolhapur spirit'

During the officiating two months period, I had discovered that for administering the district well and earning goodwill of the people, I had to be careful on two fronts: First, the people of Kolhapur – this applies equally to the leaders and the ordinary citizens – have a genius for managing their affairs, provided they are kept busy with developmental activities. Second, they have a genius for hard work. When a Kolhapuri starts working, he does not stop unless he achieves his objectives and completes the task. He may not claim to be intellectual – but when he takes into his head to do something, his grit and determination does the rest. This applies to all aspects of his life, whether it is constructing small dams and wells to store and utilize every drop of water or to bring under sugar cultivation land that no agricultural scientist would imagine or advise to be used for sugarcane, or setting up sugar factories and industrial production, poultry farming, milk diaries etc. In agriculture, in many respects, he resemble a peasant from Punjab. It is, therefore, no surprise that only Kolhapur has the peasant stock in Maharashtra who can compete with the Punjab farmers.

This character equally applies to the field of sport like wrestling and this is why Kolhapur has produced a number of India's famous wrestlers. Same applies to the field of arts and crafts. First cinema in India was produced by Dada Saheb Phalke in Kolhapur. Likewise in fine arts. Think of any field, and once a Kolhapuri takes into his head, he does not rest till he has achieved what he wants. Unfortunately, this also applies to his temper and once he resolves to finish an enemy, he would go after the target with a single-minded purpose and finish him to the end. Kolhapur and the surrounding areas had, therefore, earned a notoriety for a district with a record number of murders.

Over next three years, I would unconsciously imbibe that Kolhapur - spirit of enterprise, hard work, grit and determination. I would shed my poor Poona personality and become a good communicator, an energetic district officer and above all an all round human being.

Kolhapur not only shaped my career but also my life. Whatever I achieved in later life, whether in India at international levels, I attribute to my learning days in that district

Chapter 16

Dealing Feudal India
- Of Princes & Maharajas

In my very post as an Assistant Collector, I had met some specimens of the Princely India. During stay in Mount Abu, I had dealt with a small time Raja at Danta, a Rajput whose subjects were tribal -bhills. He lived and behaved as a raja and his former subjects were not aware that they lived in independent India. Their deity is Ambaji and every Dassara (on Vijaya Dashmi day) was celebrated by sacrificing a bull. A ghastly sight indeed. I had to be present as a part of duty.

At Abu, I met Maharaja of Sirohi, a gentle soul who led dignified life and was a specimen of old world charm and quiet dignity. Also some other minor feudal. The major ones avoided me, as it was not correct protocol wise. Also with V. Shankar as Collector, they had no need to 'pay any respects' to his assistant. Mostly they sent their ADC's with a basket of fruits.

At Palanpur, my wife and I occasionally met the Nawab and his Begum, a gracious English lady. He was suave, tall, handsome and polished gentleman. He had played a significant role in shaping India's western boundaries by stopping moves by certain rulers, including some Hindu ones to accede to Pakistan and the Nawab of Bhopal. He had also brought prosperity to Palanpur state by constructing, as an war effort, an air-strip for landing of small aircraft that was used mainly for flying diamonds and merchants from Bombay. A large number of diamond merchant families from Palanpur had been settled in Amsterdam, and that city remains hub of unpolished diamond trade - controlled by Indians and jews. Some called activities in Palanpur as smuggling, but the British rulers encouraged it because the Resident of the Viceroy was handsomely rewarded by presenting his wife with a diamond necklace.

My collector, V. Shankar ICS behaved and acted as a maharaja. Having worked and trained by him, I was familiar with mindset and behaviour of the ruling class of the former states, what was known as the Princely India. On arrival, I was briefed about idiosyncrasies of Kolhapur's feudal gentry. Fortunately for me, the collectors residence was the former British Residents residence. Built in 1848, it was a solid double storied red-brick structure with as many as six bed rooms, a large Reception hall, a Banquet hall and a Ballroom. Each bedroom had attached bath and ground floor beyond the Banquet hall were two very large size bedrooms with attached anterooms and baths. Only the Governor or the Viceroy was put up there.

The Residency was furnished with Persian carpets and old furniture mostly imported from England. In those days we had staff who were relics of the Raj, well trained, well dressed with turbans and starched white uniforms with red-gold cummerbands (belts/ sashes). They kept the Residency in top condition and served new masters well. With all that attention, no doubt a collector felt overwhelmed. Fortunately, my wife and I, having had experience of feudal, did not have any problem. What did overawe me was my office table. It was almost 16 by 10 ft and was meant to impress the visitors, mainly feudal gentry. Behind the august chair was on the wall mounted carcass of a Tiger, with head as big as two footballs. I felt distinctly unforgettable.

My predecessors had reservations to meet the Maharaja. I suffered no such complex, when I found that in the year 1957, I was considered a true successor to the Residency. My previous two predecessors - Dr A. U. Shaikh and G. R. Reddy - were promoted officers and not of the caste of a regular IAS recruit. An old timer did not fail to point out that The Residency was situated adjoining the New Palace on an elevation so that the flag of the Resident flew a few notches higher than the Maharaja's. With a garden larger than the New Palace and the top of my residence higher, I was supposed to act as a superior. I did not fall into a trap in which my predecessors had unwittingly fallen.

The Maharaja of Kolhapur, Shahaji Raje, was an institution by himself and I very soon realized that having him as my supporter would strengthen my hands in dealing with the district. His Highness Shahaji Raje, then a Lt Colonel of the Indian Army- later elevated to a Major General--- looked and behaved as a Raja, who was successor to the legacy of Shivaji the Great. With his thick upturn moustache, during my first meeting with him, I came away with an impression that he was almost play acting. Later when I got to know him better, I found that under that superficial play acting was a brave and intelligent human being, trying to adjust himself to the loss of power and pomp that he had lost so recently.

He was rightly proud of his lineage. The kingdom of Kolhapur was founded when Shivaji in 1659 A. D. captured the Fort of Panhala and adjoining Fort of Pavangad. After Shivaji's death, he was succeeded by Sambhaji who, unfortunately, with his eldest son Shahu fell into the hands of Aurangazeb and met with a cruel death. Shahu was kept in Aurangzeb's captivity and the kingdom fell to his younger brother Rajaram, who succeeded in turning the tide of the fresh invasion of Mughals. After Rajaram's death in 1700 A. D., his heroic widow Tara Bai conducted the administration in the name of their minor son. She is regarded as the founder of Kolhapur dynasty and even today tales of her valour are recounted with pride in Kolhapur. Her statue stands majestically at the entrance to the city.

I learnt that another name that not only Kolhapur, but Maharashtra remembers with gratitude is that of Shahu Maharaj. He reigned for thirty eight years from 1874-1912. Like many of his predecessors and successors, he had been adopted from the families of Ghateges of Kagal, a small Jairdari of Kolhapur. He was a true man of vision. Well brought up but not highly educated, he learnt by observation and had a perception of his surroundings and a vision for the future. Like other princely states, he did not stop after building show pieces like town halls, hospitals and palaces in the capital. He went to the villages and undertook development works like construction of small tanks, drinking water wells, school buildings and a host of other projects, which would directly benefit the people.

He undertook construction of a huge masonry dam across the river Bhogawati in the valley of Sahayadri mountain ranges. He introduced sugarcane cultivation in the land under the irrigation of the dam and laid the foundations for future prosperity of Kolhapur district. He permitted growth of trade and established markets for traders, named Shahupuri in Kolhapur and Jayasingpuri near Sangli. He encouraged traders from Gujarat to come and settle there to engage in trade and commerce. He established spinning and weaving mills in the state.

Shau Maharaj's greatest contribution was in building human resources through education and social reform. He introduced compulsory primary education. He devoted his energies to the reduction of social inequalities and undertook removal of untouchability and up-liftment of depressed classes by giving them equal opportunity to receive higher education. For that purpose, he built a number of hostels where students belonging to poor and depressed strata of society could come and live in Kolhapur. At the time of the independence and immediately thereafter, most of the prominent Maratha personalities on the political scene were products of institutions created by Shahu Maharaj. Dr. Babasaheb Ambedkar, the architect of India's Constitution, was personally picked up by Shahu Maharaj, who gave him scholarship to go England and become a Bar-at-Law. Yashwantrao Chavan, a poor peasant's son from the adjoining district of Satara, could get his education and become a graduate and get law degree.

His Highness Shahaji Maharaj was rightly proud of his ancestor, but I soon found out that he was not very popular among his former subjects. While the Jagirdars and Inamdars and their families because of their devotion and loyalty to the "Gaddi" (the throne) would never speak ill of him, I noticed that the people in general and the Congress leaders in particular were full of distrust. I very soon found out the reason.

A few weeks after taking over of my post at Kolhapur, my wife and I went for a formal call on his Highness and the Maharani. We were received with great pomp and formality by his Private Secretary, also named Yashwantrao Chavan and his ADCs. We were escorted upstairs where the Maharaja and Maharani received us with great courtesy. I was young, rather too young, to deal with a Maharaj who was regarded as the Head of the sixteen Maratha Princely States and who was a descendant of Shivaji the Great. I was, therefore, little reserved. Perhaps unconsciously, I was putting up a front to convey to Maharaja that I was successor to the Residency and as a representative of the Government of Bombay I was a notch higher in position.

It was to the credit of Maharaja that with his informality he made us feel at home and relaxed, by telling stories and anecdotes, for which he was well known. He also impressed on me his special status as a descendant of the House of Shivaji and how he was received by the top people in Delhi. Yashwantrao Chavan, being a Maratha and one who had received the benefit of education because of the bounty of his Highness's family, was of course someone who would do anything that Maharaja wished him to do.

He also claimed closeness to Morarji Desai the former chief minister who was now the Finance minister. He told with great humour how each time Morarji met him, the former would lecture him to give up drinking alcohol, and how his Highness in turn try to teach Morarji the benefits of alcohol. Once on visit to Kolhapur, Desai was invited to stay at the Palace. He was put up in a suite adjoining the Clock-Tower of the New Palace. That night, Morarji was kept awake by the resounding tolling of bells, each quarter hour. Next morning when they met at breakfast, as anticipated by His Highness, Morarji Desai bitterly complained about lack of sleep and asked His Highness to stop the bells tolling for the duration of his stay in Kolhapur. Maharaja told him that it was not possible to do so unless he dies, because as per old custom the sounding of the bells could be stopped only when a ruler dies. Instead he suggested to Desai, 'Why don't you try a peg or two of whisky before retiring to bed. I am sure, you will sleep soundly !, He added, 'Now you would appreciate why I have to douse myself with alcohol'. His Highness laughed loudly at his joke at the expense of Morarji Desai.

As we were about to take leave, he suddenly became serious and said, 'Pradhan Saheb, please do not forget that I have not surrendered my kingdom. I have only given up administering it. I am still the Chattrapati of Kolhapur. I hope you will keep in mind that unless I approve of, nothing can be done in Kolhapur, He was trying to browbeat me. I stood straight, added a couple of inches to my height and said with all seriousness, 'Maharaj, of course you have all the power within the compound of your Palace, but please note that outside as the agent of the Government of Bombay, my authority will prevail."

He did not like it, but a gracious person as he was, he saw me off with a smile on his face.

Very soon I learnt from the Palace sources that my words had their effect. Maharaja had greatly admired the way in which I had spoken without being offensive. A few weeks later, we were invited for a private dinner. Both he and the Maharani were kind to me and my wife and remained friendly to each other till his demise.

Later, I was to get involved in his family matters. Once as a trustee of Princess Padma Raje, the daughter of the late Maharaja, and second time when Shahaji Raje wanted to adopt his daughter's son. At the wedding of Padma Raje, my wife and I were seated next to the chief minister and his wife, Venutai. As a Trustee, I had to sign some papers. On the latter occasion, when the matters were really getting complicated, as the Maharaja wanted to adopt his daughter's son – not allowed under Hindu traditions - I helped him as an intermediary with Y. B. Chavan. He could thus adopt the present Maharaja, who is also named as Shau. He countinues to consider me as his well wisher - that I am.

ଔଓଔଓ

Chapter 17

Earning Chavan's Trust
- Facing Challenges

Y. B. Chavan had kept himself closely informed of what was happening in Kolhapur, but he never interfered with my work. He left me alone for the first few months to work in my own way and devise my own working methods to handle the district, which had earned some notoriety on law and order front. On my part, I never tried to contact him and seek advice. Moreover, in those days, it was not customary for collectors to leave their districts every now and then and visit the state capital. I was, therefore, on my own, engrossed in my work. While I had come to admire him like millions of others for the manner in which he was conducting the affairs of the greater Bilingual State, I had no particular feeling of affinity towards him. Also, there was no occasion for developing such a feeling. It was his convalescence following an operation for removal of gall bladder stones, some time late in 1958, that would set in motion events, which would bring two of us close to each other.

Along with several development activities in Kolhapur district, I had taken up a project for development of the

Panhala fort as a hill resort. Many prominent people including rich industrialists had acquired land within the Fort, but had done nothing to build houses or do anything for the development of the hill station. They had invested in the land, knowing that one day prices would appreciate. In a somewhat brash manner, I started issuing orders confiscating their plots. At the same time, I took up projects for cleaning up the Fort, development of old gardens and restoring historic buildings. That required pulling down of several unauthorized structures, which had been constructed, over centuries, by the so-called wardens and keepers of the Fort.

Very soon, complaints had reached Chavan. However, instead of asking for a report, he decided to come over for couple of weeks rest for convalescence. Chavan came accompanied by his wife, Venutai, whom I had not met. Since doctors had advised him complete rest, I noticed that he had brought a large number of books, rather unusual for a politician. He was staying in one of the bungalows belonging to an industrial family from Bombay and gave strict instructions that no one should disturb him.

In order to be available to CM, along with the civil surgeon of the district, I stayed in the Inspection Bungalow situated on a mountain spur, by the side of old building in which Shivaji the Great had once taken shelter when he was being hounded by the Mughal troops. During his 8-10 days stay, each evening he would call me for a chat for an hour or so. That was the time I got to know him as a widely read person with intellectual underpinning to his political personality. He talked about himself, his childhood, his education and his politics. It was a revelation for me to find that he was not only fond of reading books on history and economics but he had a deep intellectual perception and understanding of the socio-economic processes of development. I realised that he was no ordinary politician.

He went round in the evenings and saw what I had done to develop Panhala. He learnt that I had been able to do all the cleaning up without raising any controversy. I took no special credit and told him that all that I had done was a part of my duty as the President of the Panhala Municipality. Perhaps he liked my modesty. Just before he left, fully rested and rejuvenated, Chavan called me over and said 'I am deeply impressed by the way you are handling this difficult district. See what you can do for the agriculturists of Kolhapur.'

That set me on a task that brought me really close to Chavan. Also, I could leave behind to Kolhapur something really big and unique: The Shau Market for Jaggery, the first and the biggest Agriculture Produce Market in the Bombay state.

ಬಿಂಡಿ

One evening, while we were talking about development of agriculture and marketing of agricultural produce, Chavan asked me whether I knew that a scheme for regulating market for jaggery and other agricultural produce had remained unimplemented for over a decade because of the opposition of the Shahupuri merchants. I had never heard about that. I only knew that Sahupuri was the biggest jaggery market in India, where jaggery worth four-five crore of rupees was traded each season. I had not been told about any project to establish a regulated market for the same because that subject was handled by the Department of Co-operation and the collector had nothing to do with it. I immediately took stock of the situation and started preparation of a project to set up a market-yard that is a place where all jaggery brought by agriculturists had to be offered for sale.

Fortunately, I found a stalwart of the cooperative movement of Kolhapur to help me: Tatya Saheb Mohite, Chairman of the Kolhapur District Shetkari Sahakari Sangh. A self made man, he was responsible for starting village co-operatives in Kolhapur and since 1939, he was the Managing Director of the Sangh. A down to earth individual, he commanded great respect of agriculturists and equally strong distrust of the merchant community. He had been trying to establish the new market-yard but not finding any response from the administration had almost given up the idea. Therefore, when he found that I had picked up the challenge, his enthusiasm knew no bounds. Very soon, we were spending our days and nights together to work out detailed plans. We decided that the market must become operational by the beginning of the next jaggery season – eight months hence. When the merchants came to know about the scheme, most of them sniggered. They knew that we were talking of something, which was impossible. But working day and night, we had roads and sheds to hold auctions completed. Our next challenge was to get 100 telephone connections and a railway siding. For that I decided to visit Delhi to meet S. K. Patil the minister with a letter of introduction from Y. B. Chavan.

On reaching there, I went over to S. K. Patil's residence on Ashoka Road. When I met his private secretary, and showed him the letter of introduction, he promptly arranged my meeting the minister. I had never met S. K. Patil and had known him only by his great reputation as the political 'dada' of Bombay. When I told him that I had come from Kolhapur, he was somewhat incredulous. He looked at me and said : Since when the Government of Bombay has started sending their District Collectors to deal with the central government?

I was taken aback. Unthinkingly, on the spur of the moment, I said, "Sir, I have not come to the minister of the central government on behalf of the government of Bombay. I have come to meet Shri S. K. Patil, who I know belongs to Kolhapur's neighboring district – Ratnagiri."

He was equally taken aback by my approach and decided to give me patient hearing. I explained to him my predicament about the railway-siding and the telephone connections. That very afternoon, he called all senior officers and explained the situation and told them that since the chief minister of Bombay had sent Pradhan all the way and the schemes were of great interest to the agriculturists, there was no question of saying 'No'. He ordered that the rail-siding should be ready within six weeks and a telephone exchange with hundred telephone connections should be provided, to be operational one week before the market would open for trading on 1st December 1958.

When I returned to Bombay and reported to the chief minister, he was taken by surprise. Merchants of Kolhapur did not believe that S. K. Patil had ordered that both the rail-siding and the telephone connections would be operational at the opening of the market yard. They, therefore, decided to adopt the only alternative, namely to pressurize the Government of Bombay at the political level.

We were not aware in Kolhapur of what was happening in the cabinet in Bombay. However, about ten days before opening of the market, I was suddenly summoned to meet the chief minister. Ministers from Gujarat closely examined me on the state of preparations for opening of the market yard, provision of facilities for agriculturists as well as merchants. Since they knew that the Chief Minister was in favour of regulated market, they had apparently decided not to oppose the new yard, but to weaken it's functioning

On 1st December, I went to the market yard at 9 a.m. Since, despite our efforts, neither the chief minister nor any one of his minister could be present for the opening of the market yard, we decided to start the operation without any formal ceremony. There were reports of deep resentment within the cabinet and the ministers from Gujarat were unhappy that the interests of the merchants of Kolhapur had not been taken care of in shifting the market to the new yard. I guessed that even those ministers who were sympathetic about our efforts were doubtful whether we would really succeed in the end and no one wanted to be associated with an activity in which ultimately only the agriculturists would suffer and the Government get blamed.

This is how without any inaugural function, the biggest market yard in India started functioning.

Within a month, the situation was normalised and the market with the biggest turnover in jaggery was finally set up. That was possible because of strong support and steady political direction given by the chief minister to a young and inexperienced district collector. Also that is how a strong life-long bond of understanding and mutual trust was established between us.

Unfortunately, that struggle for securing remunerative prices for agricultural produce claimed life of Tatya Saheb Mohite. On 5th December, 1958, when one could discern the first break in the ranks of the merchants, Tatya Saheb suffered a severe heart attack. Despite his illness, he continued to guide the Sangh from his bed. On 27th June 1959, he suddenly collapsed at his home in his village Yulgud. In his death, we had lost a leader and a great fighter for the cause of agriculturists. I had lost a good friend. He had stood by my side and taught me many lessons of practical administration.

The day he died was my thirtieth birthday. There was no cheer in my heart.

Chapter 18

Transition to Bombay Secretariat

As the 1959 was coming to an end, I had completed many of the projects that I had taken in hand within and outside the Kolhapur city. I was comfortably settled with all-round good-will of the people. I had also received strong support from the government. There was no dearth of publicity of what I was doing. It was not of my seeking. The whole atmosphere was such that wherever I went and whatever I did attracted a great deal of public notice and often admiration. I knew that I had finally 'arrived' in Kolhapur and in the minds of people.

I decided to embark on some new projects and one of these was beautification of Rankala Tank in the city. It was a huge mass of water around two sides of which the old city had grown up. On that side, there were several temples and other places of worship. On the opposite bank, Rajaram Maharaj had built a palace, named Shalini Palace surrounded by a large garden and situated on the way to Panhala. Over decades, due to pollution, the environment around the tank had deteriorated. I thought of laying out a garden around it as had been done around the Kankaria

Lake in Ahmedabad. I had first seen Kankaria when I was posted in Ahmedabad and witnessed how the Municipal Corporation had undertaken its beautification. I learnt from friends how in five years a filthy mass of water had been converted into a place of beauty and recreation for the people. I sought Government's permission to visit Kankaria to study its development, which was promptly granted.

While spending one day at Bombay en-route to Ahmedabad I went to see V. Prabhakar, IAS, who was private secretary to the chief Minister. Prabhakar was one year senior to me in service and we had formed good friendship and mutual respect for each other's abilities. As soon as I stepped into his office, he told me that he was in fact trying to locate my whereabouts in Bombay because the chief minister wanted to see me. He refused to tell me for what purpose.

I was ushered into Chavan's office. After a few minutes of desultory talk about Kolhapur, Chavan said, 'I am looking for an officer to replace Prabhakar. I have you in mind'. I did not reply. When he saw some hesitancy on my part, he said, 'I do not want to force you. You think about it and tell Prabhakar.'

I told CM that I was on way to Ahmedabad and whether he would mind my giving a reply four days later on my way back. He liked that and asked me to talk to Prabhakar about the nature of work. He had been working for Chavan for over three years and from his career point of view, it was important for him to work as a district collector as he had no experience of district administration. He was right from his career point of view.

I had however doubts whether it was good for me to start working for the chief minister, when I had no experience whatsoever of working in the State Secretariat. Also, I had got myself so thoroughly involved in Kolhapur's developmental activities that I could not think of leaving it when several projects initiated by me were still incomplete.

During my four days visit to Ahmedabad and the overnight journeys, I gave a great deal of thought : Chavan had extended personally to me strong support throughout my tenure there. If I had been able to accomplish several tasks and won public acclaim, it was because of him. Moreover during his convalesce at Panahla he had given me an insight into his mind. His mental make up was not of an ordinary politician. He had revealed an intelligent mind capable of give-and-take in any discussion.

On way back I met him in the Secretariat and told him, 'If you want me, I am ready to come.' He was happy and asked me to choose my timing.

It was the beginning of January, 1960. Chavan was preoccupied with final stages of political discussions and arrangements for the bifurcation of the Bilingual State. He wanted me to start working with him on the day Maharashtra would be inaugurated. I therefore requested for two months' earned leave from the beginning of February, which was promptly granted by the government and the notification stated that 'my further posting will be indicated later'. Apparently, Chavan did not want to disclose that I had been selected to replace V. Prabhakar.

Everyone in Kolhapur was greatly puzzled as to why and how I have suddenly decided to proceed on leave.

Unfortunately, I was not in a position to tell them, since Government had not formally informed me of my proposed appointment. I also thought it prudent not to speak about it. On 4th February, after bidding farewell to some intimate friends, accompanied by my wife and two children, I quietly slipped out of Kolhapur by train.

When I had come there, I had only one son. My second son Vivek was born on 19th June, 1959 in Kolhapur. After a few days' stay at Bombay, we went to Delhi to spend the holidays with my in-laws. It was a happy family reunion.

At the beginning of April, I joined the Chief Minister's Secretariat as an understudy to Prabhakar with a designation of 'Officer on Special Duty'. As soon as that news was announced, a great many persons from Kolhapur visited me. They were angry that when I left Kolhapur, I didn't tell them that I was going on transfer to become the private secretary to Chavan. Some of them felt let down that I had not given them an opportunity to bid proper farewell. All this was part of great affection and love, which they had for me. Fortunately, I have continued to enjoy the same throughout my career and even after my retirement. Even today when I visit Kolhapur, a number of people visit me. I proudly declare that I am from Kolhapur.

Chapter 19

With Y. B. Chavan
- The Chief Minister

Foundations of my future relationship with Chavan were laid one day rather unconsciously. Soon after I joined I started interacting with Chavan freely. While discussing a case he said "Loyalty is a two way street and only those who are ready to give loyalty deserve to receive loyalty." He added, 'This is how we are going to work.' That was the foundation of our working relationship.

I believe that this concept of loyalty was ingrained in his thinking, because later as Defence Minister, while replying to the debate on NEFA reverses on 21st December 1963, he said : 'May I tell you that this quality of leadership is not a one-way traffic? It is a two-way traffic. As the leader expects loyalty from his followers, the followers also must have loyalty from their leaders. When they are under fire, the gun or the bullet does not make any distinction between a leader and his follower.'

By the time I joined Chavan as the Officer on Special Duty, most of the major decisions relating to the bifurcation of the bilingual Bombay State had been taken. The legislation to be introduced for the purpose was getting ready. However, within the Secretariat, one could sense an atmosphere of suspicion and distrust not only in the minds of the ministers from Gujarat, but also senior ICS officers who had been allotted to that State.

Amongst the Gujarat ministers, Jivraj Mehta, who was the Finance Minister of the Bilingual State, kept a close watch on each and every decision being taken, howsoever minor, in any department. Normally, any decision taken by the government has financial implications and no decision can be notified unless the Finance Department gives its approval. Jivraj Mehta had taken upon himself the task of being the 'watch dog'. He had one great asset in undertaking that task – being an insomniac, he hardly slept. Any file coming from him had not only been carefully scrutinized by him, but if the department concerned had failed to number the pages, he would do himself in his own bold hand-writing. He had plenty of time on hand.

At the officer's level, it was somewhat pathetic to see individuals who had worked till then as colleagues were bickering on small matters like allocations of typewriters, pencils, stationery etc. Officers going to Gujarat were naturally more aggressive because what they would not take with them would become property of Maharashtra State on May 1, 1960.

There was another type of contention among the officers: those belonging to Gujarat and Saurashtra region had hardly any option and were straightaway allotted to that state. Since the number of ICS and IAS officers from that region was much smaller than that State's requirement, some officers belonging to other states of India, who had worked all their life in Bombay state, had to be allotted to Gujarat. In the case of these officers, it was decided that those who had received their earlier training as supernumerary assistant collectors in Gujarat and had started their career there, such as H. K. L. Kapur, G. S. Baveja, Ashok Bambawale, A. S. Gill, all senior to me and S. Shivagnyanam from my batch, were thus allotted to Gujarat. On that score, I should have also gone to Gujarat. Moreover, I had started my career at Ahmedabad and spent first three and half of the service period in Gujarat region. However, in my case, as private secretary-designate to the chief minister of new State of Maharashtra, it was decided to make an exception. That meant that instead, one officer, who could have remained in Maharashtra, perhaps by right, was sent to Gujarat. The matter of allotment was dealt with in such a secrecy and speed that even I didn't come to know the name of that officer. I owe him an apology.

I did notice a certain degree of jealousy in my colleagues that I had 'escaped'. So far as I was concerned, I would have been equally happy if I had been allotted to Gujarat. In fact, in 1956, following the recommendation of the States Reorganisation Commission's Report, when Gujarat was to be formed as a separate State, I was provisionally allotted to that State. I had fallen in love with the Gujarat peasantry, where I found the village life was much more organized and disciplined that in Maharashtra. They were generally more prosperous. Also Mahatma Gandhi's principles and precepts had greatly influenced their minds and that was reflected in their daily life and community life.

I was, however happy that I would be working with Yashwantrao Chavan, whom I had come to like and respect. V. Prabhakar was to remain as the private secretary till the end of April 1960. He attended to most of the urgent and important matters. As the Officer on Special Duty (OSD), I used to see all the papers going and coming from the chief minister and also got acquainted with the senior officers with whom I would be dealing on my own, very soon.

S. G. Barve, ICS, Secretary of Public Works (PWD) and Irrigation Departments was functioning as an advisor to Chavan on matters concerning division of assets and liabilities between the two states. Chavan greatly depended on his expert knowledge of finance, economic affairs and his excellent contacts in Delhi.

Time passed too soon and in the second half of the month of April a train full of staff and the records was to leave by a special train for Ahmedabad. The officers, who remained in Maharashtra, went and said goodbye to their life-long colleagues leaving Ahmedabad by the special train. It was emotional parting.

A few days later on April 27, 1960 ministers of Gujarat were to leave Bombay on by Gujarat Mail for Ahmedabad. That day happened to be the 300th Birth Anniversary of Shivaji the Great. Chavan and his Marathi speaking Cabinet colleagues had decided to visit the Shivneri Fort, in Poona district where Jijabai had given birth to Shivaji, to celebrate the event. For Marathi speaking people, the new State of Maharashtra was a successor of the Maratha State found by Shivaji in the 17th Century. Chavan and his colleagues, like millions of Marathi speaking people, thought that the new State should seek blessings of Jijabai and Shivaji Maharaj. Among the ministers, Shantilal Shah, the Minister for Labour, who was the only Gujarati Minister from Bombay city was asked by Chavan to see off the Gujarat ministers. I was asked to see them off on his behalf.

At the station Shri Sri Prakasa, the Governor of the Bilingual State was present to see off the ministers. With his usual charm and graciousness, he talked to the ministers and made the parting as sweet as possible. I went round and conveyed the best wishes of Chavan. When I bade farewell to Jivaraj Mehta, I found him sullen. Generally, he was always pleasant and considerate.

ಐಲ

On the formation of the new State, a fresh breeze was blowing in the corridors of the Secretariat that was renamed as the Sachivalaya. That change was evident both in the functioning of the bureaucracy as well as in the working of the political leadership.

I quickly settled down to new work and routine. I had learnt that my position required me work in office and outside, with no limit on hours of work. Also when my colleagues were working on files, I was involved in policy matters as well. S. G. Barve was asked to formulate policy framework for the new state to be announced by Chavan on May 1, 1960. I was asked to assist him, probably because of my recent experience of ground level conditions in districts. For me, it was indeed a rich experience to participate in the late night meetings at Sahayadri and observe interaction between a brilliant civil servant with a highly sophisticated mind and a politician with an equally sharp analytical thinking process and down-to-earth practical approach. During those three-four weeks, I received education in political administration. Also in real politick.

At the time of the formation, K. L. Punjabi, ICS was the chief secretary. I knew him well from Ahmedabad days. He represented ethos of the old Bombay state. Polite, polished and suave, he commanded respect. A few months later N. T. Mone, ICS, from the Madhya Pradesh cadre succeeded him. He brought with him the style for which the officers from the erstwhile Central Province were well-known. He was always relaxed, humane in dealing with others and free from tension. That was opposite to style and behavior of many Bombay civilians, who believed in rule- bound administration and acted in detached manner. Morarji Desai who was a deputy collector before joining the freedom movement was prime example of that type of civil servant. Many were rude, somewhat dry, stern and always conscious of their position and power.

A prime example of that category was Dahejia, ICS, who on the bifurcation had gone as Secretary in the Ministry of Finance in New Delhi. A brilliant but hard-hitting officer he did not mince any word nor suffered fools. D. S. Bakhle, ICS was highly intellectual, but equally unpredictable. V. Shankar, ICS, my former Collector, considered himself intellectually superior and was positively rude to his colleagues, although, surprisingly, to B. G. Deshmukh and me, he was always kind and gracious, because we had been his assistant collectors in Banaskatha district.

M.G. Pimputkar, ICS was known for his blunt and ruthless ways of working. Most officers considered walking into his room like entering a tiger's den. There were others who were humane and pleasant to work with. Foremost amongst them was M. R. Yardi, ICS, the Finance Secretary who worked very closely with Chavan on the question of the division of assets and liabilities on the bifurcation of the State. He was polite and gentle, but very correct. One could not expect any latitude in either going round the rules or overlooking precedents.

There were others who brought great scholarship and dignity to their office. Among those were Bedekar and Dravid of the ICS. They were always correct and so straight-forward that even Chavan found them sometimes difficult. We had also a lone Englishman Mr. Bowman, ICS, who soon after the formation of Maharashtra, resigned and joined the Bombay Chamber of Commerce as its Secretary. Amongst the younger ICS were D. D. Sathe and R. C. Joshi.

In the process of bifurcation, we had also lost some brilliant officers. V. Iswaran, ICS, the Development Commissioner, had gone to Gujarat to become the chief secretary. As Development Commissioner he had worked ceaselessly over years for making the Community Development Project a great success. He was always helpful and never failed to reply to a letter from collectors and even junior community project officers. He was devoted to his task. He oriented a wooden and rule bound administration to be effective instrument for development. That's why Gujarat has outstripped other states in many areas in development.

With Y. B. Chavan

My former Commissioner, G. L. Sheth, ICS, had also gone to Ahmedabad. As a young officer, he had helped set up the Civil Supplies Department in the erstwhile Bombay State during the Second War and also to introduce the rationing in Bombay city. Likewise, B. P. Patel, ICS, whom I knew as the first Municipal Commissioner of Ahmedabad Corporation had also gone to Gujarat.

Among the IAS officers, we had lost H. K. L. Kapoor, who was later to become the chief secretary of Gujarat and in that capacity steer the State for over seven long years. Amongst my batchmates, while Shivagnyanam had gone to Gujarat, B. K. Halve, who had originally been allotted to Madhya Pradesh from the erstwhile Central Province, had come to Maharashtra. A number of officers, who had come from Marathwada- erstwhile Hyderabad state- in 1957, were slowly being inducted in the Secretariat in higher positions.

I also got to know what happens when a civil servant becomes a politician. At that time, the most widely known name in Sachivalaya was that of S. G. Barve, an exceptionally brilliant officer, whom Chavan used to describe as a wizard. He was also politically oriented and very soon his political ambitions were to take shape. He would resign from the ICS, contest the election in 1962 and become the Finance Minister of Maharashtra. I had known him when I was in the IAS Training School and he was a joint secretary in the ministry of Finance. Later when I joined the chief minister and found how greatly Chavan depended on him, I was slowly drawn into Barve's orbit. As a politician and later a cabinet minister Barve did not shape as well as expected of him. Lifelong habits and discipline of a civil servant could not be got rid of that easily. I learnt that a civil servant has a right to get involved in public service but should not aspire to become a politician.

My ideal of civil servant was A. L. Dias, ICS officer, who was close to Chavan. A quiet, refined gentleman, he was clear-headed and firm. Chavan first came to know of him as the District Magistrate of Satara during 1942 Movement, when Dias put him behind the bars. Chavan found him humane and sound in handling men and matters. He appointed A. L. Dias as his Home Secretary. Chavan's judgment of Dias was later borne out when Dias as the Governor of West Bengal successfully steered the state for over ten years during turbulent years in 60's.

On the political side, some very well-known figures had left for Gujarat, including the three stalwarts: Dr. Jivaraj Mehta, Rasiklal Parikh and Ratubhai Adani. Their places were taken up by moving up the political ladder the ministers from Vidarbha: Kannamwar, who was to succeed Chavan as the chief minister, Vasantrao Naik, who would succeed Kannamwar and rule as the chief minister for a record period of over eleven years and Sheshrao Wankhede, Bar-at-Law and a man with great sense of humour and sporting attitude to life. Later he would become the Chairman of the Cricket Association of India for several years. They had brought with them the charm and relaxed attitude to life of the old Central Provinces.

From Maharashtra, Chavan's strong arm was D. S. (Bala Saheb) Desai from Satara, whom I had come to know very well during my tenure in Kolhapur. Endowed with an imposing personality, he commanded respect and ensured that he received it. He was somewhat high-handed in dealing with officers in public. However, in private, he was always reasonable and kind.

P. K. Sawant from Kokan was another supporter of Chavan. Unfortunately, there were not many ministers from western Maharashtra, because in the 1957 elections, on the issue of Samyukta Maharashtra, the Congress had practically been wiped out in many districts. Ministers from Marathwada obviously did not have much experience of administration and many of them had come in the Cabinet for the first time in November 1957, when Marathwada, on separation from Hyderabad, had been merged with the Bilingual Bombay State.

The brightest and most hard-working amongst those ministers was Shankarrao B. Chavan, who had joined as Deputy Minister and become a Minister of State on the formation of Maharashtra. Later he would become chief minister of Maharashtra on two different occasions and also the Union minister of the Defence, the External Affairs and the Finance Minister. He was also the Deputy Chairman of the Planning Commision for some years. In last phase of my career, I worked with him when he was the Union Home Minister. He was a man of character. Meticulous, relaxed and polite, he studied files with care and gave orders in writing. He was highly ethical and follower of Satya Sai baba of Putuparthi.

When I first entered the Secretariat in 1953, it was a compact well oiled machine that worked by the clock,

9 am to 5 pm. After that officers were free to go to clubs and socialise. Because of the prohibition in the State, all parties were sober and hardly any officer was found awake after 11 pm. Morarji Desai had decreed that all shops and establishments must close at that hour as only criminals and trouble makers --- described as goondas-- remained awake past mid-night.

On formation of Maharashtra, the environment within and outside the Sachivalaya changed rapidly. With officers from the Vidarbha and the Marathwada region, with distinct administrative culture and way of living, we experienced a more tension-free life. Chavan himself was a relaxed and efficient administrator, who believed in not quarrelling with his tools. He had developed a style of extracting the best from officers and give them a feeling of partnership in tackling issues. That made officers more responsive and also responsible as they knew that they were part of a team. I became a member of that team and followed throughout my career what had learnt from him and others.

One distinct feature of those times was absence of corruption. Money was not a motivation to seek career in civil service. After war, rupee had depreciated. Yet there was hardly any one in Secretariat with any taint of corruption. Education, high moral values and straight thinking was a legacy of the British administrators. Unconsciously, officers then working inherited those values.

Another feature was a clear distinction between private and government. Even the chief secretary would drive in his private car to office and park it in garage below the

Sachivalya. Most walked or came by BEST bus. Luncheon boxes were brought from home by officers or some by peons from officers home. All hospitality in office was paid out of one's pocket. Office notes were generally hand written and options for ministers decision were clearly set out. Over years, all this was to change in stages and the character of administration would change.

All change was not bad, as progressively a rule bound and impersonal administration got closer to the people. What happened at district level when I was in districts percolated upwards to the Sachivalaya. All that was inevitable and not bad. Three decades later, I had a role to play in transforming district administration and widen the scope of the welfare state. If today people all over remember me, that was because of change in me and what I did to serve Maharashtra.

Chapter 20

Lessons in India's Democracy
- Getting to Know the PM

Third General elections were announced for the beginning of 1962. That was my first education in electoral politics and electioneering. Also how leaders of industry were involved in financing elections. R. D. Birla was their leader in Bombay.

Since the birth of Maharashtra, Chavan had given increasing attention to the Congress party that had received serious setback during the past five years. On his deft handling the issue of the creation of new state for the Marathi speaking people with Bombay as the capital, Chavan had emerged as a young and dynamic undisputed leader of Maharashtra. On the national scene, he was a man to watch. Because of his close involvement in the freedom struggle and high intellect, he endeared himself to many politicians in other parties as well. On his appeal, a number of political workers from other parties joined the Congress. Chavan appointed Mohan Dharia, who was earlier in the Socialist Party, as the General Secretary of the Maharashtra Pradesh Congress Committee (MPCC) and Yashwantrao Mohite, another and upcoming political worker belonging the Peasants and Workers Party was inducted as a deputy minister. Both of them distinguished themselves in their later career. A number of young educated Muslims were attracted to Y. B. Chavan and worked under his leadership. These included Rafique Zakaria and A. R. Antulay both Bar-at-Law.

Chavan was accepted as the supreme leader of the MPCC. He had also carved for himself a base in the Bombay city and very soon he was sharing power with S. K. Patil, who was till then the undisputed leader of the city. For activating the organization and workers to be educated in party's philosophy and historical role, a number of conventions and meetings were organized. In the summer of 1961, a state level convention was held at Mahabaleshwar, a hill resort in western Maharashtra. These meetings were an opportunity to younger political workers to participate and prove their organizational abilities and communicative skills. Mohan Dharia was increasingly involved in election related work. In that connection, he was a frequent visitor to my office. That gave me an opportunity to learn a great deal about the State politics and mechanics of electioneering.

I did not know then that after retirement I shall be involved deeply in planning and organizing several elections at the national level for the Congress party. My education for that started in 1961. I recollect very vividly three aspects concerning those elections.

I was not involved directly in the party work. However, as Chavan's Private Secretary I could not help dealing with some aspects of his political work, as it was not always possible to make a fine demarcation. Nor was I expected to do so, if I was to work with him.

Late in 1961, when possible candidates for the Lok Sabha were being considered, name of M. C. Chagla, former chief justice of Bombay High Court was suggested. He had then just returned from the United States, where he had been India's Ambassador. But as luck would have it, the Prime Minister felt that Chagala should go as India's High Commissioner to the United Kingdom. One afternoon, Chavan was contacted by the Prime Minister over telephone to persuade Chagala to accept the High Commissionership. With some effort, I learnt that Justice Chagla, who was fond of playing Bridge, could be in the Card Room of the Willingdon Club. I went there and requested him to kindly come over and see the chief minister as soon as possible. Chavan conveyed to him the Prime Minister's message.

Chagala was not pleased. He was hoping to settle down in Bombay after his three years absence in Washington and was expecting help from Chavan to secure some accommodation. He was visibly upset at the suggestion but with great sense of dignity told Chavan to inform the Prime Minister that he will do whatever the Prime Minister wanted of him. Thus the way was paved for Krishna Menon. Despite some grumbling within the BPCC, Krishna Menon was nominated. The Prime Minister himself came to canvass in the city for him and addressed in one afternoon as many as six meetings. Krishna Menon was duly elected.

Accommodation in one of the old luxurious villa was found for M. C. Chagla so that on return from London he would not have to look for one. As destiny worked out, he was to spend several years in Delhi in high positions at ministerial level.

The Prime Minister very much appreciated all the help and efforts that Chavan made to ensure Krishna Menon's re-election. For him, that election was very important, as evident from his letter written a few days prior to polling. PM wrote that 'the Bombay election is not merely a personal mater, but it is a combined effort of all reactionary elements and those opposed to our policies to make every effort to defeat our candidate Krishna Menon.' Considering the national and international important of the election, the Prime Minister had urged Chavan to do everything 'to counter the activities of these reactionary elements which are opposing us'.

Chavan who was personally close to Krishna Menon and shared his left- leanings felt gratified that PM had appreciated his work. That also helped him to assert his own position vis-à-vis the Bombay Congress Committee and thus slowly assert the position of the MPCC over the BPCC.

Krishna Menon became a friend of Y. B. Chavan. As defence minister, whenever he visited the city, he did not fail to drop-in to see Chavan. Like a fresh breez, Menon was always on move and set aside all protocol that normally marks a defence minister's office. Always dressed in white starched dhoti, worn in south Indian way and immaculate long shirt, he was always fresh looking. Later when I went to Delhi, I learnt from his personal staff that he would bathe five times and changed his clothes.

Chavan liked Krishna Menon and respected him for his intellect. We were to find his real stature in politics later. Because of Menon's visits, I came to know several Naval officers in Bombay. Two were from Maharashtra. One was Rear Admiral Karmarkar, a real old salt. Other, Vice-Admiral D. S. Soman, who would become the Naval chief one day. Both gave me insight into working of Navy and its role. Both remained my life long well wishers.

ಙಲ

Personally for me, during elections, the most exciting experience was accompanying the Prime Minister for four days on his tour of Maharashtra, including visit to Poona, Kolhapur and Nagpur. I traveled with Chavan in the Prime Minister's IAF plane and looked after all his requirements at the various places. It was an added pleasure to make arrangements for PM's visit to Kolhapur where I had been a Collector two years earlier.

I had observed that even in company, he preferred to eat without talking to anyone. I had, therefore, arranged a table for him on one side of the dining room where he sat alone and ate slowly. After his meal, he thanked me for letting him eat in peace. While in Kolhapur, Chavan had talked to him about great many activities that I had carried out. That evening, after dinner, before attending to official papers, he called me and asked me to tell him everything about the Agricultural Market Yard. He was fascinated with the story. Next morning, he asked Chavan to tell me how much he had enjoyed hearing about the successful struggle on behalf of the agriculturists. For me, that was the greatest reward.

After that, our relationship became more personal. I knew what he liked and whom he disliked. I made sure that he was put in good mood in his hectic electioneering schedule. A small matter but worth recalling. Immediately after lunch, as a habit he would go to his suite and come out almost to the minute at the appointed time. It was exhilarating to see him fully refreshed with vigour of a youth. I made sure that at the entrance fresh pink or red rose was offered to him on a saucer, which he would promptly put on his jacket. There was always a smile and a 'thank you' for me.

Later in my career I would have close working relations with him. That was when he was in the twilight years of his life.

What has remained in my memory is his fresh and smiling face, with a red rose.

෩෬

In that election, Congress swept the polls and Chavan emerged as powerful and the undisputed leader of Maharashtra. By that time, I was working with him for over two years and we had come close to each other. True to his word, Chavan did not hide anything from me ; on my part, I worked with him with single-minded devotion. I had practically no personal life as such. My obvious nearness to Chavan also made many politicians to use me as a conduit to convey him something, which they did not wish to do themselves. Some would also come to ask favours or to 'fish' for information. I had made a practice of meeting everyone and I had no difficulty, thanks to my experience in Kolhapur, to sift the grain from chaff.

Immediately after the general elections, I was flooded by some good friends and many other visitors with a request to bring their names to Chavan's notice, 'at the appropriate moment', when Chavan would draw the list of members of his Cabinet. It spoke well for their confidence in my ability when a couple of them did get berth in the cabinet. In those days, the procedure was rather simple. As I witnessed it, immediately after the results were known, Chavan and I left for Delhi by Indian Airlines. On the plane, he took out a piece of paper and put down some names. He asked me to have a look. I interacted, a couple of names were scored off and a couple added, and the list was ready. On reaching Delhi, Chavan drove to PM's residence. Showed him the list. PM glanced at it and said, 'That seems O K. Do what you think best.' That was the end.

On the return journey, Chavan worked out the tentative allocation of portfolios. This was little complicated and for that purpose, I had carried a copy of Rules of Business of the State Government, including the list of various departments. By the time, we reached Bombay he had tentatively made up his mind. Consultations began almost immediately after reaching Shayadri.

Thus I got to know the process of forming a Cabinet. The most sensitive task was informing those who were no longer to be continued as ministers. It was always a sad moment and I soon found that for a politician used to power, it was almost like being sent to exile, if not sentenced to death. I also experienced touching moments when individuals were informed that they were being inducted in the ministry. I would never forget one incident. That night after return from Delhi, well past midnight, Chavan asked me to get in touch with a young man who had worked hard in his field (not necessary to mention name). With great difficulty Dongre, Chavan's personal assistant, could get in touch with him and it was almost 2 a.m. when he came over to Shayadri. I was sitting on a chair next to the sofa on which Chavan was sitting. As soon as the gentleman entered, Chavan said, 'Welcome, minister for…………..'. The young man looked as if he had received a severe electrical jolt. He stood there motionless and speechless, soon his eyes started rolling and he fainted. Just in time, I could manage to catch him from falling down. I sprinkled some water on his face and soon he came round.

Chavan asked him to sit by his side. He gave him a strong cup of coffee and then told him quietly that he wanted him to join his cabinet as minister for………. With tears of joy rolling down his face, he said, 'Yes' – by merely nodding his head up and down. He was a genuine party worker who had worked selflessly without ever aspiring to be a minister.

I then learnt that post-election period could also be a traumatic one for politicians and that being dropped from office was often deemed as a 'death sentence'!

PART III :

In Defence Ministry

Chapter 21

India-China War
- My Transition to Delhi

Most unexpectedly, in November 1962, along with Y. B. Chavan, I left Bombay for Delhi to begin a new phase of my life. That came about because of a national crisis that would soon turn into a national catastrophe. Along with my minister's fate, my destiny was leading me into an arena at national level.

That tensions building between India and the Peoples Republic of China was reported in the Press early in 1959. On the north-eastern frontier, India assumed that the McMahon Line was the settled boundary with Tibet. By the middle of 1959, in the north-west as well as north-east, the border had become 'live' and it was clear that China would not hesitate to use force. There were reports about the Chinese build-up behind the Thagla Ridge that was boundary of the Northeast Frontier Agency (NEFA). The Chinese had started infiltrating down the southern slope of Thagla. Matters came to a head on 20 October. Early that morning, the Chinese struck along the Namka chu at the Dhola Bridge and overcame resistance by the Rajputs. Likewise, at Tsangdhar nearer the tri-junction of

Bhutan, China and India, they mounted a fierce attack on the Gurkhas. They also attacked at Tsangley on the western flank and the Indians had to withdraw via Bhutan. On the eastern side, the Chinese attacked the Khinzemane post and overran it.

By this time, the criticism of Krishna Menon, the defence minister had reached a crescendo. The Opposition as well as several members of the Congress Party were strongly criticizing his handling of the Defence portfolio. There were also rumblings within the army and Krishna Menon submitted his resignation. On 1st November 1962, the Prime Minister took over the Defence Ministry. The stage was set for Y. B. Chavan's entry on the national scene.

Just at that time, I was in Delhi as my father-in-law had expired on October 30. As his only son was in the US for completing his MBA at the New York University, I, as the only son-in-law, had to perform all rites. On November 5, the Prime minister had convened the National Development Council to discuss the crisis. I attended the meeting with Chavan.

By that time, the nation had learnt of the humiliation of the Indian army. There was an all-pervading atmosphere of gloom. That evening, Chavan attended a meeting in the Prime Minister's office in the South Block along with four other chief ministers - K. Kamraj of Madras, Pratap Singh Kairon of the Punjab, Sanjiva Reddy of Andhra Pradesh and Biju Patnaik of Orissa. As usual, I accompanied him and sat in his private secretary Khanna's room that was adjoining the PM office. The meeting lasted almost one and a half hours, at which the chief ministers had done some plain talking. As was his practice, the Prime minister came into Khanna's room to see them off. I stood up and greeted him. In return, he gave a wane smile. He was in deep thought. As we left Nehru's office, Chavan said to me, "Frankly, I am worried about the Prime Minister. He is facing a tough situation".

The next day, during a break in the NDC meeting, the Prime Minister took Chavan aside to discuss the previous evening's meeting. He was upset that Pratap Singh Kairon had dared to talk so bluntly. He said, "You see, they want Menon's blood. If I agree, tomorrow they will ask for my blood."

Nehru's apprehensions were proved right. The very next day, at a marathon meeting of the Executive Committee of the Party, senior Congress parliamentarians indicated that no one was bigger than the country and Menon had to go.

On the afternoon of 6th November, Nehru called Chavan in Bombay over the telephone to ask if he was ready to come to Delhi and work with him at that critical juncture. No portfolio was mentioned. The Prime Minister only asked him whether his reply was 'yes or no'. He also cautioned Chavan that the suggestion was tentative. Chavan talked to me over phone and told me possibility of his visiting Delhi and asked me to come over to Bombay.

Saturday, 10th November was an eventful day. Late in the afternoon, we left for Delhi by the evening flight. As we drove into Teen Murti House, Chavan was in a somber mood. It was pitch dark and an eerie winter silence had enveloped the Prime Minister's residence.

Vimla Sindhi at the Reception deskmet and escorted us across the large reception hall. Lal Bahadur Shastri and Indira Gandhi were waiting for Chavan to take him up to the PM's study. I sat on a sofa at the foot of the staircase. With all the tensions of bereavement and rushing around I was tired and fell asleep on the long sofa oblivious that I was in the drawing hall of the PM's residence till I was woken by Chavan. By his side were Lal Bahadur Shastri and the Prime Minister. They were looking at me with an amused smile. I got up with a jerk and apologized.

At that moment, I did not realize that I was also awakening to a new reality and exciting period of my life.

ಜಾಡ

After his appointment was formally announced by the President of India, Chavan visited Poona to bid farewell. He spoke with eloquence and emotion and the press hailed the event as 'Sahyadri (the mountain) going to the defence of the Himalayas'.

The city of Bombay gave him a memorable farewell. Yashwantrao Chavan, the young and successful Chief Minister of Maharashtra, left for Delhi in a blaze of glory. There was joy, pride and confidence - as if Yashwantrao Chavan's taking over the defence ministry would extricate the country from the despair and defeat that our armed forces had suffered on the northern front.

I was in his convoy to the airport. On reaching there amidst jostling crowd, I saw my father along with my brothers and sisters. I was taken by surprise and steered Y. B. Chavan towards them. My father had no words to say, but Chavan understood his feelings and said, "I am taking Ram to Delhi with me to help me." My father blessed him and we boarded the flight and I sat by his side. As the plane approached Delhi, I saw Chavan becoming more pensive. We hardly exchanged a word during the flight. I awoke from my reverie as the lights of Delhi became visible. The plane had started its descent. I gently nudged Chavan to alert him.

During the flight, I noticed that a number of well known industrialists and journalists were seated around us. Amongst them was my mentor, V. Shankar, ICS. He came over and wished me success in my career. He had served India's one of the tallest leaders Vallabhbhai Patel, the Deputy Prime minister of India in the Interim government. V. Shankar was a witness of history and knew that at that moment I was poised to be participate in post independent India's history. I appreciated his blessings.

Next morning, swearing-in ceremony was simple and dignified. There was the usual photo session with the President and the Prime Minister. A few minutes before 10 a.m., the PM escorted Chavan to the defence ministry in the South Block of the Central Government Secretariat. The Defence Secretary and three Service Chiefs were already in the Defence Minister's chamber: General J. N. Chaudhuri, the Acting Chief of Army Staff, Vice-Admiral B. S. Soman, the Chief of Naval Staff and Air Marshal A. M. Engineer, the Chief of Air Staff. The Prime Minister formally introduced the officials and the Service Chiefs to the new Defence Minister.

That very afternoon, Chavan started to function almost as someone who was meant to occupy the saddle of the defence ministership. He was aware that while the 'unilateral ceasefire' by the Chinese would somewhat ease the situation on the front, his first task was to put his house in order. My task was to help him. The Defence minister's first task was to assert full control over the army and to restore proper relationship between the army and the political leadership. In order to assist him, I defined my role to ensure that the bureaucracy within the ministry and leadership of the defence forces got to know their new minister. For that, I established good working relationship with the defence secretary P. V. R. Rao and other senior officers including Harish Sarin, John Lall and M. M. Sen all of the ICS. I also built bridges with S. S. Khera, the cabinet secretary and M. J. Desai, the Foreign secretary. Over a period, I had much to do with them and they were also aware of my close relations with Chavan, who had emerged on political scene as a sound administratrator. In parallel, I built relations with Gen. J. N. Chaudhuri, the Army Chief, Air Marshal A. M. Engineer, the Air Chief and Admiral B. S. Soman, the Naval Chief. Over a period and even much later when I had moved on to other fields, they remained friendly and my well wishers. I was aware that unless I had my own network, I could not be effective. For that, I established good relations with Susheetal Banerjee and Subhas Mukherjee, both deputy secretaries in the cabinet secretariat. In the Foreign A. P. Venkateshwaran, my batchmate who was in charge of the China Desk. In my ministry, S. Krishnaswamy and S. Sounder Rajan, two brilliant officers were closely identified with Krihna Menon. They helped to get the Indian army, indigenous automatic rifle.

ଔଷଔଷ

Chapter 22

Some Memorable Visits
- Unforgetable Brush with Indira Gandhi

For me, the visit to Tawang in the northwest corner of the NEFA in November 1963 would remain etched in memory. It was almost a year since it was occupied by the Chinese. The defence minister was enthusiastically welcomed by the Monpa population, who were Buddhist and of Tibetan stock. At the Tawang monastery, he was received by Rimpoche, the head lama, and the monks of the monastery with the traditional exchange of scarves, the clanging of musical metal gongs and blowing of long Tibetan trumpets. It was all very colourful. As this was the first visit of the defence minister - for that matter of any minister - after the Chinese withdrawal, the people of Tawang presented a welcome address. While there was eagerness on their faces and a show of great enthusiasm, one did not fail to sense how shaken they were by the events of the previous year. They had seen the Chinese overrun the whole territory and the Indian army fleeing from the area. One could also sense the skepticism, specially among the young, whether they would again be left at the mercy of the Chinese in future.

Chavan addressed them with a great deal of emotion and admired the way in which they had faced the aggression. However, he came away with a feeling that mere talk would not help to restore their confidence. Much hard and patient work had to be done to regain their trust. While departing, the Rimpoche presented me two paintings of Buddha done by him. They are in my treasured collection.

During this visit, I met some Officers who were by then well known for their role in the development of India's north-east frontier: Col. P. N. Luthra (Retd.), the Commissioner, Maj. R. Khathing (Retd.), the Security Commissioner and Maj. K. C. Johori (Retd.), who was the Political Officer of Kameng Frontier Division. It was a pleasure to see that within a short time, these dedicated officers and their colleagues had largely succeeded in soothing the feelings of the people on the border and in restoring their faith.

I really enjoyed that visit. It was exciting to fly in an Alouette helicopter at a height of sixteen thousand feet over the Se La top and spend a night at Bomdi La in the freezing cold. However, it was depressing to fly over the Dirang-Dzong and Tenga Valley and see remnants of the Indian army's vehicles, personnel carriers and heavy equipment lying scattered all over the narrow valley.

I did not know then that twenty-five years later, I would be visiting these areas again, as the first governor of Arunachal Pradesh. It was wonderful to see that officers whom I had casually met in 1963 had become legendary names and were still being talked about two decades later. I would also renew my acquaintance with some of them.

Some Memorable Visits

This second visit to NEFA was pleasantly memorable. But the first one had a bitter memory for me.

Prime minister decided to visit Assam on December 5, 1962 for the first time after the debacle. Along with Chavan, I accompanied him. Susheetal Banerjee also came. Late in the afternoon, the Prime Minister and his party went to the headquarters of IV Corps, located in Tezpur for briefing. It was winter and it was getting dark. Susheetal Banerjee, Deputy Secretary in the Cabinet Secretariat and I, followed the Prime Minister and Chavan. Mrs. Indira Gandhi was a few steps behind. Lt. Gen. Sam Manekshaw was at the entrance of the map room to greet the VIP's. Seeing Mrs. Gandhi behind us, Susheetal and I gave her way at the entrance. Manekshaw stopped her and said, "Madam, I am sorry you cannot enter the map room since you have not taken the oath of secrecy."

Chavan immediately understood the situation. The Defence Minister did not want to let down his Corps Commander. So, instead of talking directly to Mrs. Gandhi, he looked at me and said. "Ram, you better keep company with Indira ji."

Susheetal looked at her and told Chavan, "I also better keep company with them."

Mrs. Gandhi was quickly escorted to a lounge in the adjoining building. Susheetal and I were disappointed that we were denied the opportunity of a first hand 'super-secret briefing' in the map room on the Chinese incursions on the northern borders. We could also sense the seething anger building up within Indira Gandhi. She sat there with folded arms across her chest staring out of the window. Susheetal and I sat on either side of her sofa looking at each other, not knowing whether we should say anything at all. After a few minutes, Susheetal picked up an old issue of Time magazine from a rack and handed it over to her. Without even glancing at it, she promptly placed it on the table in front of her. Susheetal looked at me. We could feel her hurt and anger. We decided to keep quiet.

After a few minutes, to break the ice, I asked Mrs. Gandhi whether she would like to have a cup of coffee or tea? Without speaking, she shook her head and signalled 'No'. Then Susheetal and I asked for some tea for ourselves, got hold of some magazines and spent the next one and a half hours, waiting for the briefing in the map room to be over. Mrs. Gandhi did not utter a word during all that time. She felt greatly humiliated at being turned away at the entrance to the map room. She was right. Perhaps she would not have minded if the Corps Commander had told her discreetly earlier that she should not come for the briefing.

I think that Mrs. Gandhi never forgot that long lonely and humiliating evening in the Mess. In retrospect, I felt that as a young officer, I should have made efforts to humour her and break the silence. But we were apprehensive that she might snub any such effort.

Several years later, when I was the Governor of Arunachal Pradesh, I got confirmation that Mrs. Gandhi had not forgotten that evening and that I was a witness to her 'humiliation'. I had invited Sharad Pawar, the chief minister of Maharashtra to dinner. Over drinks, he suddenly asked me whether there was anything that had created misunderstanding between Mrs G and me. In his style, in an oblique manner, he wanted me to recount what had happened. Instead I asked him, "What have you learnt". He said that Mrs G had told Sadique Ali, the governor of Maharashtra, about my 'behavior' that evening.

I was right that she had not forgotten, although the incident was much before she became the prime minister. I had noted many years later when I became the chief secretary, whenever she came to Bombay, she avoided talking to me directly. Perhaps she had not forgotten that humiliation, that I had witnessed. To me, that explained many small matters in my meetings with her later in my career.

༄༅

Another memorable visit was to Gangtok in April 1963. That was memorable for altogether different reasons.

An officer of the Indian Foreign Service, Bahadur Singh was India's Political Officer in Gangtok and we stayed with him at the Residency. On the night of our arrival, the Maharajah had invited the Defence Minister and his party for dinner. We were received by the Maharajkumar who had recently married Hope Cooke, an American national. She and the Maharajah's daughters were seated at one end of the large darbar hall. Naturally, everyone crowded around, at the other end where the Maharajah was seated. Noticing that the ladies were alone, and being the youngest member of Chavan's entourage, I gallantly decided to keep them company.

I started the conversation by casually asking the Princess if she had been to Sikkim before her marriage, if she liked Gangtok, etc. Princess Hope answered the first few questions in a nasal twang loud enough to be heard at the other end of the hall where the old Maharajah was conversing with Chavan. There was an exchange of hard looks from the Maharajkumar, who was seated by Chavan's side. I suddenly found that something was wrong with my hearing. While Princess Hope's lips were moving, I hardly heard her voice. I soon caught on and started moving my lips soundlessly. Princess Hope obviously had a shrill voice and had been advised to speak softly.

She was trying to speak so softly that I could hardly hear her. I did not want to break her resolve. I therefore decided to talk so softly that she would not hear what I said.

At the end of the evening, when I was taking her leave, she graciously smiled and told me that she had very much enjoyed talking with me. She knew, and I knew, that there had been no talk!

We also visited Nathu La, situated at a height of 14,500 ft. above sea level. In those days, it was the only route to Bhutan in the east and to Tibet in the north. The Indian garrison at Nathu La received us with great warmth and briefed us on the Chinese deployment. It was a clear day and we could see the Chinese with our binoculars.

We stood beside the commemorative tablet set on a concrete pillar which read:

Some Memorable Visits

Shri Jawaharlal Nehru Prime Minister of India

Accompanied by Maharaj Kumar Lt. Col. P. T. Namgyal

Arrived Nathula by motor vehicle on
18th September, 1958.

We got ourselves photographed for posterity.

Chapter 23

Henderson- Brook Report

The NEFA debacle is actually a sad account of what happened in the Kameng Frontier Division of the NEFA during five days, between 16-20 November, 1962. The prime minister had made a commitment to Parliament that the debacle in NEFA required investigation. The question was, who should undertake the investigation, and of what?

The debacle in NEFA raised countrywide protests. The press and the public demanded an explanation. Parliament was angry and vociferous. Senior Opposition leaders Acharya Kripalani, Hem Barua and Atal Behari Vajpayee mounted relentless pressure. The prime minister had to face an angry Lok Sabha; even the Congress Party MPs led by Mahavir Tyagi and Raghunath Singh demanded an explanation for this humiliating situation. There was no choice but to order an enquiry.

Soon after assuming office, Chavan realized the sensitive nature of such an enquiry. He decided that the enquiry would be ordered by the COAS on the basis of a directive from the Defence Minister himself. Accordingly, it was the COAS who ordered Lt. Gen. Henderson Brooks and Brig. P. S. Bhagat, VC to undertake the investigation.

Chavan shared with the Prime Minister and other senior colleagues his apprehension that such an enquiry might get out of hand and result in the army blaming the political leadership for its state of unpreparedness and also point to political considerations on which the army was alleged to have been deployed without adequate notice.

The report of the enquiry panel was submitted to the COAS in May 1963. The Chief of Army Staff presented the original along with a summary and his own report to the defence minister on 2nd July 1963.

The Cabinet Secretary, S. S. Khera, who was also the Principal Defence Secretary, was entrusted with the task of studying the report and preparing the draft of the statement to be presented to, Parliament. The next day Chavan told me it was not the way he would like to present the report. "It has no political touch." He then asked me to attempt a draft.

I said, "How can I prepare a draft unless I go through the main report?" He appreciated that and said, "All right, if we do not count the President, you will be the fifth person to see the report. That will still be within the number I had stipulated."

Almost apologetically he added, "I have not shown the report to you earlier for security reasons. Had there been a leak, I did not want it to be attributed to my office." It was really not necessary for him to say so, since for my own selfish reasons, I had not wanted to know its contents. In sensitive state matters ignorance is often a blessing.

It was already the middle of August and Parliament was expecting the report to be tabled during that very session. I was under pressure of time. I could not take the report out of the ministry. Moreover, my days were filled with meetings and with visitors walking in and out of my office. I spent three nights in the office. The night duty staff and the security personnel were naturally wondering what I was doing in the ministry until the early hours of the morning. I prepared a draft in my own hand and discussed it with Chavan. After several revisions and redrafts we finalized it. One night with the help of my trusted personal assistant, who had high security clearance, a typewritten text was prepared.

The next question was how to handle the draft. Chavan was determined not to place it before the Emergency Committee of the Cabinet (ECC). He thought that if the draft was shared, then someone might ask for the report as well and the chances of a leak would be greater. His main concern was maintaining secrecy.

He went over to the PM with the original draft of the statement and delivered it to him. No copy was kept. On his return, as in the case of the President, he instructed me to take the main report and hand it over to the Prime Minister. A few minutes before the Prime Minister was due to leave for lunch, his private secretary, Khanna rang me up to come and get the report. I went over to his office with several volumes wrapped in a cloth bundle. I was promptly ushered into the Prime Minister's office. He looked at the bundle in my hand and signaled me to place the volumes in a steel box kept on one side of the table. After I had done that, he carefully took out a key from the pocket of his achkan, locked the box in my presence, looked at me and asked, "Have you read the report?"

I answered, "Yes, Sir." He smiled and said he would let me know when to come back for it.

A couple of days later, I received a message asking me to collect the papers. While handing me the volumes, Nehru didn't utter a word but gave me a knowing smile that indicated that now, both shared the super secret.

Very soon, the draft of the statement also came back in a sealed cover bearing green seals, as required for the handling of top secret classified documents. I opened it in Chavan's presence. There was a small note attached on the top. The PM had written, "No comments. I do not think I should improve on it."

I went over the draft with Chavan and found that Nehru had not changed even a single comma. That was most unusual because normally no draft came back from the Prime Minister without modifications. Sometimes, he even dictated a fresh draft himself and sent it to the officer concerned to be issued under the officer's signature.

I asked Chavan whether he was sure that the PM had not made any improvements because he wanted to keep himself aloof. Perhaps he had not liked the way Chavan had decided to handle the report. I therefore pressed Chavan to take the draft to the PM to make sure that he really did not have any suggestions for improving the draft. I requested Chavan to draw Nehru's attention to the last paragraph in particular. I had indulged in some rhetoric while drafting it.

Within half an hour, Chavan was back. He told me that the Prime Minister was completely satisfied with the draft. However, when Chavan had brought the last paragraph to his notice, he had reflected for a moment, then taken out a slip of paper and written an alternative draft in his own hand.

My original draft read:

...it may sound rhetoric, but I must add that Britain had its Dunkirk, the United States its Pearl Harbour and we had our Se La and Bomdi La. These were results of deceit and treachery which brought initial success to a totalitarian regime bent upon a policy of naked aggression at the expense of peace loving neighbours. We are now on the alert...

Nehru had neatly deleted this portion by placing a bracket around it and written in his own hand:

'What happened at Se La and Bomdi La were severe reverses for us, but we must remember that other countries with powerful defence forces have sometimes suffered in the initial

stages of a war. The aggressor has a certain advantage, more especially when the aggression is sudden and well-prepared. We are now on the alert...' He had also not failed to notice and correct a superfluous capital letter. With his penchant for under-statement and flair for penmanship, the Prime Minister had improved my draft a hundred-fold.

That draft is my most precious memento of my service career.

Chapter 24

Laying Witch-Hunt to Rest

Chavan laid his statement regarding the NEFA enquiry on the table of the Lok Sabha on 2nd September 1963.

On September 19, the Lok Sabha chamber was full to capacity. The public and press galleries were packed with expectant faces watching the treasury benches. For me, the most memorable speeches were those of Nath Pai (Maharashtra) for the Opposition and K. C. Pant (U.P.) for the Congress.

In his reply in both the Houses, Chavan explained why he had ruled out a witch-hunt from the outset. Chavan elaborated his own thinking and perception on various issues facing the defence services. He laid particular emphasis on the quality of leadership and the need to build up a new relationship between the officers and jawans. It was widely noted that neither the prime minister nor Krishna Menon had intervened in the debate. Later it was learnt that Krishna Menon had tried to get some time from Satya Narayan Sinha, Minister for Parliamentary Affairs. Sinha had firmly refused Menon's request.

After the debate, the very next day, Chavan asked me to draft a directive stating that no suggestion for action against any of the officers involved in the NEFA operations for acts of commission or omission should be made. He had made it clear to parliament that the officers were asked to give evidence on the understanding that no action would be taken against them since the enquiry was in the nature of a military appraisal.

That was how the witch-hunt for the NEFA debacle was finally buried. But for me, that was not the end. The Report remains to date as the top secret document.

A question that is often asked is when in the Central government nothing remains secret how is it that the Henderson Brook Report has not been leaked out? Let me throw some light on that.

At the end of 1964, I started thinking of my own future. I had joined Chavan in the beginning of 1960 with a clear understanding that I shall work with him for three years. Before relinquishing charge, he asked me to ensure that all papers connected with the Henderson Brook Inquiry to the NEFA Reverses were catalogued and stored properly. He did not want my successor to have a look at that report.

Till that day, the original of the report in seven volumes along with the appendices were lodged safely in a steel cupboard in my room. After the debate in Parliament on the NEFA reverses in September 1963, there was no occasion to refer to the report. In January 1965, the day before I handed over charge, I reminded Chavan that one set of the report was still lying in my office in a steel cupboard and the only other set was with Gen. J.

N. Chaudhuri. Chavan asked me to get that set from the COAS. In my presence, he told General Chaudhuri over the telephone to hand over his set to me. I took those volumes to my office, carefully checked and placed them in the cupboard. When I left Chavan in January 1965, I handed over both the sets to my successor. I had put my personal seal on the packages. Chavan did not want my successor to see the report.

Late in 1966, there was talk that Chavan might not continue in the Defence Ministry for long. I was then working in the Commerce ministry. One day, he called me and asked me to hand over the two sets to D. S. Joshi, ICS, the cabinet Secretary. Accordingly, I carried the papers to the cabinet secretariat located in the South wing of the Rashtrapati Bhavan. I opened the seals and showed Joshi each document listed. Joshi got the volumes again wrapped in cloth bundles and put his own seal. The two sets of reports were placed, in my presence, inside a safe in the Cabinet Secretariat. I believe the report remained there undisturbed for over two decades.

Last time I saw that report was when as the Governor of Arunachal, I raised certain matters with in 1987 that required checking the situation on the border at the time of the unilateral declaration of ceasefire in 1962. Arun Singh, the Minister of State for Defence opened in my presence some volumes. Otherwise, it has remained where it was lodged and have remained super secret.

Chapter 25

Three Foreign Visits
- The USA; The USSR; The UK

The US Visit

In the middle of April 1964, it was decided that Chavan would visit the United States to hold discussions with Robert McNamara to secure US assistance in the implementation of the five-year defence plan. Chavan and I were guests of Ambassador B. K. Nehru at the Embassy residence at 2700 Macomb Street. At the Pentagon, he was received by Robert McNamara, with full ceremonial honours.

During discussions in his inimitable style, McNamara was direct and hard-hitting. While Chavan felt uncomfortable, I noticed how Ambassador B. K. Nehru, deftly with his suave diplomatic finesse, intervened with anecdotes and helped. It was education for my future diplomatic career. After three days, Chavan found McNamara, true to his reputation insensitive, almost inhuman. Strangely, before leaving Washington D.C., we were to experience McNamara's human face as well.

That day, after the discussions, as Chavan was taking leave of McNamara, the latter looked at me and said, "Young man, I hope you have seen our capital. Washington D.C. is a beautiful city."

In his style, I told him that I had not seen much, because I had been kept busy with him. "Neither has my Minister seen the city," I added. McNamara pressed a buzzer and asked his staff to arrange a one-hour helicopter ride the next morning for the Defence Minister of India and his Private Secretary. It was an enthralling experience to see from the air several monuments and the enchanting countryside around Washington D.C. After one hour, we landed on a helipad on the lawns of the Pentagon, almost next to McNamara's office. As soon as we entered his room McNamara asked me, "What struck you most about Washington?"

Without a moment's hesitation, I replied: 'The parking lot of the Pentagon.' He looked at me with surprise. "Mr Defence Secretary, I have never seen so many thousand cars parked at one place," I added in explanation.

McNamara laughed and told me that over 20,000 people worked in the Pentagon but the parking lot had place for only 10,000. So at least 10,000 employees had to arrange for a ride with someone else or ask their wives to drop them early in the morning. Then with a smile, lie added, "You must see the traffic jams in the evening. These are unbelievable." I was not being flippant when I told McNamara that what impressed me most was the parking lot of the Pentagon. The matrix formed by over 10,000 cars in varied colours was unimaginable. Several years later when I had occasion to meet him in the Rajiv Gandhi Foundation, I recalled that and he had a hearty laugh. I noted that after seeing poverty of third world countries as the President of the World Bank, Robert McNamara had become more human.

That visit was to lay foundation of my friendship with B. K. Nehru, one of the most respected and high profile member of the ICS, I had not met prior to that visit. From what I had heard from colleagues, I had formed an impression of an ambassador was aloof, somewhat impersonal and haughty. Perhaps it had something to do with his being a Nehru. But before departing from Washington D.C., I had to revise my view.

On the morning we were to leave Washington, I went to the Chancery to draw allowances for the Minister's tour. While the papers were being prepared, Ambassador Nehru called me over to his office. He briefed me about the places Chavan would visit and also the persons he should be meeting. Then he casually asked me, "I hope you are aware about the practice of tipping in America."

When he found that I was a little perplexed, he said, "Do you know how to tip?" I didn't reply but looked questioningly at him. He said, "Do you know what 'Tips' means? To-ensure-Prompt-Service?" "When you tip a person, you are also assured of better service". While explaining that, B. K. Nehru looked at me with an amused smile and said: "Now make sure that you are not stingy in tipping. After all, you are going to tip on behalf of India's Defence Minister."

I had remained silent and perhaps looked at him somewhat cynically. He sensed that something was bothering me and asked, "I hope you are carrying sufficient money for yourself?"

I blurted out, "Sir, now that you have asked me, I must tell you that while I have sufficient money to pay on behalf of the Minister, I have hardly any cash for myself."

When he asked me why not, I confessed to him, "Because you were good enough to put me up as your guest." There was an incredulous look on his face. I said, "When I left India I was told that I would draw my daily allowance from the Embassy. On coming here I found that you had generously made arrangements for me to stay with you as your guest. I am not therefore entitled to full daily allowance. Under the rules, I am to get only twenty-five per cent of my daily entitlement."

Just to dig in the point a little further I added: "Sir, if I follow your advice on tipping, I do not think my one week's allowance will be sufficient for even one day's tipping."

Ambassador Nehru picked up the telephone. In a few minutes, A. K. Dar, and the Minister said, "I want you to know that Pradhan was not, repeat not, my guest in Washington." Just to ensure that Pradhan got his allowance, as due to him, the Ambassador wanted the Head of the Chancery to know that while Chavan was

Three Foreign Visits

his personal guest, Pradhan was not. I was richer by fifty dollars.

Encounters with McNamara and B. K. Nehru had many a lesson for me at that young age. The human touch is what separates the great ones in high places from others. B. K. Nehru became a friend and well-wisher and has continued to remain one.

On May 27, in the last leg of our visit, we were at the Broadmoor Hotel in Colorado Spring, Chavan was in rooms 16 and 17 and I was in the adjoining 15. I was in deep slumber when I heard someone knocking on the interconnecting door. I opened the door and saw Chavan standing there in a disheveled state, with a blank gaze in his eyes. He was greatly agitated. I thought for a moment that he had been taken ill. He looked at me with tears in his eyes and with a quivering voice said, "Talbot, the Assistant Secretary of State, rang up a few minutes back and told me that Prime Minister Nehru is dead."

I said, "Sir, we must leave for New York and catch the first flight for Delhi."

Chavan asked, "What about the work here and my meeting with President Johnson?" It was fixed for the morning of 28 May.

I explained that with the death of the Prime Minister, he had ceased to be a minister. He must return to India without delay. It was already 2.30 a.m., local time; there was a time difference of eleven hours between New York time and Indian standard time and it would take a few hours flying time to reach New York. Chavan said, "Do whatever needs to be done. I want to be in Delhi to pay my last respects and attend the cremation."

George Hannha, our liaison officer, made a few telephone calls and told me that we would be boarding a US Air Force plane at Peterson Airfield, flying to New York at 4.30 a.m., 27 May 1964.

Within a few minutes, we were ready to leave for the airfield. George had already arranged for the vehicles.

Just as I was getting into the car, I called the bell-boy who had taken our baggage down, took out a five dollar bill from my pocket and pressed it in his hand. With tears in his eyes, he declined the tip, saying, "Sir, we are sorry to hear of your great Prime Minister's death. We share your sorrow." Coming as it did with all sincerity, it truly reflected the feelings of the common American citizen in India's hour of grief.

The first thing I did on board the flight was to send messages to Mrs. Indira Gandhi and to the President of India.

I also drafted a message addressed to President Lyndon Johnson from Chavan informing him of his plans to fly to New York en route to New Delhi and greatly regretting that their proposed meeting could not take place.

While we were on our way to New York, we got a message on the tele-printer from Washington that a Boeing 707 was being placed at the disposal of the defence minister. Also that Dean Rusk, the Secretary of State, and Ambassador B. K. Nehru would be accompanying the minister. Phillip Talbot received Chavan and took him to the lounge where Chester Bowles, the US Ambassador to India, who was also in Washington, as well as Mr. and Mrs. Galbraith were waiting. Service attaches of the Indian Embassy and other officials, and several other US Service officers were also present to offer their condolences. McNamara spoke very feelingly about Nehru. Chavan was too shattered to engage in any small talk.

Soon after take-off, Dean Rusk who was seated in the front portion of the plane, changed into a bush shirt, moved down the aisle and met each one of us on board. It was a very graceful and considerate gesture

On landing in Delhi, Chavan came down the stairway and waited for Dean Rusk to say words of thanks. A moment later, Dean Rusk turned towards Chavan and said, "Mr. Minister, I and my colleagues thank you very much for bringing us along with you."

Chavan was speechless. It was the gesture of a diplomat and a gentleman.

The USSR -Encounter with Khruschev

After the visit to the United States in May 1964, a visit to the United Kingdom was under discussion. However, before going to London, Lal Bahadur Shastri, the Prime Minister felt that Chavan should visit the USSR and see what kind of assistance India could obtain from the Soviets.

Accordingly, on August 8th, 1964, Chavan left for Moscow by an Air India flight. His party included Mrs. Chavan, myself and two members of his personal staff. An official-level delegation, consisting of H. C. Sarin (leader), General J. N. Chaudhuri, COAS, Rear Admiral S. M. S. Nanda, Deputy CNS and others, was already in Moscow.

Chavan and his wife were received by Marshal Rodion Y. Malinovsky, Soviet Defence Minister and Madame Malinovsky and presented a full military honour-guard. Ambassador T. N. Kaul, accompanied by other members of the Indian embassy and the Indian delegation, was at hand to receive the minister. Chavan was driven to a villa in Lenin Hills, on the right bank of the river Moskva in the south-west of the city.

The Indian embassy was situated in a beautiful old style building with a number of smaller buildings in the compound. At the rear of the embassy, at one end of the garden, was a small building called 'Napoleon's Dacha'. We were told that during his occupation of Moscow, Napoleon had stayed there for a few days. It was all very impressive. The most impressive part of the embassy was, however, the Ambassador himself. T. N. Kaul had already established himself as an able diplomat and was widely respected in the Soviet hierarchy as well as by the diplomatic community. Short in stature, smoking a pipe, a smile on his lips and a sharp eye, he looked impressive and shrewd. Rikhi Jaipal was a complete contrast to the

Ambassador. He was quiet, suave and soft-spoken. In fact, when he spoke I had to strain my ears to catch his words. There was no doubt that he was well informed and knew what he was talking about. Listening to him, one felt comfortable and confident. His later career in the Indian Foreign Service would justify the reputation that he had already built up.

Chavan's meeting with the Chairman of the USSR Council of Ministers, Nikita S. Khrushchev had been fixed for 9th September, 1964. The previous evening, Marshal Malinovsky had hosted a dinner in honour of Chavan.

The dinner was in a villa, apparently a place where the Soviets entertained visiting dignitaries. We arrived at the villa a few minutes before 7 p.m. and were soon joined by Marshal Malinovsky and Chavan. In the entrance several glasses of milk, yoghurt and tomato juice had been arranged on tables for guests to help themselves to before going to the dining table. The party soon got into a swinging mood. Since all the senior members of the delegation on both sides were toasting each other with eloquent speeches, we soon lost count of the number of 'dodnas' (bottoms up), and the quantity of vodka gulped down—all in the nation's cause!

After a sumptuous dinner, Marshal Malinovsky, Chavan and some senior members left the party. It was already nearing midnight. The vodka had lifted our spirits and everyone was singing loudly and cheerfully. In between, the partners on either side kept changing. I was thoroughly enjoying myself when I distinctly heard the person to my right whispering into my ear, "Your minister will get everything that he wants tomorrow morning. He must, however, insist." I looked at him in surprise. I had seen that gentleman earlier from a distance, sitting with the Soviet delegation. From his appearance and the place he was occupying at the table, I never thought that he could be someone important. I was obviously mistaken.

Late that night after the party, we drove to the Embassy where T. N. Kaul was waiting for us in his office. He asked whether there was anything significant that had been mentioned by anyone during the course of dinner. When I told him, rather hesitatingly, all that had been whispered into my ear, he smiled. The meeting with Khrushchev was held on 9th September, 1964 in the Chairman's office in the Kremlin. It lasted for over a hundred minutes. Marshal Malinovsky was present on the Soviet side. Chavan was assisted by Ambassador T. N. Kaul and H.C. Sarin.

On 11th September 1964, just prior to the end of Chavan's official visit, President Dr. Sarvepalli Radhakrishnan came on a State visit to the Soviet Union. He was accompanied by Mrs. Lakshmi N. Menon, Minister of State in the Ministry of External Affairs, Mr. S. Dutt, Secretary to the President and Dr. S. Gopal, Director of the Historical Division of the Ministry of External Affairs.

The banquet in the Kremlin was a memorable occasion. It was held in the grand Kremlin Palace, which stood on the slope leading to the river Moskva. High at the top of the building was an inscription saying that it was the headquarters of the Supreme Soviet of the USSR.

Three Foreign Visits

While we were in the reception hall, I noticed a great deal of whispering and agitated consultations among the senior members of the Indian delegation and our embassy officials. It was about the seating plan, copies of which had been exhibited at the entrance to the banquet hall. The Soviet Foreign Office Protocol had obviously overlooked that H. C. Sarin, the Secretary, was a very senior officer. They had placed him at the lower end of the table amongst junior officials of the Indian Embassy. Because of these errors of Soviet protocol, I found myself seated six places on the right of President Ananstas I. Mikoyan. On my left was a member of the Politburo, whose name I never caught. On my right, I found the great Comrade Suslov who, I discovered, could understand English. An interpreter was seated behind us.

Dr. S. Radhakrishnan was seated opposite President Mikoyan. On his right was Khrushchev. I thus found myself seated diagonally across Khrushchev. Chavan was to the right of the Soviet President Mikoyan. Initially, finding myself seated way above my real protocol ranking, I was somewhat self-conscious. I knew that the senior members of the Indian delegation must be resenting the place given to me. I therefore tried hard to be as inconspicuous as possible and hid myself between the two relatively burly Soviet leaders.

The food and the service were excellent. Toasts were exchanged with fruit juice and, as expected, President S. Radhakrishnan made an extempore speech, which was brilliant in its eloquence. We felt proud of our President.

Beyond Expectations

Coffee was being served on small elegant tables, around each of which sat three or four guests. I was seated with two Soviet officials, who unfortunately did not speak English. After some time, the two Presidents departed and Khrushchev got up to say goodbye to the Indian guests. In his waddling gait, he moved from table to table and soon he approached the table where I was seated. He was followed by a Soviet interpreter. When he learnt that I was Private Secretary to the visiting Indian Defence Minister, he shook me warmly by the hand and told me what a great job my Minister was doing and that I must be working very hard for him. Just as he was about to move to another table, he turned round and said something to the interpreter, who asked me whether I was impressed with what I had seen in the Soviet Union. I was a little dumbfounded. Throughout that evening, seated in between the two distinguished Politburo members, eating out of plates fit only for royalty and now seated in a gilded chair, I was wondering as to how all these opulent surroundings could be consistent with Marxist-Leninist principles? I asked the interpreter to convey my question.

With all seriousness, Khrushchev looked piercingly at me and said: "Young man, do not forget that we are successors to the Tsars. All this now belongs to the people of the USSR. No one can run away from one's past. Nor should one be ashamed (of the past)."

He smiled, shook me warmly by the hand and moved on.

That night I reflected on Khrushchev's remark. We in India were removing statues and other landmarks of the

British and consigning them to the dustbins. Was it right? There was however a difference; while the Tsars were Russia's Russian rulers, the British were foreigners, who had imposed their imperial rule on India. Nevertheless, we could not run away from our past - whether colonial or otherwise.

Khrushchev, with the commonsense and pithiness of a peasant, knew that today's rulers would be tomorrow's past rulers. Within four weeks of our return, we learnt that he had been dethroned. I wondered whether Khrushchev knew what was in store for him. He was soon to be relegated to the dustbin of history.

The United Kingdom - at 10 Downing Street

On Chavan's return from Moscow in mid-September, where he had been assured of a supply of frigates and even submarines, if India so desired, there was rethinking in the navy. Until that time, Britain had been the sole supplier of naval equipment.

Lal Bahadur Shastri felt that before making any commitment to the Soviets, the Defence Minister should visit Britain to find out the attitude of the British Government. Apparently, the situation had become favourable with the advent of the Labour Party under Prime Minister Harold Wilson.

When Chavan called on Harold Wilson at 10 Downing Street, I accompanied him along with Dr. Jivraj Mehta and a couple of other officials. Inside No. 10, the atmosphere was staid and somewhat gloomy that winter morning. Punctual to the minute, Chavan and Dr. Jivraj Mehta were ushered in to an office adjoining the Cabinet room to meet Mr. Wilson. The rest of us sat waiting in the Cabinet room. After the interview, Harold Wilson came out to escort the Defence Minister to the door. We were briefly introduced to him. The reception, the interview, the farewell were all businesslike. No pomp. No show. No waste of time on idle talk. Of course, the result was as anticipated: no assurances of aid.

The communiqué issued at the end of the talks papered over the failure. It emphasized the British ministers' awareness of the fact that Britain had in the past been the main supplier of military equipment to the Indian defence forces. Their anxiety at India's recent efforts to cast her net further a field for defence supplies was subtly referred to. The last paragraph of the communiqué reaffirmed the importance which they (the Indian and British Ministers) attached "to the closest possible cooperation between the services" and expressed the hope that within the spirit of the Commonwealth partnership, close liaison would continue to be maintained between them. It was clear that while Britain could or could not assist, India was not expected to seek help elsewhere. Chavan's visit had been a great disappointment.

ಐಂಬಐಂಬ

Chapter 26

My Decision to Quit
- Farewell to Defence Ministry

By the end of 1964, I started thinking of my own career. I have had an unique experience of working at political level. I was hardly thirty two years old and had ahead another twenty six years of working life in the IAS. I had also fulfilled my promise to work with Chavan for three years – actually I was about to complete five because I had come with him to Delhi.

I had, apart from what I have recounted, seen the world and had honour to shake hands with some great personalities. I was with my minister when he visited, London, Washington, Moscow and again London. I had met Robert McNamara, the whiz-kid of the Kennedy administration; B. K. Nehru, the great civilian and diplomat; Professor Galbraith; Averell Harriman; T. N. Kaul Ambassador and Rehki Jaipal, IFS, one of the most talented diplomat, in Moscow. I had even shaken hand and a brief talk with Nikita Khrushchev in the Kremlin and had dinner in gold plates of Queen Catherine the Great. In London, I had visited the 10 Downing Street and met Prime minister Harold Wilson. In Washington, Dean Rusk and Philip Talbot.

I had learnt several lessons. Some trivial and some profound. In the latter category was Khrushchev's profound statement: No one can run away from one's past. Nor should one be ashamed of the past.

All this was on the plus side but what about my future in the IAS? One day, I talked to Chavan and shared my dilemma. Fortunately, he agreed that I should leave the job as soon as I had got a replacement and inducted him in duties of a private secretary. I soon found in Sharad Kelkar of Maharashtra cadre of the IAS, an able successor and decided to bid good bye to Chavan. That was not easy.

On January 25th, 1965, I showed all secret documents in my cupboards and signed papers handing over the charge. I felt relieved and almost felt liberated from bondage. Chavan was waiting in his office. As I entered the room through a small passage that connected his office with mine, I straightened my jacket and saw him seated at his huge table writing something on his small memo pad. Weather being cold he was wearing a long coat with the usual white cap on his head. I had decided to bid a business like farewell.

I stood on right side of table to say my piece. But words would not come out of my mouth. I did not know what to say in breaking our relationship. Instead tears started flowing out of my eyes. He got up from his chair and patted me on the back and said. "Ram, control your self".

My Decision to Quit

I went over to the wash room in the passage and with cold water splashed my face. When I re-entered the room I found that Chavan was wiping tears from his eyes. It was my turn to put my arms around him and console him. I told him that I was not permanently leaving him and that I shall come over and meet him whenever he wanted. That calmed him down. He opened right hand drawer of his table and handed me some papers. He said "Ram, this is the historic Statement that you drafted. I can never forget your contribution to save the government and Padit ji".

I opened the papers and saw the original of the Statement with the Prime minister's correction in his own hand. I also saw Chavan's notes in his own hand, in red colour made by the Cross pen on the Henderson Brook Report that he had studied, almost like a student appearing for an examination. I have treasured those notes all these years. Now that the event is over fifty years old, I am reproducing that Statement as an annexure.

I briskly shook hand with him and found all my staff waiting to say good bye to me. Some of them including S. N. Dongre, B. P. Joshi and R. K. Khandekar had come to Delhi along with me from Bombay. They would continue to work with Chavan till the end of his life. Khandekar and I remained in close touch when I was working with Rajiv Gandhi and he with P. V. Narsimha Rao, the Prime minister of India between 1990–95 and later till his demise.

I did not realize that I was embarking on to a career that would change my life forever.

PART IV :

International Trade and Diplomacy

Chapter 27

Launch into Economic Field

That I would spend almost one-third of my service career in diplomatic and international affairs was again a matter of luck.

I was asked to join the Ministry of Commerce as a deputy secretary on January 27, 1965. I handed over charge of the post of the Private Secretary to the Defence Minister, on January 25, 1965. I enjoyed along with the family the Republic Day Parade. My wife and I also attended the reception at the Rashtrapati Bhavan. Next day, I reported to D.S. Joshi in the Ministry of Commerce.

On entering Udyog Bhawan, I found myself in a totally different environment. The ministry of defence was located in the South Block, constructed as a symbol of British Raj in 1920s. Built with red and pink sand stones, North and South Blocks stand majestically on a slope that leads to the last Rashtrapati Bhawan located on top of Raisina hill. Corridors of the two blocks are truly majestic and represent power and pomp of the Raj. In contrast, Udyog Bhawan was built by the Central Public Works

Department (CPWD) in 1950s and while the outside facade was intended to be in tune with the architecture of the two blocks of the Raj era, the inside was like any other functional office complex. Long corridors with cubicles on either side looked monotonous and uninspiring.

I was completely ignorant of the working of the Commerce Ministry and total stranger to that field. Moreover, except for the secretary D. S. Joshi, I did not know any other officer in the Ministry. Joshi was as usual polite and businesslike. He told me that I was being appointed as deputy secretary to look after trade with the Western Europe. It would be an interesting assignment and a good beginning to get initiated into the ministry. In the absence of S Vohra (1940 ICS of Punjab – later of Haryana), the Joint Secretary, Joshi asked me to find my way about with the help of under secretary V. A. Padmanabhan and a junior research officer named Raju Makil. They had been alerted by Joshi's secretary and were waiting outside the door of his office to greet me. I was escorted to a small room on the second floor. Office table was covered with dust and bundles of papers were lying on the floor. Apparently, the room had been got vacated rather hurriedly for my use. After getting my table in some shape, I went through printed material and briefing notes connected with India's trade with Western Europe. A map hanging on the wall was useful in getting acquainted with geography as well as relative size of countries of that region. A week later I was also placed in-charge of GATT and UNCTAD. Padmanabhan briefed me on the two organizations namely, the General Agreement on Tariffs & Trade (GATT) and the United Nation Conference on Trade and Development (UNCTAD).

Launch into Economic Field

As my immediate superior Joint Secretary, S. Vohra, ICS was abroad, before he returned, I digested as much material as was dished out to me. He had gone to attend a meeting in New York in connection with setting up of a new United Nation's Organization named the UNCTAD. The name itself signified that there was considerable reservation on calling it a specialized agency such as the World Health Organization (WHO) or the International Labour Organization (ILO). That explained the word conference in UNCTAD. Since there was already a body known as GATT (General Agreement on Trade and Development) in which all matters relating to trade were discussed and in which trade negotiations were organized, it was the view of developed countries that UNCTAD should provide a forum for deliberations and discussions and should not become another body for trade negotiations. It was authorized to organize periodic conferences to discuss issues of interest to developing countries.

Within weeks of my joining the Ministry of Commerce, two events took place that determined the shape of my future career. One day I was told to prepare myself to meet Ambassador K. B. Lall, ICS, India's Ambassador to the Court of Belgium as well as to the European Economic Community (EEC). There was a great excitement as the ambassador was regarded as one of the stalwarts in international economic diplomacy who wielded great power and authority. There were hectic preparations for briefing him on several issues connected with the trade with the western Europe and economic matters dealt by the United Nations. Since I was a novice, I was not too much troubled nor I was in a position to engage in meaningful discussions. Couple of days after the ambassador had had round of briefing sessions, I was told that he wanted to see me. Introducing myself I told that I was new to my job. He said, "Are' Bhai, I have called you to see me and I know who you are. Now sit down and tell me what you are going to do to help me?"

That was my first test of what I came to know as KB Lall's way of testing young officers. I told him that I knew nothing about my subject. He laughed and told me that he liked my frankness and would look forward to work with me. He, with his peculiar style added, "After all I am only an ambassador who works under instructions from deputy secretaries in the government."

I never encountered that kind of sense of humour in the defence ministry where I found senior officers were dour, somewhat rude and full of self-importance especially in dealing with junior level officials. After a few minutes talk about my experience in the ministry of Defence, KB as he was known, told me he would like me to come over to attend the next annual session of GATT in Geneva scheduled to be held within ten days or so. I took leave of him and on entering my room asked the under secretary to brief me on GATT. Till that moment, I was concentrating on learning geography, history and economies of the countries of western Europe.

Next day, I was called by D. S. Joshi, who looked at me and said, "Pradhan, I did not expect you to seek deputation abroad so soon after joining the ministry. KB told me that you will join him in Geneva to attend the next GATT session". I was taken aback. I told the Secretary that there was no question of my wanting to go abroad. I did not even know what GATT or UNCTAD stands for. It was the ambassador who suggested that I must come over to attend the annual GATT Session. In order to make sure that there was no misunderstanding so soon after my joining the Ministry, I added, "Sir, I do not wish to make a fool of myself. Please do not send me abroad until I have fully learnt my job." Joshi was good enough to accept my word. Makil and Padmanahan undertook to complete visa and other formalities.

A week later, I left on Air India flight to Rome with an Official Passport, with white cover instead of blue one for normal citizens of India. That was the beginning of my career in the field of international trade diplomacy.

ಸಂಚ

Air India plane arrived at Rome early in the morning. I was happy to see Anant Datar IAS, First Secretary, in the Indian Embassy, handling trade matters. He took me to his home and on way back to airport he showed me some tourist spots and took me to the famous Treni Fountain. At Geneva Airport, Hukum Singh, a thirty five year old Sikh, who was personal assistant to India's Resident Representative to GATT, escorted me to Hotel Du Rhone, a first grade hotel, on the bank of Rhone river that flows out of Lake Lehmann a few hundred meters from the hotel.

Late in the afternoon, B. N. Swarup, IAS, who was India's Resident Representative to GATT, rang up to invite me to dinner at his home. He introduced me to his wife Usha and learnt that her father V. Shankar ICS, was my first collector and district magistrate in Banaskatha. Ambassador K. B. Lall and V. Shankar both belonging to ICS, were brothers-in-law, married to two sisters. Swarup undertook to take me to GATT next day.

I can never forget my first visit to GATT Secretariat. It was then situated in a Swiss-type villa, named Villa Bocage, on grounds adjoining the United Nations sprawling estates on the shores of Lac Lehmann. It was over two hundred year old building residential villa. Swarup introduced me to Wyndham White who was the Director General since founding of the GATT Organisation. A man of a few words, he was respected by all delegations not only for his advice but also for his ability to deliver what was expected of him by major trading nations. Swarup also introduced to me to several senior officials of the Secretariat, including an Indian M. G. Mathur. Madan belonged to the Indian Revenue Service (IRS). A very quiet, serious looking, soft spoken and shy with a razor-sharp brain and great understanding of trade issues.

After these formal meetings, Swarup took me to the UN Palais. I was overwhelmed by its vastness, long corridors in polished Italian marble and impeccably clean and orderly maintenance. Facing Lake Lehmann length-wise and situated in midst of sloping and beautifully tended lawns leading all the way up to the water of the Lake, it is one of the most imposing and beautiful building. Since the end of the Second World War, the Palais has become a hub on all international activities in Europe.

In the next couple of days, I got familiar with the working of the Consulate General of India, which was then situated in Place des Eaux Vives, almost in the center of the town on the left bank of the lake. It was then that I realized that I had embarked on a new career.

A day prior to the starting of the GATT session, Ambassador K. B. Lall arrived from Brussels. We had a pleasant dinner at Swarup's place with Savai Madhav Singh of Jaipur joining for drinks. On return to the Hotel, I went along with him to his room to say goodnight. After that good wining and dining, I was feeling sleepy. KB had however decided to start my training. He asked me to see him at 6 am with the 'pad' and brief him.

I was somewhat taken a back, as Swarup had not shown me any papers nor had he mentioned any pad for the Ambassador. It was already midnight. Instead of disturbing Swarup, I rang up his young personal assistant Hukum Singh, and explained to him my problem. Typically a Sikh, he told me "Sir, please do not worry, we shall get the task done." He took me to the Consulate and in next two hours he got the 'pad' ready. I was back at the hotel at 3 a.m. and asked the hotel reception to wake me up in a couple of hours. At 6 a.m. sharp, I reached the Ambassador's room and rang the bell. A booming voice said, 'Door open, come in'.

On entering, I saw KB standing, upside down, on his head, in 'yoga' posture wearing only an underwear. He asked me to brief him. I sat on a chair facing him and in that somewhat ridiculous posture I briefed India's Ambassador Extraordinary and Plenipotentiary to the European Economic Community. That was KB's way telling me that work with him was not going to be all fun.

I soon learnt that he was not only a hard task master but one who believed in training younger officers into their task. That was his way of building a cadre of officers who would serve India in the field of international diplomacy and loyal to him. Next morning, at the Palais, I learnt the importance of being K. B. Lall. I was struck by his easy informality and flattered when he introduced me as his colleague.

On another occasion, one morning he asked me to join him at a lunch with the British Ambassador at Pearle du Lac, one of the very well-known restaurants. As soon as we were seated, KB asked me, "What is the brief?" In all innocence, I replied, "What brief? I thought you asked me to join you at the lunch."

He looked at me intently and said, "Please remember that all lunches and dinners, which one gives in diplomatic capacity, are paid for by the President of India, that is the people of India. These are not for personal enjoyment. When one is invited or one asks another diplomat over for lunch, one must have an agenda and a brief that must clearly indicate what you want to achieve out of the conversation at the table." He produced a piece of paper with about ten lines neatly typed and showed me what he meant.

The way he taught the lesson was unforgettable and after that, all my life, whenever I entertained any one officially for lunch or dinner, or for that matter met anyone for discussion, I never did so without having a piece of paper in my pocket - a kind of brief. Later when I went up the ladder, I insisted my juniors doing the same. That's how the Service traditions are passed on.

Launch into Economic Field

On another occasion, he asked the Ambassador of Brazil to send one of his assistants to discuss some matter with me. Since we had to report next morning the outcome, I invited young diplomat to have a drink at the Hotel Du Rhone that evening. Although only a second secretary, he tried to impress me with his importance as normally Brazilians do. I asked him what whisky he would prefer. He mentioned 'that' to the waiter and also asked for some snacks. Next morning when I furnished report to KB about our talk and showed him the bill, he carefully studied it and said, "Look, you are new to this but why did you have to offer the costliest Chivas Regal whisky and caviar to the second secretary? In future make sure that as host you decide on what to order." Very reluctantly he signed the bill for payment out of delegation's entertainment allowance. That lesson guided me throughout my diplomatic career.

At the end of the visit, I was to learn yet another lesson. KB asked me to draft a report for GATT session and asked me to fly over to Brussels to get it approved by him I had to work on that draft five times before he found it satisfactory. Then he told me that it is not that your drafts were not accurate but remember that the Ambassador's report to the ministry must communicate not only what happened but issues on which the ministry must carry out studies and prepare instructions on how to handle that particular subject in future. Since you are new in the field, I wanted you to start thinking not at the level of deputy secretary but at the level of an ambassador. Saying so, he dictated in my presence a letter to the commerce secretary extolling my contribution to the Indian delegation, and complimenting me for preparing such a fine report. That was KB's way of shaping young officers. For me, that first induction in the international field was important. I learnt a great deal. Later I was also to unlearn a lot as well.

I learnt that if I was to make a mark in a field in which I was complete novice there was no substitute to hard work and developing my own style of working. Diplomacy did not mean trying to be cleverer than the other party and trying to deceive others to achieve one's own objective. To be really successful and effective, both in bilateral as well as in multi-lateral area, one must earn respect and trust, especially with those with whom you negotiate. These lessons proved useful to me and over a period, I earned reputation as a negotiator.

Next few months, I devoted to learning about GATT Treaty as well as about the newly founded United Nations Conference on Trade and Development (UNCTAD) founded at the conference convened by the UN, attended by enlightened leaders from western countries, such as Edward Heath from the UK and representatives of John Kennedy's administration. Their main interest was to preserve primacy of GATT as the forum to administer rules of international trade and the only body to arrange trade negotiations. UNCTAD was agreed upon to provide a forum to allow developing countries to periodically meet and discuss matters of development interest to them. It was agreed that while the Conference shall meet periodically after four years, in between, the work will be carried out by a committee named 'Trade and Development Board'.

As Director of Foreign Trade in the Commerce ministry, I had to handle negotiations in GATT known as the Kennedy Round, so named as these were launched at the initiative of President John Kennedy. These were on basis of mutual benefit. You offered concessions and in return you negotiated for better access to market of other members. All based on concept of mutuality. India was required to table a list of items on which we could offer reduction on custom duty. To identify those items, I had to work closely with the ministry of Finance, especially the Customs Department because cuts in tariffs would mean loss of revenue and also result in increased import of foreign goods, which in turn may affect sale of domestic products that may not be able to withstand competition. Our aim was to obtain to seek tariff concessions from individual developed countries so that India's products could find entry to affluent markets.

All that required intensive consultations with the Industries Ministry and a number of Export Promotion Boards, such as the Association of Textile Exporters in Bombay, the Indian Merchant Chambers Bombay, the Engineering Export Council in Calcutta. Discussions with the office bearers of these bodies and trade organizations were greatly educative, especially visits to the Commodity Board for Coffee, Spices in Cochin and the Coir Board enabled me to learn great deal about agricultural products, their cultivation, processing and marketing. As I was in-charge of trade with the Western Europe, I had also to prepare for periodical discussions in Brussels with the Commission of the European Community (EEC). For that, I had to study the Rome Treaty, as well as, the philosophy and history of formation of the European Community as also about intense competitive interests and conflicts within the Community.

ಐಡ

In 1966, during one of the visits to Geneva, I was suddenly asked to fly to Madrid to attend a conference of jute producing and jute manufacturing countries. One evening, I landed in Madrid. In the evening, I had dinner with the Indian ambassador Madanjit Singh who briefed me about the Conference. It would be a grand gala occasion because some of the richest people in Scotland and Belgium would represent jute manufacturing industry. As a major jute producing country, I would be expected to respond to a toast that would be raised by the Jute industry. I was advised to equip myself with a black- tie dinner dress. Instead of hiring a dress I decided to wear buttoned up black vicuna Indian jacket, which I was fortunately carrying with me.

That evening's dinner was an unbelievable exhibition of wealth. While men were uniformly dressed in black ties, the ladies exhibited all their finery and were decked out in diamond jewelry. Dinner was a seven course one with the choicest wines and liquors. There were toasts with champagne. Most interestingly, as a representative of major jute producing country and a relatively younger man, my black closed collar jacket, with silver buttons in nirmal*- work of Hyderabad was much admired. After dinner there was dancing and my taking the floor to dance cha-cha-cha and samba drew applause. It was like being transported back to the era of the French Kings.

That visit to Madrid opened my eyes to wealth and super rich class that had flourished for centuries by exploiting raw materials exported by India and East Pakistan (now Bangladesh). I decided to fight for reduction of high tariffs on jute manufacture in Western Europe and prepare a

Launch into Economic Field

strong case to secure concessions for India's handloom and handicraft products in the Kennedy Round.

※○≪

While enjoying work in a totally new area of work, for which I was not equipped either through education or work experience, one day I suddenly faced reality of life and death. Kennedy Round, UNCTAD and GATT meetings required me to visit mainly Geneva and Brussels. During first twenty-four months, I had to visit Geneva seventeen times.

On one occasion, I and Muchkund Dubey were to travel to Geneva from where, he was to proceed to New York. That morning, Muchkund apologetically mentioned to me that he would not be able to accompany me as he was suffering sever bellyache. Knowing Muchkund as a conscientious officer, with a view to make him comfortable, I told him that we should delay our departure by two days. Next day I spent with family and decide to take my wife to see a picture.

Next evening, the 6 p.m. All India Radio broadcast announced that the Air India flight from Rome to Geneva had crashed in the Alps. Amongst a number of passengers, the most prominent one was Dr. Homi Bhabha, the great Indian Nuclear Scientist. On hearing that news, my wife and I were in a state of shock.

Homi Bhabha's death had a sequel. It would be twenty years later that bodies of persons on that unfortunate Air India flight would be found on the top of Mount Blanc.

Even now I shudder to think of that flight and wonder whether I would also have laid there for all those years on that highest mountain top of Europe- but for a bellyache.

Chapter 28

Tripartite Negotiations
- Pioneering Task

For me, 1966 was an eventful year. Mrs. Indira Gandhi, Prime Minister of India, President Nasser of Egypt and President Tito of Yugoslavia had met at Brioni, Tito's, private island . Just as some western countries were forming trading- blocks amongst themselves that excluded countries outside post- world- war Europe. In their declaration, it was mentioned that the three countries shall negotiate among themselves a Free Trade Arrangement. Later other developing countries may join. The three countries had totally different tariff regimes. The only common point being all the three were members of the Group of 77 in UNCTAD. As Director of Foreign Trade, I was in-charge of the negotiations by D. S. Joshi.

The first meeting of the officials of three countries in Belgrade in June 1966 clearly showed that there were differences of perceptions on how to proceed on the modalities for negotiations. It proved non-productive as the negotiators could not agree either on the modality or procedure. They could only agree to meet in Cairo a couple of moths later. For me, Belgrade was of benefit as

Beyond Expectations

I met there two persons whose friendships I have retained throughout my life. One Dr Said Talaat Harb of Egypt and the other Pran Neville of India's foreign service. Said belonged to the commerce ministry of Egypt. Coming from a rich and politically influential family, he was educated in Switzerland and obtained his doctorate in Economics from Friebourg university. Pran belonged to the Indian Foreign Service and had spent most of his service career in the Socialist Countries. Over years, he became an expert on trade with these countries and was highly regarded for his erudition and practical knowledge of the working of the economic and trade organizations. He gave me a good understanding of Yugoslavian economic and trade structure and institutions.

On return to India, my main task was to find a way to push the Tripartite discussions and evolve something concrete since the leaders of the three countries were expected to review progress by the end of the year. With the political mandate at the highest level, there was no question of our not producing a tangible arrangement. One day, when I discussed the matter with D. S. Joshi, he asked me to have a talk with Dr. I. G. Patel who was the Chief Economic Adviser in the Ministry of Finance. IG heard my experience at Belgrade meeting. Three countries, because of their diverse economic structures as well as protective interests, could not contemplate even modest reduction of customs duties on an across-the-board basis. He came out with a novel concept. Why not each country first work out a list of products on which it could offer tariff reduction to the other two countries. Later, a common list of products featuring in three lists would be prepared and countries would agree to exchange across-the-board reduction on those items. It was totally a new concept on which I started working immediately.

Since the concept of common list was itself a novel one, I was asked to prepare a 'Concept Paper' for approval by the committee of secretaries. However, because of the novelty of the concept and refusal of the Industry ministry to lower protection and the Custom Department to agree to anything that involved sacrifice of revenue, no agreement could be reached within our government. I was therefore asked to launch the idea in Cairo and work on concept later. That was a clever way of higher ups not owning any responsibility for failure.

For the first two days of discussions, while we tried to fish out ideas from each other, I kept the Common List concept up my sleeve. On the third day, the delegates were taken to Aswan Dam which had been just completed. Since I had seen the site in 1961, when the work had just begun, I was not interested in wasting a whole day. Instead I spent the day in meeting some very high Egyptian officials to impress on them the need for making concrete progress in Cairo. Hussein Khled Hamdy, Secretary of State for ministry of Economy and Trade was good enough to see me. He was a friend of India and knew intimately KB as well as D. S. Joshi. I explained my predicament that the three leaders cannot be told that officials could not find a technique and therefore there was no trade arrangement. He and other officials fully appreciated my point of view and could see the danger to their careers, because Egypt was under strong dictatorship. They promised support to any constructive proposal made by India. That night on return of delegates, I put across on tentative basis the proposal of a

Common List of products. Since it was novel one, Yugoslav Deputy Minister (official of Additional Secretary's rank) told me that he could not proceed without instructions from Belgrade. Egyptians also held a similar view. It was agreed that the delegations would recess for next thirty six hours and meet to resolve the issues. Said Harb helped his Ministry to quickly prepare a list. The Yugoslav delegation found themselves in a confused state since they could not proceed without instructions. They also found it difficult to communicate the concept without knowing modality.

On the eve of prior concluding the talks, the Yugoslav Deputy Minister and his Counselor met me privately. They found themselves in a difficult spot. While India had offered some modality to negotiate and Cairo was ready to accept that as a basis, Yugoslavs could not respond. Time was running out. Obviously Cairo was keen to let the press know that this round of talk was a successful one and three countries were determined to conclude a treaty in their next meeting.

When I told the Yugoslavs that in case they could not subscribe to the modality, the press release may have to state that while the delegations of Egypt and India were willing to proceed, the Yugoslavs could not respond. I told them that I could not return to Delhi without some positive outcome. Ljubisa Milanovic, the Yugoslav Counselor, was in tears. He told me that in that case he might lose his job as President Tito had taken the initiative when the three leaders met in Delhi. I sympathized with him and agreed to work out a Press communiqué that should protect him since he was not in a position to either accept or reject the proposal tabled by India. We worked out a draft which

Tripartite Negotiations

took care of respective positions and declared that the three Delegations would meet couple of months later in New Delhi.

By the time we met for the third and the last meeting, officials of the three delegations were deeply conscious that time was running out and we had to produce a draft treaty. Fortunately, the idea of common list gave enough latitude to each country to protect its trade and at the same time, seek access in two other partner countries. We worked out appropriate rules and phraseology to meet GATT's requirements and document was ceremoniously signed in the Ministry of Commerce on December 23, 1967 first by me and officials of two countries and later by KB- who by that became the Commerce secretary – and his counterparts from Egypt and Yugoslavia.

I received considerable praise for working out an arrangement based on a novel idea. I. G. Patel was happy that his idea had been put to practical use. In the ministry, my prestige went up and I was promoted to be Director of Foreign Trade.

Chapter 29

UNCTAD- II in Delhi
- Recognition as a Negotiator

The Second UNCTAD Conference was scheduled in January- February of 1967 in New Delhi and the commerce ministry was overseeing all arrangements. Certain officers were earmarked to look after the physical infrastructure and logistics while some others for carrying out preparations on substantive matters for deliberations at the Conference. By that time, I had come to know K. B. Lall well and got used to his method of working. He involved me in several areas of deliberations, especially the trade in manufactures and the expansion of trade among developing countries. For manufactures, I had acquired a great deal of knowledge and expertise because of the Kennedy Round and for the latter because of my involvement in the Tripartite Agreement.

The inaugural function of the Conference was held in Ashoka Hotel by an address by Mrs. Indira Gandhi, the Prime Minister of India. After that, plenary session of the Conference was held in the Vigyan Bhawan, and the work was taken up in several committees. While the Commerce Secretary remained overall in-charge of the deliberations in all the committees, other officers were designated to lead the Indian delegation. I was asked to look after the work of a Committee on Trade Expansion and Economic Co-operation among the Developing Countries. We had a clear definite objective: to work on principles on which such trade expansion and economic co-operation should evolve in future. There were great differences among the various groups of countries based on geography, level of development and their then prevailing trade arrangements.

We in the Committee worked hard with a series of discussions each day beginning at 10 O'clock in the morning and ending some time after midnight. Fortunately, I had got to know well some colleagues from Latin America, especially from Brazil and Chile, as also a few from Africa mainly from Ethiopia, Nigeria, and Egypt. Through our respective regional groups and discussions among the regions, we worked out a document to represent a unified position of the developing countries. Although a number of countries had reservation, we succeeded in securing support to developing countries working out inter-regional trading arrangements on the condition that countries that supported, will be free to take their national position in GATT, to safeguard interest of their respective regional groups. On the basis of that position, we started negotiations with the Group of Developed countries and a couple of days before UNCTAD II was to end, narrowed differences to three points. Draft relating to wording on those matters were put in "square brackets", a technique which is adopted in the United Nations to highlight words or sentences on which there is no agreement, it being presumed that the rest of the draft was acceptable to negotiating parties.

Beyond Expectations

On eve of the concluding session, KB told me to come to the top floor of Hotel Oberoi (now Inter Continental) that night to attend meeting of top negotiators, known as the Everest Group. I was expectantly looking forward to witness how such negotiations are brought to an end. It being the last night, the top negotiators were expected to concentrate only on square brackets and clean up draft resolutions to be placed before the Plenary next morning.

On entering the big lounge, I found that the scene was like a bazaar, - a market place. On one side were lined tables loaded with choicest drinks and food. All over hall, leaders of delegations were sitting around in groups discussing differences that existed. They, and only the specially invited individuals, who had authority to negotiate on behalf of their group, were present. On one side of the hall sat Dr. Raul Prebisch, the Secretary General, who acted as a kind of referee, because he had the responsibility to bring successful end to the Conference. Along with my piece of paper, KB met the Ambassadors of UK and USA in one corner and explained in a couple of minutes differences; while the British Ambassador was willing to give up, the American would not budge on 'one' particular word found in the text. He had strong objection to inter-regional arrangement for trade expansion amongst developing countries since that would be against GATT. He was equally vehement that any arrangement must be liberal one. I soon found the word 'liberal' had a different connotation for Americans and to the British. Liberal trade is almost a religion for the Americans and they could not compromise unless that word was clearly spelt out for evolving any trade expansion amongst developing countries. My draft was as good as dead.

UNCTAD-II in Delhi

Within a few minutes, the draft was taken to Dr. Perbisch who, with all the majesty of his office, suggested that Americans could accept the draft on the understanding that they could reserve their position by making a statement in the Plenary. KB agreed to delete one square bracket as a trade off for removing the other one. The matter was settled within a few minutes and I was amazed the way it was done.

Later in my career, I found that in all international conferences, at the end, consensus are reached by quick trading and by technique of statements in the plenary by those who cannot reconcile with the final draft. In all respects, the process of negotiations was great education for me.

At the end of UNCTAD II, I felt that I had found my place in India's international economic diplomacy, especially on reading what the Hindustan Times reported:

Mr. R. D. Pradhan who is in Working Group II (dealing mainly with problems arising out of "trade expansion and economic co-operation among developing nations") is relatively young in the Indian delegation. He is only 39, but not in experience, nor in the record of his achievements. He was, for instance, largely responsible for the negotiation of the tripartite agreement with the UAR and Yugoslavia – an agreement which is pioneering effort in the field of inter-regional trade expansion.

Mr. Pradhan is Director of Foreign Trade ("Trade Policy Division") in the Ministry of Commerce. He joined the IAS in 1952. In January, 1965, he joined the Commerce

Ministry as Deputy Secretary dealing with GATT and UNCTAD matte's. He has since then been a member of the delegation to the annual GATT meetings, and was responsible for the preparations at "head-quarters" in connection with the Kennedy Round of trade negotiations and bilateral discussions at Geneva. India's work in Working Group II, he says, is engaging developing countries' minds in economic co-operation, particularly in inter-regional and regional agreements.

The conference was not all work. In the evenings there were cocktails and dinners. I invited quite a few colleagues to my home with their spouses. My wife and I got to know some well. That was soon to be useful asset. There were lighter moments aplenty. My good friend Adebanjo of Nigeria gave the most memorable quote. In the last plenary he said, "For most countries UNCTAD stands for: Under No Circumstances Take A Decision".

At the end of Conference, I did not know that I was soon to find myself representing India in Geneva, both to UNCTAD and GATT. In a strange way, my destiny was pushing me in that direction.

B. N. Swarup, IAS, India's Resident Representative in Geneva had been there almost four years. With help of K. B. Lall he expected to get another extension for at least one year to pursue tasks arising out of UNCTAD II. As Director in-charge of Trade Policy Division in the Ministry of Commerce, I was asked to initiate a proposal for granting another extension to Swarup. By the middle of the Conference, that proposal was being processed in the Ministry by B. D. Jayal IAS (UP – 1948), joint secretary in-charge of Administration belonging to the UP cadre.

UNCTAD-II in Delhi

One evening, most unexpectedly Bidu Jayal told me that there were certain difficulties in Swarup's further deputation, and my name was being mentioned as a possible successor although the Foreign Office was exerting considerable pressure to nominate one of the IFS officers. Going abroad at that stage was far from my mind. My two sons were getting education in the best school in Delhi, the Modern School, and my wife had a job as a librarian with the American International School on a salary four times my salary. Also at the end of the usual period of deputation of five years to the Government of India, I wished to revert to Maharashtra. Going abroad was not something that attracted me especially since I had noticed how difficult it was for Indian diplomats to live in a costly place like Geneva on their meager salary and allowances.

Suddenly one evening K. B. Lall called me and told me that my name had been approved for deputation for two years assignment in Geneva to replace Swarup and I should get ready to leave in a couple of weeks time.

৫০০৪

In the last week of April 1968, we landed in Geneva. My sons Rajiv and Vivek were twelve and eight years, respectively and our newly-born daughter Sarita was eight months old. The Consulate had arranged our accommodation in Hotel Century, very near the Consulate General Office situate in the Place des Eaux Vives. It was a family accommodation with two bed rooms, a living room and a kitchen. That was to be our home for the next three months.

I had not visited Geneva for the past 4-5 months, as I was busy with UNCTAD II. During those months, a new

Counsul General had taken over, who invited us for lunch. That was our first meeting with N. Krishnan and his wife Lalitha. They were not only hospitable but also greeted us so warmly that our two families became close friends. N. Krishnan was one of the brightest of Indian Foreign Service. A great gentleman, he was candid and transparent in all his work and dealings with others. He became one of the most popular Indian diplomats in Geneva and as he and I became friends, the working atmosphere within the Consulate changed. Instead of discord and disharmony that prevailed over protocol and security, the Consulate General started working as one team. Later in his career, N. Krishnan became India's Permanent Representative to the United Nations and after retirement, United Nation's General Secretary's Personal Representative for South Africa. Lalitha and he were not affected by the high position that he occupied and they remain the same warm and friendly individuals, now happily settled in Bangalore.

We were to meet several Indians who had settled down there. They were all helpful in suggesting accommodation and schooling etc.

Chapter 30

Into Diplomacy

In my earlier visits, I had seen how, in diplomatic life, much time and energy can be wasted on trivial mattes, especially where protocol is involved and that the best way of getting along in a multi-lateral organization like the United Nations is to be correct and friendly and not be pompous and throw about weight. One's importance is judged by others on one's contribution in evolving consensus, and conducting negotiations. Not much weight is attached to one's place in hierarchy. In fact, although I was only at the rank of Counselor, soon I was being treated as one at a level of Ambassador by even such delegations as the UK and the USA, who otherwise observe strict protocol.

I had established a close personal relationship with Dr. Raul Prebisch. We became good friends and he made me a member of select group of eight diplomats, who would meet each Thursday afternoon over lunch to discuss UNCTAD's work. Raul Prebisch, a great gourmet and who knew all the good eating places in and around Geneva, decided where the next lunch could be arranged and hosted by whom. Thus, I got to know these places, their specialties and also got great education in choosing food and wine.

During the first four months, apart from calling on several diplomats and establishing my credentials as a Resident Representative of India, my days were spent in finding residential accommodation. I got a spacious four bed room apartment in Parc Bude, a colony which was springing up near the UN Palais that was meant for foreigners who had then started settling down in Geneva in large numbers. Although the rental for the apartment was somewhat higher than what the Government of India had approved, my wife and I liked the apartment so much that we agreed to pay the difference of rent from my salary. It was perhaps the best decision that we took because adjoining Parc Bude was a school where a large number of foreign students were receiving education and which offered intensive courses in French language, to bring them up to the required standard. My sons got a sound grounding in French and have remained fluent all these years.

My apartment on the seventh floor of Parc de Bude facing Inter Continental Hotel became an object of envy of many diplomats. My Indian colleagues were jealous because it had not only four bed rooms but each had an attached shower and the apartment had a room for a servant as well. Our immediate neighbor was Nari Dastur, Regional Manager of Air India for Western Europe. His wife Katy and Nari, both friendly and intensely India-centric individuals, became our good friends and have remained so for all these years. After retirement, Nari launched holiday package for Air Mauritius to Mauritius and to Goa from Europe. Their daughter Gulsarin is today running a flourishing business in tourism and air industry.

Diplomatic calendar in Geneva starts beginning each September, since month of August is a sacrosanct holiday month for the Europeans. They are mostly out touring all over Europe and enjoying sunshine by the sea. September onwards, there was a busy schedule of meetings of GATT and UNCTAD. As I was already a familiar figure in the corridors of the Palais and personally known to many, it was easy for me to get into a groove. Over the next few months, along with diplomats from a small 'group' of countries, I came to be identified as an important member of the Group of 77. This small group consisted of Brazil, Argentina, Chile from Latin America; Nigeria, Egypt and Ghana from Africa, India, Pakistan, the Philippines from Asia. Along with representatives from some countries such as Mexico, Syria, Indonesia, we found a formidable group. Developed countries recognized our abilities as well as nuisance value in negotiations. We were therefore consulted on all matters within UNCTAD by the Secretariat. Within this group emerged a sub-group with Brazil, Chile, Nigeria and India, which came to be known as a 'mafia' within the Group of 77. Once we decided on a course of action, we developed a technique of 'pincer move' by the Asian, the African and the Latin American countries in conducting negotiations with developed countries and mostly succeeded in achieving what we wanted. For example, in a negotiation such a move could be initiated by Brazil, promptly supported by Nigeria and when arguments were put up by group of developed countries, India or Pakistan would ably counter them. All of us had done our home-work, secured backing of our respective regional groups and reached some degree of consensus within the '77'. All these maneuvers kept me actively involved in diplomatic activity, five days a week, almost working round the clock. Weekends were for family and friends.

For the next three years, my working life revolved around negotiating tables. I found that even casual contact amongst diplomats was a kind of negotiating gambit, where each one tried to assess strength and weaknesses of others; also judge flexibility that a representative had while negotiating. Much of the work of this nature was done over lunches, cocktails, dinners, including social evenings that included wives.

As India's representative, I enjoyed certain advantage. Although as representative of a country one had to work within objectives and instructions set out by one's government, Indian delegates enjoyed great deal of latitude. In those years, the only means of communication with Delhi was a single tele-printer machine which connected the Consulate General with the Foreign Office in the South Block. Telephone connections were erratic and seldom used because of cost. Thus, we were left to work out our own modality to achieve what was stated in briefs furnished by the Ministry. That kind of lack of means of communications enabled delegations, especially from developing countries, to conduct negotiations on their own, rather than seeking instructions all the time from the headquarters. Unfortunately, the delegations of developed countries, especially from the US and European countries, did not enjoy such latitude because of their efficient lines of communication and disciplined way of functioning. Of course now with information-technology revolution and instant communication devices, diplomats have lost their flexibility. In our days, individuals were more important than the system. I took full advantage of that to build a formidable reputation in negotiations conducted in Geneva as did several others, such as Muchkund Dubey in New York.

In my 4-1/2 years career as a Representative of India in Geneva, I was involved in all negotiations in the field of trade within UNCTAD, as well as GATT. Those were the hay days of furthering international economic relations between the developed and developing countries and economic diplomacy was at its height. UNCTAD had been identified as a premier forum for achieving breakthrough in a number of economic fields and many new concepts were being worked out in the field of trade, such as preferential or differential tariff regime for the developing countries; also trade expansion and economic co-operation among developing countries. Several new areas, which were completely outside the GATT regime, such as the shipping, the insurance and monetary and fiscal policy were being intensively studied and discussed within UNCTAD. Later, this work would shift to other specialized organizations such as the International Maritime Organization (IMO) and the IMF.

In all this work, I represented India in all committees of UNCTAD including those on commodities, manufactures, the shipping and several ad hoc committees. Delegations from Delhi included high level experts such as Dr Manmohan Singh or Dr Honavar on finance and Dr C. P. Srivastav for shipping. Likewise in GATT, where the work was carried out in working parties set up by the contracting parties on a variety of subjects, very often S. S.

Marathe, secretary Industries and Economic advisor to the commerce ministry came over. During my years in Geneva, a number of Socialist countries of Eastern Europe such as Hungary, Rumania, Poland, Czechoslovakia became members of the GATT, after intensive examination of their economy and tariff regimes. That helped me to learn a lot about economic and trading organizations in these countries. Also to make friends behind the iron curtain.

ೞΩ

Very soon after my coming over to Geneva, I had to represent India's case to secure acceptance to the Tripartite Agreement between Egypt, India and Yugoslavia. As described earlier, on the face of it, the Agreement violated GATT Rules. As I was deeply involved in laying down the principles and working out details of the Agreement, the three countries gave me the responsibility to seek GATT's waiver, that is a decision of contracting parties to permit deviation from the GATT rules. It took several rounds of discussions, negotiations, and diplomatic efforts to bring around major developed countries to support, on an experimental basis, what the three countries had done. United States remained opposed to the end and was finally isolated, but wisely agreed not to register a negative vote but instead to express strong reservations through a statement. KB had given me a free hand to deal this matter and I took full advantage to hone my negotiating skills and obtain GATT's waiver.

In November 1968. KB wrote, "Thanks are due to you for your untiring efforts in getting 'legal coverage' for the Tripartite Agreement." He also defined further work in his inimitable style by stating "On our part we propose to bend our energies to make the agreement work and yield dividends. On your part, please seek its expansion to embrace other parties or integration with some multilateral arrangement to be elaborated within the framework of the Trading Negotiating Committee (TNC)."

After all these years, it appears to me the Tripartite Agreement proved more a fight for a principle rather than an instrument for trade creation. Each of the three countries was at different stages of development and faced diverse internal and external obstacles. Also our political systems were widely different. What we shared, was the political will that guided relationship of the three countries for over two decades. It is strange but true that decades later, the Tripartite arrangement has provided a framework to its main opponent, namely United States to enter into several free trade arrangements (FTAs) with geographically distant countries in Latin America and Asia. The Tripartite waiver has provided a legal cover for these trading arrangements.

If I was to describe my one single achievement as a negotiator, it would be the Generalised System of Preferences (GSP). Right from UNCTAD-I, India had led a fight for developed countries offering preferential treatment to developing countries by a lowering their tariffs for import of goods from the latter. That was intended to offer comparative advantage to products of developing countries in developed country markets. The issues involved were complex. Firstly, different developed countries were at different degrees of industrial development. Their import structure and protective interest varied differently; also politically, it posed sensitive issues for their government as opening of markets would result into closure of domestic industry and result in wide-scale unemployment. Also, led by the United States of America, all these countries were strongly wedded to the most-favoured Nation (MFN) Rule of GATT and were philosophically opposed to any deviation from that principle. Thus, advocating GSP in favor of developing countries had to be discussed both at conceptual, as well as at practical ground level, to make it operational.

At the policy level, very reluctantly, the developed countries had agreed in UNCTAD-II in New Delhi to examine feasibility of GSP in a special committee. As anticipated by K. B. Lall, India had to assume the main responsibility with support of Brazil, Chile, Mexico, Egypt and Nigeria and a few other countries from Asia such as Pakistan, Indonesia and the Philippines. Most developing countries were either exporters of a single commodity or had hardly any interest in export of manufactures. Developed countries took advantage of this situation and tried their best to manipulate these countries by offering them arrangements for commodity access and to provide fair and equitable prices. India's main task was therefore to keep the Group of 77 solidly united in seeking differential treatment for manufactures.

I was fortunately placed in important role because in recognition of India's efforts in New Delhi, T. Swaminathan, ICS, India's Ambassador in Brussels and Permanent Representative to UNCTAD and GATT, was made chairman of the Special Committee on Preferences. That allowed me to function as a point- man to the Indian

Delegation. By then, I had established my own personal position within the diplomatic community and requisite trust amongst the delegations. At a crucial stage of these negotiations, I was chosen to chair the Group of 77 and to conduct these negotiations on behalf of the developing countries.

After several round and diplomatic maneuverings, a small Group of negotiators on behalf of the developing and the developed countries agreed on a scheme of preferences. My main task was to secure support of developing countries. I could fortunately obtain that after some emotional drama and strong reservation of several African countries, who did not expect to gain anything out of the Generalised System of Preferences. On my word to support their claim for access to market and fair price for commodities, they finally agreed to the GSP. One early morning at around 2 O'clock, the Committee of Preferences unanimously approved implementation of the Scheme. That was a memorable session over which Ambassador T. Swaminathan presided. In his own way, he had played an important role in making the negotiations smooth by taking position of a fair and neutral chairman, although India was in the forefront of the struggle on behalf of the developing world. As negotiations proceeded, I found that he was getting increasingly jealous of my popularity and appreciation that I was receiving from all quarters. He became somewhat petulant and reserved.

In the last Session of the Committee, where leaders of various Groups, as is customary, praised contribution of the Chairman and the Secretary General, for successful outcome, when it came to my turn, I said, "Leaders of all the Groups have already showered praise on Ambassador T. Swaminathan for guiding the work of the Committee. I would have liked to do so on this historic occasion. However he and I belong to a civil service in which, from young age we are taught not to indulge in praise of one's superior, at least not in public. I am, therefore, compelled not to say much on this occasion."

My words were unconscious reaction to certain attempts by T. Swaminathan to down-size my work. An acknowledged authority on industrial development in India and good reputation, he however suffered from a certain degree of inferiority complex. At times, he would be extremely affectionate and friendly, but he could never countenance a junior officer taking the limelight. This was experience of many who had worked with him. That was completely opposed to K.B. Lall's style of working, who thrust juniors in limelight and encouraged them to perform often much beyond their rank or ability. In the end, KB's style equipped more civil servants to work at policy levels to serve India; also, who would also remain personally loyal to him to the end. In that respect, I decided to follow KB.

Later I felt genuinely sorry that I had misjudged T. Swaminathan. He had every right to be conscious of his position as an Ambassador of India. He also enjoyed in international community great deal of respect, and above all, trust. By then, I had learnt that in any negotiations, trust was the most important quality that a negotiator must possess. Indians in general were known as clever and often regarded as untrustworthy. KB knew how to get along with every one and build negotiation positions, but his manners and convoluted way of negotiating, put the other party on alert. They were not sure whether they were being taken for a ride.

On the other hand, T. Swaminathan invoked trust. I observed that whenever T. Swaminathan (known as Swami) said anything, the Commissioners of the European Economic Community took that more seriously. I witnessed this at the end of the Kennedy Round. On the last day, in the last hours of concluding session, T. Swaminathan asked for an appointment to see the Chairman of the Commission. He agreed to give only three minutes because pressure of time was working and the clock was ticking away. Negotiations had to be completed by mid-night. I accompanied the Ambassador. As soon as we entered the room, without wasting any time on formal greeting, Swami said, "Mr. President, I have come here to convey India's disappointment on the outcome of the Kennedy Round, especially the role of the European Economic Community, which is our major trading partner. I am aware that at this moment, you cannot offer me any concessions across the table, but I am leaving a list of items on which we feel aggrieved." With these words, Swami and I walked out of the room.

Next day, before the final plenary session of the Contracting Parties, the President of the EEC gave a letter to the Ambassador stating that the Commission had taken a serious note of feelings expressed by him and had decided that although the Kennedy Round might have formally come to an end, the Community will continue discussions with India in Brussels, on points raised by the Indian Ambassador. This was an exceptional gesture and it was solely due to T. Swaminathan's credibility and trustworthiness. At that point, I decided to emulate his example rather than KB's so far as negotiating techniques are concerned.

At the end of 1968, trust that I had earned was expressed by T. Swaminathan in a letter that he wrote to the commerce secretary. While sending a Report of the 25th Session of the Contracting Parties to GATT, he wrote, "This (Report) has been prepared by Pradhan and has undergone only very minor verbal corrections... I wish to avail myself of this opportunity of telling you that Pradhan is shaping extremely well in his assignment. He is very active both in and outside the Conference Room, takes the initiative in negotiations and in drafting papers, has greatly increased and improved his already good negotiating abilities, and, what is especially important, has earned trust and confidence and respect for his technical competence universally." He was good enough to send a copy to me.

Chapter 31

All Purposes Task man

On becoming the chairman of the Group of 77, I was involved in all negotiations - whether I knew the subject or not. For example, on shipping, which is a highly specialized field, when our delegation would consist of highly competent experts, especially C. P. Srivastava, chairman of the Shipping Corporation of India (SCI), who would a few years later become the chief of the International Maritime Organization, London and occupy that post with distinction for many years. He would be knighted by the Queen for his services to shipping industry and also conferred Padma Vibhushan by the President of India. Rajawar from Shipping Corporation of India, (who later became Chairman of SCI) was a more frequent visitor. He and his colleagues would brief me on intricacies of international shipping and equip me to plead case of developing countries. I felt somewhat elated when experts from the British shipping industry would complement me on my knowledge. I alone knew that it was all borrowed one, just like a brief that an advocate holds for a client.

I can never forget one meeting of the Committee on Shipping. In the midst of the morning session, I got a telegram that my father had expired that morning. I kept it in my pocket and during lunch break went home and informed my wife. I had met my father a few months earlier in Poona and could sense that he was nearing the end. Nevertheless, the news was a shock. I was not in a position to travel as I did not have the money to buy a ticket on Air India. Over telephone I told my brothers to perform the last rites without waiting for me. In the afternoon, I went to the Palais and made a statement on behalf of India that was much applauded. Only after that session, I broke news to my colleagues on delegation. They were amazed that at that moment of sorrow I performed my duty.

Since childhood and later after joining IAS, it was dinned into us that: performance of one's Duty must come above everything else. That was Lord Krishna's advice to Arjun on the battle field. Perhaps, I had also become immune to sorrow, after I had witnessed the long illness and death of my mother suffering from cancer. In my subsequent life, I have been much misunderstood by friends and relations that I have hardly expressed grief at someone passing away. At an early age, I came to accept death as inevitable and not something to unduly grieve about - except in case of untimely or accidental one.

Next two years were occupied in continuing round of negotiations and attending meetings. There were three events that were significant and enabled me to earn a special place not only among the Group of 77 but with leaders of delegations from developed countries, including the United Kingdom and the United States.

All Purposes Task man

One of the most difficult issues being agitated in UNCTAD was the subject of Transfer of Technology by developed countries to developing countries. We in India were in the forefront of launching joint ventures and had a great deal of experience as to how developed countries mainly the United Kingdom, United States and the West. Germany, while forming joint ventures (J Vs) denied to us the most critical technology Likewise in countries such as Mexico and a number of Latin American countries where the United States had gone about establishing subsidiaries of its multi-nationals, there was no provision of transfer of technology. In that kind of situation, Group of 77 were pressing that the subject of transfer of technology should be intensively studied and discussed within a separate Committee to be established by the UNCTAD. All developed countries were united in opposing this move. Their basic theme was that these matters should be discussed in the new organization founded by the United Nations in Vienna, namely the United Nations Industrial Development Organization (UNIDO). Also transfer of technology was matter in which governments of developed countries had no say, since commercial agreements were negotiated by multi-national companies (MNC's)and other industries directly with industrial units in developing countries. Socialist countries of Western Europe took a stand that since their industrial collaboration arrangements were always worked out at government-to-government level, there was nothing to discuss in UNCTAD.

Developing countries were fortunate that at that point of time, there were two individuals within the UNCTAD Secretariat who had deeply studied the whole subject, both from conceptual as well as practical point of view. One was Mr. Malinowsky from Poland who was Director of a Division on Shipping and Invisibles. He was ably assisted by Surendra Patel from Ahmedabad who had joined the UNCTAD from the outset. We found in Surendra an economist of outstanding ability, highly motivated and who would prepare basic documentation and studies on transfer of technology. He was perhaps the first one who put together an economic model to establish in qualitative and quantitative terms 'brain drain' from developing countries to developed countries and set out a theory of reverse transfer of resources from the former to the latter. We could thus argue that this was a matter of trading, and as UNCTAD had been established to discuss trade matters of interest of developed countries, the transfer of technology ought to be dealt within UNCTAD so far as the trade related aspects were concerned.

In the 70s, after a number of hard and heated discussions, suddenly we sensed that there was a crack in the united front of the developed countries. Strangely, signal came from an Italian, named Ponti, who was relatively a junior officer in the Ministry of Industry in Rome. Italian industry was interested in forming JVs in India and identified a number of opportunities for industrial collaboration. Ponti indicated to me that his government was not opposed, and would support us in Geneva. I conveyed willingness to recommend my government to look into problems facing Italian industries in India.

One day after clearance from Rome in the Negotiating Group, he made a statement stating that perhaps there was a case for examining issues of transfer of technology within UNCTAD. That opened a flood-gate and very soon, we found that many smaller developed countries, especially, the Scandinavians openly supporting us. A Committee on Transfer of Technology was set up within UNCTAD to examine trade related issues on the transfer of intellectual properties.

Setting up of Trade Negotiating Committee (TNC) for expansion of trade among developing countries was a land mark. After the Tripartite, KB had given me the task of elaborating to promote trade expansion among developing countries. That was of true benefit to me. I got recognition as an expert and a few years later when UNIDO asked me to prepare a scheme for South-South co-operation. It was, however, the Generalized System of Preferences that launched me into the international civil service.

Another significant land- mark was work on Commodities. At that stage, India's trading interest in commodities was limited. Except for Tea and Jute we had no agriculture products to offer. Tea had a well developed auction system. Jute could only be sold to countries who had jute manufacturing industries, mainly UK and some EEC member states. Despite that, I had to take active part on behalf of African countries and some Asians such as Malyasia that was interested in Copper and Rubber.

This work brought me closer to several officials of the EEC's Commission. Relationships with the Commission's officials were always on a basis of reciprocity. If I sought their help, they would also expect my help in return in negotiations. Without compromising position of Group of 77, one had therefore to find a way of facilitating the task of the Commission's spokes persons, who, because of the complexity of seven nations that constituted the Community, faced tremendous pressures and pulls from the member states. It was also a fact that without their co-operation, we could not exert pressure on the United States who was implacably opposed to the scheme of Preferences.

In the Commodity field, the Commission's point-man was one Mr. Tran Van Thin, a Vietnamese by birth. In one such negotiation relating to commodities, a subject of vital interest to the EEC, I had an important role to play on behalf of the developing countries in building bridges with Tran. It was easy for me to do as India did not have any great problems in that field. My help was greatly appreciated by the Commission and on their behalf, Tran Van Thin sent a message to me that he repeated to KB in Delhi: "Pricing policy and trade liberalization. Your spirit of co-operation, acute political perception and mastery of problems of world trade will greatly assist international community reach definitive – not merely virtual – agreement on both these thorny problems at tenth UNCTAD board session, thereby providing people of good will on all sides compelling argument in favour of responsible, concrete and realistic approach to problems of development."

KB, in turn, as was in his style for encouraging young officers, wrote to me, complimenting me for break through in the Committee of Commodities at the international level and expressing satisfaction stated: You have now acquired a gratifying grip on problems of National and International policy. I would like to compliment you on this achievement.

What more could a young officer expect from his boss? I could repay by working harder and achieving more at the international level. Fortunately, I could do so.

When T. Swaminathan returned to India in 1970, he was succeeded by B. R. Patel, ICS in Brussel. BR was an altogether a different personality. At an early stage of his career, J. R. D. Tata had picked him to head the Air India. BR had proved himself as a doer and a no nonsense man. He had a sharp intellect and a phenomenal memory. He believed in calling a spade a spade. As a result, mentally he never adapted to the working of multilateral diplomacy, where there is no straight talk. He left me to work in my style and always came to my aid whenever I sought his assistance. He also encouraged me to work on my own.

B. R. Patel was easily the most popular and party going ambassador in Brussels and always threw large parties in Geneva in my spacious apartment. My wife and her mother, who was visiting us, was once shocked when BR walked in with a beautiful lady and introduced her as Princess of Sharma. She was the center piece of the party as she was wearing a see-through dress on top! Because of his Air India association, BR was a much sought after escort. He was generous to a fault and helpful. He was totally different type of civil servant who lived by his mores, did what he wanted openly. He was shrewd but could never appreciate 'diplomatic' way of saying one thing and meaning totally different. I had to take care of that and, schooled under KB, I could never aspire to work in the maharaja style as BR did. But I did learn that he was taken more seriously by the Americans and the British delegates who instinctively trusted him because they knew that he was sincere and well meaning. They perhaps never realized that with a mini-computer in his brain he was three steps ahead of others in his thinking.

At that point of time, having seen differing styles of K. B. Lall, T. Swaminathan and B. R. Patel all of ICS, I decided to emulate Swami's low key style with straightforward, sincerity of BR Several years later when I negotiated accords on Assam and Mizoram at political level, it was that that helped me to clinch these political deals.

Chapter 32

Into International Civil Service

By the beginning of 1972, I was about to complete five years in Geneva and planning to return to India. One day, Perez Guerrero, former Minister of Venezuela, who had succeeded Raul Prebisch as Secretary General of UNCTAD, called me over for a lunch and suggested my taking over a project to help developing countries to benefit from the Generalised System of Preferences (GSP). Since I was not only the negotiator for but also chairman of a Working Group that had worked out the Rules of Origin to administer this scheme, he felt that I was the right person to disseminate information and train officials of developing countries. I explained to him that I had already exceeded normal tenure of an officer on deputation abroad and the fact that I was reaching a stage where I ought to work in the State government so that I could become eligible for higher appointments in the Government of India. However, he persisted and his task was facilitated by a peculiar co - incidence.

Lalit Narain Mishra, a politcal heavy weight from Bihar who was very close to the Prime Minister Mrs Indira

Gandhi had succeeded Dinesh Singh in the Commerce Ministry. He was very fond of visiting Geneva where he had contacts with all kinds of people from trade and industry, Indians as well as foreigners. On each occasion, he would entertain Perez Guerrero at dinner and offer him a suit length of hand-woven khadi silk. In one year, Perez Guerrero had collected four pieces. Over that lunch, he mentioned that when next time the minister visited, he would like to host a dinner in the minister's honour. After the dinner, before Lalit Mishra had presented him another suit-length the Secretary General told him that unfortunately he could not make use, as it was very costly to get suits tailored in Geneva. The minister, who was genuinely fond of Perez Guerrero, asked what he could offer in place of a suit- length that he had brought at the dinner. Secretary General took him aside and requested to spare Pradhan's services for UNCTAD for at least three years. In a generous mood, the Minister gladly agreed and I found that my fate had been decided on trade -off against a piece of suit length of khadi- silk!

By that time having been associated with international organizations for about seven years, I knew that the level at which one joins the UN hierarchy was important. I was expected to head a team of international experts to handle a large-scale global project on behalf of UNCTAD for which finance would be made available by the United Nation's Development Programme (UNDP). Seniormost officials in UNCTAD occupied a grade known as D-II level, the highest for a career bureaucrat. I told Perez Guerrero that I could accept his offer, only if, I was offered a D-II level post. Perez Guerrero, being a shrewd diplomat, asked me to discuss the matter with Mr. Marshal, the head of the

Into International Civil Service

Personnel Department at UN headquarters and he made arrangements for me to visit New York. Marshall told me that United Nations wanted my services but he had a difficulty in offering me a D-II level post because I was too young for that, being 42 years old. On his assurance that UN would upgrade the post one year later, I agreed to his suggestion to join at D-I level. He kept his word.

An international team consisting of a Frenchman, a German, an Egyptian and an Argentinean, was formed, with me being designated as a Director of UNCTAD -UNDP- Global Project on GSP. It was the first large-scale project in the trade field with a budget of five million dollars, solely at my disposal. That led to considerable heart burning within UNCTAD. Strangely an Indian colleague, who was a Director at D- I level, tried his best to ensure that I do not get that post at that level nor full control over those funds. But my personal clout with SG of UNCTAD and very helpful role by his Special assistant, Vitteri, made sure that I was given full autonomy. Fortunately, within UNDP, which was funding the project, I had strong support. My well wisher was Dr I. G. Patel was then the chief of UNDP.

Our first task was to organize ourselves as a team before offering our services to developing countries. We undertook intensive study of the GSP and the Rules of Origin, an area in which developing countries required assistance. Briefly, these Rules are intended to define goods which should be regarded as really originating in a developing country. The most important criteria was that raw materials or semi-finished products imported in a developing country must undergo substantial transformation in a developing country, to be eligible for tariff preference when imported into a preference giving developed country. All these were highly technical matters and we had to take precautions to carefully analyze our own presentation so that we did not create any problem for exports of manufactured goods from developing countries, when imported into a preference-giving country.

A word about my colleagues on the Team. J. Brandenburg of Federal Republic of Germany was a senior official of the Ministry of Finance conversant with the Custom Regulations Rules and tariffs structure of the European Community. M. M. A. Monsalve of Argentina, had wide experience of undertaking consultancy work in the field of trade and had been seconded to the Project by the International Trade Center, Geneva. M. Nashat of the UAR had worked for several years in UNIDO and was expert on industrial- development. Jacques de Miramon of France, a brilliant economist who was working with the OECD, an inter-governmental organization based in Paris that specialized in analyzing economic and fiscal developments. Each member was selected carefully and the truly international GSP Project team was considered a highly specialized and talented one. My main task was to get them to work as a team and there were some real difficulties. Also to handle political management of project activities, because in UN there is nothing apolitical, and GSP Project was sensitive for most preference-giving developed countries. For GSP, it involved both sacrifice of customs revenue and possible political backlash from trade and business adversely affected by imports from developing countries.

Into International Civil Service

I can take some credit for welding these diverse individuals into a truly international efficient team. Along the work, we made sure that we behaved towards each other with respect and understanding. Also to take care of each other's family and their problems. Moreover, to ensure that our visits should not degenerate into all play and no work; also to ensure that these were all work and no play.

Our Project Work was such that it required constant moving about to different parts of the world; that also meant long absence from home in Geneva. That created several problems. During those five years, my children were mostly brought up by my wife. Bringing up three children with absentee father created its own problems but she handled them. Over years, she had built up her own network or friends in the Indian community as well as the British and Americans, as she took active part in the work of American Church Library, the hub for English speaking people in Geneva, to meet and also to borrow English language books, which were at that time hardly available in shops. Having been a librarian in the American International School in New Delhi, my wife was much sought after, and she gladly offered her services on honorary basis.

While we were organizing our work, one day Niaz Naik of Pakistan, who was then a Minister in Pakistan's Permanent Mission at Geneva, came over to see me. He said that his Government was very happy that an Indian, and moreover, Pradhan had taken over the Project. He desired that the Project should begin its advisory work by visit to Pakistan. This was sometime in the beginning of June 1972. The scars of December 1971 conflict between

India and Pakistan that led to the creation of Bangladesh were still raw. Mrs Indira Gandhi and Zulfiqar Ali Bhutto, prime ministers of India and Pakistan had met a few weeks earlier and entered into Simla Pact. I appreciated personal feelings of Niaz Naik with whom I had friendly and warm relations. I therefore told him that I could consider a visit, only if, an official invitation in writing was received from his Government. I did not expect to receive such letter. To my surprise, within a week, the Ambassador of Pakistan came over to see me with a letter of invitation. We decided to launch the Project activities by visiting Pakistan in the first week of September 1972.

As an extension to that visit, I planned a visit to New Delhi as well, for consultations with the Government of India. Also a visit to Bangkok to seek co-operation of the UN's Economic and Social Commission for Asia and Pacific (ESCAP), for organizing a seminar for its member countries.

Activities of the Project were organized with the help of the United Nation's Economic commissions of various Regions and other UN and non-governmental bodies, by arranging seminars, work -shops and discussions. During the five year period, the Project organized as many as a dozen such activities. Over the same period, the Project undertook Short- Term Advisory Missions to as many as fifty countries spread all over the Latin America, Africa and Asia and also prepared several hand-books for developing countries.

For me, it was truly an experience to cherish life-time. I never imagined that I would undertake such world-wide activity with the five million dollars at my disposal. Also, in the course missions, I met ministers, top officials, and industrialists in all the countries that I visited. I was personally known to many of them because of my involvement in the international trade field and more as Chairman of the Group of 77 in Geneva, while handling some landmark negotiations. It was also a great opportunity for me to learn economic, industrial and trade structure of these countries and appreciate special problems that existed in promoting trade and industrialization in developing countries. This was later of practical use to me to undertake work relating to promotion of Economic Co-operation among Developing Countries (ECDC) and South- South Co-operation in Trade and Industry.

Chapter 33

Memories of Places

Visit To Pakistan

Our Project undertook visit to a country only on invitation of government. These offered great opportunity for tourism as well. Whatever place we visited, the host government would arrange visits to tourist spots, some times even to distant places within the country.

During our first visit to Karachi, we were feted with the traditional hospitality. I found Karachi was almost an extension of Bombay. S. K. Kriplani, ICS from Sindh was Bombay state's first chief secretary after independence. In college, I had several friends who hailed from Karachi. Likewise, visit to Lahore was significant for different reasons.

My wife had been brought up in what is now the Punjab Province of Pakistan and for several years prior to the independence, her father worked there as Secretary of the Public Works Department. My wife left Lahore just a few days before the Independence Day and her parents on August 14, 1949. With riots raging all over, they left

Memories of Places

their fully furnished home with all their goods and effects and were driven from Lahore to Amritsar in a convoy led by a colleague of theirs, N. M. Bunch ICS, who himself drove his car from Lahore to Amritsar. He was their close friend, and my well wisher till his untimely death in 1955. His sons Mahesh, Girish and Mahindra – three brilliant brothers, joined the IAS.

There were several other friends of my wife who asked me to visit the official colony and the homes that their parents occupied when they suddenly left Lahore in August 1947. I was given a list of several addresses. Pakistani officials gave me an escort to visit these officer's colonies, adjoining the famous Lawrence Club. What surprised me was name of roads and lanes were the same as the time British left India. On couple of occasions, I stopped the car and stood outside at the gate of the house not being sure whether to take a photograph of the gate showing the number of the house and name of the occupant. To my surprise, on one occasion, the official staying in the house came out. When he learnt that my wife lived in their house as a girl, he not only invited me and showed the place around but asked me to take any number of photographs. The same thing happened at another house where C. N. Chandra ICS lived. I had promised his daughters that I would bring photograph of the house of which they cherished happy memories of their girlhood.

Affinity of people and affection in person-to-person relationship was in contrast to the state of hostility in which the two governments had developed their relationship after the Partition. This point came to me strongly at an official reception hosted by the Pakistan authorities at the Lawrence Club, where we met the then Mayor of Lahore. When he learnt that my wife had received her education in the local school and the high-school named Sir Ganga Ram High school, he publicly declared that he would like to host a dinner on behalf of the Lahore Municipal Corporation for Mr. Pradhan and the Project Team. Next night over 150 persons were invited to a dinner. Addressing them, the Mayor pointed out that the dinner was in honour of the son-in-law of Lahore city. Could there be a greater show of affinity?

Latin Ametica

For me, the most fascinating region was the Latin America. As a representative of India and Chairman of Group of 77, some time in the month of September 1970, I had an occasion to visit Lima (Peru) in connection with the preparations for the Ministerial level meeting of the Group of 77. A few months earlier a powerful military Junta had taken over. We stayed in a hotel in the center of the city. In the night, one could hear bombs exploding around the hotel and army chasing miscreants, who we learnt were people who opposed the rule. Lima, situated on the western board of the Atlantic, With Humboldt current passing along the coast, has a peculiar pleasant climate with even temperature all round the year with misty spray of water floating around in the atmosphere, especially in the night. Populated mainly by mixed descendents of original Aztecs and the Spanish Conquistadors, its ancient culture and civilization that is found in mountains rising high all along the Pacific coast is remarkable. Ruins at Macchu Picchu, a high mountain hideaway, is unbelievable testimony to highly developed Aztec civilization and of their past. Incidentally, mines in Peru produce the purest silver graded internationally as 99.9 percent.

As chairman of the Group of 77 in Geneva, I had an important role at the preparatory meeting for the Ministerial level meeting held in Lima. That was my last representational act. At that meeting. I was given a special position on the main rostrum and differentially consulted by ministers on issues to be raised at UNCTAD- III. That was the high water-mark for my work for Group of 77. At that meeting the Group of 77 adopted resolutions to form basis of negotiations at Santiago (Chile), where UNCTAD- III would meet a few months later in 1971.

We found that while Buenos Aires (Argentina) is the most European city in Latin America, mainly habited by people of Italian origin, on the other side of the Andes Santiago (Chile) is very much English. Lying over a stretch of over 2000 kms along the Pacific going all the way down to the South pole, Chile developed trade with British colonies to the east, across the Pacific. Much influenced by that, especially in Santiago, one gets a feel of England while strolling in shopping galleries in the city, as these are replicas of those in London. At the time of my first visit in 1971, Chile had a record of being most liberal country in Latin America with longest democratic rule. Later, it was to come under strong military dictatorship under General Pinochet.

I have many pleasant as well as unpleasant memories of Santiago. My second visit was immediately after joining the international service to attend UNCTAD- III. Indian Delegation led by the then Commerce Secretary, H. Lal,

ICS, and comprising of senior officers whom I knew well were staying in Hotel Carrera adjacent to the Presidential Palace La Moneda. I spent several pleasant evenings with the Indian delegation, including Dr. Manmohan Singh, N. K. Singh, Muchkund Dubey, and Romesh Bhandari. I still recollect one evening when the Indian delegates visited a night club. Show was as expected, but what was shocking was the behaviour of some seniormost officials. After imbibing generous quantity of alcohol, they started behaving in lewd manner. Manmohan Singh and I got disgusted and marched out along with N. K. Singh. At midnight, we walked to our hotels in silence. We found awkward to discuss what we witnessed. After that, our seniors would avoid looking into our eyes.

During that stay, I renewed my contacts with the officials of the Economic Commission for Latin America (ECLA). Also Dr. Raul Prebisch who entertained me to a lavish lunch in a Spanish restaurant named Forresta. We spent three hours recollecting our association in Geneva.

Santiago had another connection for me. Hugo Cubillos, who had been close advisor of late presdent Allende' came over to Geneva. One day, I accosted him in the Palais and found out that he was without a job and living on his savings and help from father, who had been Chile's Ambassador to Britain and settled down in Ecuador. In addition to Monsalve, GSP project did require another expert to work in Spanish. I talked to Perez Guerrero and offered a post at a relatively junior level. Hugo's joining UNCTAD /UNDP project was a puzzle to many because he was a persona non-grata to the Pinochet Government.

Visit to some of these countries also brought home what happens when there is an unbridled inflation such as the one that prevailed in 70's. Undertaking a mission to Buenos Aires, we had sent Marcos Monsalve in advance to make arrangements for our visit. That night, when we went out for dinner, Monsalve carried a brief case full of currency to settle our bill. We met with similar experience in Santiago where prices in the market were unbelievably low when converted into US dollars, a currency in which we were paid by the UN. I picked up a well-tailored three piece suit for less than ten dollars and several objects de art for a song, especially the Lalique glass. Most old families were selling antiques and family heirlooms to buy food. That was an unbelievable experience.

Visit to Bogotá, Colombia, was another unique experience. Deeply forested and rich in resources, tragically under several military dictatorships, its natural resources have been squandered. Colombia's mines are rich in gems and precious stones and its deep green emeralds are the best in the world. In 1972 when we visited, it was relatively a peaceful country, but a few years later, it was struck by insurgency. Smuggling of cocaine into Mexico and some other countries for processing into heroin posed such a threat that the US has waged war against drug mafia inside Colombia. Even today, people continue to suffer from lawless conditions.

Another fascinating visit was to Mexico where Julio Faesler, who in 1990's came over as the ambassador of Mexico in New Delhi, was the Head of the Department of Trade. He was a known colleague from Geneva and he gave us a memorable treat as host. But my memory of Mexico city is of another type. We were put up in an old elegant hotel named Hotel Geneve in the center of the Zona Rosa, a lively down town area. Since the weather was very pleasant, I kept the window of my room open at night. Next morning, I found that my lungs breath was smelling petroleum fumes. This is a common experience for most visitors. Mexico city is situated in a bowl surrounded by high hills, in which petroleum fumes from cars are trapped and in the night all these settle down in the center of the city. Only late afternoon, winds carry them out of the bowl.

Asian Countries

Visit to Asian countries was a different type of experience and for my western colleagues, a somewhat unsettling one. Our very first visit to Manila remains an unforgettable one. We were put up in a hotel facing the Pacific near the old Manila Hotel, which was the headquarters of General Mc Arthur during the Second World War. As soon as we checked in, we were given a letter from the UN Resident Representative warning us not to step out of the hotel after 7 p.m., as several gangs freely moved out and robbed foreign tourists. In the hotel itself, elaborate instructions were given as to how to look for strangers in the corridors of the and what precautions to take. One night, in the lobby of the hotel, there was an attempt on the life of the Mayor of Manila. Several foreign visitors were injured. Those were the unusual times for the Philippines. President Marcos ruthlessly dealt with these unruly elements and restored law and order.

Each country that we visited had its own problems, economic, political and social. At the same time, in the

70's, the prospects of international co-operation were encouraging. While developing countries were seeking access to markets of developed countries, that also provided an opportunity to the latter to seek concessions as a quid pro quo. As an answer to that, Dr. Raul Prebisch had propounded at UNCTAD–I that export earnings would serve as engine-of-growth for developing world provided the developed countries opened their markets, not on the basis of strict reciprocity, which was the rule of the GATT, but on basis of broad mutual benefit. In theory it was good model but without basic reform of political and economic structures that promote enterprise and investments it was not possible to reap benefits of opening up of markets.

That was very much evident when we visited several countries in a region and could look at each country, in the context of what was happening within that region. For example in Asia, Thailand, a monarchy ruled by the army could have benefited but Bangkok and much of the country had become a play field for the United State's soldiers fighting in Vietnam. The whole country was being used during the Vietnam war as a rest and recreation camp which brought in considerable easy money and pleasures. This also led to creation of great infrastructure for tourism for which Thailand is famous now. It also brought many social evils and health problems such as the AIDS.

After observing this, I once asked with Dr. Raul Prebisch, if the aim of such economic development was intended to bring prosperity to a developing country through exports, could not the same be achieved by promoting tourism instead through setting up unviable manufacturing capacities. His answer was straight and simple. Along with trade in goods, he was also advocating trade in service and trade in invisibles including tourism. That explanation helped us in our advising certain developing countries not to waste their resources merely to set up manufacturing produces for exports for which they had neither the natural resource base nor trained manpower, but instead to promote tourism. This was especially true for countries, which depended on production and export of a single agricultural commodity. As we were to experience in India, without a strong domestic market, it is not easy to set up production solely for exports.

We visited Bangladesh on three occasions between 1972 – 76. That newly formed country was a case study by itself. Having secured independence from Pakistan's autocratic rule, there was much eagerness to project Bangladesh as a sovereign nation with democratic policy framework for economic development. All international institutions, World Bank, IMF and UN were keen on helping that new born country. GSP Team was invited to visit Dacca mainly because several senior Pakistan officials who had represented in Geneva found themselves at the helm of government there. As representatives of Pakistan, they had actively participated in discussions on better access to markets and for GSP. Naturally, they wished to avail of the advantages available, but these officials lost sight of the fact that they now worked for that part of Pakistan whose industrial manufacturing industry was still at nascent stage. Till that time, industrial units were mostly located in West Pakistan and there was hardly any industry in East Pakistan. During our visits, after finding the situation obtaining on the ground, we explained that there was not much for Bangladesh in the GSP at that stage. Also their structural problems including depth of poverty was so intense that a project like this could hardly be of any relevance. Moreover, their traditional products such as jute, hand-woven handloom-products, handicrafts were already enjoying duty free access to developing markets.

On the other hand, a small city state such as Singapore was poised to greatly benefit from GSP because it had trained manpower and economic strength to set up new industries in technologically advanced areas. We could undertake very useful advisory missions to Singapore and often felt that we were learning more from Singapore bureaucrats, as compared to advice that we offered to them.

Sri Lanka was another story. I had a large number of friends from that country, which has always been active in the international forum. Their representatives, bright young diplomats, could easily work in the larger interest of the Group of 77, since as a small South Asian country, they could generate more trust among other Asian countries, compared to India and Pakistan. Sri Lanka took full advantage of that and in 70s, a large number of international organizations were headed by Sri Lankans. They adopted a good model of economic growth, a mix of industrialization in selected sectors along with development of infrastructure for tourism. The country had a very bright future but internal problems had retarded growth. The country however remains a democracy and has successfully battled insurgency.

There were some countries, which were keen to invite us and we had to respond although we knew that there was hardly anything that we could advise. As an illustration, I may mention Jamaica and Afghanistan. Georgetown is a pleasant place and we were put up in a very good hotel Pegasus. After a two days work and usual round of talk, we found that their main interest was in export of alcoholic products such as rum and some liquors. These did not benefit from GSP. Their main manufactured item was well-tailored exotically printed cotton shirts which were so much in demand in the United States, especially in seaside tourist resorts that duty concession was not required. In case of Afghanistan, except for hand-knotted wool (duty free) carpets and dry fruits, it had hardly any product to offer. In case of Jamaica, we could at last discuss promotion of tourism which had been badly affected because of the then prevailing law and order in Georgetown, where after dark it was not advisable to walk on the streets. In case of Afghanistan, we did not want to take risk of suggesting any item. We knew that there main exports were narcotic drugs and guns.

Visits to Developed Preference-giving Countries

As a counter-part of our Missions to developing countries, we had to be in close contact with officials in preference giving developed countries, to keep them informed. In that connection, as a Project Director, I had to visit London, Brussels, Washington and several other capitals. The United States and the European Economic Community, as then constituted, were main markets for products of developing countries. It was important for GSP Project to have good working relationship with the concerned authorities, who could help to resolve practical difficulties and who could advise their administrations for improving the preferential arrangement.

Memories of Places

I was fortunate in establishing close relationship with the US Trade Representatives Office who is the Principal Adviser to the President on all issues connected with international trade. I had got to know some officials during the Kennedy Round and some others during negotiations on the GSP. Although at that time, we had fought for our cause and on several occasions strongly criticized lack of political will, we were aware that we were working in representational capacities and as such, we were doing a job. During our meetings in Washington, they were not only polite but also constructive; having implemented their scheme of preferences, they were keen to ensure that developing countries took advantage of greater access to US market. For them, it was both good economics and perhaps much better politics. I got full support from the Department of Treasury when Mr. Bushnell, who was First Secretary in Geneva, had suddenly been catapulted to the office of Assistant Secretary in-charge of Latin American countries in Nixon's Administration.

Swedish International Development Agency (SIDA) and the Canadian International Development Agency (CIDA) supported the Project by financing certain activities. I had to visit Ottawa and ---- to explain our case. Finland, though a small country, made available services of their experts. For me, it was a pleasant experience to meet several colleagues in their country's capital and enjoy their sauna and nights with light, as if it was daytime. My brown skin served an attraction for young ladies and several times I was greeted on the road just to find out how one could acquire that shade.

As Project Director, I had to pay visits to the Socialist countries of Eastern Europe as well. These were intended to find out whether they could work out some preferential arrangements. As they had no tariffs, officials of these countries explained that they already accorded preferences through their purchase policies. The goods from developing countries were not only considered as preferred sources of supply but their public sector organizations gave a higher prices as well. Apparently, trade was connected with politics and these countries' linkages with developing and other countries were more politics than economics. Thus, while we could not achieve much in substance, there was great deal to be achieved by establishing good will and smooth relations with the officials in the capitals.

Visits to the Socialist block countries were enjoyable because there was not much by way of substantive work. Moscow, where we were lavishly entertained, one could notice that the officials who were in-charge of our visit and senior officials of ministries used the occasion to entertain themselves. They also had a different work culture. In most public sector organizations where we were taken first thing in the morning, we were offered brandy which was generously consumed by the officials and by lunch time, several officials were under strong influence of alcohol.

In Bucharest (Rumania) or Budapest (Hungary), although these were Soviet block countries, their working, drinking and eating habits were greatly influenced by Latin culture. Apparently, Danube waters had been greatly influenced life of people in these countries. They were more open, communicative and sophisticated. We were lavishly entertained and escorted to several tourist places. In

Hungary, it was interesting to hear several Sanskrit words and sounds. Rumania was different. It had preserved old world culture, dance and folk dance and music.

All this travel added considerably to my knowledge and also how different societies had developed, each with distinct traits. It was a unique experience.

In London, I was always welcomed at the Board of Trade, where I had several friends. Several had known many ICS officers of the RAJ era and respected an IAS.

In Geneva, I got to know a few from the Foreign Office as well. I can never forget one young officer, named Richard Abbot. Four generations of Abbots had served in India in the ICS, and as political officers, were probably heroes that Kippling described in the Kim, who governed lawless lands in the north-west. (Several exploits of Abbots are vividly described by British author Charles Allen in his book titled: SOLDIER SAHIBS ----- The Men Who Made the North-West Frontier). Unfortunately, I lost touch with the young Richard Abbot. Language and old imperial connection were useful bonds in multilateral arena; these were put to good use by the British diplomats. They knew the ICS and could spot young one's of IAS, whose friendship might be useful and profitable in future. I was always impressed with their hospitality at the most exclusive clubs in London, which one could see later on television in the "Yes Minister" serial.

During 1970's, Sir Eugene Melville, KCMG, was Ambassador for the United Kingdom of Great Britain & Northern Ireland. A die hard diplomat, he made sure that he was the focal point for most Commonwealth countries. Only India and Pakistan were out of the ambit of his influence. He treated me with special respect on learning that my previous posting was PS to Defence Minister of India. In the UK, an officer who worked as PS was regarded as one with bright future. There was another reason why the British respected Indians: mastery over their language. In UN, in all negotiations, deftness in using English that was important for drafting purposes and Indian representatives had built up formidable reputation.

India's economic diplomacy since independence was centered around Washington, London and later Moscow. In late 50's, Brussels started emerging on scene.

When I was launched into international trade field, Brussels was emerging as hub of economic activity. In 70's, the Community was still in formative stage and original member states, France, Federal Republic of Germany, Italy, three Benelux countries, Belgium, Netherlands and Luxembourg, were evolving into a tariff free area and were starting process of dismantling non-tariff barriers to trade amongst the member States. However, trade, economic and political significance of integration was already evident and the Americans were worried about emergence of a powerful trading block within Europe. They apprehended threat to their economic and political dominance over post-war Europe. UK was not sure where their interest lay. Many developing countries, members of the Commonwealth, had started charting their future, by loosening linkages with UK. India had bargained its 'Imperial Preferences'* in course of the Kennedy Round, and my personal contribution had been recognized. We had taken a conscious decision to change direction of our

* Special tariff rates

trade. UK, West Germany and USA were our trading partners, in that order. After those negotiations, we were aiming for the USA, the EEC and the UK in that order. Thus, role of Brussels had become crucial.

Chapter 34

Treasured Personalities

Geneva was a great place to meet colourful personalities and for that UN Palais was the venue to be in. Working long hours, and eating lunches, drinking at cocktails was a routine. Inevitably delegates got to know each other. Sometimes too intimately. I had my share of casual acquaintance growing into deep friendship. I still remember some.

One day I was taken aback when an Ethiopian accosted me and spoke in Marathi. He was Ghebre Chidan Alula, First Secretary in his country's mission. Alula had studied for over five years in the Ferguson College in Poona and fluently spoke my mother tongue. His country's interest in trade field was small, but since the headquarters of the Organization for African Unity (OAU) was at Addis Ababa he was required to participate in UNCTAD's work. I liked him immensely for his candidness and somewhat simpleton approach to complex issues.

Scandinavians were a class by themselves. They were in Europe but not in the EEC. As small countries, their clout was limited, but that also allowed them to play important role in all negotiations. They inspired trust and we could share our real difficulties with them. I had several friends in Denmark, Norway and Sweden. Magna Reed of Norway, who led the developed countries in GSP negotiations, and his wife became our close friends.

I cannot forget role that some Ambassadors from Africa played in shaping my career. Amb Benie Nioupin from Ivory coast was a highly cultured and good conversationalist; he was equally fluent in English. Amb Marc Nan-Ngema of Gabon was a colourful personality. Short, with a goatee and always smartly dressed in three piece suit, he reminded me of the French artist Henry Luterec of the Moulin Rouge fame. Another one was Armand Razafindrabe of Madagascar. All three represented small countries that did not have great stake in international trade, except for one or two commodities. But belonging to the Group of 77, I can never forget the role that these three played in concluding the GSP negotiations.

After Magna Reed, on behalf of developed countries and I, on behalf of Group of 77, had cleared the final draft of resolution, I was told that the African countries had decided to abstain. That implied that the EEC may go back on concessions offered by them in order to protect interests of these African countries. Also, it was a clever attempt to break unity of developing countries with the objective of weakening UNCTAD. As soon as I learnt of that, I asked for adjournment and requested the three ambassadors to get all representatives to meet in the hallway, outside the Plenary Assembly Hall.

In a few minutes, I was surrounded by fifty to sixty delegates, right in the middle of the magnificent passage of the Palais overlooking Lake Lehman. Some diplomats were angry and asked me: What is there in GSP for African countries? Why should they lend their support to a scheme that would benefit Asians and Latin Americans ?

I decided that at that last hour, it was past mid-night, there was no point in giving a reasoned reply. They were in no mood to be convinced. Instead, I addressed them through Amb Nan-Nguema of Gabon, as most delegates were French speaking. I offered them a bargain: in return for their support to GSP, the Asian group shall extend full support to issues relating to the Commodities. It was for them to accept or reject. Saying so, I walked out of that crowd. It was left to the three Ambassadors to argue and convince that it was a genuine offer. After thirty minutes – that seemed to be long wait - I was invited to join them. With tears flowing down his cheeks, ambassador of Gabon said: Mr Pradhan, we trust you and accept your word. Although Africa will not benefit from GSP, we have decided to support. I solemnly repeated my assurance. That's how the GSP was finally accepted in UNCTAD.

On my part, I kept my promise and became a friend of African countries. I have already described how with support of Tran van Thin, I secured a good deal and UNCTAD became main platform for negotiations on commodities. Later my successor in Geneva, Inderjit Chaddha, IFS, played a significant role in commodity agreements and was rewarded for that by offer of the post of the Director of Commodities, in UNCTAD. He held that post with great distinction.

Treasured Personalities

Over ten year stay in Geneva I made innumerable friends, in far off lands. I recollect many and their association. In multilateral diplomacy, where delegates have to work closely, one meets many individuals and their families, knowing all the time that we are all birds of passage. One is always welcoming or saying goodbyes and promising to meet sometime, somewhere. But that mostly remains a wish.

In my case, whenever I had occasion to visit Switzerland, I visited Geneva to meet Vinod Rege and his wife Shyamal who entertained me at their home for dinner and it was a pleasure to see their son and grandson. Vinod was with me in the Ministry of Commerce as a Research officer. Very bright and hardworking, he helped me learn about GATT. When I went to Cairo for the Tripartite, he accompanied me along with his newly wed bride. We were put up in the famous Shepherds hotel on the bank of Nile. With our punishing schedule Vinod did not find any time for his bride. I apologized to her for that. It was a matter of some pride for me that Vinod went up the ladder in GATT and retired as a Director. After retirement, he continues to work for the Commonwealth Secretariat in Geneva. Unfortunately, a couple of years back, his only son died in Goa of heart failure.

My research assistant in the ministry of commerce, Raju Makil, worked with me in the Mission as Second Secretary. He assisted in UNCTAD work. A bright Keralite, Raju worked his way up and eventually retired as Director General of the International Trade Center (ITC) Geneva, a post that has been upgraded to level of Assistant Secretary General. A high honour indeed. He and his English wife Mona are happily settled in a large villa near Coppet. I had known Mona as secretary of R. Krishnamurti, who worked as Director of Manufactures Division of UNCTAD.

Krishna was one of the old timers. He had worked in ESCAP, Bangkok, before Dr Raul Prebisch picked him to be his Personal Advisor on trade. Krishna and his wife, Meena were our close friends. Now, as old great grand parents, they live in Toronto, where their eldest son Raju lives. Their daughter Indira incidentally is married into a Pradhan family of Uttar Pradesh. We occasionally e-mail each other.

Amongst Indians, one couple that was unique was Madan and Collette Mathur. Madan was a Director in GATT when I first met him in Geneva in 1965. An officer of the Indian Revenue Service (IRS), Madan went up in GATT secretariat and reached post of the Deputy Director General. He was a pillar of strength to developing countries and enjoyed trust of all. He was a great friend and true international civil servant: frank, discrete, objective yet helping to find solution to complex problems of developing countries, from within an organization in which not many developing countries reposed much trust, by using his influence with developed countries. Collette proved a great source of strength to him. They had two handsome children, a boy and a girl. Collette carved a career for herself in the World Economic Forum, one of the most powerful platform to bring together world leaders, Presidents, Prime Ministers, leaders of industry etc. She was in charge of India and by now well known in India's industry and business circles.

Treasured Personalities

Our closest friends in Europe are Jacques and Helene de Miramon in Paris and Fernandez-Espinars in Madrid. In recent years, we have visited Madrid and Paris three times just to meet them. Edourdo and Maia-Teressa are warm Spainards and we spend hours at their residence, when in Madrid. Both Jacques and Edourdo are fond of India and have large collection on India. We exchange family news over internet from time to time.

One colleague and friend with whom I have lost contact is Said Harb. After retiring from the International Trade Center, he has gone back to Egypt. An exceptionally intelligent and sophisticated individual, his first wife was a real life heroin. Fatima, young and beautiful, was with Ben Bella, revolutionary leader of Algeria. He had adopted her as his daughter. After independence, she came over to Geneva. She and Said got married and were one of the most attractive couples in Geneva. Fatima and my wife became friends at our first meeting and she shared many a family matters with her. I recollect at one dinner when someone expressed doubt about her actual participation in Algeria's war with France, Fatima boldly lifted her skirt and showed deep marks of bullet injury on her upper thigh. While she was a socialite and unconventional, Said was an aristocratic Arab. She was flamboyant while he was low key individual. Their marriage was doomed and ended in divorce. Unfortunately, a few years later Fatima succumbed to cancer.

৪০৬৪

On shifting to Commerce Ministry and later during my posting in Geneva, I met a number of persons whom it would be difficult to forget. Some shaped my life and some gave abiding friendship.

Sharada Shankar Bajpai belonged to the ICS of the United Provinces Cadre in pre-independence India. He was brother of famous Sir Girija Shankar Bajpai, ICS, who became the first Secretary General of the Foreign Office. His son Katyani Shankar is my batch mate who had equally distinguished career in the Foreign Service Both father and son were erudite scholars and civil servants of high character and intelligence.

Girija Shankar's younger brother Sharada Shankar Bajpai was a different person altogether. Educated at the famous public school at Dulwich and the Balliol at Oxford, he was an elitist. After independence, he preferred to join the Indian Foreign Service and eventually retired as India's Ambassador in Rome.

He took in hand my training in food and wines, in which he was both a connoisseur and gourmet. Sharada Shankar belonged to era and style of living that is no longer found to be in India. My greatest fortune was the affection that he and his wife extended to me, my wife and to my children. Despite their very fastidious taste, they would welcome us, who belonged to a different strata of Indian society. Over years, we learnt from them grace, good living and much about the French food and wines. His tuition and later my study of wines helped me to be regarded as some kind of connoisseur.

Sharda also introduced me to someone who was a part of India's History at time of Parition. One evening he took me to visit Sir Raghavan Pillai ICS, who had been private secretary of the prime minister Nehru, head of the Foreign Office and a Cabinet Secretary as well.

We also owe to Sharada a friendship that we continued to cherish in Bombay. One day, he rang up to say that a couple, Adi and Minoo Dubhash would be visiting Geneva. They became our good friends and through we met several in Bombay; prominent amongst them were Jim and Shirin Chagla. Unfortunately, Shirin died early and my wife lost a dear friend.

Amongst other Indians that my wife and I came to know and whose good wishes we enjoyed throughout their lives, were D. S. Joshi and his wife; K. B. Lall and Indrani, T. Swaminathan and his wife and Dr. Nagendra Singh and his wife. All belonged to the ICS and were outstanding. Their wives were equally talented.

Geneva was the place where almost all top industrialists of India came from time to time. They had extensive connections in Europe and Geneva / Zurich were generally the meeting places. JRD Tata was a regular visitor and I was often invited by Nari Dastoor to join him at lunch.

Other regular visitors were B. M. Birla and his wife. I had known Brij Mohan Birla from my days with Chavan. Another Birla that we came to know were Ashok and Surekha. Young and vivacious. Ashok, who lived in the Birla House on the Malbar Hill in Bombay, was a different type of Birla. We mourned their death in the air-crash at Bangalore Airport.

In mid-seventies, a large number of Indian families who had migrated to UK and Europe from East Africa, came over to settle down in Geneva. We met Prakash Hinduja and later on return to India, I came to know brothers Srichand, Ganga Prasad and Ashok as well. They were different kind of entrepreneurs and financiers.

Fatima Ahmed and P. K. Banerjee's love affair is out of a story book. Purnendu Kumar Banerjee was an exceptional person. Highly educated in Calcutta, New York and Harvard, he was a polished diplomat. He represented the best of Bhadralok of Calcutta (now Kolakata). He was recruited to the Foreign Service early after the independence in 1948 and had served as the acting high commissioner to Canada, India's Permanent Mission to UN in New York and embassies in Tokyo and Peking. In Geneva, where PK came over somewhat reluctantly, at a party he met Fatima. Their attraction for each other blossomed into a love affair. We kept in touch with Fatima from time to time and it is always a pleasure for me to meet her in her apartment where she shared the twilight years of PK, who died a few years back. In many respects PK was an exceptional person. He was the grandson of Sir Asutosh Mookerjee, who was an scholar, a teacher, a lawyer, an educationist, a legislator, a Judge and finally Chief Justice of Calcutta High Court. PK represented some of his qualities.

Amongst my dear friends in Europe, were Babu Gouri and his wife Susheela. Gangadhar S. Gaouri was brought up in Belgaum, when it was part of Bombay state. He did his post-graduation and Ph.D. from the School of Economics of the Bombay University and did post-graduate work at Oxford University. When he was doing his Doctorate, he and I stayed in the same University hostel opposite Marine Lines Station in Bombay. We then knew each other slightly. He later joined the United Nations and went up the ladder to become a Director in the United Nations Industrial Development Organization (UNIDO) in Vienna. A brilliant economist, he was a popular figure and his wife Susheela added charm and grace. Her father was M.P. Patil, who was a minister in the erstwhile Bombay Government in 1950s. Susheela was always full of mirth, energy and one who really enjoyed in extending their hospitality to every Indian official who visited Vienna to attend UNIDO conferences.

Another Indian whose friendship and affection we enjoyed was M. F. Husain. Long before we left Delhi, we got interested in Indian art. By the time we came over to Geneva we had acquired a few paintings of Shanti Dave, Laxman Pai. On advice of Dhoomal gallery, we also acquired a couple of M. F. Hussain's canvasses and we helped some friends of ours to acquire Hussain canvasses, which we could not afford to buy. After I joined the UN and had some money to buy art, we got quite a few Husain canvasses from Kali Pundole of the Pundole Gallery in the Fort area. Kali introduced us to Husain. We became friends in Geneva and remained till his death in exile.

All that travel and interaction with several personalities with diverse interests added considerable spice to my life.

Chapter 35

Good-Bye to International Career

Early in 1976, I was approaching my five year tenure with the United Nations. I was 48 years old and I started thinking about my future. In ten years, time I would retire from the Service. During the previous two years, there had been some changes in my family life. My father had died and although all my brothers and sisters had got married and settled, I felt that I had aliened myself from the family. I had been away from them since I joined the services in 1952. From my career point of view, I had left the State Government November 1962 and if I was to make a career in the IAS, I had to go back to Maharashtra. In 1976, my wife and I started to discuss our future. Fortunately, for me, there was an option.

I had a good innings in the United Nations on the top of D-II level, which is the highest for a career bureaucrat. After that, at higher levels, the recruitment is mainly on political considerations. UNCTAD/UNDP wanted me to continue either as a Project Director or some other equivalent post in the United Nations. I had a career to look forward to in the IAS, provided I worked in my

Good-Bye to International Career

State Government and obtained good reports so that I could be considered eventually to become a secretary in the Government of India, highest level that Service office could aspire.

All this talk led to my wife and I thinking seriously about our children. Rajiv had done extremely well in the American International School in Geneva and deserved to go in for higher education in Oxford or Cambridge. Vivek was more versatile in sports, his friendships and extra activities; in his studies he was good but not in the same class as Rajiv. His one great asset was that having received education in French language and within the French system, he was proficient in language and was much admired for that. Sarita was seven years old and we had to plan her future. If we were to go back to India she could start her schooling there; otherwise, a few years later she would not fit in the Indian system. While we were still to make up our mind, we decided that Sarita should be given a break in India because if she grew up in Europe, she may have problems of adjustment in later life.

Fortunately, we had come to know Dr. Shoumi Das, the Head Master of the Lawrence School, Sanawar, situated at Kasuali on way to Simla. Thanks to Das's, she settled down and over years, made a number of friends who are now spread all over the globe. The net-work of Sanawar is indeed remarkable, whether in Delhi, Mumbai or New York. Over the years, Sanawar did good to Sarita. The schools motif is: Never Give in. She is representative of that.

Late in 1976, I told the Secretary General of UNCTAD and UN Administration of my intention to go back to

IAS. They were somewhat surprised because normally all, especially the Indians, at the end of their tenure, try to stick to their UN jobs rather than leaving. In my case, they wanted me to serve UN and offered some alternatives. One of them was the Director of the International Trade Center, (ITC), Geneva.

Victor Santapillai, who had been the Director of ITC from its inception, was due to retire. He wanted to go back to Sri Lanka in an important position at political level. He pressed me to accept his post. He had already informally got clearance from all concerned to my name. I was tempted and many friends, including Said Harb who had become a Deputy Director in ITC, pressed on me to accept the post.

My wife and I decided to stick to our decision to go back, for reasons that no one would ever appreciate. Having joined the IAS, early after independence, and having been brought up in the ethos of freedom-struggle, I belonged to a generation with the high sense of duty to the country. In my case, having joined the IAS, when no one expected me to be selected, I felt that I had an obligation to India. I was firm in my resolve to return and work in whatever capacity I was accommodated in the state government. The feeling was from my heart and it was not easy to describe. However, I was determined because of another altruistic consideration. After joining the service, we had been told that only 7-10 per cent could aspire to become secretaries in the Government of India, which is the highest level. Cabinet Secretary's post goes mostly by seniority and I knew that I had no possibility of occupying that post nor had I the possibility to become chief secretary to the State government, since there were several who were senior to me and by the time my turn came, I would have already reached the age of retirement. Nonetheless, strong motivation ultimately prevailed and with full support of my wife, I decided to leave Geneva and not fall prey to any temptation.

My leaving Geneva was of direct benefit to Dr. P. C. Alexander, IAS who had taken voluntary retirement after Mrs. Indira Gandhi's government had lost in the general elections in 1976. He was frustrated at the way he was treated by Morarji Desai who succeeded as PM and with his contacts within the UN, he found a post at a D-1 level in the ITC. When I declined the post, Victor Santapillai offered to Dr. P. C. Alexander who was perhaps more qualified having been Commerce secretary in the Government of India and worked over long periods in the field of commerce and industry. A few months later, that post was upgraded to the level of the Assistant Secretary General and my declining the post was a direct benefit to him.

I had no regrets because my decision was based on my personal considerations and I was well aware that with my records of service, I could aspire to go back to UN at political level one day. I did not know then that a door would be opened four year later for me to do so.

Having decided to leave Geneva, last four months of our stay was devoted to winding up our household. In nine years, we had accumulated considerable goods and effects. We decided to take only those items that we could use in India and distributed many to charities in Geneva. We gave over 700 books to the American Church Library. After handing over our stuff to movers, we shifted to a small apartment near the Palais which belonged to the Ambassador of Afghanistan. He used to come occasionally to Geneva and gladly offered on a small rental his furnished apartment for our use. My wife and I were thus free to bid farewell to innumerable friends and also visited some places in France and Italy. Before we left, we learnt that Mrs. Indira Gandhi had lost power.

For me, Morarji Desai taking over the post of Prime Minister was in a way good news. He was not the most popular leader nor one who hungered for popularity. He lived by certain principles and believed in following his own path. He had got fond of me since early in my career and I had kept relationship of the direct and honest talk with him that he greatly appreciated. I was happy for him that at a ripe age of 84, he had attained one ambition that he had nursed since 1963, i.e., to become the Prime Minister of India.

So far as Morarji Desai was concerned, he did not hide his ambition,; nor played any dirty games. The way he conducted himself on both the occasions made me a greater admirer of Desai.

Just about the time I decided to leave United Nations, I learnt that the Prime Minister Morarji Desai was to visit London to attend the Commonwealth Prime Ministers Conference. That was in the beginning of June 1977. I visited London in connection with some work with the British Government and sought an appointment with him, which was promptly given. I met Morarji Desai at the

Good-Bye to International Career

Indian High Commissioner's residence in the Kensington Palace Garden. Desai, as expected by me was happy that I had decided to return to India to work in the IAS. He was more happy that I was not going to ask him for a posting in Delhi but to go to my State, Maharasthra. He appreciated my confidence and wished me well. At the end, he told me in affectionate, but admonishing manner, "Ram, you have not met me all these years. Now that you are coming back, you must meet me when you visit Delhi. Do not forget."

After meeting Morarji Desai, I felt much better. After all, he was the Prime Minster of India and through relentless struggle, he had achieved his ambition after failing on two occasions to get the support of the Congress Parliamentary Party.

As the Air India flight took off, my wife and I were in wistful mood. Geneva, one of the most beautiful cities in the world had been our home for ten years. When we arrived, our children were young. Now Rajiv and Vivek were in their youth. Geneva would always remain in our psyche as a place where we brought up our family.

How Geneva's geography, history and enchanting beauty became a part of our life were thoughts that raced through my mind as we flew over Alps and headed towards Rome en route to Bombay to begin a new chapter in our life.

ଔଇଔଇ

PART V :

Back to the State

Chapter 36

Return of the Native

On return from deputation to the United Nations in March 1977, I was asked to report to the chief secretary of Maharashtra. I had been away from the State since November 1962. Several senior colleagues and my well-wishers had suggested that after my diplomatic and international career, I should be more useful to the Government of India in Delhi. I was, however, looking forward to re-building my career in the Indian Administrative Service and I knew that I had to return to my grassroots. Since my departure in 1967, India had changed and far-reaching changes had taken place in my own State.

Maharashtra State was born on May 1, 1962. I had left for Delhi on November 19, 1962 for an eventful career. During my absence for over fifteen years, as expected, there had been rapid industrialization all over the State due to forward-looking policy adopted by the State government. Surprisingly, Maharashtra had also made great strides in the agriculture field, thanks to the Green-Revolution. In Western Maharashtra, the sugar industry had developed far beyond one's expectation. In the Vidarbha region, cotton had flourished. This was all due to forward looking policies of chief minister Vasantrao Naik, an enlightened agriculturists, who had practical outlook. A well educated and soft spoken individual, he was universally liked by all sections of the society and especially by the bureaucracy. Naik had a way of getting the best out of individual officers. Administrators, engineers and agricultural experts worked with great enthusiasm that had led to prosperity of Maharashtra. State earned well deserved reputation for governance along with political stability. I therefore looked forward to return to serve the State. After my meeting with Morarjee Desai, the Prime Minister, in London in June 1977, I was convinced that I had taken right decision.

On reaching Bombay, I met B. B. Paymaster, ICS who was the chief secretary. I received a somewhat strange reception. Paymaster's first remark was, "Pradhan, I think you have been foolish in leaving lucrative assignment with the UN and returning to India." I was little taken aback. He knew me since 1956 when I was Additional Collector of Poona and he was the Director of Local Authorities. (Having abolished the post of divisional commissioners, the government had created these posts for officers of equivalent seniority.) I had gone with the expectation that Paymaster would welcome my return and discuss my preference for posting with the State Government.

I did not feel it worthwhile to explain why I had decided to return to India. I replied, "Now that I have taken a foolish decision, I would like to know where the Government would like me to work." In reply to his enquiry, I told him that my preference would be to go to districts as a Divisional Commissioner. May be, Nagpur or Pune. Certainly not Bombay as I wished to get myself familiarized with changes that had taken place at the rural grassroots.

The chief secretary asked me to meet the chief minister and accordingly, I got in touch with B. K. Chougule, chief minister's secretary and went to see Vasantdada Patil. I felt nostalgic while going up to the sixth floor and walking down the corridor, where fifteen years ago, as a young officer, I had wielded power and authority. The chief minister' chamber was the same and I felt at home when I was greeted warmly by two Jemadars (head peons): Mehmood and Vithal, who had worked with Y. B. Chavan.

Vasantdada Patil invited me to join him in a private room adjoining his formal office. He was warm and friendly. I had known him since the days I was the collector of Kolhapur in 1950s and he was emerging as a political leader in the adjoining Sangli district. He was a well-known freedom fighter who had received gun-shot injury in his thigh while escaping from the police dragnet. He was a real hero of a revolutionary group who had set up a parallel government in Satara district during 1942 freedom movement. By 1976, he wielded much clout in Maharashtra and on Mrs. Indira Gandhi losing the Prime Ministership, Vasantdada had maneuvered to get Shankarrao B. Chavan, the chief minister removed and get himself installed.

After some polite talk about me and my family, I told him about my talk with the chief secretary, especially my desire to work as a Divisional Commissioner. Vasantdada had some other ideas about me. He wanted me to be the Home secretary in the state government. I was taken aback, as becoming head of the law and order department was far from my mind. I explained my predicament and pleaded to send me out of Bombay to any post. The chief minister was firm. He said, "I have taken a final decision and you should join at the earliest." In order to assuage any hurt feelings, he added I have talked to Yashwantrao ji (Y. B. Chavan, who was then Leader of the Congress Party in the Lok Sabha) and he agrees that at the present times Pradhan should be the Home secretary.

As a last resort, I told Vasantdada Patil that I had seen the working of the Home Department in the State and at the Center and I was firmly of the view that no officer can function as home secretary unless he has total confidence of the home minister. Also, both of them must share common thinking on handling of law and order matters. Dada agreed to that and said, "Sharad is our man. He is close to Yashwantrao Chavan and you will have no difficulty in working with that young man. He is in Poona, and I shall ask him to see you tomorrow morning in Bombay. Only if you are satisfied that you can work with him, you should accept the position that I have offered." That afternoon, I got a message that Sharad Pawar will be meeting me next morning at his residence in Ramalaya.

As background to interview, I got some information about Sharad Pawar. I had not even heard his name. Vasantrao Naik former chief minister told me that Sharad Pawar, a young educated man hailed from a good agricultural family of Baramati in Poona district. In fact, he had inducted him into politics and in the Cabinet in 1967. He was mature for his age and would prove worthy of traditions laid down by Y. B. Chavan.

Next morning, I met Pawar. He had traveled by car late in the night just to meet me. I found him polite, cool-headed and suave. When I told him about my talk with the chief minister, he said, "You do not know me but we know a great deal about you. I am looking forward to our working together."

Then he told about his own induction in Maharashtra politics by Y. B. Chavan, his education at the Brihan Maharashtra College of Commerce in Pune, of his family in Baramati, especially his political lineage of belonging to the Peasants and Workers Party, and he being inducted in the cabinet as the youngest minister. He told me plainly that since I was out of India during the Emergency, I was one of the very few officers who could look into many complaints of excesses by the police and objectively advice on action. Many officers, who could be considered for home secretary's post, were involved in some sordid deeds or other that had taken place even in enlightened State like the Maharshtra. I was impressed with Pawar's earnestness and the soft and low pitch in which he talked to me. Before taking leave, I said, "If I have to work as home secretary, I want to be assured that I shall get your unstinted support and trust because on several occasions, the home secretary must function without seeking instructions or advice of the home minister." Pawar assured me that he appreciated what I had stated and he was convinced that we can work cordially as a team.

From Ramalaya, I drove to the chief minister's residence Varsha and told Vasantdada Patil that I was ready to accept the position. Very next day, I assumed charge and got myself involved into an area of work which was far different to the one in which I was immersed in the past twelve years. For the next three years that I worked, Sharad Pawar was as good as his word and there was no occasion on which we had any disagreement. Credit for that must be given to his administrative ability and strong common sense. What he wanted to get done, he got done, in a subtle way without my knowledge. Any way, those were not the matters on which the home secretary need to waste any time.

A home secretary's life is governed on day-to-day basis, mainly on what had happened in the previous twenty-four hours, what was expected to happen on that day, or may be in the next twenty four hours. In this respect, I soon found that Sharad Pawar's antenna were very powerful. Those were not the days when telecommunications worked - if at all. There was no television, no telecommunications except antiquated telephone equipment that connected the State headquarter with district officers on telephone and divisional headquarters by tele-printer. Police at headquarters in Bombay and in districts found it expedient to send information by courier. But even in that situation, Sharad Pawar had built up his own networking and he would inform and alert me about possible law and order matters. That led to foundation of our relationship.

In 1976, Maharashtra could boast of a sound police administration. E. S. Modak, Indian Police (IP) was the Inspector General of Police (IGP). In Mumbai, V. V.

Choubal, IPS was the Commissioner of Police who joined the police in the first batch after the independence and worked for several years with the Intelligence Bureau in the Government of India. Mature and intellectual, I found him greatly different to the IGP Modak, an old timer from the last batch of the Indian Police Officers of the Raj, and a strict disciplinarian. He ruled by letter of law and regulations. That was understandable because that was how the officers were expected to carry out their duties.

Twenty years after Independence, many things had changed. People had become conscious of their rights and governance had gone into the hands of politicians. especially in dealing with the police administration. The Emergency had played havoc and the police had been used blatantly by the Congress Party government for carrying out dictates of Sanjay Gandhi. Soon after taking over, I learnt with shock how even in Maharashtra, the law and order machinery had been utilized to enforce programmes dictated from Delhi. Government of India had set up a Commission of Enquiry under Justice J. C. Shah, a retired judge, to investigate excesses committed during the Emergency. Commission officials had made list of several cases of illegal detention, of irregular action by police and enforcement of family planning programme by the district and lower level officials. They asked the states for information and I was required to review those cases and decide in consultation with the Commission's officers whether these were worthy of Justice Shah's attention. I soon found that information was being leaked by officers who had suffered and bent on revenge. In order to keep morale of officers I had to work as a devil's advocate. Only then I realised why I had been appointed to the post. I could be objective since I had been out of the State during Emergency.

My task was also to review several cases of detention under the Maintenance of Internal Security Act (MISA). Under that legislation several political leaders, social activists, as well as criminals had been sent to jail, without recourse to normal judicial process of being produced before a magistrate on arrest. High level officers from Delhi were monitoring progress of action by state governments and I spent much time in carrying out those reviews. Fortunately, most of the political persons detained under MISA had already been released.

However, so far as smuggling was concerned, I learnt how money power had got stranglehold on Indian economy. Most of smuggling related to gold via United Arab countries and several traders in Bombay acted as conduit for selling and distributing smuggled goods. Several well-known jewelers in Bombay were consumers of smuggled gold. This kept me busy for passing detention orders on persons apprehended by the Central Excise and Customs. A great deal of time and energy was spent as my orders were subject to review by the Advisory Board presided over by a retired High Court Judge. This work helped me to learn quickly how far the underground and criminal activities had spread widely in Bombay and other urban centers of the State. This also brought home as to how weak was antiquated police machinery and methods to deal effectively with these and other sophisticated crime. That helped me to launch a program for modernization of Maharashtra police.

In fact, the Ministry of Home Affairs at the center had not only prepared plans but got funds sanctioned from the Planning Commission to help the states. The only condition was that the state government must make matching contribution. In this respect, Maharashtra was found wanting not because it had no funds but because it did not want to ask any grants from the central government. As a financially well-administered State both at political and administrative level, government had worked so far without expecting any assistance from the central government. I found that old time administrators did not want to be accountable to the officers in Delhi. As a result, the State was deprived of many centrally assisted projects.

I became aware about modernization schemes only when Joint Secretary of Home Affairs (MHA), J. C. Somiah, IAS visited to brief me about the central schemes. With the help of some bright officers in my department and some enthusiastic police officers, we worked on a scheme to cover the whole state with VHF wireless. Also setting up of a Police Housing Corporation to build residential quarters for police constables. Later we prepared schemes for modernization of police stations, police equipment ,including forensic laboratories. In case of Bombay city, several new police stations were set, taking into account shifting of population density from south to north Bombay and provisions of setting up training centers for additional manpower. Modak, Choubal and all senior officials enthusiastically helped in implementation of the scheme. At political level, Sharad Pawar ensured necessary clearances from the Finance.

For me, modernization of police did not merely mean equipping them with modern and scientific tools. I found that Maharashtra from time to time had gone through communal tensions which at certain places such as Bhiwandi, Jalgaon, Malegaon and Akola erupted in communal riots. These were manifestations of underlying communal disharmony and intolerance. I felt it worthwhile to get objective study prepared by scholars to identify issues and situations that led to communal riots. On consultations in Delhi, I found that the Center for Research and Development headed by Raschpal Malhotra in Chandigarh had carried out similar studies for the Ministry of Home Affairs. I invited him to undertake studies in Bombay and some other selected places. Those provided valuable input in understanding problems of minority community and why trifling matters led to serious rioting. For example, playing of musical instruments on a street facing a mosque, meat pieces thrown in front of Hindu temples, a muslim boy eloping with Hindu girl in love with each other or a trifle matter such as persons chewing betel nut leaf spitting on a wall lead to stabbing incidents. Basically, over years after partition, both Hindu and Muslim communities had ceased to hold dialogue and communicate. Muslim community in particular had gone into a shell and in most cities lived in ghetto, like areas. What was needed was establishing forums where leaders of both the communities could meet from time to time, exchange information on matters that may lead to tension and, in case of eruption of violence, quickly act to quell the same with the help of the police. I think over a period, with enlightened leadership, particularly in the city of Bombay, much more cordiality was brought about by setting up of Mohalla committees. My colleagues Julio Rebeiro and Satish Sahaney have rendered great service in keeping these committees working even today.

The basic problem was economic. As a rule, Muslims were denied posts in the government and especially the police force. At that time, there was no policy of reservation except for the Constitutional provision for scheduled castes and scheduled tribes. Except for expression of goodwill and appeal to maintain harmony, not much was done at the political level. Perhaps, as a consequence, many young from the Muslim community engaged in smuggling of goods and worked as hawkers for selling those goods. They were easy prey to mafia led by Haji Mastan, Yusuf Patel and Karim Lala, who controlled smuggling. Haji Mastan controlled all smuggling within the Bombay docks and no one would come forward to depose. Several of his minions were detained by me but there was hardly any evidence to book the top man. All these mafia dons had been detained during Emergency and unless fresh evidence since after their release was collected, nothing could be done legally. Later, over a period, they succeeded in establishing linkages with politicians in power and Haji Mastan even floated a political party. He got close to chief minister and started visiting Varsha openly. On that score, later when I became chief secretary of Maharashtra, I had serious confrontations with the chief minister Vasantdada Patil.

Chapter 37

Between Two Power Centers
- Congress(O) and Congress (Indira)

While I was working out my own way to improve the law and order machinery, two political events shook the State. There was a split within the Congress (O) at the Central level and the Organization was split into pro-Indira Gandhi and others. Y. B. Chavan, who was the Leader of the Official Congress in the Lok Sabha, opted for the faction named Congress (O). Other faction was named as Congress (Indira), later abbreviated to Congress (I).

This led to split at all levels in Maharashtra. Vasantdada and Sharad Pawar opted to remain with Congress (O). Some leaders mainly from Vidarbha, such as Vasant Sathe and Nasikrao Tirpude, considered as loyalists of Indira Gandhi, opted for Congress (I). Some leaders who were ambivalent decided to float their own political set up, such as the one formed by Shankarrao B. Chavan, former chief minister during the Emergency.

As a result, the Congress ministry in Maharashtra was re-constituted as a coalition of Congress (O) and Congress (I). As expected, Nasikrao Tirpude who belonged to the scheduled caste, and who was a strong advocate of

Vidarbha Region as a separate state, insisted on becoming Home Minister and also to be designated as Deputy chief minister. It was for the first time that such a post, which has no constitutional sanction, was created in Maharashtra.

Nasikrao Tirpude, a small stature dark skin individual was a powerful orator. As a Home minister, he decided to ride roughshod over the police administration. With patronage, threats, and help from some police officers, he divided the State police into factions. As Home secretary, my job became much more difficult because I had to work closely with him and also be totally loyal to the chief minister. Since everyone was aware about my relationship to Y. B. Chavan and Vasantdada's total trust in me, Tirpude was cautions and was polite and socially affable. As bullies normally do, he would often humour me. On day-to-day working, I had to take decisions and also implement minister's directions ensuring that I was not doing anything irregular and also to keep the chief minister informed of important matters concerning the Home department. On occasions, I had to confront Tirpude. He was careful in not pushing me beyond a point because he was aware that I knew some unsavory aspects of his life when he was a young deputy minister in Y. B. Chavan's Ministry in 1960s.

Sharad Pawar, former Home minister, had become minister for Industry. In his own way and through his network, he kept himself informed of Tirpude's activities. He was also carefully watching Vasantdada Patil's changing attitude. Dada as a Maratha strong man would not brook any slight. A proud man, though gentle in behavior, he took quick offence. Tirpude made it a point of talking in offensive way and working with a view to provoke him. Perhaps, he expected Dada to quit the chief ministership, as he had an ambition to become the chief minister of the State.

Very soon, this led to open confrontation when Tirpude insisted on holding a mini-cabinet meeting of the Congress (I) ministers prior to the formal meeting of the State cabinet. Thereafter, instead of individuals expressing fairly and frankly their views on agenda, Tirpude made it a practice of voicing the view of Congress (I) as a group. This was a subtle way of confronting the Congress (O) ministers, and especially the chief minister. As cabinet takes decisions by consensus, under the principle of joint responsibility, no cabinet minister is expected to express publicly a contrary view, once a decision was taken. Nasikrao Tirpude's functioning was contrary to that, as he made it a point to announce to the press the views of the Congress (I) ministers.

I used to attend all the cabinet meetings along with the chief secretary and soon discerned Vasantdada getting impatient to the erosion of his authority. Other ministers used to be discreet and not confront Tirpude. With the help of police and other officials within the administration, he prepared 'files' on some of the senior ministers. All this vitiated cordiality and decision-making by discussion and compromises within the Cabinet.

As Home secretary, I had privilege of handling transfer and posting of Indian Police Service (IPS) officers. At the outset, I had devised a system under which the IGP of the State would propose and the Home department carefully examine the same. I would then meet the chief secretary and discuss the proposals before seeking the chief minister's approval. Vasantdada Patil normally approved or suggested in discussion some modifications. Thus all postings of IPS officers were finalised between the home secretary and the chief minister. In the process, the home minister was not normally involved although on occasions I would share my thinking with him and also accept his suggestions in some cases.

One day in June 1978, I went to see Sharad Pawar, Industry minister, in connection with police protection sought by certain industries for taking out finished products from factories despite objection by the labour. At that time, there was strong labour unions led by Datta Samant and others who were taking advantage of the post-Emergency pro-labor policy of the central government. They were disrupting industrial production and holding industrialists to ransom by stopping movement of the finished products out of the factory premises unless their demands were fulfilled. As a policy, we used to give police protection for exports goods, as it was a national obligation.

After a few minutes discussion, just as I was about to leave, Pawar said, "I understand that you have finalised postings of certain senior police officers at the deputy inspector level. I would advise you to wait for 7 - 8 days before issuing formal orders."

This remark was out of context and it bothered me. I called over the deputy commissioner of police in Bombay dealing with the Intelligence and asked him if something was happening at the political level in Maharashtra. In my mind, there was some connection between Nasikrao Tirpude's behavior, chief minister's frustration and Sharad

Pawar's remarks. Deputy commissioner (Intelligence) mentioned that he sensed that something was afoot but he did not have any specific information.

Next day during a meeting with the chief minister, I tried to find out whether he was aware of any political development. Without specifically mentioning the remark of Sharad Pawar, I asked whether the CM had heard anything about Pawar's meetings with several non-Congress politicians. Dada told me brashly, "Sharad Pawar is our man, do not bother about his activities."

Those words haunted me when within a week, Sharad Pawar had carried out a coup, dislodged both Vasantdada Patil and Nasikrao Tirpude and formed a ministry with support from all other political parties, including Jan Sangh, the Praja Socialist Party, Peasants & Workers Party, S. B. Chavan's Party, the Communists and several independents. Anticipating the loss of majority support within the party, Vasantdada Patil resigned. Sharad Pawar promptly put in his claim to the post of chief minister and met the Governor with the list of MLAs from various parties supporting him. Vasantdada was deeply hurt that a young Maratha whom he was grooming to take over his mantle had stabbed him in the back. Y. B. Chavan whom I spoke soon after the event, was equally taken by surprise. Much later, soon after the death of Y. B. Chavan, Sharad Pawar started telling audiences in Maharashtrra that what he did was with the knowledge and tacit approval of Y. B. Chavan. This, I honestly believe was untrue. Tirpude was deeply upset at the turn of event and his losing the post of the deputy chief minister so suddenly. Sharad Pawar had carried out 'operation toppling' with such speed and such finesse that even the home minister could not sense of the conspiracy that toppled the government. When I met him just before he demitted office, Tirpude bitterly complained about the police intelligence services and assured me that very soon on return of Smt. Indira Gandhi to power at the center, he would come back as the chief minister of Maharashtra.

Tirpude profusely praised my services at that difficult period and wished me well. We remained on cordial terms and whenever I visited Nagpur, I made it a point to meet him. He realised that he was gradually becoming unwanted colleague even within the Congress (I). He resorted, from time to time to raise the bogey of separate Vidarbha State to attract attention. Because of his behavior and style of functioning, Tirpurde had made himself irrelevant in the Maharashtra politics. As a bright scheduled caste person and oratorical skill, he could have been effective in the state politics for a much longer period, had he functioned with restraint and built up his own stature within the Congress (I).

In the politics of reservation, that was to dawn in 1989, I have no doubt that Tirpurde could have emerged a powerful Dalit leader. At the end, he remained isolated even within the Dalit politics and remained as certain nuisance value within the Congress (I). With Sharad Pawar's coup, a new era in Maharashtra politics had dawned. The monolithic hold of the Congress in Maharashtra had broken and a new power game and politics of opportunism was born; that is continuing for past thirty years.

ఐఇఐఇ

Chapter 38

Renaming of a University
- Atrocities on Dalits

Just couple of days prior to Sharad Pawar's coup, a motion had been moved in the Maharashtra Legislative Assembly to re-name Marathwada University as Dr. Babasaheb Ambedkar Marathwada University. Vasantdada Patil and most of the Maratha leadership within and outside the Congress was opposed to such re-naming. But with the new alignment of political forces that was taking place at that time, no one dared to openly oppose the passing of the resolution, which was passed by the Legislative Assembly unanimously. Those who were opposed expected the resolution will remain on paper and nothing would be done to rename the University. However, no one anticipated violent reaction that would take place in the Marathwada region and especially in Aurangabad city.

I got some reports from the State intelligence machinery that trouble was brewing and a serious law and order situation might arise. Thus, at the time, Sharad Pawar was engaged in forming his coalition ministry, there was no effective governance to take control of the situation at the political level. I decided to visit Aurangabad along

Renaming of a University

with V. V. Choubal who had succeeded Modak as the Inspector General of Police for the State. We flew by the State Government plane and on reaching Aurangabad, we reviewed the situation with local officials including the Commissioner of the Revenue Division, the Deputy Inspector General of Police, the District Magistrate and Superintendent of Police.

We learnt that several Dalit houses were being set on fire and some persons had been killed. Marathas had considered renaming as a insult to their community. For them renaming of the University set up specially for the Marathwada region and attaching the name of a scheduled caste leader was insult to Maratha sense of pride and Maratha leaders were determined to get the Assembly resolution rescinded. While in Aurangabad, we learnt that serious arson and looting incidents had taken place in Nanded. While Choubal and myself were planning to fly to Nanded to review the situation there, we got information that Sharad Pawar and his ministers were likely to be sworn-in in a couple of hours time. As protocol required the IGP's presence on the occasion, we flew back to attend the Swearing-in ceremony, just in time.

Sharad Pawar, the new chief minister decided to convene a meeting of the Cabinet soon after the ceremony. In the meantime, I had orally briefed him and alerted about the seriously developing law and order situation in Aurangabad and Nanded, which was likely to spread in the adjoining areas.

All ministers were present although no portfolios had been allotted. I took Choubal to the cabinet meeting. For us, time was running out. Already we had received reports of some incidents of lynching and houses being set on fire. I quickly briefed of ground situation and expressed certainty of rioting spreading to other cities and towns. Ministers were aghast to be greeted with that news minutes after getting sworn-in. After all, they had celebrated a few days earlier the unanimous passing of the resolution in both houses of the Legislature to rename the Marathwada university. Instead of getting kudos, they were finding the majority community in that region opposing the renaming. As politicians, they did not know what to do. They asked my advice.

After a word with IGP Choubal, I asked for authority to deal with iron hand. I told that in a civilized society, one can not allow citizens to be lynched. Nor Police stations to be put to torch, as learnt by us, while we were in the cabinet meeting. Maharashtra's reputation as a well administered state was at stake. I also asked if any ministers were ready to visit Aurangabad and appeal to people. None was willing as the majority community was on offensive.

After half an hour, Sharad Pawar, the chief minister said that the situation should be brought under control by the police and civil administration with all means. No politician should interfere. With that assurance, police started acting ruthlessly and many areas, instead of dalits, police became object of wrath.

Riots over the issue were great shame to Maharashtra. For over a fortnight, rioting spread from Aurangabad to Nanded, Parbhani, Osmanabad and Beed districts. Maximum number of violent incidents were in Nanded area. Assault on neo-Buddhist and burning of houses was rampant. But the most inhuman was the burning of individuals. I was working almost round the clock and when a gruesome incident was reported, I would walk into the chief minister's office to brief him. As soon as he saw me entering, he knew that I was the harbinger of a bad news.

Sharad Pawar kept his cool. He also kept his word, not to interfere. In fact on couple of occasions when I asked him whether he would like to visit the riot affected area, he declined. In fact on that issue, no politician was ready to risk making any statement or help us. When I approached Y. B. Chavan to visit, he advised me not to allow any politician to enter that zone, as instead of cooling down tempers they might say something that would add fuel to fore.

After that, I tried to find out whether some respected social worker or religious leader will help us. We approached Sant Tukdoji Maharaj of Vidharbha region. He declined. We could not find a single person who could appeal and lower down tempers of Marathas.

I must record that the police authorities, assisted by efficient armed State Reserve Police (SRPF) acted with alacrity and brought rioting under control. Over the three week period, the leaders were either tired or found it futile to fight on the streets over an issue that had been triggered by their representatives in the State Assembly. The fight had to be taken there. It was long and bitter fight.

It would take over fifteen years to implement the Resolution to rename the university as the Baba Saheb

Ambedkar Marathwada University. It was Sharad Pawar, who was again the chief minister, who deftly judged the mood of people and chose the right time for announcing that decision.

The way I, along with the senior police officers handled the law and order situation, was much admired by the Parliamentary Committee that visited Bombay to examine the matter, as it were some of the most heinous atrocities on Dalits after independence. I candidly spoke to them and explained limitations of force to bring under control such situations. They perhaps liked my advising them to observe restraint and think before taking decisions on such emotive issues.

ಸಿಆಸಿಆ

PART VI :

The Director General of Shipping

Chapter 39

A New Area For Work

By the middle of 1979, I started receiving signals from my well wishers in Delhi that since I had completed two years of 'cooling down' period in the state, I was eligible for deputation to the Centre. When I informally enquired, I was told that no secretary level post in New Delhi was then available but I could be accommodated in the new post of the Secretary for the North-East Development Council based in Shillong.

My wife and I did not find it attractive to leave Bombay and live in another far off place. It had taken us two years to adjust to living in our own apartment in the Lalit building situated hardly ten minutes walking distance from the Mantralaya. Moreover, my second son Vivek was completing his A-levels in the Lancing College, Sussex. We did not want to be away in case he decided to return to India for further education, which he actually did. I was told that I could be accommodated in the post of the Director General of Shipping which was then occupied by S. B. Bhave, IAS from Maharashtra cadre, who was likely to be appointed as chief secretary to the State Government.

After consulting Bhave, I decided to opt for the post of DG Shipping. Accordingly, I took over in the beginning of October 1979.

My interest in shipping was not new. As India's representative to UNCTAD, I had studied international shipping, maritime laws and also taken part in several negotiations on behalf of the developing countries. C. P. Srivastav, then chairman of the Shipping Corporation of India and Rajawar, a joint MD of SCI, used to visit Geneva on behalf of the Ministry of Shipping. Over the years, I had educated myself on shipping matters. In fact so much so that the negotiators from the United Kingdom, the frontline UNCTAD member on all shipping matters, were genuinely under the impression that I was a 'shipping man' – which I was not. I acted more like an advocate who pleads a case on the advice and brief of the Solicitor.

I was happy to find that I was welcomed by the shipping fraternity who had heard about me from C. P. Srivastav, who had by then become the Chief of the International Maritime Organization (IMO) in London. They greeted me in a press statement with the words, "In the prevailing challenging times for shipping, Shri Pradhan with his sound and variegated experience, would no doubt prove helpful in resolving the various problems of the shipping companies to enable them to improve their operational economies and thus create a favourable atmosphere for strengthening and further development of our national shipping. We extend to him greetings from the industry and wish him all success in his new assignment".

Fortunately, I had very good support from S. M. Ochaney, who had worked in the Directorate General of Shipping since its inception in September 1949 and had risen to the post of the Deputy D. G. With his long experience, he was a great asset and my main support and advisor.

A young colleague of Maharashtra IAS, Kuljit Singh Sidhu, was second Deputy Director General. He was in-charge of dealing with owners, shippers and Seamen's problems which involve considerable tact. Sidhu was excellent in that respect having had served for five years for a Short Service Commission in the Indian Artillery Regiment.

On the administrative side, I had two other colleagues who were highly professional, Captain Barve, the Nautical advisor and Captain Gill who looked after training. They briefed me on ships, shipping and actual operations. Also about a training ship named 'Rajendra' that was in Bombay harbour that used to train each year over 100 seamen. Only after that, they were eligible to get jobs on Indian and foreign ships on obtaining a document called 'seamen's card'.

The shipping industry was then dominated by three shipping companies, the Shipping Corporation of India (SCI), a public sector company, 'The Scindias' and The Great Eastern Shipping Co. in the private sector.

The Scindias was an extraordinary enterprise. The Maharaja of Scindia of Gwalior had taken great deal of interest in shipping. He journeyed each year, at least a couple of times from Bombay to Liverpool and back on P&O's passenger ships. After knowing that there were no facilities for constructing even a medium size sea going vessels, the Maharaja thought of setting up a ship building yard in Bombay. He also proposed setting up of an Indian shipping company.

Walchand Hirachand, an enterprising industrialist, set up high technology industry in a place, which is known today as Walchandnagar, in Ahemadnagar district of Maharashtra. He was entrusted to set up the shipping company. Since the Maharaja of Gwalior had taken the initiative, Seth Walchand Hirachand named that Company 'The Scindia Shipping Company'. Actually the company was run by Walchand Hirachand family and the doyen of that family Smt. Sumati Morarjee was the Chairman when I became the DGS. She invited me to visit the Scindia House in the Ballard estate and acquainted me with the problems of the shipping companies in the private sector. The other company based in Bombay namely The Great Eastern Shipping Co. belonged to the Seth family and from its inception, Vasant Seth was the Chairman.

I soon found out that while the Scindias were the old tradition bound bureaucratic organization, the Great Eastern was run by a entrepreneur who had better knowledge of modern shipping than anyone else in India. Incidentally, I later found that Vasant Seth was the son-in-law of the great Malaviya and his wife, hailing from Allahabad, belonged to that family. The Great Eastern was mainly in carriage of oil in bulk.

The only other major private shipping company was the India Steam Shipping Co of the Birlas with headquarters in Calcutta. Capt. J. C. Anand was the CEO of that company. Over years, I would have much to do with Capt Anand in his role as the head of the Indian Register of the Shipping, Bombay.

A New Area For Work

Thus the main players were Rear Admiral Krishan Dev, Vice Chairman and MD of SCI, Smt. Sumati Morarjee, Vasant Seth and Capt. Anand. T. M. Goculdas of the Scindias was the president of the Indian National Ship Owners Association (INSA).

My next three years in shipping as DGS were spent with these persons. All of them highly cultured, affluent and products of old value system that was fast disappearing.

༄༅

Even before I had time to settle down in the job, we faced an emergency. The Forward Seamen Union was holding up operations in Calcutta port. They would not allow loading of cargo until their demands were met and on slightest pretext they would hold up working; as a result, a large quantity of cargo started accumulating in the port area. Shipping companies, shippers and shipping agents were fed up and declared their intention to stop operating the Calcutta port.

By end of December1979, 40,000 tonnes of jute goods, 84,000 tonnes of engineering goods and 60,000 of tea were awaiting shipment. The ministry of Commerce pressed the panic button and threatened the ministry of Shipping to get the export shipments cleared. Otherwise, India would lose export markets and substantial loss of foreign exchange. They were worried about Sri Lanka taking over the tea market in the UK and loosing the engineering markets to competitors. As an old commerce man, I could appreciate their plight.

The problem in Calcutta was a political one. The Forward Seamen's Union was controlled by a minister in the Jyoti Basu government. The port authorities could not perform their tasks without help of police as seamen indulged in hooliganism on slightest pretext. Police could not act without instructions from higher ups. At the Centre, we had no governance, as the Charan Singh cabinet was, on last leg. The Shipping minister was a well intentioned Socialist, Jyaneshwar Mishra, who had no influence on the communist led state government in Calcutta. It was an untidy mess.

In that situation, along with K. S. Sidhu, I visited Calcutta, where we a highly experienced officer N. Chakraborty, as the Principal Officer of the Mercantile Marine Department. It was end December and Calcutta was in traditional X-Mas celebration mood. Even the chief secretary was not available. I decided to directly approach the chief minister, who was good enough to give me appointment to see him in his office in the Secretariat. At appointed time I was ushered in and I found a relaxed, fresh looking and cultured person welcoming me. It was my first meeting with Jyoti Basu, the great Marxist. I had to seek his help to 'break' a strike called by his coalition partner.

I decided on a frank and head-on approach. I presented the grim picture on export front. I pleaded that if he could ask his minister to lift the ban on loading export cargo, I shall use my good officers to get the grievances of labour looked into. CM called his minister and in my presence, told him to call off the undeclared strike and allow lifting of cargo. I told the CM that I shall personally work out a time table and supervise the operation.

On 31st, I met the Shipping line's Representatives, the exporters and the Export Promotion Councils and informed them of my intention to visit Calcutta very soon with a concrete plan and time table. Shippers had also complained about inadequate sailings from Calcutta, as many foreign shipping lines were avoiding that port because of labour trouble. I agreed to look into that as well.

We arranged a meeting with wide representation of several interests, as their role and cooperation was most essential. T. S. R. Subramanian, joint secretary ministry of commerce (who would one day rise to the post of the cabinet secretary) and S. R. Shah, Director in the Transport were two persons, whom I had met in my earlier stint in Geneva. They gave me full support. From the shipping circles, other than Capt J. C. Anand, V. D. Chowgule was present as the President of the Shippers Council. I knew him well from my days with Y. B. Chavan in Bombay. On the Export promotion side, I had Dr R. K. Singh from the Engineering industry and representatives of the Jute, Tea interests. Newspapers did not fail to report that the Chairman, Port Trust, nor his staff attended the meeting.

A few days later, I visited Calcutta and declared setting up of an "Operational Group" and announced targets for lifting different variety of cargo. We monitored each day and soon the cargo started moving. A meeting held in Calcutta was attended by P. K. Kaul, IAS, the Commerce secretary. He praised our performance and publicly thanked the Operational Group for helping to reduce India's trade deficit. That was a great boost to all. I had established a position for myself in the Shipping Industry. I also attracted the attention of Delhi. Soon a diplomatic assignment would focus glare on me.

Chapter 40

On a Diplomatic Assignment
- To Basra and Baghdad

In the very first year as DG Shipping, I had to handle two difficult assignments that called for diplomatic skills and invited the central government's attention.

The first was on the outbreak of Iran – Iraq War in 1980. In a previous war in 1971, Iran had occupied a couple of small islands in the Persian Gulf near the outlet at Shatt-al-Arab that was exclusively under Iraqi control. In mid-September 1980, we received a report that more than 25 Indian shipping vessels had been locked inside the Iraqui Shatt-al waterways and the narrow exit to the Persian Gulf was closed by the Iraqis who would not permit any vessel to sail without a permit and only after a thorough search. Over 300 Indian seamen, who were manning mostly the sailing ships, which ply from Jamnagar or Porbunder to the Gulf were locked inside the waterways. Also, while the actual fighting had stopped by intervention of the Security Council, the ships could not travel down the narrow strait as it was heavily mined and only Iraq could arrange safe passage.

Romesh Bhandari, IFS, who was an Additional Secretary in the Foreign Office, briefed me on the problem and requested me to see how the Indian sailors and Indian ships could be repatriated from the embargo by the Iraqis. S. Y. Ranade, IAS secretary, Shipping called me over to Delhi to meet the minister who directed me to visit Baghdad and do the needful. Accordingly, one day I flew to Kuwait City. I had visited that place twice when I was working for the UN and knew some officers in the Kuwaiti establishments where all senior posts were manned by persons from the Ruler's family. I was informally briefed by them about my visit by road to Basrah for which the Indian Ambassador had already arranged a visa to enter Iraq and to re-enter Kuwait. The Ambassador also arranged for a local Indian gentleman, one Mr. Shah in construction industry, who would escort me to Basra and back.

While on the way to Basra, I saw the gulf and narrow passages to enter the Shatt-Al waterways that were heavily mined and movement controlled by the Iraqis. At Basrah, I met officers of a couple of Indian ships that were stranded on the other side of the waterways. They had left skeleton crew on board and come over to Basrah, to await news about sailing of their vessels. They explained their difficulties as they were not allowed to go outside the port area nor were any facility for replenishing their supplies available. I discussed with the local officers who told me that they were under instructions from Baghdad and they were helpless. I motored to the other end of the Shatt-al-Arab and met captain and officers of an Indian ship stranded there. They were determined not to leave their ship. They were idling with quantities of beer and playing cards. I admired their grit and morale? I also shared their modest meal and assured them help. For that, I decided to visit Baghdad and accordingly informed the Indian ambassador in Kuwait.

It was a four hour drive from Basra to Baghdad and the entry to the city was by crossing the Tigris, a name familiar from the Arabian Night's fables. The city itself was an admixture of the old and the new. The houses in the old town were mostly of earth and limestone, all washed in white lime or ochre. Modern houses were mostly one storied. The ambassador was hosting a lunch for some senior Iraqi officials. He and his wife received me warmly. She was the daughter of A. L. Dias, ICS whom I had known over two decades and who was then the Governor of Tripura. She recalled meeting me at her parent's place in Bombay.

The lunch was a social affair. On knowing my mission, the Iraqi officials present advised me that the task was indeed a tough one, as the civilian officers had hardly any discretion and in military matters, all decision emanated from the top.

Next day, the Ambassador had arranged my meeting with some officials in the Iraqi foreign office. Fortunately, I could also meet some Iraqi officials who used to visit Geneva to attend UNCTAD meetings. I represented to them the human aspect and the fact that sailing ships were a means of livelihood for thousands of sailors who are unfortunately trapped in the gulf war. Recalling age old India-Iraq relations, I strongly requested their intervention to get the Indians out of the Shatt-al-Arab. I was advised that the matter will take some time and I need not wait in

Baghdad. In the afternoon, since I had no work as such, my Iraqi friends took me around to show the old town that revived memories of the Arabian tales. I was also entertained to a lavish dinner.

Next day, I left by road for Basra onwards to Kuwait city. In between, the driver of the private taxi pointed out to me on the left hand side of the road, a huge dome under construction, which on my enquiry; he told me was Iraq's nuclear power generation set up. Years later, it would become the center stage of the US-Iraq conflict. On arrival in Kuwait, I informed Romesh Bhandari that I was hopeful of Indian vessels being released but could not indicate the time table.

Very soon, we learnt that 16 Indian vessels were allowed to exit. Cases of others were under examination but they generously allowed the sailors to be air lifted to return to their homes. I remember that number of those sailing vessels would slowly rot and become unfit for sailing. Romesh Bhandari wrote to me a very warm letter of congratulations and thanked me on behalf of the Foreign Office for securing a good agreement from the Iraqis.

The other case that attracted a great deal of publicity in shipping circles was a very unusual matter. Nilhat Shipping, a small company, carried cargo to London. Beginning of March 1980, we received a report that the crew of 'Alexandra' of the Nilhat Co had seized the ship for non-payment of wages and approached the British Admiralty Court. That Court had seized the Alexandra and ordered its auction for paying the salaries of the crew. The auction was due on 18 March.

There was panic in the Shipping ministry. Auction of an Indian ship in London would bring shame to the country and the government, who could do nothing because the matter was a private one between the owners and the crew. The owners had no money to pay their crew and told me plainly that they did not mind auctioning of their ship in London. The then minister of shipping, A. P. Sharma, was greatly worried that the news would finish his political career. The PM will not pardon him if the auction takes place – after all, the Alexandra, named after the British Royalty, was flying India's tri-colour. He frantically telephoned and asked me to do whatever could be done to avert auction.

I called the owners of Nilhat, who explained their plight. They were small ship owners and had no funds to ply their ship. If not London, then somewhere else their ship would meet the same fate. How long could they avoid its sale? They had been facing financial problems for quite some time and had no solution. I learnt from them that their another ship had been seized in Bombay port and the Maritime Union of India as well as the Indian Seamen's Union would press auctioning that ship.

The situation appeared to be hopeless. I called Captain J. C. Anand, the CEO of the India Steam Shipping Company, for consultation. I decided to play the patriotic card. I knew all the prominent Birla's since my days with Y. B. Chavan. I told Capt. Anand that his company belonged to the Birla's, who were very much part of India's freedom movement. Could they not consider bidding in auction and buying Alexandra?

Beyond Expectations

Overnight, after consulting his owners, Capt Anand informed me that the India Steam Shipping was willing to buy the Nilhat ship if an agreement was negotiated in India.

I called the owners of Nilhat and Capt Anand and reached an agreement between them and got that signed 48 hours prior to the auction. However, time was running out as we could not approach the British Court without the agreement of the Maritime Union of India and the National Seamen's Union, Calcutta. My advisors and I worked non-stop for thirty six hours in my office to sort out and approached the solicitors in London to agree to postponing the auction. We got it almost at the last moment and by saving Alexandra, we saved India's honour. The press gave me fulsome praise and the shipping fraternity was full of it. That created some ill will in the ministry, where some babus unfortunately including my good friend, S. Y. Ranade, the Shipping secretary, became jealous when they found that the Minister A. P. Sharma was overjoyed and personally thanked me profusely.

When I visited Delhi next, he told me of a letter that he had asked the Shipping secretary to write to me and convey government's appreciation for what I had done. I received a letter in bureaucratic language stating that, 'We note that your efforts have culminated in the settlement….. But for this, the sale order passed by the Admiralty Court, London and withdrawal of case could not have been possible.' He added: I am directed to convey to you Government's appreciation for your endeavours and efforts in this behalf.'

Minister expressed to me that the letter was too formal and did not fully reflect his instructions. He grandly assured me that he would recommend my name for Padma award. I knew that it did not mean much, as the next years award were too far away. By that time both, the Minister and the secretary shipping would change.

ಸಿಂಕಿಂ

Chapter 41

Coastal Shipping
- Pradhan committee

Mahtma Gandhi, as back as 1930, had made a remark to reserve coastal trade for Indian company, as there was no foreign competition. The Government of India soon after independence had acted on Mahatma Gandhi's demand, yet, the Ministry of Shipping, which had been supporting through a fairly vigorous programme of expansion of overseas tonnage, had over years neglected the problems of coastal shipping. Result of that was evident. In fact the coastal shipping may have been in much worse condition but for the social responsibility that the two government owned shipping companies, the SCI and Mogul Lines, had to bear.

I hailed from the Konkan coast of Maharashtra where coastal trade had an emotional angle. Economics of trade were making it progressively uncompetitive. In April 1980, I decided to look into problems of coastal shipping as I found it odd, that the salt from Saurashtra was being transported by rail to east coast and coal was moving from the east to west coast by rail when both the bulk commodities should have found coastal shipping faster and economical. Main hurdle appeared to be the structure of freight rate. Where railways offered concessions and subsidy in rate, coastal shipping lost the cargo. The shipping rates had also not been revised. On the recommendations of DGS, government decided to permit coastal operators to raise the freight rates on carriage of coal from Calcutta/Haldia complex to Madras, Tuticorin, Cochin and Saurashtra coast by an average of 60%. The government's announcement was the result of the initiative taken by me as the DGS, and the examination of the cost structure of coastal shipping by the Bureau of Industrial Cost and Prices (BICP). However, because of strong lobbies, the Government did not increase freight rate on salt, a commodity which accounted for more than 25 per cent of the dry cargo of 9 lakhs tonnes that moved along the coast. Therefore, while recommending an increase in the freight rate, I had also proposed that the whole coastal trade required to be studied and examined in depth and accordingly, the central government set up a committee under my chairmanship.

We found that the end of December 1979, we had only 57 coastal vessels with a total gross tonnage 2.5 lakhs; of these 35 were dry cargo vessels but only 18 or so of them were employed exclusively for coastal trade. It was observed that dry cargo coastal trade had nose divided from 35/40 lakhs tonnes a year in the 60s to 9/10 lakh tonnes. General cargo, including cement that moved along the coast, also dropped significantly. The same applied to the salt cargo. But the steepest fall was in the carriage of coal that had fall from nearly 20 lakhs tonnes to less then 5 lakh tonnes.

Beyond Expectations

It was natural that with the steep increase in fuel prices, the economics of coastal shipping in relation to other modes of transport bulk cargo had to change. But unless the trade and industry found it more economical to move cargo by coastal shipping than by road transport and, in certain cases, even by railways, they would not opt for the former. The issues were thus clear.

Over a period of a few months, the Committee received submissions from the Indian Coastal Conference (ICC), explaining their difficulties and setting out their perceptions and also suggestions for reviving coastal shipping. All those were technical matters and the Committee examined in depth the various issues. We also estimated future traffic potential. Based on detailed studies and projections of anticipated coastal shipping traffic, the committee proposed several items for reservation for coastal shipping for transportation from production points to the user ports.

In mid December 1980, we presented the Committee's report to Veerendra Patil, Union Minister for Shipping and Transport at a function arranged by Smt. Sumati Morarjee, Chairman, Indian Coastal Conference. The report was hailed as path finding and practical. It was promptly named as the Pradhan's Committee Report, even by the Ministry of Shipping.

Several years later, as a member of the Maharashtra Legislative Council, I had an opportunity to review Coastal trade. It was in a sorry state for want of vessels, ports and adequate handling machinery. I found that while emotionally everyone used to get worked up on coastal shipping, actually in practice, not much was done. I took up the matter with Rajesh Pilot who was then Minister of Shipping in Narasimha Rao Government. He thanked me for bringing the report to the notice. But nothing was done. The Pradhan Committee Report had been consigned to the archives of the Ministry of Shipping. I think that is where it is still lying.

During those years, I had not only acquired a great deal of knowledge of the Shipping industry but also learnt a lot about seamen's training and also about training of officers for the merchant marine. The industry was growing with a large acquisition of cargo and tanker carriers by enterprisers. Foremost amongst them were Ruia brothers from Madras. They were experts in spotting almost ready tonnage in construction yards and negotiated cleverly to acquire those ships. All these had to be personally cleared by me as DGS. I admired their enterprise and can claim to some extent their emerging as a premier industrial house under the banner of the "Essar". Likewise, I extended help to a number of smaller shipping companies to grow. For me, it gives special pleasure to meet some of those today in Mumbai. They do not fail to recall my help.

But my efforts to set up an Marine Engineers Training School/ Institute in Navi Mumbai when I became the chief secretary of Maharashtra brought me again in close touch with the shipping fraternity. I also helped to set up the training institute of the Registrar of Shipping in Powai facing the lake for which initiative was taken by Capt. Anand.

As the DGS, I was the chairman of the National Shipping Board, which met periodically to review various aspects of shipping. One of its meeting held in Jamnagar is memorable. People of my generation had heard a great deal about the Jamsaheb of Jamnagar and role he played in getting the prince's India to merge with the independent India. At a meeting held there, the successor of the great Jamsaheb invited all members of the Board for breakfast at the palace. When he learnt that My wife and I were close to late N. M. Buch, who was the first Regional Commissioner for Saurashtra, he had a long separate meeting with us. He personally took us round the palace and showed us their treasure. Also the secret record room where five hundred old records were stored. For me, it was great pleasure to meet a kin of the legendary cricketer, Ranji. He presented me two books on him.

After two years, I had settled down to a comfortable position and I expected to be called to Delhi to become the secretary of Commerce for which I had been groomed. But the fate willed something different.

PART VII :

On International Assignment

Chapter 42

On a Globe Trotting Assignment for UN

Somehow, between June 1977 and in the middle of 1979, while I had tried to distance from the United Nations, my friends and former colleagues would not allow me to do so. While I was the Director General of Shipping, I got a pressing invitation to undertake a comprehensive review of a large-scale UNCTAD/UNDP Project to assist developing countries to develop trade with the Socialist Countries of Eastern Europe. UNDP wanted me to make an assessment about the efficacy of that Project in the light of my experience of the GSP Project.

In UNCTAD, the Project was headed by Pran Neville, who was an old colleague and a friend since my visit to Belgrade in 1966. He wanted me to undertake the evaluation because a senior Indian official would be in a better position to hold consultations with the governments of Socialist Countries. I also had very good contacts with all the major developed government countries especially in their departments of Trade and Commerce. On Neville's insistence, I undertook to evaluate his Project on the understanding that Hugo Cubillos, my former colleague on GSP Project, would also join me on behalf of UNDP. That suggestion was approved both by the UNCTAD and UNDP Administrations.

With Hugo, starting with a briefing at Geneva, we visited EEC in Brussels, London and Washington for six weeks, to get an idea as to what was the attitude of their Governments towards the Project that we were required to evaluate. While the EEC and the Department of Trade of United Kingdom were neutral, Trade Representatives' Office in Washington thought that it was a waste of resources because the trade with Socialist Countries was best done on bilateral agreements that were the outcome of political relationship between individual developing countries and the Socialist Block.

From Washington, we flew via Alaska to Tokyo where I had an occasion to renew acquaintances with my old colleagues. After visiting Manila, we had consultations in Bangkok with the Economic Commission for Asia and Pacific (ESCAP). From there, we went to Egypt via New Delhi. So far as New Delhi and Cairo were concerned, they were all for developing countries establishing close relationship with the Soviet Block. From Cairo, we had planned to visit Beirut for consultations with the United Nations Office in Beirut but we could not visit because of war-like conditions there. We therefore skipped Beirut.

After visiting Latin American countries, including Santiago (Chile), for discussions with the Economic Commission for Latin America (ECLA) we finalized our report in Geneva. In fact, the report was intended to only prove and set out some evidence on what has already been decided by the UNCTAD and the UNDP.

For me and Hugo, it was an opportunity to spend those six weeks in each other's company, which we always enjoyed. My friend Pran Neville was particularly appreciative of the efforts made by us to prolong the life of his Project. He became an acknowledged authority on Trade in Socialist Countries and even after the Project was wound up, his services were in great demand mainly because over fifteen years of his career in the Indian Foreign Service had been spent working in Soviet Block countries. There was no Indian who had such unique experience and expertise. I was, therefore, happy that I could associate myself with that task.

After that Mission, there were several offers from the United Nations requesting me to undertake similar missions. However, I did not respond to their requests. In a way, I was resisting my destiny. Incidentally, for that review, I was given a high sounding title of eminent International Trade Economist!

Chapter 43

Again to United Nations
- Pushed out of IAS

I had voluntarily left international career, but it would not leave me. On return, I received two letters. In letter dated 18th July 1977 from Br. Bradford Morse to Mr. N. K. Mukarji, Cabinet Secretary the Administrator of the UNDP stated:

"At the occasion of the return of Mr. Ram Pradhan to your Government I wish to express my great appreciation for his services to UNDP. The project has managed to do this with an extremely high standard of competence and efficiency, thanks in large measure to the personal qualities and dedication of Mr. Pradhan. May I express again my very sincere appreciation for the extremely valuable services which Mr. Pradhan has rendered to the international community which reflect great credit on him and on his country."

In his letter dated 22nd April 77 to Mr. M. L. Dharia, Minister of Commerce, Gamani Corea, Secretary General of UNCTAD, wrote :

Again to United Nations

"I should like to stress that the competent and devoted manner in which Mr. Pradhan conducted his work in the GSP project made him gain a respect and admiration of all those who had the opportunity to work with him..... His services were secured in the first instance by my Predecessor Mr. Perez Guerrero, and I myself was readily willing to secure him extension of his appointment in the Project. He is now going back to his region and his country, and I already anticipate every success in his future endeavours".

I was aware that those kind of letters were usual manners of the United Nations system. But it was clear that I left the international career when they wanted me to continue.

Much as did not want to serve the UN again, my destiny was leading me in that direction. In the next three years, the ministry of Commerce wanted to sponsor my name against a Director's post in UNCTAD. I politely declined. In fact, twice the new Director General of GATT, during stop over at Bombay, invited me to dinner at the Taj to find out whether I would come as a replacement for Madan Mathur. Again my answer was no. I had firmly decided not to accept any UN assignment, because I was aiming to become a secretary in the central government, an ambition that every IAS officer nurtures from the day one joins the Service.

One day, the cabinet secretary asked me over telephone to meet him in Delhi. C. R. Krishnaswamy Rao Saheb, IAS of the Andhra cadre, was a confidant of the Prime Minister, Mrs. Indira Gandhi. He had been her Principal Secretary and on his appointment as cabinet secretary, Dr. P. C. Alexander, IAS succeeded him.

Rao Saheb, as he was generally referred to, explained to me that they were considering my deputation to the United Nations in New York to take a high level post in the newly created department dealing with trade and economic issues that was headed by a Frenchman appointed as the Deputy Secretary General. I was greatly surprised, as I was expecting an offer for a secretary level post in Delhi, since I was about to complete five years in Bombay. When I appeared somewhat hesitant to give direct reply, he asked me to see Dr. P. C. Alexander.

Dr. Alexander came straight to the point. It seemed that on retirement of C. V. Narsimhan, Under Secretary General in New York, there was no senior Indian in position. This matter was taken up by the Prime Minister during visit of Kurt Waldheim, the UN Secretary General, who had anticipated such a request. I was told that my name had been mentioned by the Secretary General as a person who would be acceptable to him at the Headquarters. PM had asked Alexander and Rao Saheb to pursue the matter and hence, they had launched the subject. With that background information, he asked me to see the cabinet secretary again.

Rao Saheb, whom I had hardly known, was surprised at my reaction and asked me to seriously consider the matter as the decision had been taken at a high level. He bluntly advised me that in case I refused, I should not expect offer of any secretary level post in the Government of India. I shall have to serve in the State government till the date of my retirement, knowing fully well that I had no chance of becoming the chief secretary in Maharashtra.

I returned to Bombay and seriously thought over the matter. Fortunately, my wife had left the decision to me. By curious coincidence, one Mr. Naik who was a senior official in the State Bank of India in Bombay came to see me one day. Ever since my meeting him a few years earlier, he was requesting me to show him my horoscope. My father, as a tradition in those days, had cast the horoscope on my birth in June 1928. I got in touch with Naik and hesitantly showed my horoscope. After few calculations, he told me that I was destined to go out of India on international assignment and I should not avoid that. Strangely, my horoscope also showed that whatever post I occupy in future, I had to be in a leadership role and I would have to deal with army or personnel in uniform.

A few days later, I went to meet the cabinet secretary. I knew that my options had been closed. Rao Saheb was happy that I had agreed to their suggestion to go on deputation to the UN. However, he put a condition that since my deputation would be second one to the UN, I must offer my resignation from the IAS. I was somewhat shocked and took his permission to check the Rules with the Establishment Officer in the Ministry of Home Affairs. S. P. Bagla, an IAS from Punjab was very helpful but insisted that as an Establishment Officer he had to follow the Rule and that I must seek voluntary retirement, if I wished to go on second deputation to UN. While checking up the Rules, I had noted that an officer must give 'not less than three months notice' to the Government about his intention to seek voluntary retirement. With that knowledge, I went back to the cabinet secretary and told him that I felt somewhat aggrieved that I was being sent to the UN against my wishes and also being asked to retire from the IAS. I added somewhat sarcastically, "Rao Saheb, I think that is immoral".

As soon as I uttered those words, Rao Saheb, who was a highly ethical minded person, looked up at me and said, "Why do you think it is immoral?" I replied, "Immoral because you are thrusting your desires on an officer who is not attracted by high salary and high position in the UN. He wants to serve at a modest salary without asking for favours. You are asking him to go, and at same time asking him to retire. In my view, that is an immoral act."

Rao Saheb looked at me and said, "Pradhan, what you say is not wrong, but we cannot afford to lose the UN post." I made one suggestion that normally an officer seeking voluntary retirement has to give a notice of not less than three months and that is interpreted to mean that at the end of three months, he stands retired. I requested Rao Saheb that in my case, can the Government agree to a notice period of six months. Cabinet secretary quickly consulted Bagla over telephone and agreed to my suggestion.

Next day, I met him and handed over a hand written letter. While taking leave of him, in a somewhat off-handed manner, I made a remark: Rao Saheb, I have asked six months because that is long enough period for me to work out my contract with UN. That is also a long enough period for the Government of India to really decide whether they did not want my services any more. He looked at me in surprise. I walked out of his room with my head high wondering all the time what astrologer Naik had predicted.

Again to United Nations

One day, in March 1982, along with my wife and daughter Sarita, I landed in Geneva. United Nation officials had asked me to get a briefing there and then meet them in New York. We were familiar with Geneva and since I had been advised that the new post in New York in the rank of the Assistant Secretary General would be available in the month of July, I was asked to assume a non-existent job in the United Nation Secretariat in Geneva on salary that I would receive in New York. I was, in keeping with the status, given a large size office along with two young lady secretaries. Except for meeting some officials over a cup of coffee I had no work.

I quickly hired an apartment, bought a car and three of us would leave Geneva on Friday afternoon and return on Monday morning after visiting several tourist places in Italy, Austria, West Germany and France. During the week, except for some discussions and so called consultations, I was free to do whatever I wanted to do to prepare myself to meet the Secretary General of the United Nations, who would be visiting Geneva to attend the Annual Session of the Economic and Social Council (ECOSOC), that meets in Geneva in the beginning of July each year. Those three months of the early spring were enjoyable, but I felt wasted. No one would define my work and therefore all I did was to study old reports of the Economic and Social Council of the UN. The only thing that I was assured was a high post and high salary. At the UN Headquarters that I visited, they were still not very sure about my role. Being a political appointee, that was for the Secretary General of UN to decide.

ಸಂಚಿಸಿ

PART VIII :

Chief Secretary Maharashtra

Chapter 44

Unexpected Recall
- Que Sera, Sera

On June 27, 1982, my wife and daughter celebrated my birthday. Next evening, we were having dinner on the terrace when the telephone bell rang. A voice at the other end said, "I am Babasaheb Bhosale, the chief minister of Maharashtra. We have not met but I have been asked to talk to you on an urgent matter."

I was somewhat perplexed because I had not kept track of news in Bombay. I did not know that Barrister A. R. Antulay, who was the chief minister, had been replaced by one Babasaheb Bhosale. So in all innocence, I asked as to what was the call about. Since this led to interesting conversation, I propose to recall it word by word.

Babasaheb replied, "There has been a minor mutiny in the Bombay police. We have decided that you should come over take the charge as the chief secretary."

I asked, "Who has decided?" He replied, "I am speaking from Delhi. The decision was taken in a meeting held by the PM, in which both Dr. Alexander and the cabinet secretary were present".

I said, "Since I have never met you nor heard about you in political circle, how do I presume I am talking to the chief minister of Maharashtra?" I suspected that it may be a prank.

He replied, "You can check that up with the cabinet secretary."

I told the chief minister that I would have no difficulty in doing that but as the Central Government had sent me on deputation, it would be for the Government of India to inform me that they would like me to return to India to become the chief secretary". I advised him to request the cabinet secretary to send a message to that effect to the Indian Mission in Geneva. Chief Minister gladly approved the suggestion.

We spoke on a Thursday evening and I had planned to go out of Geneva for next three days to visit the Loire valley in France to see chateaux of the Middle ages, I assured the CM that I shall give him a reply on next Tuesday evening at 9 pm Bombay time. He gladly gave me a private telephone number, where he would be available at that time.

My wife and I quickly re-assessed the situation. In my wildest dreams, I had never thought I would become the chief secretary to the State Government because my seniority would never allow me to occupy that position. Obviously five IAS officers who were senior to me were superseded in proposing my appointment. The decision had been taken in a meeting held in the Prime Minister's Office. The call had been made by the chief minister, because as explained by him, there had been a mutiny in the police force of Bombay Police. It was felt that I was the right person to handle the State when the Police force of Maharashtra State was greatly agitated and was being influenced by many irresponsible leaders to make all kinds of demands on the streets. Discipline was greatly eroded. Was not this a historic opportunity for me to take over the chief secretary-ship of the State? Also surprisingly, was not the situation similar to one described by astrologer Naik? We decided to return.

Immediately after talking to Babasaheb Bhonsle, I spoke to Krishnaswamy Rao Saheb, the cabinet secretary. He confirmed the decision taken at a high level meeting and that the chief minister had been asked to persuade me to return. I told him somewhat curtly, "I do not need any persuasion to become the chief secretary. You are very well aware that I was sent out much against my wishes." I requested him to send me a tele-printer message through the Indian Mission in Geneva to confirm the request.

Having taken the decision, my anxiety was to seek the confirmation, which came over on the tele-printer message to the Indian Mission over the weekend. I also faced the task of telling the UN Secretary General. Despite having conveyed my approval to joining UN, I had to back out because my own government wanted me to return to India. I requested the cabinet secretary to inform the UN through our Representative in New York and Geneva. I quickly briefed aide of the Secretary General. He approved my not accepting the job and wished me well. My colleagues and friends in the United Nations were greatly surprised that I was declining the post. Indians in Geneva were equally surprised why I have opted to become a small bureaucrat on a small modest salary when I was destined for a higher job and much higher salary in the United Nations.

Four days later, as promised, I rang up Bombay punctually at 9 pm The chief minister was happy that I was agreeable to give up my UN assignment and return to the State. He also readily agreed to my request to give me a couple of weeks to wind up my affairs in Geneva. The very next day, I informed the United Nations to cancel my meeting with Mr. Kurt Waldheim, the Secretary General, since I did not wish to offer myself for the high level post for which I had been sponsored.

I returned to India to serve my destiny and to serve India.

Chapter 45

To Bombay as Chief Secretary
- Police Mutiny and Moral

On return to Bombay on the 19th August, I was informed that a meeting had been fixed with the chief minister at his residence. On reaching there, I was received by Venkat Chari, IAS, who was working as a Secretary to the CM. He escorted me to the room where the chief minister was working on files. He greeted me warmly and briefed me about the situation obtaining in the State and especially in the Bombay city due to the agitation by the police. He candidly told me that his own experience in politics and administration was a limited one although he had been working in public life. He promised me the fullest support to run the administration and to restore its high reputation and morale, which had been badly affected during the tenure of his predecessor.

On 21st August, I assumed charge as the chief secretary, knowing that I enjoyed the full confidence of the chief minister. Also a feeling that the person was genuine one as opposed to a professional politician. Babasaheb Bhosale was true to his word. We readily established a relationship of mutual trust and mutual respect, so necessary for a chief secretary to work effectively. I also found soon that while he had rightly claimed that he was a novice to administration, he possessed a strong common sense and a quick mind to grasp the essence of any problem. So important for success at that level.

My first priority was tackling the disaffection running deep in the police, especially the constabulary in the Bombay city. I held a series of meetings with the then Director General of Police K. P. Medhekar, IPS and senior officials and we worked out a package of measures, administrative as well as financial, to ameliorate the difficulties faced by the constabulary. We also revamped the then existing structure and provided better opportunities for promotion and reward for good work. Many of the grievances of the policemen were genuine, e.g., they would work long hours on 'Bandobust duty' (deployed on duty to maintain law and order on streets), sometimes for several hours without a provision of any food or drinking water. Some grievances were petty, e.g., whether to pay for laundry charges for washing of the clothes or continue to provide soap.

These and several other matters were sorted out to mutual satisfaction without engaging in any formal negotiations with unionized bodies of police. In all these matters, the chief minister who was kept informed of our discussions fully supported the administration. He also scrupulously abstained in getting into formal discussion with so-called unions of policemen. It would have been tempting for a politician to get into such a role. It was to his credit that in the larger interest of the administration and the discipline within the police ranks that he did not do so.

To Bombay as Chief Secretary

All this working contributed to building up a relationship of understanding and trust between the chief minister and myself. He would interact and consult me on several matters which were not strictly official. I had no hesitation in talking to him because I had formed my own judgment that he was not in the usual mould of politicians. He was a genuine person who could talk and laugh without affectation. He had a sense of self-respect but not of arrogance. His greatest and endearing quality was the ability to laugh on his own foibles. Politicians rarely do so.

CM and the chief secretary working as a team, like two wheels of a chariot, helped in re-establishing a relationship of mutual respect and cooperation between the political leadership and senior bureaucracy, which are unique features of Maharashtra. Babasaheb Bhosale was working with greater degree of confidence in tackling problems at political level. He was also securing good support from his colleagues, some of whom were exceptionally able. In particular, I was impressed by young Dr. Shrikant Jichkar, who was the Minister for General Administration, Home and host of other Departments. I found him exceptionally intelligent and he was proving himself to be a very useful aide to the chief minister. In my career, I had not come across someone with so many string of post-graduate degrees. He was a scholar of Sanskrit and Vedas. An exceptional human, it was unfortunate that he died at an early age.

From the outset, I was on the top and thoroughly enjoying my work. As the chief secretary, like others in such a post, I had to be ready to face the most unexpected and at the same tim to have my own agenda for action. That kept me busy almost eight to ten hours in the office during the week and out of Mumbai over weekends. I developed a style of working in a transparent manner and interacting with the press and the people. Instead of keeping my door closed, I kept myself accesable to any visitors during certain specified hours that in a way opened a window for me to learn from non-officials many matters that I would not have come to know in the normal course

Babasaheb Bhosale, a relative novice in power structure, had a cabinet that was weak in administrative experience. That created many problems and headaches to him. He made it a habit of passing on those to me.

One day, unannounced, Vasantdada Patil, with a couple of workers, by his side dropped into my office. He spoke to me about the problem faced by a sugar industry because of certain excise surcharge levied on molasses and on alcoholic spirits in the budget. Normally, there was a demand for molasses outside Maharahstra and great quantities were exported to other states. Levy of surcharge had made Maharashtra's molasses uncompetitive and huge stocks were accumulating in the sugar factories. A stage had reached where for want of storage, factories were compelled to dump molasses in the rivers. That caused pollution. Similarly because of high price, the sale of spirits and alcohol was badly affected.

The problem was a practical one. Surcharge had been imposed by the Finance Minister, Dr. V. Subramanian, a former IAS officer, without realising the problems that the industry may have to face. I was convinced of the seriousness of the situation. Water supply was already posing big problem in rural areas and pollution of rivers would aggravate that. I assured Vasantdada that I shall take steps to get the decisions reversed within a week.

After talking to the chief minister, the matter was taken to the cabinet, who, despite the Finance Minister's opposition, decided to remove the additional excise. Vasantdada was happy that I had acted fast to give the relief to sugar industry.

I took the issue as pragmatic and practical one caused by a taxation measure that was ill conceived. N. Raghunathan, the Finance Secretary, with his knowledge and field experience, fully supported me. As expected, Dr. V. Subramanian, who regarded himself as an expert on financial matters, was unhappy. I observed that he started opposing several suggestions made by me. I knew that not being from the political class, he suffered from a certain degree of inferiority complex while dealing with a service colleague. That reservation continued for several years and was again evident when he was the General Secretary of the Y. B. Chavan Foundation and I as a Trustee made several suggestions to make the Foundation work more effectively to promote the ideas of late Y. B. Chavan.

That behaviour reinforced my conviction that a Service officer, after retirement, may join politics as public service, but should not become a minister. I had seen how S. G. Barve had lost support of his former colleagues. As a politician, he started behaving as one of the political class. He soon found himself a stranger to both, the administrative as well as to the political class. That was a lesson for me for future. As luck would have it, I faced that option a few years later, when Sharad Pawar offered me a ministership.

Every day brought its own quota of problems, some big, some small, but nonetheless important and brought me into limelight. Publicity was not of my choosing. It came without my seeking. I should recall two- three incidents.

One morning, I received from the Meteriological Department a warning that western Maharashtra, especially Mumbai, is likely to be hit by unprecedented stormy cyclone, which, after having hit Gujarat, was moving rapidly down the western coast. In Veraval and Surat, the pre-cyclone winds had played havoc. Electric and telephone poles had been uprooted and over thirty persons had lost their lives. Waves stretching over ten kilometers were hammering the coast, over 400 fishing boats had sunk without trace and over 1600 fishermen were missing. It was anticipated that the cyclone would move towards Mumbai.

During a few hours that were available, with the help of police and homeguards we organized a massive relocation of people living along the coastline and several hutment dwellers were forcibly shifted to safe places. Police and homeguards, along with officers, were sent to different areas to warn the population and arrange their shifting by mobilising trucks and other public transport. To keep informed the people about developing situation, I decided to go on air by radio broadcast. In the absence of televisionin those days, that was the only way I could communicate with the people.

I also requested the Mayor, Dr. Prabhakar Pai, to do the same. He mobilised a municipal administration. Fortunately, by the evening, the cyclone turned to different direction and instead of moving towards Mumbai, it moved northwards. As the chief secretary, I got much cudos in the press for the way the administration was mobilised. For me, it was also a great lesson: how to prepare to face emergencies. A few months later, that was useful when we suddenly faced more serious problems.

Another incident worth recalling is personally humbling. George Fernandes, the charismatic labour leader, who was a specialist in calling strikes that were known as 'Bandh' s. He was the undisputed leader of the BEST workers' union. Bus services run by BEST – Bombay Electric Supply and Transport Company – along with the Local train services, are life line of Bombay – now renamed Mumbai. Lakhs of people commute to work because of these two efficient services and to earn their livelihood. One day, the BEST Union declared intention to go on strike, with hardly three days notice. One deputy of George Fernandes was determined to show his hold over the Union and also his muscle power. Perhaps he wanted to prove that Datta Samant was not the sole leader of workers in Bombay. The Rail Workers Union led by George Fernandes also announced their joining the "Bombay Bandh".

Both services were essential services and Babasaheb Bhosale, who claimed that he was also a labour leader, felt that it was a challenge to him. But apart from issuing appeals he could not do anything. I told him that after the police agitation, the administration cannot buckle down because the so called leader of Police union was also making noises. In consultation with Julio Reibero, IPS, the Bombay City Police Commissioner and K. P. Medhekar, IPS, the Inspector General of Police, a strategy was worked out to confront striking workers who indulged in hooliganism to enforce the strike.

We decided that three arterial roads leading to Fort area of Bombay must be kept open to the movement of vehicular traffic. All roads leading to these roads would be blocked by deploying strong contingent of police, including the gun wielding SRPF. Home Guards would be deployed in places where normally police are stationed. No breach of law and order would be allowed and if it however occurs, it would be dealt with sternly. Trains would run as best as the Railway police could manage with help of Home Guards. We mobilized forces from across the state and made arrangements for their stay, food and other necessities. We wanted to impress on them that the administration was humane in treatment of constabulary. That would reassure them after the police agitation a few months ago.

My going on the All India Radio on a few occasions had reinforced my confidence. I addressed the citizens of Bombay and assured them full protection and invited them to travel for their work. We arranged Maharashtra government staff living in certain clusters in Bandra and Chembur to be transported in the State Transport buses to the Fort area. Fortunately, the State government staff union gave us support and issued appeal to its members. In return, I promised to look into their grievances.

A few Best buses were stoned while exiting from their depots and few workers beaten. But, the life lines were open and cars were safely moving. By 4 pm it was apparent that the Bandh was a Flop. In the evening, the chief minister rang me up to tell that George Fernandes had sought a meeting. I told him not to respond, till we let the people judge that the administration had successfully faced the challenge and that the strike had failed. Services of the Police deserved to be publicly recognized, by the people, so that their moral gets a boost.

Late that night, when I found that everything was as planned by us and there was peace, I requested the chief minister to invite George Fernandes to Varsha, his official residence. It was 11 pm in night, when I reached there.

Babasaheb Bhosale was seated in the private seating room on the first floor. I quickly briefed him of situation and asked him to leave talking to me. He should watch and if he has anything to tell me we could go into adjoining room. Scenario worked as planned.

George came along with couple of colleagues and started complaining of police high handedness. That was anticipated by us and I told him that a Bombay city cannot be brought to standstill on issues that can be discussed with the Labour Commissioner. Having lost face, he wanted a way out to secure release of his lieutenants and large number of others who were in police custody. I told him plainly that we may consider that only if he was willing to give a public apology to the people of Bombay. When he said, he could in his way out do that, looking at CM who was enjoying dialogue, I said that would not do. I gave a paper and pencil and told him what we would like him to state. We wanted a statement in writing. His saying something to the press was not acceptable.

George Fernandes, being a practical man knew how I was trying to find a face-saving formula. I dictated him a five line statement word-by-word. My UN drafting ability was evident to him. He agreed and CM nodded in approval. I think that was the end of George Fernandes's undisputed reign over BEST workers Union.

All senior police officers met me the next day and congratulated me. I thanked them for all the hard work put in by them and the police force of the state. It was an achievement of the co-operation between the political masters and the bureaucracy that was the hall mark of the Maharashtra administration from days of Y. B. Chavan.

As usual, there was one dissenting voice. That was Vasant Nagarkar, IPS. He was a freedom fighter and, after independence, drafted into IPS. He had worked for over two decades in the Intelligence Bureau specialising in labour matters and leftist movements. He was then the Inspector General of Home Guards. In our preparatory meetings, he had expressed strong reservation to use of force to handle law and order. I brushed aside his objections in an open meeting with all senior officers present. He remained a sullen colleague thereafter.

Chapter 46

Assembly Session in Nagpur
- CM's Imprudence

In the latter half of November 1982, as usual, the ministers and senior officials went to Nagpur for the session of the Legislature, where the government shifted for the winter session. I was visiting Nagpur after over twenty years and it was a pleasure for me to work with the chief minister in the same building, named as Hyderabad House, in which as private secretary to Y. B. Chavan, I had set up in 1960 the chief minister's secretariat.

The chief minister was in great form. He was by then comfortably settled in office and he was enjoying the Legislative work and hospitality extended by Nagpur city. In the legislature, he engaged the Opposition in debate and repartee, of which he was a master. In India, one rarely came across politicians capable of a good memorable repartee. That requires an intelligent grasp of opponents argument and equally quick response in a short pithy manner. I had found that Babasaheb Bhonsle was a master in that respect. He not only enjoyed the beauty of the Marathi language but was often carried away by the sound and delivery.

One day in a debate, the chief minister used some words which immediately provoked the opposition and invited attention of the press. That very evening when I met him, I told him that perhaps, he was carried away by his rhetoric. He should now better watch out for the reaction. In a gallant manner, he laughed the whole matter off and again repeated for my benefit how much he had enjoyed what he had said on the floor of the House.

Unfortunately, both the opposition and several members within his own ranks did not take kindly to what he had said. The next day, the press played up those words and all those who were waiting in the wing to dislodge the chief minister came out of their hibernation. In the next few weeks, several other problems were unduly magnified and a determined effort was made to dislodge Babasaheb Bhonsle from office.

One such problem arose out of the acute drinking water scarcity obtaining in several thousand villages. To be truthful, everyone knew that this was something over which the government had no control. The administration was doing all that was necessary to provide drinking water to thousands of villages affected by draught.

It was sad to witness how because of pressures of interested groups working against him, Babasaheb Bhonsle had to demit office early in February 1983. I believe that he provided a very stable and supportive leadership to the administration at a time when the morale of the bureaucracy was severely damaged during his predecessor, Barrister Antulay's regime. In his own way, he restored the balanced relationship between political executive and administrative bureaucracy.

After the furore in the Legislative Assembly, as expected, political developments moved fast. Delegations of Congressmen started visiting Delhi to complain and seek change of chief minister. There were several aspirants. One of them was Vasantdada Patil, who was the General secretary of the All India Congress Committee. He was keen, but decided to wait for a signal. After usual internal squabbles, AICC sent observers to get opinion of the legislators. They had apparently come with instructions from Mrs. Indira Gandhi, the Prime minister. After usual charade of consultations, Vasantdada Patil was declared to be the choice of the legislators.

In the Mantralaya, we were closely monitoring political developments and preparing for transition. Fortunately, Babasaheb Bhosale was taking the whole matter in a sporting spirit and spent his time, clearing pending files in his office. I had told him and his secretary not to take any major decisions as I had already instructed the secretaries of the departments to keep all such decisions in abeyance till the new government takes over.

Sporting nature of Babasaheb Bhosale was evident when he told me that, "Mr. Chief Secretary, I have been the Chief Minister, and till my death I shall remain ex-Chief Minister of Maharashtra. No one can deny me that privilege". With that spirit, we were assured that the transition would be smooth. The day he laid down office he profusely thanked me and in his own style said, "My greatest satisfaction was to receive blessings of Indira

Gandhi. She made me the chief minister". He again repeated how he shall always be an-ex CM. He laughed heartily and bid me good bye.

Chapter 47

Vasantadada Patil as CM
- New Style and Challenges

Vasantdada Patil's election was widely anticipated and for me it represented an opportunity to carry out several measures to get the State administration to regain its high reputation after great damage inflicted by A. R, Antulay and weak political leadership of Babasaheb during their regime. I had known Vasantdada since 1957 when I was the Collector of Kolhapur. Dada was an important Congress party functionary and was then involved in setting up a sugar factory in Sangli. He was a well known freedom fighter who had actively involved in the Patri Sarkar, a parallel government in Satara District. Vasantdada was a man of few words, little education but tremendous practical commonsense.

As chief secretary, I had a prominent role in swearing in of the chief minister and the cabinet. Y. B. Chavan specially flew down from Delhi and attended the ceremony. Everyone, being aware about my special relationship with Chavan, was hopeful that I might also play a part in the formation of the ministry. I had played my bit when I was his private secretary in 1960s. As the chief secretary in the

1980s, I scrupulously kept myself away from the political process although I had been kept informed of what was happening.

Just before swearing in, I had met Vasantdada and briefed him about several problems facing Maharashtra. The biggest challenge was the drinking water crisis that would take place couple of months later. According to official assessment, out of 30,000 villages, over 17,000 villages were facing drinking water scarcity. As a politician, Vasantdada knew that unless the urgently needed measures were taken to face that crisis, his tenure as chief minister may be as short as the one of Babasaheb Bhosale.

As soon as the swearing ceremony was over, Vasantdada, instead of proceeding to the Mantralaya, told me that he proposed to come over to my residence to discuss and work out a programme of action to meet the water scarcity before convening the customary first meeting of the cabinet next morning. He also wanted to interact with me about allocation of portfolios for junior ministers. An hour later, accompanied by B. S. Chougule, the Home secretary and S. P. Mohoni, the Secretary to the CM, he came to my apartment in Lalit Building near Mantralaya. In a one hour meeting, we briefed him about the situation and shared with him several proposals that we had discussed at the official level to meet the threat of water scarcity.

Dada, with his penchant, was working on a broader canvas and wanted a programme of action that would reassure the rural population. He asked us to prepare overnight a programme to utilise every drop of water from all available sources to ensure that no housewife will have to walk more than half a kilometer to get drinking water. During previous weeks, I had several discussions with experts in the Public Works and Irrigation Departments. Next day, at the cabinet meeting, Vasantdada got approval to the programme. That caught the imagination of the people.

Our job in the administration was to ensure that the programme was translated into projects and implemented at the ground level. For the next four months, the Maharashtra Government, including the chief secretary, was engaged in a kind of war to face the water scarcity. This took me to almost every district of the state. Each week-end, my wife and I and couple of officers from the Revenue and Rural Development Departments visited different district headquarters to hold review meetings with the field officers. We ensured that instructions given on the spot were recorded and orders handed over before we left the place. That inspired the district officers to push the programme with vigour. I was always accompanied by my wife and that gave us opportunity to meet families of district officers over a meal and everyone got a feeling of belonging to a family. Generating that spirit was important for me to get unstinted cooperation and support of district officers. I was a stranger to most as I had been away for a long time.

In the next two and half years, if I could establish a name for myself and reestablish reputation of the Maharashtra administration, it was solely because of the restoration of that spirit and unstinted support that I received from officers at all levels and all departments. The Administration was applauded by the people for all that, and given due credit. I believe I also earned a place in the heart of the people. Even today, almost twenty five years after my retirement, wherever I go in Maharashtra, people come over to meet me and talk about 'those days'. Nothing has given me more fulfillment.

By the time Vasantdada's Government was formed, I had settled down. I had also formed a team of officers on whom I could fully rely. In any Administration, the chief secretary has to have a band of senior officers, on whom he could depend for advice and trust their ability to deliver results. In doing so, I did not want other secretaries to find themselves outside that small circle. I belived that I succeeded in creating an atmosphere of trust and dedication amongst senior officials within the Mantralaya, as well as outside.

That style of functioning was also in tune with the style of the chief minister. It was routine for Vasantdada to meet over hundred visitors a day when he was in the office. A large number of people also visited him at Varsha, the official residence on the Malbar Hill. In fact, on occasions, even his bedroom was occupied by 15-20 senior level politicians. On many occasions, when I entered Varsha to meet the CM, passing from the entrance varandah, the main living room, the sitting room upstairs, up to his bed room, I had to greet a swarm of people. His bedroom was the place where he met many visitors. When he wanted to have a one to one talk with me, that I insisted on occasions, he would enter his bathroom. He would majestically occupy the top of the WC and ask me to sit on a chair facing him. It was somewhat ludicrous to find a chief secretary talking to the chief minister in that room, but it was perhaps the

Vasantadada Patil as CM

only place where no one dare disturb him and he could finish the discussion without waste of time.

Despite a rustic background, Vasantdada was always conscious of time especially for senior officials. His ability to comprehend even complicated matters was phenomenal and he could see the real issue cutting through the peripheral matters. He was not only clear headed but firm. Once he had taken a decision it was almost impossible to get him to revise. On that score alone, many ministers started using my good offices as they found that he was receptive to suggestions made by the chief secretary and was even willing to change his decisions. It was the reflection of the trust and respect that we nurtured for each other. A few months later, cracks developed in our trust, all on account of problems in his household.

ॐ☙ॐ☙

Chapter 48

The Longest Textile Strike
- Dealing with Datta Samant

Eight months prior to my arrival in Mumbai, Dr. Datta Samant, a militant labour leader, had launched an indefinite general textile strike in January 1982. On assuming the office, I found that the textile workers were in no mood to return to work. Rashtriya Mill Mazdoor Sangh - RMMS that represented the textile workers as a whole was steadily losing ground to Datta Samant.

By September 1982, it was clear that Samant enjoyed wide support from the textile workers. It was also known that he had a group of musclemen at his command to ensure that the strike was strictly observed. He wanted the government to recognise him as the sole spokesman for the textile workers and not deal with the RMMS that had close relations with the Congress party. This was not acceptable.

As Dr. Datta Samant had made unreasonable demands for increase in the wages and allowances and as these demands were clearly not acceptable to the textile mill owners, the strike had dragged on. The Central Government was keen that the contentious issues be resolved amicably as India's exports of textile fabrics were suffering. Shivraj Patil, who was the Union Minister for Commerce, had announced in the Parliament in the month of July 1982 that the workers would get an advance of Rs.650, returnable in equal instalments as adhoc rise of Rs.30. He had also announced formation of a tripartite committee to look into this demand.

Soon after I took over as the chief secretary in August 1982, a delegation of mill owners met me. They grudgingly said that though they could not afford a fresh burden, they were prepared to accept the formula so that the economy did not suffer. There was no response from Dr. Datta Samant.

In order to get him to change his stance, the government had thought of derecognising the RMMS by scrapping the Bombay Industrial Relations Act. Before taking such a legal measure, it had to be ensured that Dr. Samant was ready to withdraw the strike. To that end, efforts were on way to create a rift between him and his associates. We found that the workers had rallied soildly behind Samant and would ignore the communists, as well as the socialists led by George Fernandes. Moreover, Datta Samant refused to budge from his demands and was not ready for any dialogue.

In such a situation, disaffected Congress party workers were increasingly becoming hostile to Babasaheb Bhosale. To meet their challenge, on the eve of Diwali, the Chief Minister announced a generous package. In response to that, about 45,000 workers joined. By end of November 1982, it was clear to me that there was no further role that state government could play to bring about settlement of the textile strike and there was a danger that the strike could spread to other industries as well. Datta Samant and his team were already spreading disaffection amongst workers of engineering industries especially in Navi Mumbai area, and it was anticipated that by the time the State Assembly met in Nagpur in mid- December, the strike may spread.

I decided to brief Delhi and seek some help from the highest quarters. Fortunately, I personally knew Pranab Mukerjee, the Finance Minister, since his earlier days as the Commerce and Industry minister. He had kept him fully informed of the situation in Mumbai. According to his advice, I approached Dr. P. C. Alexander, the Secretary to the Prime Minister, who met me along with Dr. Arjun Sengupta, who was looking after economic matters in the PMO. Fortunately, I had known both Alexander and Sengupta and had excellent rapport with them. They could envisage the PM getting involved to resolve the issue, in case Datta Samant was persuaded to openly declare that in the national interests, he would accept anything the Prime Minister offered. Alternatively, the formula for virtual takeover of the mills by the Government was discussed. That was administratively and legally feasible. However, this was not found politically expedient, especially because of the recent debacle for the Congress in Andhra and Karnatak assembly elections.

The strike continued with sporadic incidents of law and order at the behest of Datta Samants. Despite that, the state government was firm in giving assistance to the mill owners who requested for police protection for taking out their finished goods from factory premises. The Bombay police did a commendable job. Unfortunately, when the administration was getting into shape, the political situation was deteriorating. This was evident in the Nagpur Session held in December 1982.

By the beginning of January 1983, Babasaheb Bhosale was on the way out and Vasantdada Patil was sworn in. As a shrewd political leader, he knew how to divide the workers and strengthen the role of the RMMS. With him at the helm, I was assured that the administration should handle the strike firmly. I had to be equally firm with the mill owners, some of whom wanted to start dialogues with Datta Samant and give-in to his demands. I made it clear that since they had already got the state government and to great extent the central government to face Datta Samant's strike, it will be wrong in their part to break ranks and we shall not offer any police help. They got the message.

Results of all these developments led to a stalemate and the strike continued. In 1984, slowly some workers started resuming work. Many others, who had gone back to their villages, found that instead of living in shanties in Mumbai, they could live a much better life in their own villages and decided not to return. We encouraged them to shift work in cooperative textiles units for manufacture of yarns that were being set up in southern Maharashtra and elsewhere. The disastrous strike continued because it was never called off by Dr. Datta Samant. It was however clear that he had progressively lost the support of the textile workers.

That indefinite strike eventually fizzled out. That also sounded death knell to Mumbai's textile industry. Even today, after over three decades, textile workers are suffering. Government is still grappling with problem created by huge vacant lands and rehabilation of workers. The main benficieries are the textile mill owners who are reaoing huge profit with unimaginable escalation of land prices. In my view, that issue has been badly handled mainly because poilticians in Mumbai and the state are in close cohort with building lobby to make unimaginable fortunes for their future generations.

It is worth recalling what an analyst wrote in the Economic Times (17th January 1983): *"In the history of trade union movement in the world, one will look in vain to find parallel to the Bombay textile strike Here is a strike about which, if anything is definite, is that it is indefinite; brought about by a stranger to the textile arena; declared right from the start as illegal by the State government; practically ignored by the center for quite a while."*

Chapter 49

Testing Times
- Relationships and rewards

A chief secretary is not only at the top of the administrative pyramid but a visible face of the administration. During my days, in most of the states, the chief seretaries effectively functioned as the chief executive of the state administration, although over the last fifteen years, or so, the chief ministers have progressively started assuming that role. Seperation of politics and bureucacy was a great British legacy to India. Mixing of the two has led to a decline in both.

Fortunately for me, during that period, we had a dedicated team, both within the Secretariat and outside. N. Raghunathan, IAS who had suffered during Antulay's chief ministership and had been shunted out to a not-so-attractive field posting in Pune, had been brought back to the secetarait by my predecessor, P. G. Gavai, IAS. PG hailed from the Nagpur region of the state and belogning as he did to the scheduled caste, had strong moral streak. During Antulay era, he was fortunately posted on deputation to the central government post in Mumbai, as the Director General of Shipping, a post that I had occupied between 1978-81.

N. Ragunathan, known as Raghu to colleagues, was intellectually outstanding and vocal. He was a graduate of the Cambridge and I found that he had very good knowledge of the finance and monetary matters. He was alert and wathched over Maharashtra's precarious finances with a hawk's eye. He was aware that a financially surplus state had been driven to a deficit one because of the unwise spending spree and a lack of vigilance by the Finance department. Each morning, he would enter my room and brief on finacial health of the State. He spent sleepless nights if there was any withdrawals, over and above the limits set by the Reserve Bank of India. He was ruthless in cutting down expenditure and examined proposals made by other departments so thoroughly that soon other secretaries and ministers started complaning. It was left to me to sort out their grievances, as the chief minister did not wish to get too much involved in inter-departmental feuds. In fact, as the chief coordinator at secretary level, I found that much of time was devoted to sorting out those conflicts. I did not find anything unusual in that, as that showed, that each secretary was preparing proposals with due application of mind and ready to defend the same. It was my task to see how these could be accommodated within budgetary constraints and priorities set by the Planning Commission of the Government of India. I found that once I had taken a view, Raghu was amenable to find a way out. I admired him for that because at a young age I had seen how an obstinate finance secretary like M. R. Yardi, ICS had made himself not only unpopular, but made the task of the then chief secretaries difficult. Unwittingly as private secretary to the CM, I had to get involved. Chavan was capable of understanding the complicated financial issues, but that could not be said of either Babasaheb Bhosale or Vasandada

Patil. Of course, Sharad Pawar was in a different class.

Raghu was not all that negative, as he seemed to his many colleagues. Being intellectually bright and educated in intricacies of finance, he was sometimes ruthless and called a spade a spade. In a way, that helped me play my role of an elder, conciliator and one who saw the bigger picture. I earned the admiration of ministers and the loyalty of colleagues for that, a trait and reputation that helped in my next posting as the Union Home Secretary.

I also depended on some other colleagues: D. Sukhthankar, Sadashiv Tinaikar, Sharad Kale all at secretary level and Lalit Doshi, who was then a joint secretary. I made it clear that I did not have any favorites. Not even B. K. Halve, the Additional chief secretary, who was my batch mate. My doors were open at certain hours for any officer to walk in. I made it known that we were collectively responsible for administering the state. Very soon each felt the he was involved in decision making. I also found that that was in my interest. Having been away from Maharashtra for decades, I had no experience of working in field as a commissioner, head of a department or a joint secretary in Mantralaya.

I also appointed bright young IAS officers as Officers on Special Duty in my personal office. I had Jairaj Phatak, Ramani and Benjamin, A. P. Sinha in succession. They also benefitted from getting an overview of the state administration and of decision making at high level. All of them did very well in their future careers. I am proud of them all.

Chapter 50

All for Bombay / Mumbai
- Summer 1952

Having visited a number of metropolis in several countries, I decided to take in hand planning of projects for Bombay city that would soon become a mega-city. A major problem is proliferation of slums. Even footpaths meant for pedestrians were occupied in several areas. Antulay, the chief minister in early 80's had taken initiative to remove slums on footpaths. Unfortunately, the action was taken at the height of monsoon. That caused great misery and several NGOs approached courts for relief. By the time I came over as the chief secretary, the matter was already in the Supreme Court and remained there till almost the end of my tenure in January 1985. Thus, the slums remained as they were and proliferated wherever open space was available. Sixty percent of people in Mumbai today live in slums. I had seen worse in Rio de Janeiro, the then capital of Brazil.

On the question of slums, my colleague S. S. Tinaikar, IAS had studied the problem in depth and formed his own ideas. His main conclusion was outside the island city there were large tracts of land available for rehabilitation as well as for settlement of new migrants to Bombay City. So far as the existing slums were concerned, instead of demolitions and providing accommodation in multi-storied buildings, he was of the view that the government should provide infrastructure such as streets, water supply, drainage, latrines, street lights etc. and the slum dwellers encouraged to carry out improvements to the shanties built by them. Over a period of years, many existing slums could thus be made livable at an affordable price both to the slum dwellers as well as to the government. His thinking was on the right line because, as proved later, wherever government made efforts to provide alternate accommodation in multi storied buildings free of cost, the slum dwellers sell their apartments and continue to live in their slums. This is one problem on which we applied much thought at the bureaucratic level but failed to make any dent. Since then political parties, in and out of power, have played politics of vote banks, the slum - problem has become more acute despite government having spent thousands of crores of rupees. Main beneficiaries of several rehabilitation schemes have been the developers, builders, and local politicians.

Almost thirty years earlier, SG Barve, ICS, the far sighted administrator had anticipated overcrowding of the city and had planned a new Bombay - a city beyond the Thane Creek on way to Poona. Over last few decades, because of enterprise of enlightened officers, such as J.B.D' Souza, IAS, and PC Nayak IAS, the New Bombay was taking shape. CIDCO (City and Industrial Development Corporation) had been entrusted the task to develop infrastructure and undertake construction of housing as well. At that time, there was not much response from the private sector. When I discussed the matter with developers and CIDCO officials, I learnt that unless there were facilities to commute from New Bombay to the Fort area, people will not be interested in shifting there. The road-bridge was not sufficiently attractive as Bombay moves on the local trains, on which over 1.2 million people traveled each day. During my one of the visits to New Delhi, I took up the matter with the Chairman, Railway Board, who was good enough to assure me to carry out a survey. Six months later, their studies had established feasibility and they could plan investigations for construction of a railway bridge parallel to the existing road bridge, but considering the budgetary restraints, they could do so only if Maharashtra Government agree to share the cost, which, at that time, was estimated around Rs.120 crores. In the meeting attended by the Chairman of the Railway Board, after consulting Raghunathan, the Finance secretary, I committed the Government to contribute Rs.60 crores in a phased manner. When I briefed the chief minister about the discussions, he readily approved our action.

There is sequel to this. In 1985, when I went to Delhi as the Union Home secretary, I checked up with the Railway Board. I was told that the Planning Commission had objected to the Railways accepting contribution for the project from the Maharashtra government. On checking up with the Planning Commission, I was told that it was not a 'planned project' and the Railways could not divert Rs.60 crores from their surplus, because, as a rule, all surpluses of railways were committed to the Consolidated Fund India. In one of my meetings with the Prime Minister Rajiv Gandhi, when we were discussing some issues, as an administrator. I pointed out how our system did not allow development at a rapid pace even where funding was assured. Rajiv Gandhi heard with great interest and a few days later told me that he had sorted out the matter. Fortunately, because of his initiative, today a commuter from New Bombay can reach the Fort area to earn his daily bread. That bridge connecting Vashi to Mankhurd over the creek has also accelerated development of New Bombay, which is now a flourishing city that should qualify in a few years as a mega- polis.

There are two other infrastructure projects that I got myself interested. Some years back, it was planned to connect the Nariman Point near Mantralaya in South Bombay to Bandra. A tunnel under Malabar Hill and a bridge connecting from there across the sea to Bandra was planned. However, because of several objections and fears of dangers to ecology, the whole matter was stalled. When I reviewed the matter, R. T. Atre, Secretary, Public Works Department, a highly professional civil engineer, and I visited the Bandra and area beyond the Mahim creek and worked out a proposal for Bandra to Worli- Sea-face. That appeared feasible and one likely to meet less resistance from the various lobbies that were objecting to the original proposal. I am glad to find that an idea mooted at that time has, twenty five years later resulted in magnificent Bandra- Worli Sea Link. For that, credit should have really been given to a forward looking and imaginative person Atre but as it happens generally, the originator of an idea hardly gets recognition in our system.

Likewise, during that investigation, we found that Kalanagar Junction was a bottleneck. R. T. Atre and his team of officers worked out a 'Clover- Leaf design'. Today, that is a boon to the motorists. As luck would have it, that project caught up with me five years later when I became a member of the Maharashtra Legislative Council. One day, the former chairman of the Unit Trust of India came to see me. On retirement, he had been appointed to head the newly created corporation for financing infrastructure, named the Infra Structure Financing Ltd (ISFL). He was in search of some good projects to finance. I asked Atre to brief him of two projects conceived by him. I also talked to Sushil Kumar Shinde, who was the Finance minister. I recollect Pherwani coming over one day with a young colleague to thank me for getting the Kala nagar project for the ISFL.

All these things that I have mentioned are not traditional part of the chief secretary's duties. For me, these provided stimulants and also opportunities to do something tangible. These activities were not restricted only to the Bombay city but wherever I visited, such activities were planned. A visible example of that is the relocation of slum dwellers on the slopes of Parvati Hill, Pune, in a new township built at Bibwewadi. That was possible, thanks to initiative shown by Arun Bongirwar, IAS, who was then Municipal Commissioner of Poona and who one day would become the chief secretary. My initiative to permanently cure the pollution in the major source of drinking water supply was much appreciated by the citizens of Pune. As an appreciation the Pune Municipal Corporation honored me by inviting me to visit the PMC. Balasaheb Shirole, the Mayor, presented a statue of the Shivaji the Great on horseback and publicly thanked me. That was a recognition, but for me, the greatest satisfaction was when I visited the Bibwewadi project site in 1991 and saw how happy the residents were in their new homes where we had adopted S. S. Tinaikar's idea of constructing only one storied houses by providing bank financing. Several spontaneously came forward and took me inside their homes. For them, who had lived for a generation in the slum, it was a complete change of way of living. That held a lesson for me: Many had advocated multi- storied buildings. I was convinced that Tinaikar was right.

ಸಂಚಿಸಂಚಿ

Chapter 51

More Opportunities to Serve

Floods in Kokan

In August 1983, there were unprecedented torrential rains all over the western Maharashtra. Rivers were in flood and the Irrigation officers were afraid that some dams may develop cracks or breach. That threatened several dams. In July 1962, I had seen havoc caused in Pune by breach in the Khadakvasla dam that was caused by washing away of the upstream earthen dam across the Mula river at Panshet. Several hundred people residing along the banks had been rendered homeless. I was anxious to ensure that there was no repetition of that in 1983.

Fortunately, we had in the secretariat Madhav Chitale, a highly knowledgeable chief engineer in the Irrigation department. He knew all the river basins and had identified possible danger sites. We set up a Crisis Management Group in my office to monitor day and night water flows in several water basins spread all over the Deccan plateau. A wireless communication network was set up on dam sites and river banks to connect with the CMG. For two days and nights, officers kept a vigil with maps and charts on the walls. What was achieved can be best described from the reports appearing in the Press. To quote from the National Herald:

Catastrophe Averted in Maharashtra – Bombay August 17, 1983.

With efficiency of the highest order and administration tuned to military precision, the Maharashtra Government has successfully averted what would have been a catastrophe if the overflowing dams were allowed to flow downstream.

Today the disaster has been averted with water level in all the dams receding primarily because the top level committee took precautionary steps to shift inhabitants on the banks of the rivers and canals well in time before releasing water from the dams and thereafter the rain god came to the rescue by calling halt to the incessant downpour.

The death toll in the floods and in house collapse together could have been well above a hundred and five. If the 60,000 odd people had not been shifted the toll would have been very much higher. From prevention of floods the top level committee headed by Chief Secretary, Ram D. Pradhan, has immediately switched over to relief and rehabilitation include repairs to damaged houses, repairs of communication particularly roads, prevention of epidemics by undertaking a massive drive of inoculation and vaccination and agriculture operations which were badly affected by the sudden outflow of water from the dams.

That was the situation on the Ghats - a plateau about 1800-2000 ft. high. Kokan, a narrow strip of land facing the Arabian sea, with range of mountains running from north to south with slopes all along west up to the sea conditions were grim. Many coastal villages were inaccessible and because of land-slides, road communications from ghat to Kokan were cut off. Telephones and telecommunications were almost non-existent.

We did not know what was happening in the 800 km stretch between Alibaug and Goa. Fortunately, as I hailed from a village in the Kokan, some persons who had managed to reach Mumbai, briefed me. There was severe shortage of food supply and whatever had been sowed had been washed away and people were helpless.

I consulted N. Raghunathan and V. Ranganathan, who was Secretary in-charge of Relief and Rehabilitation, and decided that the situation was desperate and we must organize the relief at the ground level. The chief minister Vasantdada Patil was in Sangli and I could not get in touch with him over telephone. N. Raghunathan and I, along with senior officers from the Public Works and Agriculture Departments, decided instead of motoring from Mumbai all the way to Goa to fly by the state government plane from Mumbai to Panaji, Goa. Wireless communications were organized and transport to pick us up arranged with help of Goa officials.

Our first place of visit was Kudal, where a new district headquarters of the Sindhudurg was under construction. The young collector and team of his officers briefed us on the havoc. Fortunately the rains had subsided and we decided to undertake immediate relief measures that were called for. Accordingly, we started driving upwards from Kudal to Chiplun and onwards to Ratnagiri. People were happy to see that the chief secretary had come to offer relief and console them on loss of property and cattle. All along the highway, we got the food-grain godowns opened and arranged distribution of grains, so that no one should suffer from hunger. Likewise, the Agriculture Department arranged distribution of seeds and fertilizers. That night we slept in Ratnagiri. Next day, after reviewing the situation with all the district officers, we proceeded onwards towards Mumbai. Raghunathan, as was his habit, meticulously kept notes and we made sure that the local officers were given sanctions and orders signed by the Finance secretary and chief secretary to ensure that there was no complaint either from the people or from the audit authorities. Next day in the night we arrived in Bombay to brief the chief minister, who in the meantime had returned. Vasantdada, a doer himself, was very happy at the alert and promptness, and the way we had handled people's problems. Very soon the reports from Kokan started coming in and I had become a hero for them. Thereafter, whenever I had occasions to visit the Kokan area, people would recall my visit to their dilapidated homes and help in their hour of need. For me, that was reward enough for what the administration could do in their hour of need.

Chapter 52

Un-earthing FSI Scandal
- Discovery of 17 Century Cannons

Early in 1984, we came across some press reports that the Collector's office, Bombay, had issued some false certificates regarding measurement of plots of land on which certain builders had constructed buildings much larger and higher than the permissible Floor-Space-Index (FSI).

In the island city of Bombay, in those days, the FSI was 1.33, i.e., over say 1000 sq. of plot, a builder could construct 1330 sq. of built up area. Thus, much depended on the size of the plot on which a builder designed his building and submitted plans for approval of the Bombay Municipal Corporation. It was reported that while issuing certificates of area, in some cases, these showed much higher area than the land on actual measurements.

Secretary, Urban Development department mentioned to me that there seemed to be some collusion between certain builders and the Collector's Office. K. G. Paranjpye, IAS, was then the Revenue secretary and a young IAS officer, Manmohan Singh was the collector of Bombay. Both briefed me in my office with some records. One day I told the collector that I should be visiting his office and he should make available the records of 10 or 12 cases that had come to his notice. It was perhaps after many decades that a chief secretary was visiting the Collector's Office and naturally there was a great deal of speculation as to why I had decided to visit.

The Bombay Collector's office is situated in an old British regime building known as 'The Old Custom House'. Back side of the house faced the old dock yard. Adjacent to that is a fort like structure that was meant to house the British troops to guard the fort. It is a historic building where the naval mutiny that triggered India's march towards freedom had started in 1946. I had had no occasion to visit the inside of the Old Customs House and very much looked forward to get acquainted with that piece of India's history that I had learnt when I was a student in the Fergusson College, Pune.

On arrival, as a custom I was presented arms by the contingent of Bombay Police. While taking the salute, I saw that just outside the main porch of the Custom House there were four iron pillars protruding about three feet from the ground.

Paranjpye, who accompanied me, had looked into all the cases and verified from the records the basis on which the area of the plots was certified. Everything appeared to above board. I do not remember why but suddenly I asked him a question whether the bound survey records which were being shown to me were 'the original'. The Collector told me that these were the copies of the original made several decades back and on which his office had been issuing certificates all these years. I asked him to take me to the record room where the original bound survey sheets of Bombay City were stored.

Collector's office was surprised to find the CS entering the Record Room. When the original records of some of the plots for which the Collectors office had issued certificates were produced, we found that there was difference between the area recorded in the original, and area in the copy on the basis of which certificates were being issued. It was obvious from looking through the magnifying glass that areas of certain plots had been altered or over written. That discovery led to instituting an enquiry that resulted in unearthing what came to be called the FSI scandal.

K. G. Paranjpye did a magnificent job in meticulously checking all the certificates issued in the past several years to locate the staff members who could have done the mischief and also to establish nexus between his staff members and the builders. Of course, there was a another nexus between the builder and officers of the Bombay Municipal Corporation who actually authorized construction, because they were required to visit and carry out actual measurement before authorizing construction. It took over two months for a team of officers to unearth the whole scandal and identify some individuals - mainly lower level government servants. But our enquiries also revealed that they were working at the behest of some senior politicians.

On return to the Mantralaya, I called the secretary of the Public Works Department (PWD) and asked him to send some engineers to dig the plot opposite of the Porch of the

Un-earthing FSI Scandal

Customs House where I had seen four protruding steel pillars. It took them two-three weeks to excavate. One day the Secretary, PWD reported that they had discovered 23 big cannons of the British era underground. I asked all the cannons to be brought and placed at the back of the garden of Mantralaya adjoining the annex. After inspection, we found that most of the cannons belonged to the 17th century. I selected four and these are now to be seen, two on either side of the Mantralaya in the small gardens in the front.

A few years later, I mentioned these discovery to Dr. P. C. Alexander and his wife and requested them to select a few cannons for the Raj Bhavan. Akamai Alexander visited the Mantralaya selected 8/10. These are now to be seen in the patch of lawn behind the Raj Bhavan building fronting the Arabian Sea. That lawn is used for holding Republic Day reception and those cannons are a great attraction.

I had found that Manmohan Singh, the young collector of Bombay had performed his duty with honesty and diligence. He was a fine and sensitive young man who was quiet and did not brag about what he had done. I liked him and when I found that he was being marked in political circles as the one who had brought that scandal to light, I decided to shift him to a district and bring in a tougher individual. Arun Bhatia, IAS was then the collector of Raigadh. One day, accompanied by my wife, I visited Alibaug, the district headquarters. Bhatia and his wife Preeti hosted a lunch. I informally talked to them. He was an alumina of the Scindia school in Gwalior that had a high reputation for character building. I had met two Rajwade's who were past students of that school. The elder, B. L. Rajwade was in the Indian Foreign Service and the younger one. M. R. Rajwade's a major general in the army. I also learnt that Preeti's father had retired as a major general and his was a well-known name in the northeast, where he commanded the Assam Rifles. I was impressed with that background and decided to get him over to Bombay as replacement for Manmohan Singh.

Arun Bhatia's task had already been defined and I wanted him to thoroughly investigate the fraud and tampering of old Survey and Settlement records in the Collectorate. He did that thoroughly, knowing he had full support in Mantralaya. But progressively, he went overboard. He was fond of publicity and the press found in him a new hero. He would pass on information that he ought to have first brought to S. M. Paranjpye, the Revenue secretary's notice. Knowing what public service he was performing I gave him support and protected him from jealousy. After I had gone over to Delhi, he was much harassed and shifted out. He was denied his due promotion and when he approached the Central Administrative Tribunal for justice, no one would help him. One day, he came to meet me when I was the Union Home secretary. The state government, under instructions from the chief minister, would not give him a copy of his confidential report written by me. That I found unjust and I gave him a letter about his conduct when he served under me. Because of that he got justice. I had forgotten about it till he reminded me about the same.

Arun Bhatia continued to perform public service after retirement and associated himself with several causes in Pune. He even offered to be a candidate for the Lok Sabha although he was badly defeated. He was courageous and I liked him for fearlessly performing his duty. He attracts press and publicity but that is not his fault. One rarely comes across that breed of civil servants now.

Chapter 53

Differences with Chief Minister
- In Protest CS Proceeds on Leave

In a way the FSI scandal was first 'slight crack' in my relationship of trust with chief minister. Persons under investigation were mentioning some names that were uncomfortably close to 'Varsha'. The matter was getting politicalized as well. Vasantdada did not mention anything to me. However, I sensed that he was under pressure from his household. In the Mantralaya, there was much gossiping about what was happening inside the chief minister's residence. I was not in the least interested, nor had time for that kind of news. I warned some senior officers not to do so in my presence and advised that let the law take its own course.

In that situation, reports of certain discords in chief minister's residence were brought to my notice. His family consisted of children from his first marriage and those from his second with Shalinitai, a domineering and politically ambitious person. She and her children from her earlier marriage were also staying in Varsha. Politics and money matters were at the heart of all the information coming out of the chief minister's residence. I refused to speak to Vasandada about that as it was his private life.

Differences with Chief Minister

One day in October 1983, I was informed by the Superintendent of Mahabaleshwar hill station that a large piece of government land had been given on forty year lease at throw away price to Vasantdada's daughter from second marriage. The piece of land was located on a hill slope at the entrance to the town and was a prize location. I talked to Vasantdada, who tried to play down the whole affair, as politically motivated. I was familiar with that reasoning, as that's what politicians say when any impropriety is reported. But I did not 'buy' that, as my American friends would say.

A few days later, news started filtering to the press. In February 1984, the Supreme court's judgment on a graft case against a former chief minister showed that no minister or member of legislature was above law. I gently prodded Vasantdada and hurriedly the order of grant of land was rescinded. He was a wise man and having played some role in getting his predecessor A. R. Antulay dethroned, Vasandada did not wish to offer any opportunity to his political opponents.

Just at that time, the crime situation in Bombay was attracting my attention. As expected, the Police Commissioner Julio Rebeiro was perusing crime and criminals with zest. The central government agencies were investigating a large number of persons for smuggling activities and for 'hawala' transactions (laundering), that involved sending out of the country Indian rupees and bringing back the same in foreign exchange. The Bombay port area was found under control of Haji Mastan and all kind of imported electronic items, especially transistor radios, tape recorders and gadgets were on display and sale all over in Fort area. We had also found some shops only selling these products. There was a market, known as Manisha Market, behind the Crawford market, off the Mohamed Ali Road, that was hub for imported goods.

In the absence of the laws that were available during the emergency, police and the custom authorities were finding difficult to curb these organized criminal activities. As I had worked as a Home secretary, I was familiar with these activities and also limitations of authorities. In consultation with central authorities, we decided to round up several notorious criminals and book them under the dreaded National Security Act. Under NSA, a person could be detained without any prosecution in court of law for one year. That was deterrent and relatively easy to justify.

In the month of April, some rioting had taken place in Bhiwandi, near Thane. The place had notoriety for communal trouble and knowing that, riots rapidly spread to other communally sensitive towns, it was our policy to put down communal riots ruthlessly. Some Shiv Sena leaders were identified as provocateurs. We put them in jail under the NSA. There were riots in certain parts of Bombay. Julio Reibero detained Karim Lala, notorious extortionist and boss of crime syndicate and Haji Mastan, the king-pin of smuggling in detention under the NSA. During the raids on their premises the police reported finding illegal arms stored there. Reibero publicly stated that they had definite evidence that arms were supplied to the rioters by the All-India People's Secretariat run by Haji Mastan.

Differences with Chief Minister

This strong action was welcomed by all and Reibero was given full praise for that in the press. That helped to build his reputation as a professional, no-nonsense police officer. I was happy that we had regained the reputation of a well-run administration. The Press as well as the leaders of industry were vocal in expressing their appreciation. That helped our moral and reinforced the will to plan more intensive action to curb the 'mafia'.

One fine morning, we got a shock to learn from newspapers that the State government had issued orders to release Haji Mastan, Karim Lala, and Shiv Sainiks detained under the NSA. Even the chief secretary was kept out of the loop in taking that decision. According to the Rules of Business of the state government, it was the prerogative of the Home department to always keep the chief secretary informed in advance of major decisions having a larger impact.

I was shocked to find that the chief minister refused to take any responsibility for that action. It was hinted that it was done at the behest of the central government. When I wanted to check that up with colleagues there, I was advised not to do so, as high persons and higher stakes were involved. I could only 'guess'. Vasandada Patil, having had an experience of a coup in 1978 in which he lost his chief minister ship, was sensitive to what was happening within his government. The issue of "the Loyalist versus non- Loyalist" was being raised and the chief minister, who was not regarded as a loyalist to Indira Gandhi - having left Congress (Indira) in 1978 and gone to the break up group Congress (O) - was finding that a small group, within his cabinet was spreading distorted news about happening within Varsha, and of anti-Muslim action by the administration. I had received reports of a senior minister, a legal luminary, who was encouraging dissidence. He was also known to be close to some mafia dons.

For me, enough was enough. Late in August 1984, I put in an application for six week leave and a few days later left for Switzerland. There was much speculation about that decision. Some thought that I had gone to find out whether I could get a job in the UN.

My motive was to get away from sordid happenings in Bombay. I had no intention to resign, because not many knew that I had refused a high level job in UN, when I opted to return to serve in the IAS, where I belonged. I had no intention to resign and make a martyr of self. I went to visit my eldest son Rajiv, who was posted to Lausanne. He was working for an Italian multi-national company - the Olivetti. His wife, Nutan was expecting their first child.

Lausanne is less than an hour's drive from Geneva. I used to borrow Rajiv's car and drive to meet my old colleagues in UN and several Indians whom we knew well. All welcomed me and were happy to learn from the Indian press of the attention I was getting as a public servant in India. After six weeks of holiday in that beautiful land, I felt regenerated. On return, I resumed my post.

The very next day, The Times of India reported that "Pradhan, CM rift ends." It stated: Pradhan had opted for 45 days leave as he was reported to be "unhappy" with the working of the Government at the Chief Minister's level. I

Differences with Chief Minister

refused to confirm or refute that report as before rejoining I had met Vasantdada at Varsha and had a frank talk. Times reported that 'It was a happy ending to a controversy, which had led to a lot of speculation about Mr. Pradhan's future civil service career, Government circles say.'

I did not know that in a few months, events were to bring me into greater lime light and catapult me to the post that I aspired to occupy in the central government. In the meantime, I had established an excellent relationship with the chief minister and earned respect of the political class, irrespective of their parties. That allowed me to work with greater confidence and freedom.

৪০৫৪০৫

Chapter 54

Environment Matters
- Indira Gandhi's Directives

By mid-eighties', Bombay was rapidly moving towards one billion mark in population. Construction of buildings was rapidly changing the profile of the coast line. This was also creating new urban problem as the high rise building on the frontage effectively blocked both the air and the light for older buildings. Unregulated construction along the Juhu beach had already taken place and the distance between the high-water mark and the cottages was almost reduced to less than 100 meters. That had spoiled the beaches and the orderly development that had taken place in the 1930s when only one storied bungalows were allowed to be constructed, all facing the sea.

Some environmentalists led by Adi Godrej, who had access to the Prime Minister had brought this to her notice. Indira Gandhi was at heart not only an environmentalist but had high aesthetic sense. She issued directive to all the coastal states that no construction should be allowed within 500 meters of the high water mark. Also all unauthorized construction should be pulled down. With that directive, many young people got involved in forming environmental lobbies. Shyam Chanani was then working with the Tatas who were always in the forefront of environmental matters. He was free to engage in voluntary work. He formed the Bombay Environment Group. I liked him as he was highly educated person. An IIT graduate, he was a Cambridge and the Sloan School alumni. He was in the Tata Administrative Service.

One day, Shyam Chanani came to see me in connection with a conference at Mahabaleshwar to high-light problems created by unregulated development there. He was then around 38 years old. He did not need any introduction because his late father was the chief justice of the Bombay High Court.

Mahabaleshwar meet was beginning of my involvement in environmental issues. At that time, there was hardly any consciousness that by mindlessly cutting down trees and reducing water bodies we were endangering future of our grandchildren. Politicians were all of view that it was some kind of fad of the rich to protect their property and scenic beauty around their houses. They were not completely wrong because I came across several cases where so-called environmentalist who were peddling their personal agenda. By getting the chief secretary involved, they were wanting to get local administration overruled. I had to be careful not to mindlessly support their activities.

In case of Mahabaleshwar, my knowledge was limited to couple of visits with Y. B. Chavan in the sixties to participate in congress jamborees. I did not attend those meetings and had some time to move around with local officials. That gave me some idea of the geography. History,

I knew well because we were all taught how Shivaji had killed with tiger-claws Adilshah's emissary on a plateau just below the Fort named Pratap Gadh, where the deity of Bhonsle's was installed.

The conference was an eye opener. One retired IAS officer named Russi Boga who later became chairman of the Ceat, Dr. Farrokh Wadia, a horse breeder from Poona and one Ananda Wood were the moving spirit in organizing the event. After listening to speeches and knowing what was happening to the environment, I decided to act by drawing upon my experience at Mount Abu, where, apart from being an Assistant collector, I was also the Superintendent of the Hill station. In fact, historically the post had been first created in the Bombay state for Mahabaleshwar but after independence, perhaps some collector of Satara felt that he was not getting due recognition, quietly got that post abolished. Mahabaleshwar thus came to be administered from the district headquarters.

Having found the basic administrative weakness, I promptly got the post of the Hill Superintendent revived and appointed a young IAS officer, Aziz Khan as Additional collector Satara and the Hill Superintendent. He did a magnificent job to protect and preserve the environment and the forest wealth around.

I am happy when after twenty five years, persons living in Mahabaleshwar and young brigade that launched the movement there remember my contribution. Now some have received international recognition and great national acclaim. My contribution was to use my power and authority to support their voluntary work. That has given me great satisfaction.

I had earlier got familiar with environmental issues when I was the Director General of Shipping for India between 1979- 81. We were locating a site for the Nava- Sheva container port, across the bay. Bombay port was getting over congested with all kind of cargo. Goods imported in bulk in holds of ships were loose bundles in all shapes and sizes and in shipping terminology called 'break bulk' cargo. On import, big cranes would lift and place these on quay. The port area was thus littered all over and one had to find one's way around to locate parcels. Over past ten/ fifteen years, western counties were progressively using containers to carry break-bulk cargo. I had an occasion to study that in UNCTAD, as a special convention was drafted to arrange their movement from port to hinterland. It was named the Multi-Mode Transportation Convention. When I had sought instructions, I was grandly informed that India had no interest in that Convention. On becoming the D G Shipping, I learnt how wrong we were, and how much backward in shipping cargo. Rear Admiral Krishan Dev, MD of the Shipping Corporation was at his wits end to educate the offices in the Ministry of Shipping. We were thus a decade behind in the Container shipping and realized its importance only when shipping companies of Singapore started poaching on our cargo, by carrying our cargo in containers. Now bulks of India's exports of dry cargo are moving in containers.

Nava Sheva posed two problems. One, the actual site for the port and the land required in the hinterland. A large area of land was required to be acquired under the Land Acquisition Act. That was the state government's responsibility and that is how as the chief secretary, I came into the picture. The other was the environmental issue.

Acquisition of land for Nava Sheva Port and for the City Development Corporation (CIDCO) for new Bombay brought me into limelight. The container port was absolutely essential as the Bombay Port was getting over-congested. Also container shipping was progressively replacing carriage of dry cargo in 'break-bulk' state. I had studied that matter as the Director General of Shipping.

As the chief secretary, I found that while everyone was convinced of a container port in Nava-Sheva, there was not enough support for acquisition of land for the project. Uran area in Raigad District where the project was planned was dominated by the Peasant and Workers Party (PWP). Their leader D. B. Patil, was the leader of opposition in the Maharashtra Assembly and a powerful political personality. The chief minister Vasantdada Patil had several talks with D. B. Patil but the PWP leadership was not ready to agree unless adequate compensation and other facility of rehabilitation of people whose lands will be acquired were agreed to by the Government.

So far as the price was concerned when I was Home Secretary, I had helped the Indian Petroleum Corporation Ltd (IPCL), Baroda to acquire considerable area in as many as nine villages adjoining Nagothane in Raigadh district. As a native of Nagothane, I had impressed on the people the importance of the project and kind of prosperity that they should look forward. We also obtained certain commitments for employment of local persons in the IPCL. The rate for acquisition was Rs.30,000 per acre as against the then prevailing rate of around Rs.5000 an acre. Because of my personal intervention the, villagers had agreed to part with their land for the IPCL. Taking that as a bench mark D. B. Patil had demanded Rs. 40,000 per acre and other commitments such as jobs etc. in case of land in Uran area.

As there was a stalemate in negotiations between the chief minister and D. B. Patil, one day Vasantdada asked me to personally handle the matter as he was under considerable pressure from the Prime Minister's office in Delhi.

Before entering into talks with D. B Patil, I visited Nagothane and met the project-affected families in a conference convened by the IPCL. I found that several commitments had remained on paper. For example, IPCL was willing to give jobs, but there were no qualified engineers, civil or chemical engineers in that area. All that they did was to set up a training facility to train local boys in plumbing, carpentry and certain mundane trades. IPCL had employed some of them on the project but the overall performance was not satisfactory. I was expecting that some local persons will be employed for the operation of the plant.

After studying that experience, I had a couple of informal talks with D. B. Patil at the residence of the Chief Minister. But the impasse could not be overcome. These discussions however enabled me to learn matters of real concern to PWP leader. I was fascinated with his knowledge of ground level realities and his ideas regarding development taking place in the Navi Mumbai and CIDCO areas.

The more I reflected on our talks, I almost came to feel what D. B. Patil felt. It was alright to acquire land for a national project. Monetary compensation was governed by laws and had to be paid. But the real issue was the human beings. The families who would be deprived of their land and they would certainly become landless. Their land holdings were small and how could they earn their livelihood was the real question.

I came to the conclusion that for an agriculturist and his family, land was not only a means to raise crop for their subsistence, but it was really their way of living. In the process they also earned their livelihood. What we were depriving them of was their way of living and something must be done so that their future generations would not blame them for disposing their lands for pittance. For me, it was a moral question. How to compensate an agriculturist whose land we were acquiring for a project, so that the needs of his future generation are taken care of and they do not feel cheated. Cash compensation might look attractive in the short term but that money would soon disappear.

Out of these thinking, one day in a free and frank discussions with D. B. Patil, I told him of my dilemma. He thoughtfully asked me if I had any ideas. I replied that the only way I could think safeguarding the interest of the future generation was by ensuring the 10% of the land, which was offered by an agriculturist for the project, was returned to him by the government as 'developed land' with all facilities of road, water, electricity etc. The land thus to be returned to him, need not be the part of land, which he had given to the government, but could be elsewhere in the project area. He was fascinated with the idea and promptly agreed to my suggestion.

The chief minister, who was not present at the critical stage of talk which was held in ante- room of his office, liked the suggestion and blessed the agreement. I received considerable praise in political circles and in the press for finding a forward looking suggestion to a very difficult issue. A few years later, Sharad Pawar as chief minister of Maharashtra, one day announced that instead of 10 per cent the government will return 12.5 per cent of developed land. He received kudos for that statement. I wonder how much have the agriculturist actually gained out of these political announcements. Someone needs to carry an in–depth study.

The story did not end there. One day Rajiv Gandhi, suddenly asked me to explain the idea. He liked it and he asked the cabinet secretary to incorporate it in the government of India's land acquisition policy. As the Union Home secretary, I did not have time to find out if the idea was implemented.

৪০৩৪০৩

Chapter 55

Reforming District administration

Ahmednagar Experiment

I was conscious that 1983 district administration was not the same that I had experienced when I left Kolhapur district in January 1960. After formation of Maharashtra, the chief minister Y. B. Chavan had set up a committee to study Panchyati Raj. It was under the Chairmanship of Mr. V. P. Naik, the Revenue Minister, and Mr. D. D. Sathe, ICS who was the Member Secretary.

The concept of Panchyat Raj was first advocated by S. K. Dey, who was a freedom fighter and social worker. He rightly advocated that a merely law and order administration cannot deliver development programs that the prime minister and planning commission was advocating. Unless the administrative set up was geared to become development oriented and equally people oriented, all programs will remain on paper. As a beginning, S. K. Dey had launched National Extension Service (NES) Blocks, with tehsil (Taluka) as a unit. A block development officer (BDO) assisted by a specialized staff in health care, agriculture and water management would undertake all development work. The emphasis would be on provision of health services establishing primary health center and setting up agricultural farms to introduce new varieties of seeds and training farmers in the use of fertilizers; likewise water management by digging of wells for drinking water and also a network of water channels for making the best use of water for irrigation. These were identified as the primary needs for lifting villagers from poverty and diseases that afflicted them. In the British administration, while Ryot were guaranteed their title to land by the records of rights and they in return guaranteed revenue for the government, there were hardly any development oriented policies as such. NES were the first attempt in independent India to undertake integrated development of villagers.

Later these NES blocks were extended to all the Tehsils/Talukas and converted and a group of such blocks were formed into Community Projects. I was familiar with that development process in Kolhapur district.

As the chief secretary of the State I was looking for some programme to undertake modernization of district administration. As I had extensively visited several countries and found that the district itself was a concept that the British had introduced in the Indian subcontinent and certain parts of Africa to administer their colonial empire. Nowhere else in the world people were 'administered' in developed countries where people governed themselves at the county or at municipal council levels. We were still worked with the colonial administrative set up, where anyone visiting an office had to present an application and then wait indefinitely for a reply. Even on such simple matters as getting extracts of land records, it would take three-four month and not without a certain bribe, called speed money.

One day I learned from the Commissioner of Pune that a young collector of Ahmednagar district, named Anil Kumar Lakhina had started reforming the working of the Collector's office by transforming it into a people oriented set up. Simultaneously Lakhina had also taken up aesthetic improvement of the inside of a collector's office by orderly seating arrangement, provision of adequate stationery and equipment, typewriter, lighting arrangement and facilities for staff as well as for visitors. In essence, Lakhina's 'Operation Clean-up' was to simplify relations between the government machinery and people, similar to an across-the-counter transaction in the banks. With the rational organization of work space, the creation of an uncluttered and task facilitating wok environment, simplification of the system of maintaining files and records and backed by leaflets and pamphlets for people in local languages meant to "de-mystify" bureaucratic procedures, it became possible for the people of Ahmednagar to obtain a 100 year old land record within one minute, a new ration card within an hour and a gun license within a week. One improvement that greatly impressed was orderly and neat arrangement of old records in the Record room. Files had been classified and neatly arranged in bundles of cloth of different colors.

After my visit, I formed a team of young secretaries to visit Ahmednagar to evaluate how similar programme should be implemented in other districts. They came out with positive suggestions with minimal cost to government and took a proposal to cabinet for introducing reforms, in stages in selected districts. Very soon, there were press reports of similar "miracles" beginning to happen in Pune, Nasik, Bhandara, Latur, Ratnagiri, and Yavatmal, the six districts in Maharashtra where the Ahmednagar experience had gradually been reproduced over the last year.'

We had decided to undertake similar series of drives as proposed at the Mantralaya in order that the administrative headquarters increasingly imbibe and reflect the changes initiated from below. This received excellent support of staff, thanks to my seeking help of their Staff Union, ably led by R. G. Karnik. "Operation Clean-up", during which 200 tons of paper was weeded out of the dusty files of the government yielded an income of Rs.2.32 lakhs through the sale of raddi (old waste paper). Simultaneously, after visiting the staff canteen, in consultation with experts from Institute of Hotel Management, Dadar modern cooking equipment was procured and wholesome food was dished out. Very soon the press reported that: Satisfied bellies of the Mantralaya staff already point at the impressive uplift which has already been given to the canteen situated on the mezzanine floor of the Mantralaya.

By end of 1984, the Mantralaya bore a new look. All corridors had been cleaned and appeared wider on removal of old furniture and cupboards stacked all over. On an experimental basis, we undertook new layout for interior of offices and at no cost the Public Works Department transformed its work place. Encouraged with enthusiastic participation of staff, who put in extra hours of work, without claiming any allowance, on the eve of the New Year 1985, I announced an ambitious project for the new year.

It was announced that, "By March end, it is expected that the new layout already prepared for the various departments and within each department will have been completed. From January 14,1985 a 12 day repeat of the a two week-long drive will commence to clear up the backlog of files caused by the Lok Sabha elections which kept both Ministers and the administration tied-up. Chief Minister Vasantrao Patil has asked Ministers to stay put at the Mantralaya during this period to facilitate a speedy disposal of pending matters."

Press reported:

"Procedural changes to reduce desk work so that the field staff can concentrate on the various development programs are receiving the highest priority. While following earlier directives, the task of compiling periodic returns at the field level has already been slashed down by 30 per cent, the Chief Secretary has asked Secretaries to recommend measures through which elaborate procedures could be further cut down. Perhaps for the first time ever, employees at the Mantralaya are being asked to come forward with suggestions to make the administrative system more responsive and efficient."

I announced that "I am also hopeful that with the measures that we have already taken and the ones we propose for the immediate future, Maharashtra will turn out to be a forerunner and a pace-setter in the field of administrative reforms for the rest of the country." The necessary reforms at the district and lower administrative levels, if undertaken in an intensive manner at an All India level, will undoubtedly go a long way in fulfilling the

Prime Minister's objective in creating an administration responsive to the people."

I was then thinking of what the young Prime Minister of India had said in his address to the nation on January 5th, 1985, after taking oath of office.

Chapter 56

Setting up of MIDA
- Present YASHADA

Maharashtra Institute of Development Administration (MIDA) is now well known as Yashwantrao Chavan Institute of Development Administration (YASHADA).

MIDA was established in a strange way. Traveling out of Mumbai I used to go past the Bombay Gymkhana to the Bombay Municipal Corporation (BMC). At the end of that road, opposite the old Capitol cinema there was a board titled "Administrative Staff College." In October 1983, out of curiosity along with my colleague P. P. Mahana, IAS secretary in General Administration Department, I visited the College that was intended to provide foundational training on recruitment and in-service training on promotion to officers of various state services. It had been set up in 1963 at the initiative of Mr. S. G. Barve, ICS who also was appointed as Chairman of the Governing Council of the Staff College. It was also providing training to boys and girls from rural areas of Maharashtra who wished to prepare themselves to appear for the Union Public Service Examinations (UPSCP).

Setting up of MIDA

I was appalled to see environment in and around the staff college. At the back was the Azad Maidan and in front the Capitol Cinema. After that visit, I wondered how boys and girls from rural areas who would come to Bombay for the first time in their life would benefit by that kind of environment. It was more likely that would fall into bad company or waste their time and parents resources.

After discussing with my senior colleagues, I decided to, visit Pune to find out whether any suitable piece of land was available in case the government decided to close down the Administrative College in Bombay and shift it to Pune. My first preference was the sprawling campus of the Pune University. I met the Vice Chancellor who was good enough to explain that under the statute, the university had been barred to transfer any land to any organization including the state government. I think the Governor at that time was Raja Maharaj Singh who had agreed to part with the 400 acre Government estate to Pune University wanted to ensure that it was not misused by subsequent governments. I explored several sites near about the university campus but nothing suitable was available. While going in search of land I had also visited the present Raj Bhavan across the road where the Government house had been shifted after handing over the campus to the Pune University.

I noticed that there was a piece of land which was lying vacant and it had some barracks to store the tents and horse carriage of the governor. It was more a store house for old and discarded furniture. At the very end of the plot, there were 8/10 servants quarters for housing of barbers, dhobis (laundry linen) and the Raj Bhavan staff.

I earmarked this land in my mind hoping to persuade Air-chief-Marshal I. H. Latif, the Governor of Maharashtra to part about ten acres of land for setting up MIDA. We had high respect for each other and he was always positive. He assured that he would try to see how he could help. As expected, his staff objected to parting with any land out of the Raj Bhavan estate. They pointed out that instead of 400 acre campus of the old Raj Bhavan, the new Raj Bhavan had hardly 40 acres and just not possible to cede any land out of that to the state government. Moreover, the governor has no power to give any land or dispose off any property without the specific approval of the Union Home Ministry.

Nonetheless, I pursued the matter and with a helpful Union Home secretary who approved our request, especially when I pointed out that almost half the area could not be put to any use for new construction as high voltage electricity wires were overhanging over that land. After that assurance and excellent work by Mr. P. P. Mahana we decided to approach the cabinet to close down the staff college in Bombay and to shift its activities to Pune. We also proposed that the new institution should impart foundation training in the field of rural development and public administration.

The chief minister Vasantdada Patil was as usual supportive and cabinet approved the proposal with admiration for the initiative. Later a Government Resolution was issued on 28th May 1984. I had made up my mind to inaugurate MIDA before the middle of the year. Governor Latif laid the foundation stone of the project. My colleagues were equally enthusiastic, especially Mr. K. S. Sidhu who was

Setting up of MIDA

the Revenue Commissioner at Pune. With that kind of all-round support, we planned construction of a hostel to accommodate one hundred persons and carry out extensive alterations of the tent godown to set up offices. Likewise servants' quarters were converted into residence for senior faculty and staff. We gave contract for the hostel on turn-key basis to B. G. Shirke & Co, who were the only one in India manufacturing Siporex blocks for construction. Mr. B. G. Shirke personally accepted the challenge to hand over the hostel block within 150 days. He kept his word and I became his admirer. Baburao, as I called him died recently at the ripe old age of 94 years.

MIDA was inaugurated on 31st May 1984 by Vasantdada Patil. Governor ACM Latif presided over the function. Later, Sharad Pawar government renamed it as the Yashwantrao Chavan Institute of Development Administration (YASHADA). It is today a premier institute in India

My appointing Anil Kumar Lakhina was widely welcomed. The Times of India reported:

'The initiator of the long chain of reforms within the administrative machinery is now functioning as the Additional Director at the Maharashtra Institute of Development Administration (MIDA), Pune which was inaugurated last year, to train and orient the State officials to function better."

"The institute has now become the focal point for creating the people essential for the reforms and soon its staff will be augmented to play a direct role in the implementation of the reforms at various levels." Pradhan stated.

"The necessary reforms at the district and lower administrative levels, if undertaken in an intensive manner at an All India level, will undoubtedly go a long way in fulfilling the Prime Minister's objective in creating an administration responsive to the people, Pradhan opined."

Very soon, when he was eligible, Anil Lakhina was promoted as the Director of MIDA. In Delhi, I briefed the Prime minister about MIDA and the work of Lakhina. On the next Republic Day, I was conferred Padma Shri. PM approved that and visited MIDA. The institute was recognized as a premier place for refresher training for senior officers. Nothing has given me greater pleasure than to see YASHADA flourishing as it has under stewardship of able young officers.

ೞಲ್ಠೞಲ್

Chapter 57

Modern Art Gallery, Mumbai
- Sir Cowasji Jehangir Hall

My interest in art and modern art is an old hobby that my wife and I cultivated in 1960's during my posting in Delhi. Our first oil painting was a Laxman Pai that we bought from the Dhoomimal Gallery in the Connaught Place. It was priced Rs.350 and not having that much cash to spare Ravi, the young owner of the gallery, offered us on monthly installment of fifty rupees.

An Indian artist whose friendship and affection we enjoy is M. F. Husain. Long before we left Delhi, we got interested in Indian art. Over the next four years, we acquired a few paintings of Shanti Dave, Laxman Pai and also a couple of M. F. Husain's canvasses. After I joined the UN and had some money to buy art we got quite a few Husain canvasses from Kali Pundole of the Pundole Gallery in the Fort area in Bombay. Kali introduced us to Husain.

Thus when we returned from Geneva, our modest apartment had a handsome collection on the walls. Several artists met me at various art exhibitions and many looked upon me as an art's patron. I also helped the Jehangir Art gallery to sort out its problems with the Price of Wales Museum at Kala Ghoda and its installing an air-condition plant.

In 1983, except for the Jehangir gallery, there was no place to hold any big exhibition. Many western countries wanted to bring exhibits but unless there was a fully air-conditioned, moisture as well as dust free gallery was available they could not bring old and precious art work to Mumbai. That gave me an idea to construct a modern building to house a gallery. Some one suggested using space at the Nehru Centre at Worli. I was an executive committee member and along with Mr. I. Kadri, the architect and Dr. Raja Ramanna, the General Secretary we explored that possibility but unfortunately because of several constraints we found that was not feasible. Mr. Kadri however undertook to provide a facility for holding exhibitions and thanks to his interest we have at the Nehru Centre a medium size, air- conditioned art gallery.

Just at that time, when I was working on that project, Dr. L. P. Sahare, Director of the Modern Art Gallery, New Delhi met me with a proposal to set up a branch of that gallery in Mumbai. He asked for a large size plot of land in south Mumbai. I visited several areas, including the World Trade Centre and Worli but no plot to meet his requirement was available. While doing this reconnaissance, it dawned on me that the Kala Ghoda area was the hub of the art and artists. There were four/five art related galleries or institutions around that compact area. But no land was available.

Modern Art Gallery, Mumbai

One day in June 1983, Dr. Sahare again visited my office. He was under pressure from the prime minister's office to get a modern art gallery set up in Mumbai. Mrs. Indira Gandhi's love for art was well known and several exhibitions were due to visit Delhi. I wonder what came to my mind. I invited a small group of artists and art lovers to my apartment. Around my modest dining table we had, Dr. Sahare, M. F. Husain, Ara, Keku Gandhi of the Chemould and a few others. At the tea meeting, I explained need for the new gallery to be near Kala Ghoda from convenience of art lovers. I also explained that the Maharashtra government was not in a position to allot any land in south Mumbai nor earmark funds for a building. Why not think of a building such as the Cowasji Jehangir Hall that was meant for use of Parsee community for holding condolence meetings etc. It was maintained by the state Public Works Department with certain funds placed in deposit by the Sir Cowasji Jehangir family.

It is to credit of Keku Gandhi, who took lead to secure consent of the Jehangir family. A few months later Sir Cowasji wrote a letter to me giving consent to use of the Hall to set up a Modern Art gallery, making clear that it should not be used for any other purpose. On my part, while giving that assurance, I undertook to ensure that the name of the building, namely the Cowasji Jehangir Hall would not be changed by the government of India.

That project began with my signing a Memorandum with the Secretary of the Education Department of the government of India, who happened to be Mrs. Sarla Grewal, my batchmate in the IAS. Very soon we would be colleagues in Delhi. She as the principal secretary to the Prime minister and me as the Union Home secretary. Later, after my retirement, I would have much to do to get the project off the ground, where it was stuck up in bureaucratic processes. I feel proud to have given to Mumbai, with help of Keku Gandhi and co-operation of the Sir Cowasji's family, a land mark building to start a branch of the National Gallery of Modern Art in Mumbai.

I left for Delhi in January 1985 to assume the post of the Union Home secretary. On 21st January, The Times of India wrote in an editorial:

"The Maharashtra Chief Secretary, Mr. R. D. Pradhan, who has taken charge as the Union Home Secretary, will be missed by artists and art lovers in Bombay. Mr. Pradhan has been a great patron of art and had a good collection of original paintings executed by masters like Hussain, Bendre, and Akbar Padamsee.

He had also played a notable part in organizing Krishna Reddy's workshop, when the latter took time off from a busy schedule in the U.S. to familiarize Indian artists with his unique etching techniques.

But the highpoint of Mr. Pradhan's affinity to artists was the selection of the Cowasji Jehangir Hall to house the country's art treasures. He gave the national gallery project at the hall the final touches before he went to New Delhi for the new administrative post. Bombay artists, who have spearheaded the art movement in the country, now have a dignified place to exhibit their historic works, thanks to him.

The former Maharashtra Chief Secretary had also encouraged Warli tribal in their art pursuits. A few days before his new appointment, Mr. Pradhan had fixed a tryst with the Warli master, Jivya Soma Mashe, at the latter's Dahanu Home. That meeting had to be put off because of his departure for Delhi.

He had released at the Chemould gallery a book on the paintings of Jivya Soma. After speaking in English for some time, he switched over to Marathi for the benefit of Jivya. The gesture was widely appreciated.

Mr. Pradhan also championed the cause of a better environment and took a keen interest in the preservation of the city's beaches."

That recognition gave me greater satisfaction than many achievements in my service career. On my return from Arunachal in March1990, I again got involved in pushing the project that had got mired in bureaucratic tangles. Fortunately, with a person like Mr. Bhaskar Ghosh secretary of the Department of Culture at the Centre, we got the final architectural designs of Romi Khosla approved and funds sanctioned. That's how one more landmark was added to Mumbai's art scene.

A few years back I found a letter dated 23rd June 1983, written by Dr. L. P. Sahare to my wife about that meeting in my apartment when foundation of today's Gallery was truly laid. He wrote:

"May me sincerely thank you for your very kind hospitality on June 21st, 1983. Besides a most fruitful discussion which I had with Shri Pradhan, it was, indeed, a great pleasure to see your art collection." The next day when I visited with Prof. N. S. Bendre, I had a pleasant surprise to know that the original of Mother & Child by Bendre which has been beautifully reproduced is in your collection.

I very much hope that we are able to start the branch of the National Gallery in Bombay soon, so that the cooperation of persons like you could help us to propagate the cause of modern art more effectively in the country.

We were sad to learn that very soon he died. Today, no one visiting the Sir Cowasji Jehangir Modern Art Gallery, remembers him. That's why I am mentioning Dr. L. P. Sahare.

Chapter 58

Raja Dinkar Kelkar Museum
- A landmark for Pune

As the chief secretary, I was also the chairman of Management committee of a museum in Pune. One day my wife and I visited an old 'wada' a typical residential house in Shukrawar Peth, a locality of Poona of Peshawa's regime. These wadas had a distinctive style and architecture. At the entrance was a door large enough for horse-rider to enter. Around an open courtyard were one storied buildings with doors and windows carved in wood with typical design. Inside the entrance courtyard were series of courtyards, depending on affluence of noblemen (Sardars in Peshwa days). I was familiar with that as my school, the New English School established in 1884 by Bal Gangadhar Tilak was housed in the wada that belonged to Nana Fadanavis, redoubtable prime minister of Peshwas in 18th century.

The museum that we visited was of similar pattern. We were received by an old couple, Dr. D. G. Kelkar, and his wife Kamalbai. Raja, as he was known, and his wife, with their old world charm and welcome ceremony, fascinated me. I was expecting to see an exhibition of objects belonging to the era of Peshwas. I had seen several museums all over the world and I was looking forward to a similar one. But what I saw was astounding. Room after room, in glass case after case, were objects of everyday use by millions of Indians over centuries. There were thousands of artifacts all over and I was told that more than 90% of collection were stored in go downs as there was no space to exhibit.

After that visit, with enthusiastic participation of Arun Bongirwar, the Municipal commissioner and K. S. Sidhu, the Revenue commissioner and a young collector Ashok Bhadkamkar, we acquired adjoining piece of land, arranged funding and with ceaseless supervision of Raja Kelkar, got an annex constructed. Today one enters museum through that new annex.

I started visiting the museum almost once a month and discussed with Raja Kelkar about his dream. I was fascinated to hear him talk as to how he moved around in bullock carts and on foot remote areas all over the vast continent and bought those artifacts.

One day he invited Babasaheb Purandare, a well-known scholar of the Great Shivaji's era to meet me. I was charmed by him with his knowledge and his enthusiasm. In my childhood I used to pass every day a wada, known as 'Vishram' wada, about a km from Peshawa's residence. Apparently it must have been on outskirts of city in those days and used by Peshwas and their guests for rest and recreation. His dream was to restore that wada to old days and set up a museum. Raja Kelkar offered to provide old articles and exhibits stored in his go downs, as those were too large to be shown in his museum. My contribution was to see how we could get the Wada that housed the Poona Municipality in old days and currently sundry offices including the birth and death office. With Arun Bongirwar and Bhadkamkar undertaking that task, those offices were shifted elsewhere and in few months we handed over the Vishram Wada to Raja Kelkar to set up his dream project of the hall from the house of Mastani, the paramour of Bajirao Peshwa. Several other large objects were brought to recreate old world for benefit of new generation. That is how Poona-now Pune-got another landmark.

I regret that much as I would have loved to, I could not associate with a dream project prepared by late Raja Kelkars son-in-law Dr. Hari Ranade and his sons to relocate the museum elsewhere so that all collection of Kelkar could be exhibited. I understand today hardly 15% collection is shown. Rest are still in go down.

Chapter 59

Bhiwandi Riots
- Meeting Rajiv Gandhi

The second fortnight of the month of May was hot and uncom-fortable. Most of the ministers had gone to cooler places in the State. While I was engrossed in some file work, 1 learnt that com-munal riots had claimed several lives in Bhiwandi. Precise infor-mation was not yet available at the Police Headquarters.

Bhiwandi was notorious for communal riots. Along with the Director General of Police K. P. Medhekar IPS, I rushed to the helipad on the grounds of the Raj Bhawan to visit Bhiwandi. What we saw hovering in the helicopter over the town was un-believable. A number of houses were on fire and new fires were erupting in several localities, while we were helplessly watching from the air. We returned to my office and I got in touch with Maj. Gen. Laxman Rawat, Commanding Officer for the Maharashtra and Gujarat Area, whose headquarters were within a couple of kilometers away from the State Secretariat. He responded promptly to my call for army assistance. By 10 p.m. that night, a battalion had moved into Bhiwandi and more troops were on way from Poona.

Mrs. Shankaran, IAS, collector of Thane district kept in touch throughout the night. Several hundred persons had been killed. Corpses of human beings and dead cattle were lying all over. Some local leaders had provided relief to the riot-affected-but there was not enough food, milk, and water. We organised relief on a war footing.

Five days later, Mrs. Indira Gandhi visited Bhiwandi, accompanied by a team of senior officers from the Central Government and some Muslim politicians from UP. At the end of her visit, she asked Vasantdada, the Chief Minister, how long it would take to clear all the mess. Dada looked at me. I unhesitatingly said. "Four days". The PM said, "All right. I shall send someone to check up."

During the next four days, teams of officers worked nonstop. All corpses were disposed of and debris of burnt houses cleared. Rehabilitation camps were working smoothly. Public health officials had immunized the whole population against cholera and typhoid. Teams of sanitary inspectors and even sweepers from adjoining areas had been brought over to clean up. I was satisfied with the progress and told my district officials to deal with whoever was expected to visit on behalf of the PM.

On the fifth day, Murli Deora, the Bombay Regional Congress Committee chief rang up to say that Rajiv Gandhi, the All India Congress Committee General Secretary of the Party, was reaching Bombay on his way to Bhiwandi. He said, "Rajiv would be glad to meet you and seek your assessment."

I was not sure whether I should go all the way to Bhiwandi to meet a general secretary of the Congress Party. However on reflection, I thought it prudent to be there since Rajiv Gandhi was coming on behalf of the PM. Also, if any information was needed, I would be in a better position to provide it. I decided to visit and be available at the Circuit House.

Rajiv Gandhi came accompanied by his aide Arun Singh to the Circuit House, where I was holding a meeting with my officers. Arun Singh had come fully briefed from Delhi, because he had sheet of paper with information and a list of questions. Both of them had already gone around the town and seen the work done. Local leaders had also briefed them about initiative taken by the administration to provide relief and rehabilitation. The prompt and effective action taken to quell the rioting with the assistance of the army was already known.

After a few general questions, Arun Singh whispered something to Rajiv, who asked me, whether he could have a word with me alone. We sat down in one corner of the room while Arun Singh carried out debriefing of other officers. Rajiv Gandhi was very courteous and polite. He asked me a few questions about the reasons underlying the rioting, the communal situation, and the role of politicians providing relief, etc. Apparently he was satisfied with what we had done. While taking leave he said, "Pradhanji, I am really impressed with what I have seen. How could you accomplish all this in four days?"

I said, "The credit goes to the Maharashtra administration. We know how to work as a team in a crisis". He smiled and

Bhiwandi Riots

thanked me and after a warm handshake took his leave.

A couple of days later, cabinet secretary Krishnaswamy Rao Saheb rang up to say that PM was happy about the work in Bhiwandi.

༄༅

A few days later in the first week of June, the 'Blue Star Operation' had an echo in Pune, where some Sikh soldiers had got worked up. There was a minor mutiny. Truckloads of Sikh armed personnel were on their way from Pune to Delhi. It was fortunate that three battalions were already positioned in Bhiwandi. Those troops were promptly deployed to stop the mutineers from proceeding to Bombay City and chased on the national highways. The army and the Maharashtra district authorities worked very closely and effectively to block their progress towards Delhi. This was noted with appreciation in Delhi.

In the beginning of October 84, we were looking forward to celebrate Diwali when one day astrologer Naik of the State Bank of India walked into my office and told me that I may soon have to move northwards. He had studied my horoscope and his one prediction had come true. He was emphatic that before I retire, I would be in a much higher position to be in 'lead' position. I heard him with skepticism. I was already in that position. So far uniformed services were concerned, I believed that I had made deep impact and very good friendships both with police and with the defense services in Bombay. I dismissed his prediction by telling him not to bother me.

I did not imagine that events in next two months would catapult me to Delhi.

Chapter 60

Post Mrs. Gandhi's Assassination
- Handling Law and Order

On 31st October 1984, all the senior police officers of the State were in Pune to attend a State level Conference. Vasantdada Patil, the Chief Minister, and I were also there. That morning I was visiting a village ten kms out of Pune when someone told me that the All India Radio had broadcast news of attack on Mrs. Indira Gandhi. No one was sure whether she had been injured or mortally wounded. On hearing the news, Vasantdada Patil and some senior politicians left for Delhi by the state government plane. I got hold of K. P. Medhekar and we flew by helicopter to Bombay. Our objective was clear: under no circumstances should law and order be allowed to be disturbed. By the time we entered Mantralaya, we had learnt that Sikh guards had attempted assassination. Julio Ribeiro, the Commissioner of Police, Bombay who was also in Poona had acted fast. He had instructed to cordon off areas habited by the Sikhs and Gurudwaras to protect life and property and rushed to Bombay by car. A statewide alert went out on the wireless advising similar action. Police were deployed in certain visible locations and armed police were brought in the city. Their visible presence and Rebeiro's overt leadership had the desired effect.

We received confirmation around 6.30 p.m. that Mrs. Indira Gandhi was dead. There were reports that night of rioting in Delhi that would go on for next four days and over 4000 persons would lose their lives. In contrast, quick action had averted any untoward incidents in Bombay. The rest of the State also remained relatively calm, barring a few stray incidents. Later I learnt that all this was noted in Delhi and perhaps my name came up when the then Union Home secretary Mr. Manmohan Wali, IAS was asked to take over as the Lt. Governor of Delhi.

After cremation, it was decided that her ashes would be sent in several traditional copper vessels to different capitals for each state to immerse in holy rivers of respective states of India. I personally monitored arrangements to be made within the compound of Vidhan Sabha, the State Assembly building, to place the urn to enable people to pay homage to the departed PM. Officers of the Directorate of Information, police, municipal and state administration worked overnight to prepare a stage and set up cordons for controlling crowds and ensure persons could pass in orderly ques in front of the dais. Next day early morning I was at the airport along with the Governor Latif and chief minister Vasantdada Patil. When we got the ashes to Raj Bhavan, I was given the honour to carry the copper vessel in my hands. Thanks to orderly behaviour of crowds, over a million people marched past the dais for next twenty four hours and paid their respects to India's tallest leader of that era.

Post Mrs. Gandhi's Assassination

Prime Minister Rajiv Gandhi decided to seek a peoples mandate and general elections to Lok Sabha were called in middle of November. With hardly two months to hold elections, we all got busy with preparations. Fortunately, my colleague B. K. Halve, the Additional chief secretary was an experienced officer and I was spared hectic work. Just when candidates were being selected and asked to file nomination, we learnt that Y. B. Chavan was unwell and shifted to All India Medical Institute. We did not know about the gravity and except for his loyal staff, no one was around to tell us. Those days it was difficult to reach anyone over land-line telephones. It was Vasantdada, who informed me that Chavan had passed away and his body was being flown to Mumbai next morning. I rushed to Varsha, CM's residence, and discussed about arrangements. As we had carried out only a few weeks earlier public viewing and homage, I immediately set in motion the drill to place on a similar dais the body. Next question was: where to perform the last rites. Several political leaders were asking that these should be in Mumbai, as befitted the first chief minister of Maharashtra. CM agreed and we started preparation for his cortege to be taken in procession for cremation. Late that night, Vasantdada rang me and told that people of late Yashwantrao Chavan's home town wanted to have cremation at Karad, where he had spent his youth and wherefrom he joined politics; Vasantdada Patil had to agree to their suggestion otherwise he was told that a million people from his area would converge to Mumbai.

Next morning, we received the body and brought over to Chavan's personal residence on the Marine Drive. I paid my respects along with the family as I was considered as one of them. That day I left for Karad to check on arrangements there. Next day I went along with Mr. Sharad Pawar receive the body to the air strip where it was brought by the state government plane by the chief minister. Last rites were performed on a site prepared overnight by P. D. Patil an old follower of Chavan. In retrospect, cremation at Karad turned out to be wise one and today on the banks river Koyna is a tasteful memorial visited by thousands.

Chapter 61

Meeting Mrs. Margaret Thatcher
- Post Bhopal Gas Tragedy

On the morning of 4th December 1984, we got first information of the gas leakage at the Union Carbide plant near Bhopal city. Thousands of persons were reported to be afflicted with serious breathing problems. After few days, we would learn about the scale of the tragedy in which thousands were dead. For us with our day-to-day problems, that was only news till we learnt that Mr. Keshab Mahindra, one of the senior and highly respected industrialist of Bombay, who was the chairman and Vijay Gokhale, Managing Director, had been arrested for criminal negligence on their reaching Bhopal to render relief to the afflicted. Bombay was shocked.

Almost at same time, we had a peculiar crime in the business district of Bombay. While I was entering my office, Ribeiro, the Police commissioner rang up to inform that Mr. Percy Norris the British Deputy High Commissioner had been killed by pumping one bullet in his temple. On his way to office Norris was in his car near the Ambedkar statue near Mantralaya.

Along with P. P. Mahana, the chief of protocol, I rushed to the office of the Deputy High Commissioner located on top floor of the present Mercantile Bank building opposite the Flora Fountain. We met senior staff who was not very communicative. Ribeiro had joined me there and we decided to go to the J. J. Hospital where body had been taken. We saw the wound where a bullet had pierced from left side of temple and come out on the other. It was a clean job with high velocity silencer. As the chief secretary, I was responsible for the diplomatic community and I was required to send a report to Delhi. After discussions with some experts and senior police officers, we concluded that it was a highly professional job and perhaps related to the Deputy High Commissioner's previous posting somewhere in the Middle East where he had worked for a private company. As the consulate was not forthcoming, that confirmed our suspicion that Norris was himself an undercover agent and his assassination was the job of intelligence services of the United Kingdom. Any way, after filing my report, I had nothing to do with it.

Within a few days of these two events, I got a message that Mrs. Margaret Thatcher would land in Bombay on way to Hong Kong and after an hour's stay would depart. I should receive her and see her off. Accordingly on 6th December, I and P. P. Mahana, secretary for Protocol received the British Prime minister who was accompanied by Lord Howe, the Foreign Secretary. We offered them refreshments in the VIP lounge and, as instructed by the Protocol from Delhi, conveyed greetings from the Prime Minister Rajiv Gandhi. I also told her that very day he was expected to visit Bhopal for electioneering. She asked me to convey her deep sorrow on the tragedy.

Meeting Mrs. Margaret Thatcher

I also talked to the Foreign Secretary and mentioned in her presence our sorrow on the death of their Deputy H. C. I was struck that she neither expressed any sorrow nor ask any questions about the incident. That confirmed our suspicion that it was carried out by one of their secret service agency.

About the Bhopal gas tragedy, our knowledge was from newspaper reports. Frankly, I received no briefing when I took over as the Home secretary in Delhi. Recently when circumstances in which Mr. Anderson, the chairman of the US Union Carbide was arrested and released to be flown out of India – almost on the day I received Mrs. Margaret Thatcher – several media representatives asked me to say something, as the role of P. V. Narsimha Rao, then Home minister, in that incident was under scrutiny. I had taken over as the Union Home secretary within six weeks of the tragedy. Strangely, there was no mention of any role by the Home ministry. Nor was I interested at that time as it was regarded as an issue to be handled by the state government. To the disappointment of several media persons, I refused to offer any 'bytes'. But as the story has unfolded, I have no doubt that 'someone' in the PM's setup had pulled strings and got Anderson to leave the country. PM himself was busy electioneering all over and air lifting of Anderson was too small a matter to plan and execute.

ಙಇಙಇ

Chapter 62

Meeting Young PM of India

Within a month after taking over the office of the Prime Minister, Rajiv Gandhi called for general elections to the Lok Sabha. During the next three months, I received him twice, when he visited for electioneering, as required by protocol.

In the beginning of December, soon after my meeting Mrs. Margaret Thatcher, I received him at the Santa Cruz airport. He greeted me with special warmth. After addressing a mammoth election meeting at Shivaji Park in Dadar, PM and his party were to travel by road to Thane, a distance of 30 km or so. After Mrs. Gandhi's assassination, the security for the PM had been further tightened. 1 had reviewed the arrangements along with all the senior police officers. We were not happy about the journey by road where there were several dark patches with poor lighting. I decided to travel in the PM's convoy to Thane to make sure that his security was not compromised in any manner.

Just as we were to leave Dadar for Thane, Arun Singh asked me to accompany him in his car. I had already met him in Bhiwandi and found him a quiet, decent and amiable type. That journey to Thane was to prove fateful for me. Arun Singh started asking me a series of questions – my service career, background, interests, how I looked at my own future, etc. His tone was conversational and polite. I responded to him equally frankly. One of his last questions was, "How is it that a person with your background of long experience in international trade and diplomacy is not in Delhi?" To that I gave a blunt reply: 'Perhaps, I am not wanted there!"

Next morning, I went to the airport to see off the Prime Minister. Just when he was about to board the plane, Mr. Rajiv Gandhi turned back, took me on one side and said, "Arun has told me about you. I will find out."

I was happily settled down in Bombay after almost twelve years' absence. I was the chief secretary of the most important State in the country. I had a firm grip over the administration. Politicians of all hues treated me with respect and I knew that I had found a place in the heart of the ordinary people of Maharashtra. My activist style of functioning was much admired and I loved my state and my people. I had less than two years service left before retirement and nothing was going to induce me to move to Delhi at that stage. I therefore took Rajiv Gandhi's remark as well intentioned, but hardly of any significance for me.

Rajiv Gandhi had decided to hold his last election meeting near Pen town in Raigad district. My village Nagothane is hardly 30 km away from Pen. I was happy to go there with my wife. Both of us were treated very affectionately by the Prime Minister. While PM addressed the meeting,

Arun Singh had a long talk with me in a tent behind the rostrum about my assessment of situation and particularly about A. R. Antulay. Electioneering came to a close with that meeting. As he came down from the rostrum, Rajiv Gandhi looked relieved after almost two months of non-stop flying all over the country. He warmly shook me by the hand. I wished him all success. Just before we parted company, he said, "Pradhanji you will hear from me soon."

ಬಲ

The day Rajiv Gandhi was sworn in on 5 January 1985, he addressed the nation over Doordarshan. Unknowingly I become his admirer. He spoke with sincerity. His agenda was precise and he appealed to the nation to give him a chance to push it into the 21st century. I instinctively felt that my place was to be by his side. Much as I detested leaving Bombay, I realized that my thirty three years of experience in the civil service would be more useful at the national level and especially to the youthful Prime Minister.

The call was not late in coming. Within two days, Krishnaswamy Rao Saheb asked me to urgently come over to Delhi. Next morning I met PM's Principal Secretary, P. C. Alexander. He asked me whether I was ready to come over to Delhi.

I replied straightaway, "Yes, but only as the Union Home Secretary". I had heard that some well-wishers of mine wanted me to be Commerce secretary. My background and experience qualified me for that post. But after having been the chief secretary of Maharashtra, I thought I was now too senior to occupy that post. The only post for which I was willing to leave Bombay was that of the Home Secretary.

I met Krishnaswamy Rao Saheb and Arun Singh as well. I told Arun Singh that in case the PM wanted me to be Home Secretary; I was willing to come over to Delhi. Otherwise not.

Next day an announcement was made of my appointment as the Union Home secretary. I relinquished the office of the chief secretary on 14 January, 1985 with a sense of regret that I was leaving so many tasks incomplete but at the same time that with a sense of joy that I was asked by the young Prime minister to come to Delhi to help him. Was not that what I dreamt of when I joined the Metcalf House?

14 January was also the 'Makar Sankrati', first day of Hindu calendar. I did not realize that I was stepping into a new beginning in my life.

༄༅

My sudden transfer was interpreted by media as recognition of my services. Just as there was praise, there were comments expressing anxiety. One newspaper reported:

"The transfer of Chief Secretary, R. D. Pradhan to the Centre as Home Secretary comes at an inopportune moment when the morale of the bureaucracy is at an all time low in the wake of the FSI scandal and the vague charges leveled by dissident ex-Chief Ministers of corruption against the senior bureaucratic cadre in the State.

He is one of the handful of officials who combine high administrative ability with an ingrained sense of propriety and honesty and is looked upon by younger functionaries as a fair minded arbitrator capable of restoring credibility to the organization.

Pradhan's transfer, though to a very sensitive position, is a little premature and following the repeated attempts to unseat Police Commissioner Julio Ribeiro, hints at a conspiracy to rid the city of its upright and incorruptible administrators so that the criminal underworld can subvert the law without fear of reprisal."

ಬಿಡಿಬಿಡಿ

PART IX :

Union Home Secretary (1985-86)

Chapter 63

In the North Block
- IAS Training School

Rajiv Gandhi had been sworn in as the Prime minister on the 30th October 1984. Soon after he called for the General Elections to the Lok Sabha (Lower House of India's Parliament). I had met him only once before he became the Prime Minister. After the General elections, in which he received unprecedented majority, he was sworn-in on January 5, 1985. We saw him over the television and heard his first address to the nation same evening with rapt attention. I saw in him the future of India. I did not know that my own future was also linked with his.

Within ten days of his becoming PM, I joined Rajiv Gandhi as the Union Home secretary. When he asked me to come to Delhi, I requested that instead of being bogged down with 'Babu' work, my services should be utilized for political work, which is inherent in the Home Secretary's mandate. He took my suggestion seriously and that enabled me to work with confidence. What was done is a part of contemporary history.

Rajiv Gandhi inherited three major conflicts, namely the Punjab, Assam and Mizoram. The Punjab problem had claimed his mother's life. Sikh fundamentalism was not the root factor in the case of Punjab. It only provided the focus for manipulating youth by preachers. An attempt was also made to exploit the rural-urban divide as a Sikh-Hindu divide. In the 1960s, the character of Sikh leadership had started changing from the non-Jat urban leadership to the newly emerging Jat rural leadership. In rural areas of Punjab, Hindus are in a minority.

This problem was the most serious one. It had to be dealt with in a delicate way. Operation Blue Star—the military operation carried out in 1984 by the Indian Army on the orders of the then Prime Minister Indira Gandhi to flush out Sikh militants from the Golden Temple who were amassing weapons and advocating an independent nation for the Sikhs as envisaged in Anandpur Resolution. The way the Operation was carried by tanks of the army entering the Holy Golden Temple of Amritsar and the damage that was caused had given rise to large-scale disaffection amongst the civilian population. Moreover, a sizable percentage of the Indian army was Sikh and there were mutinous acts in some places including Maharashtra. The issue required proper handling to curb hatred and secessionist activities fuelled by religious fanatics. Also, Pakistan was engaged to create chaotic conditions by infiltrating militancy with the help of certain separatists organizations founded by Sikhs living outside India who were advocating a separate nation named Khalistan.

Punjab was under the President's rule and simmering with discontent when Rajiv Gandhi took over. One did know how and when it would explode. Rajiv Gandhi showed remarkable shrewdness and boldly announced in his very first speech to the nation: "My government will give priority to the problem of Punjab.... there cannot be any concession to separatist ideologies and the cult of violence. India's unity is paramount, everything else comes after that."

When I joined as Home Secretary I got detailed briefing from senior intelligence officers and the army authorities. My wife's cousin General Arun Vaidya, MVC was the chief of army staff and I got from him more informal briefing as to why and how Mrs. Indira Gandhi ordered army to attack and flush out the terrorists who had taken over the Temple and their leader Bhindranwale was fueling their activities.

Rajiv Gandhi's speech defined parameters of his thinking on tackling the issue. That task had to be performed by the Home ministry that was the headed by Shankar Rao Chavan, former chief minister of Maharashtra. He was sound in administration but not imaginative. I had known him since he became a deputy minister in Y. B. Chavan's ministry on formation of the bigger Bi-lingual Bombay State on November 1, 1956. In Maharashtra he had functioned very effectively and had a reputation as incorruptible and strict disciplinarian. In my very first meeting with him he told me that some were talking that he had got me over to Delhi. That was not true. It was solely Rajiv Gandhi's decision. He also told me that the prime minister wanted to handle some politically sensitive important policy matters and the home ministry will have to work accordingly. He wanted me to deal with prime minister directly if needed. That showed how sincere S. B. Chavan was. Any other home minister would have insisted on my reporting to the Prime Minister only through him. Obviously, Rajiv Gandhi had spoken to him as to how he wanted me to function.

Some unorthodox means were adopted to start a dialogue with the Sikh political leadership that was languishing in several jails; as well as with the youth, mostly students, who were leading the militancy.

On his suggestion, I visited Chandigarh to familiarize myself with men and matters. I met several senior officers and editors of two English language news papers that were published from Chadigarh. Both Prem Bhatia of Tribune veteran editor of Tribune and young Rahul Singh of Indian Express had their ear to the ground and candidly helped me to assess the ground situation. I proposed the replacement of the governor, Satarawala, a very experienced civil servant, by appointing a politician instead. In a way, my recommendation was intended to start a change of approach from the top rather than tinkering with the field and secretariat-level officials. On my return in the evening, on way from the airport to my office, I handed over to the Prime Minister my brief report. Next morning, Rajiv Gandhi called me to his office in 2 Akbar Road and dramatically introduced Arjun Singh, who had been sworn as the Chief Minister of Madhya Pradesh a day earlier. Within the next 24 hours, Mr. Arjun Singh resigned from that office and was flown to Chandigarh to be sworn in as the Governor of Punjab. The rest is history.

Rajiv Gandhi was much ridiculed by the press for this sudden decision. But knowing the complexity of the Punjab problem, RG had decided to restart the dialogue with various politicians of Punjab, within the parameters so clearly defined by him, with a sincere and innovative approach.

While Arjun Singh wisely started a dialogue with politicians and reinforced civil administration, I was entrusted with some delicate tasks. With inputs from an experienced retired IAS official, R. V. Subramaniam, who was then an advisor to the governor of Punjab, we started exploring the thinking of senior Akali leaders lodged in different jails. With the unflinching support of the PM and the help of trusted aides, I could start a dialogue with militants, knowing well that if anything came out in the press, I would lose my job. Today, I can reveal the name of my intermediary: K. P. S. Gill - a brave, fearless officer of the IPS, who was later to play an important role in crushing militancy in Punjab. Late in night, he would meet student leaders who had been brought over to Delhi from the Jodhpur jail and kept in a barrack on the police headquarters in the civil lines in Delhi. After that, he would visit me at my house on the Pandara Road and brief me. This went on for some time. Often, his assistant from the IB would leave with me the tapes of conversation recorded during their talks. As I could follow Punjabi, having been brought up in Delhi in my boyhood, listening to those tapes gave me some insight into thinking of the militant student leaders. They had been soundly indoctrinated. Later, we learnt name of a professor who was their ideological guru. Bhindranwale was a preacher who could rouse masses, but real intellectual underpinning was provided by highly respected university teachers. I met two of them privately. That insight into the Sikh psyche was essential to handle the political problem. In that Arjun Singh was superb.

Large-scale riots and the killing of thousands of Sikhs in Delhi in 1984 in the wake of Mrs. Indira Gandhi's assassination had cast a shadow on the peace process. 13 April, the Baisakhi, is one of the holiest days for Sikhs, as on that day the last Guru Gobind Singh ji had formed the Khalsa, the militant wing. On the eve of that day in 1985, Rajiv Gandhi took some quick and bold steps: He announced an enquiry into the anti-Sikh riots in Delhi by a sitting Supreme Court judge and the lifting of the ban on the All India Sikh Students Federation (AISSF). In parallel with that move, when the Akali were threatening to resume their agitation from the Golden Temple on that day, the Governor of Punjab organized a national integration meeting in Jallianwala Bag as part of the 'peace offensive'. That was a wise political move.

Arjun Singh worked out the political contours of the accord based on certain understandings he had reached with Sant Harchand Singh Longowal, then President of the Akali Dal, through intermediaries, which included political leaders and academics. He arranged for Sant Longowal to visit Delhi. Along with him, I received the Sant on the steps of the Parliament House. I was greatly impressed on first sight with his humility. The signing of the Rajiv-Longowal Accord on 23rd July 1985 was a significant step to restore peace in Punjab. It was a bold step. In fact, it proved to be too bold a step.

Arjun Singh, being highly political, was a man in a hurry. All issues of concern to the Sikhs were dealt with while drafting the accord but not much time was given to study and examine how the accord would be implemented. Thus, subsequently, while its actual implementation was riddled with several difficulties, politically it gave the right signal to the silent majority: Rajiv Gandhi was sincere and determined to give justice to the Sikhs.

Implementation was the task of the Home Ministry. Issues relating to territory, water resources and the capital city of Chandigarh, that was the Union territory, faced innumerable difficulties. I have described those in 'Working with Rajiv Gandhi' in great details. At every stage, we faced serious road blocks and could not move forward despite Herculean efforts on part of Rajiv Gandhi. But during six to eight months, while we tried to implement the accord, the security forces succeeded in restoring some semblance of peace in Punjab. It also allowed us time to take some positive steps for the creation of jobs for unemployed youth and students.

It would take another five years to restore peace despite Rajiv Gandhi handing over governance to an elected government.

Chapter 64

Conflicts in the Northeast
- Assam and Mizoram

In India, with its diversity of race, religions and languages, conflicts are inevitable. These are intensified by issues related to ethnicity, economic disparities, social mores, political ideologies or sheer political opportunism.

Two conflicts in the North-East relating to the Nagas and the Mizos had a bearing on national security and territorial integrity. Assam agitation was a different in character. Rajiv Gandhi dealt with Assam and Mizoram.

Northeast is where conflicts and secessionist movements first started, which at times led to serious militancy and insurgency and even today, remains a major area of concern as is evident from other movements that have sprung up, such as for the creation of Bodoland, Gorkhaland, etc. ULFA was set up to create an independent state of Assam intended to resuscitate the glory of ancient Assam and the Ahom civilization. We learnt later that some influential politicians were behind it. They thought of fighting AASU by taking a position harder than the one adopted by the students. Each has a different history and in my experience its psychology.

The Assam problem was an old one with a different dimension, namely the problem of infiltration by Pakistani/Muslim migrants. In August 1961, a representation was made to Pandit Jawaharlal Nehru, which began with the words "The evil omen of a dangerous situation enveloping Assam, the sentinel of the north-eastern frontiers of India... The people of Assam apprehended that if the influx of Pakistanis was allowed to continue on the prevailing scale, before long, Muslims would become the majority population in the state".

By then, the strains in the India-China relationship, especially along the northern borders of the North-East Frontier Agency (NEFA), were apparent and the Government of India was more exercised about that issue. The problem of infiltration was placed on the back burner, till it found expression in confrontations and violence in the shape of student-led, anti-migrant agitation that rocked the valley in 1978–79. All Assam Students Union (AASU) had been formed by a few student leaders on the campus of the Guwahati University with some professors providing guidance and motivation. They launched their agitation for drawing the center's attention to the problem of influx of foreigners. They adopted the Gandhian way of peace marches and satyagrah and generally it was peaceful agitation although the Congress party led government led by shrewd Hiteshwar Saikia tried to provoke them by using force.

Immediately after Smt. Indira Gandhi returned to power in January 1980, P. K. Mahanta, President of AASU, wrote to her in January 1980 to draw her attention to the alarming situation. Smt. Indira Gandhi knew Assam and the ethos of Assamese well. She understood that their agitation had a national dimension and also the potential for creating a serious law and order situation in the Northeast. With her uncanny political sense, she decided to start a dialogue with AASU and invited them for talks. Apparently, there was a feeling that the 'AASU boys' would be overwhelmed by the charisma of the Prime Minister, and the issue would be resolved in no time. She soon found that the AASU boys were not novices. She passed them on to the Home Minister and a group of ministers.

They found that the issue of infiltration was intimately connected with the future of minorities, especially for the Muslim political leaders and that pursuing these talks would affect the Congress politically. Talks at the political level were discontinued in 1983. But to keep AASU engaged, Krishnaswamy Rao Saheb, the cabinet secretary, who had earlier been secretary to the Prime minister, was entrusted with the task of keeping the talks going. Sixteen rounds of such talks had taken place before Rajiv Gandhi was sworn in as the Prime Minister in January 1985. After signing of the Punjab Accord, the prime minister asked me to handle Assam. I took over a bundle of papers from the cabinet secretary who had meticulously recorded his talks with ASSU.

I was left to devise my ways to resume the dialogue with AASU. He not only gave me unflinching support but also restrained himself and other ministers, including high-level busybodies from interfering in the talks with AASU. In fact, he himself came on the scene to meet the AASU delegation when I took the final documents for his approval late on the night of 14 August 1985. Politicians of different hews were all the time pumping me for information. Except my minister, S.B. Chavan, I did not share anything with anyone, except the prime minister. Bhishma Narain Singh who was the governor of Assam and his chief minister tried their best to know what was being agreed between me and the AASU. He claimed to be monitoring discussions and advising AASU delegates and later claimed that he was instrumental in getting AASU leaders to agree to draft formulations. Actually, he had no access to any piece of paper as Mahanta and I had agreed that there would be no draft till we had agreed on certain principles. Our discussions were all oral till the final day. That was important because in highly sensitive negotiations secrecy was essential to reach a mutually satisfactory agreement. In doing so, I was drawing upon my experience in the UN, where there are really no secrets, yet in final stages agreements are reached only when there a balance of 'equal degree of disaffection'.

Rajiv Gandhi appreciated my ways. How many politicians today will show such restraint in not interfering with the negotiations? In Mrs. Indira Gandhi's regime, at one stage, no one knew who was talking to the Akalis or to AASU and how many.

The outcome of our talks was known to people of India when early morning on 15 August 1985, the Prime Minister announced the signing of the accord in his Independence Day speech from the ramparts of the Red Fort. It was wildly greeted by the nation.

ಜಾಡ

Another long-standing conflict in the northeast was in Mizoram. Mizos' declaration of 'independence' came about in an unbelievably strange way. The Mizos inhabit what are known as the Lushai Hills bordering Burma, now called Myanmar. There is extensive bamboo cultivation in the area, and these wild bamboos bear flowers once in 59 years. This increases the rat population, which after eating the bamboo seeds overwhelm the standing crops and stored grain, resulting in famines, which are called mautam. The Assam government failed to deal with the Great Mautam Famine of 1959. A retired army hawaldar, Laldenga, founded the Mizo National Famine Front to fight on behalf of the people, which led to the formation of the Mizo National Front (MNF) in October 1961. He formed an armed wing known as the Mizo National Army (MNA) and openly came out for secession and independence after a few bloody clashes with the security forces.

Mr. Bimala Prasad Chaliha, the chief minister of Assam, a very shrewd politician, saw in Laldenga the potential to neutralize the anti-Congress Mizo Union Party, a legitimate political organization. He suggested that Laldenga formally join politics and become a legitimate leader. Laldenga responded positively and managed to secure an acquittal from the charge of treason. However, in February 1966, he suddenly declared 'independence' of Mizoram and resumed insurgency.

On Mrs. Gandhi's return to power in 1980, Laldenga again started the dialogue. It continued for the next five years without prospects of coming to any conclusion and Prime Minister Rajiv Gandhi inherited that problem. In fact it was later confirmed that on 30 November 1984, Mrs. Gandhi was walking from her residence, 1 Safadar Jung to her office in the adjacent 2 Akbar road, for interview by some foreign television channel team and also to meet Laldenga, when she was assassinated by her security guards. After the Assam Accord, PM asked me take over the Mizoram issue from veteran G. Parthasarathy to whom late Mrs. Indira Gandhi had entrusted talks. I must gratefully acknowledge Rajiv Gandhi's clarity of thinking and overriding concern for national integrity. Once he felt that this was being compromised in a draft agreement worked out by G. Parthasarathy, he directed me to renegotiate without compromising on those issues. In fact, he, in his own hand, marked portions on a photocopy of the draft with bold instructions that he would never agree to those clauses. That copy was my brief and is in my possession. I shall describe conclusion of those talks in a separate chapter.

Chapter 65

Nagaland
- Why Rajiv Gandhi Did Not Deal?

I have in earlier chapter recalled Rajiv Gandhi's statesmanship in tackling the Punjab, Assam and Mizoram conflicts. Now I propose to recall a problem that he refused to deal because in this biographical account it has a place.

The first conflict within our borders was launched by the Naga National Council (NNC) in 1947. As India moved towards Independence, the Nagas did not want to join the Indian Union. NNC, in fact, declared on 14 August 1947 the formation of the 'sovereign' state of Nagalim. The Indian government did not accept this and considered the Naga Hill District as part of India. Significantly, in June 1947, a nine-point agreement was signed with Sir Akbar Hyadari, and then the Governor of Assam, when it was agreed that 10 years after the agreement, the Nagas would be free to decide their future. A group of Nagas led by militant leader Zapo Phizo did not accept this and refused to participate in the first assembly and parliamentary elections held in 1952. They took to insurgency in mid-fifties and to restore peace and tranquility, the Indian armed forces entered Naga territory in 1956.

Nagaland

Pandit Nehru, knowing well geopolitical importance of the region and bowing down to aspirations of the majority of Naga population, agreed to formation of a separate state. Accordingly Naga Hills-Tuensang Areas, which was then part B Tribal Area within the State of Assam, was formed into a separate State of Nagaland by the Constitution Amendment Act, 1962. That was consequent to agreement with the leaders of Naga peoples Convention. However that did not bring an end to insurgency. Phizo and his followers decided to fight for independent Nagaland.

I got first acquainted with Naga problem in 1963, following the 1962 debacle of the army in NEFA, Y. B. Chavan, Defense Minister of India was deputed to discuss modalities for reducing redeployment of army within Nagaland. Along with the minister, I visited Kohima. We were lodged in district officer's bungalow. I was deeply impressed by Shilo Ao and others who were then representing Nagas and were genuinely looking for ways to tackle insurgency on their own and reduce army's deployment. Their demands for autonomy had been met by insertion of Article 371A in the Constitution and they had got Constitutional guarantees to preserve their tribal identity, culture and way of life within India's federal structure. There was a small minority followers of Phizo who did not wish the talks to succeed. To prove their effective presence within Naga territory, they would fire at the district officer's residence from across a hill where they had taken positions. That was their way of showing defiance to the presence of India's Defense Minister. They did not know that Chavan had instructed army officers not to return fire. These talks paved way to restoration of peaceful conditions for some time.

During my tenure as Home secretary, there was no insurgency as such. There was some local trouble over right of Oil India, a public sector company to drill for exploring oil. Nagas objected to that. They claimed that under article 371 of the Constitution, they had the ownership of land and what was below the surface. This was contrary to the Government of India's sovereign right. There were several skirmishes between the Nagas and local police on this issue. Jamir, the chief minister, visited Delhi on couple of occasions to represent case of Nagas. We promised to abide by the judgment of the courts. I do not know what the final outcome was.

Just at the time the matter was hot, we got to know that some leaders of Nagas, who were followers of Phizo had been in contact with Jamir and the church authorities. We called Jamir to Delhi to find out what was happening. We learnt that two followers of Phizo, Isak Swu (Chu) and Muviah, who were in China, wanted to hold dialogue with the government of India. Obviously, they were impressed that Rajiv Gandhi had entered into accords with the Sikhs and with the ASSU. Probably Laldenga was in touch with them and sensing reaching an agreement had advised them to seek a dialogue.

We learnt that for Isak Swu and Muivah, the most important issues relate to autonomy for Nagas and to seek merger of Naga habited areas located presently within boundaries of other Seven Sisters namely Assam, Manipur, and Arunachal. They had a dream of larger Nagaland called a Nagalim. When their message was received, we were faced with an unusual situation in Nagaland that showed how sensitive is the issue of state boundaries is in the northeast.

Nagaland

Merapani situated on the Assam-Nagaland border adjoining Dimapur had a long history of conflict between Assamese and Nagas, since 1972. Over years, several governors and senior officers tried to work out effective solution. In 1985, what happened there was unimaginable. The central government had, in response to request of states deployed central para-military forces, mainly the CRPF to supplement law and order machinery in Assam as well as Nagaland. To our surprise, when tensions built up and exploded, not only the Nagaland and Assam police forces started firing at each other, but even the central forces deployed on both sides were firing at each other across the border. It took a lot of quick, harsh and determined action on the part of the CRPF leadership to bring fire under control. When we enquired into the 1985 incident, it was found that five members of Naga Students Federation had been arrested at Jorhat a month earlier by the Assam police. Merapani outburst was to teach Assamese a 'lesson'. That incident was a lesson for the government as well.

In May/June 1986, Isak Chu (Swu) and Muvaih showed readiness to talk, their leadership included Khaplang as well. Jamir, the chief minister of Nagaland, played an important role in bringing their offer to government of India. This was the period when it was widely known that Laldenga was reconciled to give up two decades of insurgency and that his talks with me had progressed satisfactorily and he would get an agreement. One pending issue was Laldenga's demand to merge Mizo habited tribal areas in adjoining states with Mizoram.

They did not realize that that was one matter on which Rajiv Gandhi would not yield.

In the draft agreement that had emerged out of over three years of discussions between G. P. Parthasarathy, who was Adviser to Smt. Indira Gandhi and Laldenga, one main point conceded by GP was agreement to merge Mizo habited areas of adjoining states into Mizoram. Prime minister's brief to me was specific and clear. In fact, in the draft handed over to me by him he had in bold pink marking ink had crossed out those portions stating "this will not do".

Because of those specific directions, I had refused to discuss that matter. Finally, realizing futility of trying to reopen that point, Laldenga agreed to sign accord on 30'h June 1986. That Accord brought to end not only insurgency but has enabled Mizos to become full partners in the democratic polity of India. Today, almost twenty five years later, one finds that Mizoram is one of the most peaceful states.

Rajiv Gandhi's firm resolve has a bearing on the ongoing charade of talks between the NSCN leaders and the government of India representatives that are going on since 1995. He foresaw dangers of disturbing cartographic boundaries inherited from the British. He rightly foresaw dangers. Apart from problems of Manipur and Assam, it must not be overlooked that Naga areas situated within Arunachal Pradesh are adjoining international borders with Myanmar (Burma). That lends another dimension to territorial claims in the northeast, as China, who have sheltered NSCN leaders for decades, has made its territorial ambitions known.

I may recall in this connection wise observation of B. K. Nehru, three decades earlier. As the Governor of Assam, he had called for a 'Moratorium on border claims'. I believe that this guided Rajiv Gandhi in dealing with Laldenga's claim and also his decision not to enter into any dialogue with NSCN.

A similar firm decision must guide discussion with NSCN leaders. Otherwise, we shall see beginning of a new era of Cartographic insurgency. I believe it was wrong on the part of the successor government to start talking to the secessionist leaders without prior commitments on their part. These have led us nowhere. Perhaps, now the central government has no option except to continue talking.

ಎಂ

I believe Nagaland that I first visited as a young man in 1963 has some connection with my fate-line.

One evening, in October 2009, I got a telephone call from Shivraj Patil then Union Home minister to tell me that 'they' would like me to go as the governor of Nagaland. I declined the offer. I am quoting from the letter that I wrote to him soon after that that call. I wrote:

I wish to thank you for your kind telephone call in October. As I told you, I was in Delhi a week earlier and wanted to see you. Unfortunately you were out of Delhi.

During my stay I had called on Smt. Gandhi as well as on the Prime Minister. I had not made any request. I was thus surprised and honored that you were thinking of me for Nagaland. I am familiar with conditions in the State. Also with damp climate and topography. That was not the main reason for my reply.

I sincerely believe that the ongoing dialogue is not going to lead anywhere. I am aware that it was started much before your assuming present office. My own assessment is that certain commitments that have been made may create more problems in the North East. I had to resist these demands in case of Mizoram. Late Rajivji was sensitive to the issues and I had his full backing.

I do not wish to dwell on the subject in a letter. I shall be glad to have an opportunity to meet you. In case you are visiting Mumbai please do ask your office to let me know.

Chapter 66

Farewell to Arms
- My Retiring from IAS

It was already November 1985. Laldenga was showing the effects of the soft life. Months of enforced idleness in Delhi, interspersed with occasional talks with me or courtesy calls on the Home Minister, were showing its effects. He longed to be with his people but he would not go to Mizoram, fearing assassination. Nor could he go to London empty handed. He talked to me about his wife and only daughter, who were in London. I had learnt from Swamy how they were being taken care of. As Christmas of 1985 approached, Laldenga became increasingly homesick. He was delighted when I told him that we were making arrangements for his return to London to spend Christmas with his family. Swamy had even arranged for him to take Christmas presents for the family.

While Laldenga was away, I visited Aizwal along with my wife. Lt. Governor Dubey and his wife looked after us and we met a number of political leaders. Lal Thanhawla, the Chief Minister and his lovely wife hosted a lunch for us where we met all his ministers. We attended a cultural show specially arranged in the town hall. We found the

Mizos warm, friendly and always smiling. Their young boys and girls sang religious songs to the accompaniment of guitars and were fond of jazz. They knew how to enjoy themselves. Christianity obviously played an important role in their daily lives and one could observe the beneficial influence of the Church.

I flew in a helicopter all over the southern and eastern parts of Mizoram. I was fascinated by the emerald-green forests covering rolling hills all along the Indo-Burma border. I did a reconnaissance by air of the areas where the MNA were expected to come out in the open. I had still to work out a detailed scheme for Laldenga's army to enjoy the fruits of freedom. Their leader was in London and we made sure that reports about him reached Mizoram.

In the beginning of February 1986, we got reports that Laldenga was getting restive in London. He started making enquiries at the Indian High Commission as to when the Government of India wanted him to return. He also started making some noises about wanting to go back on the agreement already reached. "If the government has had second thoughts about the agreement, it should state so publicly," he stated. When Swamy told me that in his desperation Laldenga may say or do something foolish, I spoke to the PM. We sent a message and got Laldenga back in Delhi.

For the next 10 to 12 weeks, we kept talking about the scheme to enable his army to come out. Considerable amount of detailed planning had to be done and cross-checked with the ground reality. Where would MNA enter the Indian Territory, at which place should they be met by the Indian Army's representatives; how they would lay down arms and what kind of treatment would they be accorded were matters that required careful consideration. I was in no hurry; I wanted to collect Lous from Laldenga. I was determined to encash those Lou's at the right moment.

Talking of the surrender of MNA personnel, I became conscious of the inner turmoil a 'soldier' must undergo when, after two decades of insurgency, he is asked to disarm. To ensure that there was no feeling of humiliation, I worked out a drill. As the MNA members crossed the border at Parva, situated in the southern-most point, each person would enter a hut and deposit all his arms inside. He would come out and walk for a couple of hundred meters before being met by the Indian army personnel. The act of laying down arms was to be made in privacy, so that there would be no humiliation.

Laldenga appreciated all the consideration shown to his army personnel and the facilities that would be accorded to them once they came out. Frankly, my objective was clear: to let MNA's so-called commander-in-chief know that the Union Home Secretary was a reasonable and sensitive person, he respected a soldier - even a rebel. If the accord did not come about, it was because of the unreasonable attitude of their Chief, Laldenga, who was interested in becoming the Chief Minister.

The Government was much criticized for dragging on the negotiations with Laldenga. There was a good reason for doing that. PM wanted real peace to be restored to Mizoram. That required that all arms, ammunition and equipment with the so-called Mizo National Army and the insurgents be deposited with the Government. Also, there was a real danger that the more sophisticated arms of MNA might be passed on to other rebel groups in the North-East. We had received reports that B. K. Hrangkhawl, the leader of TNV (Tripura National Volunteers) insurgents in Tripura was in touch with Zoramthnaga, the Vice President of MNP, who was with the Mizo army (MNA) in the jungles. This was also the time when TNV was becoming active in Tripura.

There was yet another reason. We were not sure whether the MNA would honour the peace accord reached by Laldenga with the government of India. For several years, Laldenga was living in comfort, far away from his hard-core followers, who were somehow surviving for over two decades in one of the most inhospitable jungles of South-east Asia. His devoted aide Zoramthnaga was at that time with the MNA and much would depend on his influence with the so-called army officers. We therefore made sure that Laldenga, through his trusted emissaries, could establish contact with Zoramthnaga and get firm assurances from the latter that all MNA personnel would come out with their arms and ammunition. Once that was assured, we could move forward to reach the accord.

I was due to retire from service on 30th June. At the beginning of that month, I told Rajiv Gandhi that the time was ripe to put pressure on Laldenga. He was passed on to Arjun Singh, the Vice-President of the Congress party for political matters. An ace diplomat, Arjun Singh kept him talking. I was personally kept informed of all the talks, which centered round transitional arrangements, in case the accord was signed. Rajiv Gandhi had already taken a view publicly that welfare of the people was more important to him, whether the Congress (I) remained in power in Mizoram or not. He had done that in Assam also.

On 25th June 1985, Rajiv Gandhi asked the Chief Minister Lal Thanhawla to be present with his entire cabinet. A political agreement was signed between Arjun Singh, the Congress (I) Vice President and Laldenga in the presence of the Congress President and the Chief Minister and his colleagues. These outlined the coalition arrangements in the Interim Advisory Council to the Lt. Governor of the Union Territory. That was the first time Rajiv Gandhi met Laldenga since I took over the negotiations, but refused to talk to him about the details of the ongoing negotiations.

That morning, before signing the agreement with the Congress (I), Laldenga came over to meet me. He was in a happy mood. He was already seeing the light at the end of the tunnel. He told me of high hopes and jubilation in Aizwal and other places in Mizoram. I took him to Buta Singh, the Home Minister and we assured him of an early solution to the pending issues. That evening the CCPA was briefed of the stage of negotiations. I was authorised to push ahead, now that a satisfactory political arrangement had been worked out.

I also wanted to complete the task before laying down my office on 30th June. I had fallen in love with the Mizos. I found myself captivated by Laldenga's enigmatic personality and the easy informality of a Mizo- now that he had begun to trust me.

June 27 was my birthday. I invited Laldenga for a cup of tea. I told him that in three days I would lay down office. It was for him to consider seriously whether he was willing to agree on the terms suggested to him. He assured me that he would go back to his legal advisor and also speak to his colleagues, most of whom were in Delhi. I did not hear from him for two days.

Around 2.30 p.m. on the 30th June, Laldenga came to see me alone. This was the first time he had done so. My table was clean. All my files had been cleared and arrangements made to formally hand over charge to C. G. Somiah in a couple of hours' time. The Home Ministry had arranged a farewell function, where Buta Singh and other ministers had been invited.

I nostalgically recalled to Laldenga our first meeting in my office and about the mutual trust and understanding that we had developed, as two individuals. Over a cup of tea, I said, "Mr. Laldenga, my wife and I have fallen in love with your land and the Mizos. Perhaps one day, very soon, we can greet you and your family there."

Laldenga became emotional. After a pause to clear his throat he said, "I wish I could have concluded the accord with you."

I said, "It's too late. In three hours I will not only leave this office but stand retired from government service."

I do not know why, but something overcame me and I said, "Laldenga, if you are ready to be flexible, perhaps we can reach a settlement before I leave this office. You could later sign the accord with my successor."

"But as a friend I ought to warn you that if you do not have a settlement with me, you may have to go on discussing pending issues with my successors for years to come. I do not know how many," I added most sincerely.

He appeared anxious and said, "Can I consult my colleagues and come back to you?"

"Please go ahead but return before 4.30 p.m. Thereafter I must go and bid farewell to the Home Minister and the Prime Minister and be back for the function in the ministry," I replied. Laldenga left in a hurry. My joint secretary and I felt that a breakthrough was in sight. He advised the ministry officials to postpone the farewell to the next day. I do not know what reasons he gave.

I spoke to the Home Minister and quickly briefed the Prime Minister. I was asked to persist in my efforts and not lay down office.

At 4.30 p.m. Laldenga came over with his team. In less than one hour we sorted out our differences of perception on outstanding matters and cleared a draft. A couple of really vital points were left for the final decision of the Prime Minister, on the clear understanding that none of the matters settled between us would be reopened by Laldenga in his meeting with the Prime Minister. I warned him that the clock was ticking away for me.

A short while later, both of us went over to 7 Race Course Road. The Prime Minister quickly cleared the two pending points. The Cabinet Committee on Political Affairs met at short notice and approved the draft of the agreement. With the task accomplished, I bade goodbye to the ministers. As

I was about to take my final farewell of the Prime Minister, he said, "Pradhanji you have worked hard in shaping the accord. I want you to sign it before you retire. Do it within half an hour so that it comes over the 9.30 p.m. TV news." I was deeply touched at the Prime Minister's gesture.

It was already 8.30 p.m. Suddenly it dawned on me that probably under the Civil Service Rules, I already stood retired after office hours. How could I affix my signature to a formal document? I mentioned that to PM. He looked at me and said in all seriousness, "Why can't I give you an extension?"

That was fully within his powers. But I had decided long back that I must retire on that day. That morning my wife had talked to me with about the exciting career we had had. Out of 36 years of my service, we had been married for 35 years. She did not want me to work anymore. Recalling all that I said to PM, "Sir, you have publicly declared that you will not, repeat not, and give any extension to any retiring officer. I would beg of you not to make an exception in my case."

Rajiv Gandhi was determined. He asked me to consult the Law Secretary in his presence. I got him over the RAX. He advised that if I had not formally handed over charge to my successor, I would stand retired only at midnight. PM was happy. He asked me to hurry over to my office and sign the accord with Laldenga.

Rajiv Gandhi asked V. George to make all arrangements for Doordarshan to cover the historic event. He wanted to witness it on the TV screen. By 9 p.m., Laldenga had arrived with his wife and his colleagues. A few ministers from Mizoram, including the Chief Minister Lal Thanhawla were already seated at the long table. Soon my wife also joined us.

In the short time available, R. Vasudevan had efficiently prepared the document titled 'Memorandum of Settlement on Mizoram'. We affixed our signatures: Laldenga for the MNF, Lal Thanhawla on behalf of the Mizoram government and me, on behalf of the Government of India.

Laldenga said a few words into the microphone. Suddenly the camera was focused on me. I was overcome with emotion. Here is gist of what I said: "I thank the Prime Minister for allowing me to handle these negotiations. I am grateful to him for giving me this unique distinction to say farewell to my service career. I would like to convey over Doordarshan my grateful thanks to the nation for all the opportunities I got to serve it and to seek fulfillment in my work. I wish the Mizo people all the happiness and prosperity on this joyous occasion."

I can never forget that gesture of the Prime minister that enabled me to bid goodbye to my service career publicly. I do not know of any other civil servant who had an opportunity to do so.

I wonder how many politicians have the generosity to make such a gesture. Rajiv Gandhi was bold in seeking to resolve three conflicts that had all the elements to frighten anyone. But he acted with single-mindedness of purpose to restore peace and democracy. Towards this end, he even sacrificed Congress party governments in Assam and Mizoram.

RG's three accords will remain a triumph of his democratic spirit over the petty interests of India's polity.

Tribune of Chandigarh, in its editorial dated 27th June 1986, aptly wrote: "Mr. Rajiv Gandhi has sought to project himself [as] an Indian first and a Congressman afterwards by manifestly sacrificing the interest of his own party."

RG in his very first address to the nation, broadcast on 5th January 1985, had stated: "The give and take of the conference table can yield victories that confrontation cannot. That was his mantra for resolving conflicts." I had successfully followed that mantra.

As I walked out of Gate No. 4 of the North Block along with my wife, I did so with a sense of relief. I had discharged my duty for the past eighteen months with the utmost dedication. I had helped a young Prime Minister to translate his hope and vision into accords in Assam and Mizoram. I had also thoroughly enjoyed working with him.

৪০ଔ৪০ଔ

Chapter 67

Dealing with Conflicts
- Within and out of Ministry

As the Union Home Secretary I was under the rules of business a link with the Rashtrapati Bhavan. In fact, on constitutional matters and ceremonials, such as Padma Awards, the Home Secretary has a role.

In April 1985, K. K. Tiwari, a Congress MP from Bihar, made a statement in Parliament making allegations that the President had links with Punjab extremists, two of whom had been permitted to stay in Rashtrapati Bhavan. Naturally the press started asking me since I was then deeply involved in the Punjab problem. I claimed ignorance and Bandopadhyaya issued a contradiction. Two days later, S. B. Chavan quoted that contradiction in the parliament. We had no information on Tiwari's allegation.

When I became Union Home Secretary, I sensed that the relationship with the President was not too cordial. Giani Zail Singh was expecting Rajiv Gandhi to look up to him for advice on all matters especially connected with the Punjab where he had had long inning as the chief minister. Rajiv Gandhi and his main advisers at that time, especially Arun Nehru, were in fact somewhat doubtful about his loyalty to the late prime minister. They had come to believe that he had a line of communication with Bhindranwale who was advocating secessionism from within the precincts of the Golden Temple. A few months later, when Arun Nehru became Minister of State for Internal Security, it became clear that he had an agenda for putting President Zail Singh in his place. He started by denying to the President copies of the Intelligence Bureaus communication, which till then were being sent to the President for perusal as a matter of routine. Arun Nehru directed IB to send him only a gist of the reports that they sent to the Home Minister. Bandopadhyaya had spoken to me about this and I discussed with the IB chief but did not consider the matter worth pursuing as in any case I also felt that gist of communications was more appropriate for the eyes of the President. I had found that mostly IB reports were often full of information but not of much use for any administrative decision or action. In any case, I had no interest in gossips and personal information that are the gist of politics in Delhi.

That was not the only matter of discord. The MOS for Internal Security also arranged placement of several IB personal within Rashtrapati Bhavan obviously with a view to getting information about visitors and inside information of the happenings within the Rashtrapati Bhavan. I came to know about it only when the President's secretary spoke to me and pointed out that some IB personnel who had previously worked with Zail Singh when he had been the Home Minister had brought this to the notice. The President was rightly annoyed and asked the IB personnel to be withdrawn. One day, I mentioned

Dealing with Conflicts

to the MOS that this kind of games might embarrass the government. I kept my Minister S. B. Chavan informed about these matters. President Zail Singh, who had his own sources, must have known these activities. He knew of my nearness to Rajiv Gandhi and may have thought that I was a party to these acts. Strangely, a few months after my retirement, these matters would play a role in my life.

At the beginning of January 1986, newspapers were reporting deterioration in the relationship between Rajiv Gandhi and the top bureaucracy. On January 9, two senior officials of the IAS were reported to be victims of Rajiv Gandhi's 'bullying tactics'. The occasion was a meeting of the parliamentary consultative committee on science and technology, at which around 30 members of parliament and at least 70 officials were present. The meeting was chaired by the prime minister who had asked for audio-visual (AV) presentation. The first AV was on rural drinking water supply. After three or four shots of the presentation, the prime minister expressed his annoyance that 'hard facts and figures' had not been presented. He publicly upbraided Mr. D. Bandopadhyaya, the Secretary, for not providing the committee with enough information to enable them to ask further questions. The next presentation was by Mr. C. S. Sastry, Secretary Agriculture, whose ministry had been asked to present an AV (Audio Visual) on Oil-Seeds program. After few questions and answers on that presentation, the prime minister suddenly asked for AV on the ministry's Dairy Development Program. Sastry pointed out that the subject had not been included in the day's agenda and he was not prepared. Prime Minister wanted both the officers Mr. Bandopadhyaya and Sastry to be sent back immediately to their parent cadres. His principal secretary Sarla Grewal convinced him to not to take that action. But the incident that had been witnessed by several parliamentarians was naturally widely reported and commented upon in the press. Unfortunately, within a few days, there was a much more high profile incident connected with the foreign secretary A. P. Venkateswaran, who was my batchmate.

A. P. Venkateswaran or Venkat, as is called by his friends, had a distinguished career in the Foreign Service and before coming over to Delhi, he had been ambassador in Beijing. When Romesh Bhandari, the foreign secretary, was about to retire, in one morning meeting, the prime minister suddenly asked me as to what I thought of A. P. Venkateswaran as successor to Bhandari. Knowing Venkat well, I told the prime minister that he would be an excellent choice and would bring fresh ideas to the foreign office. A few weeks later, when Venkat arrived in Delhi, he came to meet me to get briefing on the prevailing internal situation. After that briefing, knowing well his fondness for talking and his 'peculiar' sense of humor, I advised him to be more discreet and not indulge in needless humor. I could do so because of our friendship beginning on the day when we joined the IAS training school in Metcalfe House on April 2, 1952. That his 'public sacking' by Rajiv Gandhi would create an issue between the PM and the President Zail Singh was something unimaginable. A few months later, it came in the way of my appointment as the governor of Arunachal Pradesh.

ಬಌಬಌ

Chapter 68

To Arunachal Raj Bhavan

After retiring on June 30, 1986, my wife and I decided to visit holy places in the north before settling down in Bombay. We visited Hardwar, Kashi and Benaras. At Kashi, thanks to our old friend B. P. Singhal, IPS, whom we had known from Mount Abu days, we were well looked after in Allahabad and visited Pandit Nehru's house, 'Swaraj Bhavan'. Also performed 'Aarti' at the Vishwanath temple on the banks of the Ganges in Kashi, the holiest place for Hindus.

We had decided not to stay in Delhi, even a day longer than ninety days allowed by the rules to occupy 2, Pandara Road. Accordingly I bade farewell to Delhi on 30th October. Many friends advised me not to leave Delhi. They warned me in all sincerity: Out of sight, out of mind.

In fact, Rajiv Gandhi had not forgotten me. One day Shiv Shankar, Foreign minister visited me and asked whether I would agree to be considered for ambassadorship in Washington. PM had asked him to sound me. Having lived over ten years abroad, I had no fascination for spending another three years outside India. I declined. I think P. K. Kaul, who was appointed, was a more worthy person for that important assignment.

About my future, politics was not out of my mind but I was thinking more of public service. Although I had a much wider exposure than normal civil servants, I was aware that bureaucrats do not easily fit into active political life. Before I left Delhi, I met Rajiv Gandhi. He liked my idea and assured me that he would keep in mind my name for Rajya Sabha when the next biennial vacancies arose. I requested him not consider me for a gubernatorial position. "Later perhaps, not now" I told him.

It was midnight of 14 February, when V. George rang up. He said, "Boss is in a meeting, therefore he cannot talk to you, but he wants to know whether you would go to Arunachal as Governor."

I asked George to thank PM and convey to him: "You know what I want to do. Please do not consider me for a governorship."

Next day, early in the morning, George rang up again to say that PM was not very happy at my response and wanted to speak to me. A few hours later, I spoke to him and explained my inability. He said, "Pradhanji, I thought of you because I want you to be there, at this time, in the national interest. We may soon have problems across the border."

I said, "PM, if it is a question of national interest I cannot say no. I will go. Give me a couple of weeks to wind up my personal affairs here."

"O.K. take four weeks," said Rajiv Gandhi with obvious happiness in his tone.

I did not anticipate any difficulty to get my Warrant of Appointment. But I had become a pawn in relationship between the PM and the President.

I had accepted the PM's offer and was expecting a message to collect the same in Delhi from the President's secretariat. One day, I was told by a friend that there was some hitch as the President Zail Singh did not approve of the appointment. He had some reservation on seeing an article that I had written and published in the Indian Express on 17th February 1987 titled "Shouldn't the Inquisition Stop?" It is a classic case of some dormant prejudice stored somewhere deep inside one's mind suddenly coming out. Let me explain.

As the Union Home Secretary, I had had cordial relations with the Rashtrapati Bhawan. When I assumed the office in January 1985, I called on Sardar Zail Singh, the President, who had been, during late Prime Minister Smt. Indira Gandhi's regime, the Home Minister. He greeted me warmly and recalled meeting me when he visited Mumbai in 1983. I also met Bandopadhyaya, the President's Secretary who had earlier worked in the Home Ministry. His being there proved useful to me on several occasions.

I however found that the PM's relationship with the President was not too cordial. Arun Nehru was doubtful about Zail Singh's loyalty to the late prime minister and believed that he had a line of communication with

Bhindranwale who was advocating secessionism from within the precincts of the Golden Temple. The president knew of my nearness to Rajiv Gandhi and may have thought that I was a party to what Arun Nehru had done. Strangely a few months after my retirement these matters would play a role in my life.

A. P. Venkateswaran, the foreign secretary, during his visit to Pakistan in the middle of January 1986, in reply to a query by Pakistani journalist announced that the prime minister of India would be visiting Pakistan 'early'. Normally, announcement of such visits were always carefully calibrated. Apparently, PMO did not approve of that statement. Soon after, on January 20, Prime Minister Rajiv Gandhi met national and international press at an annual news conference. The prime minister had just finished giving a pretty comprehensive and convincing answer into a rather loaded question from Husaini on the troop buildup in the Indo-Pak border region when Husaini rose to ask a supplementary: "When are you visiting Pakistan?"

Pat came the answer: "At the moment I've got no fixed plans for visiting Pakistan:" Husaini shot back: "Your foreign secretary said you will be visiting Pakistan as the SAARC chairman." With a fixed grin on his face Rajiv Gandhi announced: "You'll be talking with the new foreign secretary soon." A. P. Venkateswaran, who was seated in the front row, as a seasoned diplomat, kept his cool.

After the press conference, he returned to his office and quietly applied for premature retirement. That started a tirade against Rajiv Gandhi. For a couple of weeks, the press was full of deplorable behaviour and about Rajiv Gandhi being a novice in handling such matters. The Foreign Service reacted by passing a mild resolution expressing how they felt deeply hurt and how deeply they regretted the circumstances leading to the decision taken by the foreign secretary etc. Going through all those press reports, I felt that the media was too harsh on Rajiv Gandhi.

I expressed my views in an article that appeared in The Indian Express on February 17, 1987 titled "Shouldn't the Inquisition stop?" which I had written a day before I received mid-night call about offer of governorship. I gave some personal instances to show that Rajiv Gandhi was not as inconsiderate as he was being projected in the press. In the concluding paragraph, I wrote, "Finally, it is time to reflect whether the current media treatment of incidents, involving senior civil servants will in any way help the bureaucracy. The present interface between politicians and bureaucracy provides enough scope for removing any misunderstanding and to clear up the present atmosphere in order to allow proper functioning of senior civil servants vis-à-vis their political masters.

The Venkateswaran affair, whatever may be the reason, was bad and will be realized by historians. Isn't it time that we relegated it to history?

This article had attracted President Zail Singh's attention and a couple of weeks later, when papers regarding my appointment as Governor of Arunachal Pradesh were submitted to him for approval, he refused to give his formal consent. He connected my appointment as a reward for that article in defense of Rajiv Gandhi.

I did not know about it till I reached Delhi on 19th March 1987 on way to Itanagar. When I met Rajiv Gandhi, he told me how he had to deal with Gianiji to make him approve of the appointment because he had made a matter of prestige. The PM was equally determined and ultimately, through some intermediaries, the President was persuaded to give his approval. That is how my appointment came through.

I was fortunate to get some firsthand briefing about the state from two distinguished civil servants who had spent many years serving in that area. On the day the appointment was announced, B. K. Nehru, ICS, who had been the Governor of Assam in the Seventies, came over along with his wife to greet us. One of the most distinguished civil servants, B. K. Nehru had been the governor of Assam, Jammu & Kashmir, and of Gujarat. They had many friends from the northeast and talked highly of the tribal culture and their way of living. That was very interesting as well as reassuring for me.

Another visitor was Nari Rustomjee, ICS, who had served as Advisor to the Governor of Assam on tribal areas. He had worked closely with Verrier Elwin to evolve a policy for administration of those areas. His wife and he were genuinely glad at the appointment, but their briefing about life amongst tribal, their eating habits and animal sacrifices was not very reassuring. In contrast to BK and his wife, who had talked of what was unique there, the Rustomjees talked of what we would not like and what we shall miss. However, they meant well. After a few months in the state, we found that while the northeast had changed, the Rustomjees remembered it as it was when they left in 1972.

The most touching was the farewell dinner that Shankar Dayal Sharma, the Governor of Maharashtra hosted at the Raj Bhawan. He invited to a banquet all the former governors who were in Bombay. We met there, A. L. Dias and his wife; I. H. Latif and Bilkis; Mrs. Renu Mukharjee; Homi J. H. Talyarkhan and Thrity as well as several dignitaries. Shankar Dayal and Vimlaji were our well-wishers. Even after he was elevated to high posts of the Vice President, and later as the President of India, he and his wife continued to extend to us their hospitality and affection and also visited Itanagar on our invitation.

On 17th March 1987, we were in New Delhi on our way to begin our sojourn in the northeast. We were put up at the Arunachal state guest house a very modest establishment as compared to other stately mansions. During the two days stay in New Delhi, while I got busy with official calls and briefings, my wife quickly glanced through several books on the NEFA in the Resident Commissioner's office. She was impressed by the number of books and publications on a variety of subjects and decided to make full use of the treasure trove of information.

A young police officer named Jumke Bagra had been sent to Delhi to escort the governor-designate. He had Mongloid features and we could not guess his age, but we found him soft spoken and bright. I decided to appoint him as my ADC. Bagra remained in that post throughout my stay there. I found that prior to joining the police, he had served as a revenue officer and worked in various districts. His knowledge was phenomenal and he became my wife's guide on matters in which as a woman, she was more interested: the life of the tribes, family, children, marriage customs, education and health. Bagra was discreet and made sure that we were properly briefed about the sensitivities of the different tribes inhabiting the state.

PART X :

Epilogue

Chapter 69

End of Civil Service Career
- Beginning of Political

On reaching Itanagar and getting sworn-in as the first Governor of the State of Arunachal Pradesh, I suddenly realized that I had reached a point of my life that many civil servants aspire but do not achieve. During previous 34 years of service in the IAS, I had worn several hats. I had been a district officer; a private secretary to a politician; a diplomat as well as an United Nation civil servant. An unique career in many respects. My appointment was greeted widely by people and media in Maharashtra.

We flew from Delhi to Guwahati where we were received by the staff of Bhishma Narain Singh, the Governor of Assam. He was also officiating as the Governor of Arunachal Pradesh. After dinner, he briefed me about political as well as other matters. The next day on 19th March 1987, we flew to Itanagar in an Indian Air Force M-8 chopper. Mr. K. N. Saikia, the Chief Justice of the Assam high court accompanied us. He would administer the oath of office to me.

Beyond Expectations

In less than an hour, we had crossed the mighty Brahmaputra at Tezpur and within minutes our chopper had entered Arunachal and headed straight for Itanagar, the capital in the foothills. We hovered for a moment over the hill, atop which majestically surrounded by vast lawns and covered with green bushes and tall trees, rested the Raj Bhavan. The helicopter gently settled down just behind it, adjacent to rear entrance. All the ministers with their wives and senior civil and police officers were present to receive us.

As we stepped out, the young chief minister Gegong Apang and his wife Yari came forward to welcome us. A light shower had just passed by and the cool air and the aroma of the plants and trees surrounding the helipad enveloped us. Indeed a refreshing experience for one attuned to overcrowded streets and unsavory smells of Bombay. While I was being introduced to the ministers, my wife turned to greet the smiling ladies with peach-colored skin who were wearing their colorful traditional tribal dress, and looking beautiful. As Yari Apang introduced each one to my wife, she discerned a sense of curiosity but no servility. Some spoke a few words in fluent English and were obviously educated in the convent schools of Assam. We found the warm friendly faces of all those women greeting us with open smiles and brightly lit eyes reassuring. Their husbands were formal and felt a little overwhelmed by the arrival of their first governor. They were aware of my work to help restore peace in Assam and to end the thirty-year-old insurgency in Mizoram. Later, when I moved about in the Northeast I found that I was some kind of hero for the people.

End of Civil Service Career

As we were led upstairs in the Raj Bhavan to get ready for the swearing-in, we fell in love with the place. What caught our attraction was the sight of a high mountain facing our bedroom window with a tall white Buddhist stupa, a bell-like structure. Itanagar was adjacent to the Kameng region in which Tawang Monastery was situated. Some enlightened Central Public Work Department's architect had designed the roof of the Raj Bhavan in the shape of traditional Buddhist Vihara, the residence for monks.

In the spacious ground floor hall of the Raj Bhawan, as the chief secretary read the warrant of appointment signed by the President of India and bearing the embossed red seal, all attention was focused at the small platform where seated were Chief Justice K. N. Saikia of the Guwahati high court and the governor-designate. He administered the Oath of Office. At that moment our sojourn in Arunachal had begun. I realized that I had just set foot in an unknown territory among complete strangers. Looking at the Buddhist-Stupa, I felt as if I had arrived there, to rejuvenate and seek in the foothills of the Himalayas, my spiritual moorings.

Sprawling along the northeastern boundary of India above the plains of Upper Assam, Arunachal Pradesh is spread along the south face of the eastern Himalayas, with international borders with Bhutan, Tibet (China) and Mayanmar (Burma). Arunachal has an international border of around 1,650 km: with Bhutan on the west, China (Tibet) in the north and north-east and Burma in the east. On its south, beyond the foothills, bordering Assam, is the Brahmaputra flowing from east to west.

In the western part, adjoining Bhutan and Tibet, the people are Buddhist with a curious blend of local beliefs. The main tribes are the Monpas and the Sherdukpens. The cultural and spiritual life of the Monpas revolves round the Tawang Monastery, founded over 350 years ago. It is by far the biggest lamasery in India, at an altitude of 3,048 meters and houses over 500 lamas. The central region, watered by the mighty Siang is inhabited by the Adis. The third group of people consists of the Nocte, Wancho and Tangsas who inhabit areas along the border with Burma to south west of Assam and sharing border with Nagaland. Both the Nocte and Wangcho have many characteristics of Naga society, including hereditary chiefs, who still wield a great deal of influence.

During our stay there, my wife and I toured all interior areas of the sprawling state that, in area, is larger than Assam. We met tribal leaders; shared their hospitality and joined them in tribal dances. We participated in cultural events and enjoyed their zest for life. I took initiative to set up a museum in Itanagar for exhibiting tribal arts and crafts from different areas. My wife set up an 'Imdad Bhawan' for women to meet and share their tribal life.

One of the important projects I undertook was the restoration of the Tawang monastery. As the sixth Dalai Lama was born in Urgyalling in 1683, for Buddhists, it has a very special place and ranks as the third after the Potola at Lahsa and the Drepung monastery.

Footnote :
I have written about the land and the people and of our sojourns in my, "Dragon's Shadow Over Arunachal". (Rupa 2008)

End of Civil Service Career

I spent three years in Arunachal Pradesh. During that period, I toured extensively and visited the remotest parts of the state accompanied my wife. As the first Governor by everywhere we went, we were welcomed affectionately in the tribal manner. We also met a large number of senior Army and Air Force officers deployed all over the mountainous tracks.

I have written extensively about my sojourn in Arunachal in my book: 'Dragon's Shadow over Arunachal'.

During my tenure in Arunachal Pradesh, I had also occasion to act as a Governor of Bihar for over three months. My stint as Governor of Bihar was too short for me to make any profound analysis of the state of affairs there. But the political scenario during those three months enabled me to see emergence of new ruling class of Bihar belonging to the ST and SC tribes. They were till then been used as fodder for delivering votes to upper class candidates. When I was there I found that a new intermediate class called 'Other Backward' class led by Lalu Prasad Yadav was emerging as a dominant political force. In the next elections, OBC would take over the reins of power and governance for the following ten years. Unfortunately, with fall of standards of morality and ethics in public life and graft, Bihar would sink into greater depths of lawlessness, poverty and lower standards of governance.

After three months in Bihar and another four months in Itanagar, I demitted my office as the Governor. I was looking forward to going back to my state and try to settle down a retired life in Mumbai/Pune. But again the fate intervened and I was called upon to serve as a political aide to Rajiv Gandhi and later after his demise with Sonia Gandhi. During that period, I also became a member of the Maharashtra Legislative Council (MLC) that gave me another career. Although I have retired from active politics, I do continue to participate in political events, especially those connected with the Congress Party.

I believe I have had a very unique career in life as a civil servant that started in the Metcalfe House in 1952 and ended with my becoming the Governor of Arunachal Pradesh. That period was nation building era for India. By the end of the twentieth century, India became a vibrant democracy.

I trust very much that the readers, especially younger generation of civil servants, will enjoy reading this book.

Index

A

Abul Kalam Azad, preface 41

Agricultural Research Institute, 14

All India Congress Committee, 383, 449,

Allahabad, 336, 501

Anandpur Resolution, 468

Anantnag, 34

Anil K. Majumdar, Foreword Page 3

Arunachal Pradesh, Foreword Page 4, 32, 186, 188, 484, 500, 505, 511, 513, 515, 516,

Assam, Foreword Page 8, 6, 17, 23, 187, 266, 412, 468, 474-479, 480-483, 491, 496, 506, 511-514

Assam Accord, Foreword Page 8, 479

B

B. G. Deshmukh, 161

B. S. Raghavan, 24

Babasaheb Ambedkar, 141, 326

Balasaheb Kher, 61

Banaskantha, 103, 107, 115, 118, 125

Baramulla, 25

Baroda, 4,6,118,125, 129, 424

Bhakra Nangal, 41

Bhopal, 138, 457, 458, 459,

Bihar, Foreword Page 5, 5, 14, 17, 267, 497, 515

Bombay, Foreword Page 3, 5, 6. Pages 4, 5 , 7, 18, 19, 32, 41, 42, 44, 53, 55-177, 191, 234, 257, 258, 265, 270-475

Bombay Electric Supply and Transport Company (BEST), 377

C

C. D. Deshmukh, 22

C. S. Venkatachar, Foreword Page 4, 44

Central Asia, 14

Chattisgarh, 17

Congress, 17, 62, 71, 130, 131, 142, 165, 168, 169, 171, 173, 180, 181, 192, 198, 305, 312, 315, 320, 322, 324, 325, 326, 383, 385, 390-392, 417, 421, 449, 450, 475, 476, 478, 490, 491, 496, 497, 516,

Congress (I), 320, 322, 325, 491,

Congress (O), 320, 322, 417

D

D. R. Gadgil, 55

D. S. (Balasaheb) Desai, 128

Dakota, 33

Dalai Lama, 32, 514

Dehradun, 34, 36

Delhi, 4 - 511

Dr. Krishnan, 13, 19

Dr. Rajendra Prasad, 125

E

Egypt, 16, 235-239, 241, 249, 252, 254, 269, 295, 356,

Fergusson College, 21, 55, 409

G

G.L. Sheth, 120, 126, 163

GATT, Foreword Page 4, 105, 222-359

Gen. K. C. Cariappa, 21,

Geneva, 18, 105, 224, 232, 223, 244-252, 265-305, 334, 339, 343, 356, 363, 368-370, 418, 439

Gobi, 14

Gujarat, Foreword Page 5, 5, 55, 64, 66, 67, 71, 72, 89, 94, 105, 106, 115, 116, 118, 120, 125, 141150, 157, 158, 159, 162-164, 376, 448, 506,

Gulmarg, 34

H

Harcharan Singh Longowal, Foreword Pg 8
Hardwar, 34, 36, 37, 501
Homi J. H. Talyarkhan, 507

I

Indian Police Service Academy, 37
Indira Gandhi, 42, 182, 185, 187, 206, 235, 240, 272, 303, 304, 311, 320, 325, 359, 383, 417, 420, 441, 449, 453, 454, 468, 469, 472, 475, 477, 479, 484, 503
Indore, 79
Islamabad, 4

J

J. D. Shukla, 5, 6, 9, 10
Jan path, 14
Jharkhand, 17
Jhelum, 25 - 31
Jivraj Mehta, 157, 213, 214

K

K. M. Pannikar, 15
K.P.S. Menon, Foreword Page 4, 15, 20
Kabul, 26
Kailasnath Katju, 44
Kannamwar, 164
Karad, 124, 455, 456
Karnataka, 55
Kashmir, 6, 23, 24, 25, 26, 34,
Kerala, 5,6
Khadakvasla, 35, 125, 404,
Kolhapur, Foreword Page 7, 129-174, 311, 385, 428, 429
Kolhapur District Shetkari Sahakari Sangha, 111
Kurd, 24

L

Lahore, 29, 33, 274-276

M

M. G. Pimputkar, 57, 75, 86, 162
Madhukar Namjoshi, 5, 35

Maharashtra, Foreword Page 4, 22, 55, 80, 117-120, 129, 136, 140, 154, 157-198, 216, 245, 300, 309-336, 348-351, 360, 365- 516

Mahatma Gandhi, 158, 348,

Marathwada, 163, 165, 166, 326-330

Meerut, 38

Mizoram Accord, Foreword Page 8

Morarji Desai, 61, 71, 107, 142, 143, 161, 166, 303-305

Mount Abu, Foreword Pages 6 and 7,102, 117, 137, 422, 501

Mussoorie, 34-36

Muzaffar nagar, 37

N

National Defence Academy (NDA), 35, 125, 126,

National Physical Laboratory (NPL), 13, 19

NEFA, Foreword Page 8, 32, 156,179, 185, 187, 192, 198, 199, 475, 481, 507

P

P. D. Kasbekar, 22, 131

P. K. Sawant, 165

Pahelgam, 34

Pakistan, 7, 30, 33, 103, 108, 138, 232, 249, 254, 271-275, 282, 283, 288, 468, 475, 504

Palanpur, 103, 108, 110, 117, 137, 138

Pandit Jawaharlal Nehru, 8, 19, 26, 40, 481, 501,

People's Republic of China, China, 7, 15, 41, 139, 140, 144, 435, 442, 444, 476

Planning Commission, 15, 16, 18, 317, 396, 400, 426

Punjab Accord, Foreword Page 8, 436

R

Rajaram, 140, 152,

Rajiv Gandhi, 4, 42, 203, 217, 400,401, 427, 448-450, 455, 458, 460-462, 467-516

Index

Rajpal, 64, 65, 69, 70, 75, 76, 91, 95, 101,
Ratnagiri, 149, 407, 431
Ratnappa Kumbhar, 131, 133
Rawalpindi, 26, 29
Red Fort, 40, 437
Rishikesh, 35, 37
Roorkee, 38

S

S. K. Kriplani, 40, 274
S. K. Patil, 148, 149, 169
S. P. Thorat, 32
S.G. Barve, 22, 159, 160, 163, 375, 432,
Samyukta Maharashtra Movement, Foreword Page 7, 130
Sangli, 141, 311, 385, 406
Sardar Patel, Foreword Page 6, 15, 16, 41
Satara, 124, 131, 141, 164, 311, 385, 422, 470
Saurashtra, 40, 98, 116, 147, 348, 349, 352
Shahaji Raje, 139, 144
Shahu Maharaj, 129, 140, 141
Shankar Rao Mohite, 124
Shankarrao B. Chavan, 165, 311, 320
Sharad Rege, 74, 95
Shau Market For Jaggery (is it Shahu or Shau?), 147
Sheshrao Wankhede, 164
Sonmarg, 35
Srinagar, 25, 29, 33,
Subramaniam Swamy, 60,
Surat, 125, 376,

T

Tara Bai, 140
Tatya Saheb Mohite, 148, 151
Tibet, 14, 32, 179, 185, 190, 513, 514
Turkey, 17

U

Udaipur, 39
UNCTAD, Foreword Page 4, 182 - 260
United Kingdom, 7, 18, 170, 207, 213, 260, 261, 287, 334, 356, 458

United Nations, Foreword Page 4, 223, 226, 230, 241, 246, 247, 261, 269, 299, 300, 304, 309, 355-363, 369, 370

UPSC, 16, 20, 21, 22, 434

US, USA, Foreword Page 2 and 8, 7, 15, 247, 289

Uttar Pradesh (UP), 107, 294

V

V P Menon, 20

V. V. Giri, 21

Vardachar, 16

Vasantrao Naik, 164, 310, 312

Venutai, 144, 146

Vidarbha, 144, 146, 310, 320, 321, 325

Vitthal Mavinkurve, 66, 73

W

West Bengal, 115, 164

Y

Y. B. Chavan, Foreword Page 8, 56, 60, 123-125, 128, 134, 144, 145, 148, 156, 169, 171, 179, 180, 182, 311, 312, 320-324, 329, 339, 345, 375, 381-385, 421, 428, 455, 469, 481

College Student

Assistant Collector & SDO Mt Abu

IAS Probationer

Diplomat

Wedding with Lopa
(17-01-1954)

With Lopa – 1954

PM Jawaharlal Nehru
inaugurating Maharashtra State
(1st May 1960)

With PM Nehru at Kolhapur

With Defence Minister Y. B. Chavan

Meeting President Zail Singh

In Leningrad with Chavan (1963)

Commerce Ministry (1965-67)

Signing historic Tripartite Agreement with UAR & Yugoslavia

Leading Indian Delegation to UNCTAD (1969)
- Dr Manmohan Singh, N K Singh

Diplomat in Geneva (1967-76)

With Ambassador Hugo Cubillos (Chile)

With Dr. Mazal (Austria) and J. Bradenburg
(W. Germany)

Chief Secretary Maharashtra (1982-85)

With CM Vasantdada Patil

With CM Sharad Pawar

Greeting Mrs. Margaret Thatcher, PM, UK

Greeting Prince Philip

With Governor Air Marshall Latif
At Foundation laying ceremony of MIDA Pune

Greeting PM Smt. Indira Gandhi

With Mrs. Margaret Thatcher at Santacruz Airport on 6th December 1984

Greeting PM Rajiv Gandhi at Santacruz Airport

In Raj Bhavan (1987-1989)
Governor Arunachal Pradwsh Swearing–in ceremony

Raj Bhavan Itanagar

Swearing-in as Governor of Bihar

Greeting The President and Smt. R. Venkatraman

Greeting Shankar Dayal Sharma, Vice-President at Raj Bhavan.

With son Rajiv & late Dr. L. H. Hiranandani (2015)

With Shri Chadrashekhar, MP

Signing Mizo Accord on 30^{yth} July 1986 with Laldenga

www.ingramcontent.com/pod-product-compliance
Lightning Source LLC
Chambersburg PA
CBHW030558230426
43661CB00053B/1765